The Antinomies of Interdependence

The Political Economy of International Change
JOHN GERARD RUGGIE, GENERAL EDITOR

The Antinomies of Interdependence
National Welfare and the International Division of Labor

edited by JOHN GERARD RUGGIE

COLUMBIA UNIVERSITY PRESS
NEW YORK,   1983

$\overset{\text{Soc}}{\underset{\text{HD}}{}}$
82
A637
1983

Library of Congress Cataloging in Publication Data
Main entry under title:

The Antinomies of interdependence.

(The Political economy of international change)
Includes index.
1. Economic development—Addresses, essays, lectures.
2. International economic relations—Addresses, essays,
lectures. 3. International division of labor—Addresses,
essays, lectures. 4. International relations—Addresses,
essays, lectures. I. Ruggie, John Gerard, 1944 –
II. Title: Interdependence. III. Series.
HD82.A637 1983   338.9   82-2123
ISBN 0-231-05724-5
ISBN 0-231-05725-3 (pbk.)

Columbia University Press
New York   Guildford, Surrey

Clothbound editions of Columbia University Press books are
Smyth-sewn and printed on permanent and durable acid-
free paper.

Contents

Preface

THIS VOLUME IS the most visible product of a colloquium, convened in the hope of clarifying an issue that is high both on the policy agenda of the international community and on the research agenda of political economists: the impact of the international division of labor on national welfare. This issue is of practical concern to policymakers in all countries, but it is particularly pressing in the developing world, which is far more dependent than the rest on foreign markets and capital. And it is hotly debated between neoclassicists and dependistas, with the orientation and arguments of each in essence constituting the mirror image of the other's. Our aim in the colloquium was to contextualize the economism of this debate in broader institutional frameworks, wherein the issue itself could be rendered in terms that reflect meaningful categories of political analysis and action.

The project began when I was asked by the Institute for World Order, in New York City, to organize a small, diverse and international group of "younger" international relations scholars, who would be willing to focus their attention and energies on this issue, and who would also form the basis for a more lasting invisible college. I was happy to oblige. The original group consisted of Barry Buzan (International Studies, University of Warwick, UK), Cheryl Christensen (Political Science, U.S. Department of Agriculture), Graciela Chichilnisky (Economics, Columbia University), Jeffrey Hart (Political Science, Indiana University), Helge Hveem (Peace Research, University of Oslo), Gerd Junne (International Relations, University of Amsterdam), Peter Katzenstein (Political Science, Cornell University), Robert Keohane (Political Science, Brandeis University), David Laitin (Political Science, University of California at San Diego), Alberto Martinelli (Sociology, University of Milan), and myself. The group met on three occasions, and exchanged research memoranda as well as draft papers between meetings. Once the final volume took shape, Stephan Haggard (Political Science, Harvard University), and Lynn Mytelka (Political Science, Carleton University, Canada) were asked to contribute to it. For diverse reasons, several of the original members could not contribute to this volume. Their participation in group discussions and their impact on the evolution of our collective thinking was profound and is acknowledged with gratitude.

Several other acknowledgements are in order. We are greatly indebted to the Institute for World Order for making this experience possible in the first place, and for their superb administrative support throughout the life of the project. We are also grateful to Juan Somavia and his colleagues at the Instituto Latinoamericano de Estudios Transnacionales, in Mexico City, who hosted our final meeting, and who participated actively and constructively in our discussion of draft chapters on that occasion. The staff of the Institute of War and Peace Studies at Columbia University, very ably led by Ms. Anna Hohri, processed my editorial work as well as my own chapters swiftly and efficiently. Lastly, I want to express my deep personal respect and affection for the other members of the group, for their willingness to detour from their own research programs, for taking seriously the charge of mutual instruction, for producing outstanding papers, and—not the least, as far as I am concerned—for their unfailing and gracious responsiveness to their pernickety editor.

New York City   John Gerard Ruggie
December 1982

About the Contributors

BARRY BUZAN is Lecturer in the Department of International Studies, University of Warwick, U.K. He was born in London, England, in 1946, took his B.A. (1968) at the University of British Columbia, and his Ph.D. (1973) at the London School of Economics. He is the author of *People, States, and Fear: The National Security Problem in International Relations* (1983), and of *Seabed Politics* (1976), and co-editor (with Barry Jones) of *Change and the Study of International Relations* (1981). His other published work concerns aspects of the law of the seas, security policy, and international organization. In 1982, he was awarded the Francis Deak Prize of the *American Journal of International Law* for an article which he published in that journal the previous year.

STEPHAN HAGGARD is Assistant Professor of Government at Harvard University. He was born in San Francisco, California, in 1952. His B.A. (1976) and Ph.D. (1983) are from the University of California at Berkeley. He has been a research fellow at the United Nations Institute for Training and Research (1978–79) and The Brookings Institution (1980–81), has conducted fieldwork in South Korea, Taiwan, and Mexico, and has written on the strategies of the newly industrializing countries.

JEFFREY A. HART is Associate Professor of Political Science at Indiana University. He was born in New Kensington, Pennsylvania, in 1947. He received his B.A. (1969) from Swarthmore College, and his Ph.D. (1975) from the University of California at Berkeley. He taught at Princeton University from 1973 to 1979, and in 1980 served on the professional staff of the President's Commission for a National Agenda for the Eighties. He is the author of *The New International Economic Order* (1983), of a prior monograph on the Anglo-Icelandic cod war, and of journal articles dealing with various aspects of international relations.

HELGE HVEEM is Associate Professor of Political Science at the University of Oslo, and has been associated with the International Peace Research Institute of Oslo since 1968. He was born in Oslo in 1941, and received the Magister Artium from the University of Oslo in 1968. He has done research and teaching in several countries, including Uganda (1969–70), France (1974–75), and Algeria (1975), and has worked as a consultant with the United Nations Conference on Trade and Development on several occasions. Among his publications are *International Relations and World Images* (1972), *The Political Economy of Third World Producer Associations* (1977), and a number of articles on dominance theory, international development issues, and the New International Economic Order. At present, he is editor of the *Journal of Peace Research*.

PETER J. KATZENSTEIN is Professor of Government at Cornell University. He was born in Bremerhaven, Germany, in 1945, and is now a U.S. citizen. His B.A. (1967) is from Swarthmore College, and his Ph.D. (1973) from Harvard University. Among his publications are *Disjoined Partners: Austria and Germany Since 1815* (1976), *Between Power and Plenty: Foreign Economic Policies of Advanced Industrial States* (editor, 1978), several other monographic studies and numerous papers on international political economy and comparative politics, as well as the forthcoming book, *The Small European States in the International Economy*. He is currently the editor of *International Organization*.

ROBERT O. KEOHANE is Professor of Politics at Brandeis University. He was born in Chicago, Illinois, in 1941. He received his B.A. (1961) from Shimer College, and his Ph.D. (1966) from Harvard University. He has also taught at Swarthmore College and Stanford University. Among his publications are *Power and Interdependence: World Politics in Transition* (co-author, with Joseph S. Nye, 1977), *Transnational Relations and World Politics* (co-editor, with Joseph S. Nye, 1972), and numerous articles in international relations theory, international political economy, and international organization. He was the editor of *International Organization* from 1974 to 1980.

DAVID D. LAITIN is Associate Professor of Political Science at the University of California, San Diego. He was born in Brooklyn, New York, in 1945, received his B.A. (1967) from Swarthmore College, and his Ph.D. (1974) from the University of California at Berkeley. He is the author of *Politics, Language, and Thought: The Somali Experience* (1977) and of a number of articles on language policy and African politics. Currently, he is completing a book entitled "Hegemony and Culture: The Politics of Religious Change Among the Yoruba."

CHUNG-IN MOON is a doctoral candidate in the Department of Government and Politics at the University of Maryland, College Park. He was born in Cheju Island, South Korea, in 1951. His B.A. (1977) is from Yonsei University, Seoul, and his M.A. (1981) from the University of Maryland. His dissertation concerns the political economy of bilateralism between the newly industrializing countries and OPEC, focusing on South Korea and Saudi Arabia.

LYNN K. MYTELKA is Professor of Political Science at Carleton University in Canada. She was born in Jersey City, New Jersey, in 1942. Her B.A. (1964) is from Rutgers University, and her Ph.D. (1971) from Johns Hopkins University. She is the author of *Regional Development in a Global Economy: The Multinational Corporation, Technology, and Andean Integration* (1979), co-author (with C. Legum, I. W. Zartman, and S. Langdon) of *Africa in the 1980s: A Continent in Crisis,* and has also published numerous articles in international political economy, regional integration, and North-South relations. She has been a consultant to the Canadian International Development Research Centre, the UN Economic Commission for Africa, the United Nations Conference on Trade and Development, the OECD Development Center, and the Junta Del Acuerdo de Cartagena (Andean Group), as well as other governmental and intergovernmental organizations.

JOHN GERARD RUGGIE is Professor of Political Science and a Member of the Executive Committee, International Economics Research Center, at Columbia University. He was born in Graz, Austria, in 1944, emigrated to Canada in 1956, and to the United States in 1967. He is now a U.S. citizen. His B.A.

(1967) is from McMaster University in Canada, and his Ph.D. (1974) from the University of California at Berkeley, where he also taught from 1973 to 1978. His published work concerns aspects of international relations theory, international political economy, international organization, and world systemic change. Columbia University Press is also publishing his book *The Structure of Planetary Politics: Ecology and the Organization of Global Political Space.* An earlier volume, *International Responses to Technology: Regimes, Institutions, and Technocrats* (1975), co-edited with Ernst B. Haas, was awarded the Harold and Margaret Sprout prize by the International Studies Association. Professor Ruggie has been a consultant on North-South relations to the United Nations Office of the Director General for Development and International Economic Cooperation, the UN Environment Programme, and the UN Office of Science and Technology.

The Antinomies of
Interdependence

Introduction:

International Interdependence and National Welfare

JOHN GERARD RUGGIE

I

THIS IS A study in the political economy of human welfare. Within this broad range of concern, we address one central question that is high on the policy agenda of the international community, particularly of its Third World members: by means of what strategies vis-à-vis the international division of labor can countries best achieve significant and sustainable welfare gains for their people? The question itself is hardly new; as we shall see presently, it has been at issue

Parts of this paper were presented in lecture and seminar form at the University of British Columbia, Vancouver, Canada, in March 1982. I am very grateful to Mark W. Zacher, Director of the Institute of International Relations at UBC, for arranging my visit and for the hospitality and stimulating conversations I enjoyed while there. For their extensive comments on an earlier draft, I am indebted to Jagdish Bhagwati, Douglas Chalmers, Ronald Findlay, Catherine Gwin, Kal Holsti, James Morley, and Howard Wriggins. The other contributors to this volume have also closely scrutinized the paper, especially my summaries of their work, but final responsibility for the interpretations contained herein remains mine alone.

at least since the time of the Industrial Revolution, and thanks largely to the so-called North-South Dialogue, the academic literature on the subject in recent years has exhibited some of the characteristics of an emerging growth industry. The combination of three attributes, however, differentiates our study from others that have recently raised the question. First, the papers that follow are "essays in trespassing" that move, reversing Albert Hirschman's formulation, from politics to economics and beyond.[1] Thus, they focus directly on the political correlates of economic strategies. Second, our approach is inductive and comparative, rather than a priori and global, and we draw on the experience of the United States and Western Europe as well as the newly industrializing countries of the Third World.[2] Finally, wherever possible, we conceive of the welfare effects of economic strategies broadly, to include not only the surrogate

1. Albert O. Hirschman, *Essays in Trespassing: Economics to Politics and Beyond* (New York: Cambridge University Press, 1981). In chapter 1, "The Rise and Decline of Development Economics," Hirschman presents a provocative and engaging account of the development economics produced over the course of the past thirty-five years by heterodox liberals—who set themselves apart from neoclassical orthodoxy by rejecting what Hirschman calls the "monoeconomics claim," that is, the claim that advanced industrial and developing economies differed only quantitatively not qualitatively, and that their study therefore necessitated no distinct analytical apparatus. However, this variant of development economics continued to hold to the "mutual benefit" claim, that is, the claim that economic relations between industrial and developing economies can yield benefits for both. For a complementary and equally spirited examination of more thoroughgoing, Third-World-generated deviations from the mainstream, which reject both of the standard claims, see Carlos F. Diaz-Alejandro, "Delinking North and South: Unshackled or Unhinged?" in Albert Fishlow et al., *Rich and Poor Nations in the World Economy* (New York: McGraw-Hill, for the Council on Foreign Relations, 1978).

2. This puts us at odds with the epistemological premise enunciated by Wallerstein and in a sense mirrored in classical liberal thought, that there is no such thing as *national* development in the modern world system, only development *of* the modern world system. Immanuel Wallerstein, "The Rise and Future Demise of the World Capitalist System: Concepts for Comparative Analysis," *Comparative Studies in Society and History* (September 1974), vol. 16. The similarity to the presuppositions of classical liberalism is pointed out effectively by Robert Brenner, "The Origins of Capitalist Development: A Critique of Neo-Smithian Marxism," *New Left Review* (July—Autumn 1977), no. 104.

measures expressed by aggregate and per capita rates of growth, though these of course are important, but also measures that reflect more directly the extent to which the living standards of peoples are actually improving.[3]

The conclusions of this study are intended to have practical value, in that they suggest the range of viable policy options. But they are also intended to be of theoretical consequence, in that they challenge both the mainstream explanations and the dependency perspective that constitutes the major critical alternative. In view of our own orientation, we are led naturally to emphasize the role of the state, which we find to be far more important than the mainstream believes and more autonomous than the critics allow. But the cases we examine also show that no single policy prescription is fully adequate to answer our central question, and no single theoretical position fully adequate to explain our answers to it. To pretend otherwise is to tread dangerously in the realm of ideologizing—about the magic of the marketplace, the immutable international hierarchy, or the omnipotent state—with potentially deleterious consequences, or opportunities lost, for the very welfare gains that are at stake.

This introductory essay briefly sets the scene for and summarizes the main conclusions of the papers that follow.

---

3. We adopt this posture because improved living standards are the universally accepted objective of the development process, but growth is not universally accepted as guaranteeing them. As the World Bank has noted, what it calls "human development" (improvements in standards of nutrition, health, education, and so on) directly contributes to growth; however, the contribution of growth to poverty reduction "appears inexact." IBRD, *World Development Report, 1980,* ch. 4, p. 35. A more elaborate analysis of this relationship by a World Bank official may be found in Norman L. Hicks, "Growth vs. Basic Needs: Is There a Trade-Off?" *World Development* (November/December 1979), vol. 7, which reaches a similar conclusion. Finally, the "Editor's Introduction" to a volume on poverty and inequality summarizes its main lesson as being "that there is no correlation between either point inequality or changes in inequality and rates of growth." Paul Streeten, *World Development* (March 1978), 6:212.

II

If the Industrial Revolution can be described as a singularity in its positive transformational effects on how and how well people live, it has also proved to be a unique agency of economic stratification. Differences in international levels of income before the Industrial Revolution were limited; the data are poor and estimates vary, but it seems to have been the case that the richest country was considerably less than twice as well off as the poorest country.[4] Moreover, until 1750 or so, the average standard of living in Europe was probably a bit lower than in the rest of the world, due to the high level achieved by China, and it had only reached parity by 1800. By the 1830s, however, the gap significantly favored what we now call the developed countries over the present Third World, and it has continued to grow ever since: average living standards in the two regions differed by a factor of two in the 1870s, three by 1900, five in 1950, seven in 1970, and nearly eight in 1977. Today, the real GNP per capita in the "most developed" industrialized countries is nearly thirty times that of the "less developed" of the developing countries.

At about the time that income differentials between the "developed" countries and the "Third World" began to diverge significantly in the 1830s, pronounced though lesser disparities emerged within the group of developed countries as well. Equalization set in before the end of the nineteenth century for the countries that began their development process before 1860.[5] But it was not until after World

4. This and other figures in this paragraph are taken from Paul Bairoch, "The Main Trends in National Economic Disparities Since the Industrial Revolution," in Bairoch and Maurice Levy-Leboyer, eds., *Disparities in Economic Development Since the Industrial Revolution* (New York: St. Martin's Press, 1981), ch. 1. Bairoch estimates pre-Industrial Revolution income gaps among countries to have been on the order of 1.0 to 1.6, though larger for what he calls "micro-regions" (areas less than 2 million population); inter micro-regional disparities may have been as high as 1.0 to 3.0.

5. Belgium, Canada, Denmark, France, Germany, Norway, Sweden, Switzerland, United Kingdom, United States. Before World War I, four of the eight richest

War II that the poorest of the developed countries experienced a substantial reversal of their relative decline;[6] and it was only in 1977 that the coefficient of variation in GNP per capita among all developed countries fell back to the level at which it had been in 1840—50.[7]

Very roughly speaking, the domestic inequalities triggered by industrialization have tended to follow similar patterns. Here, the data are of even poorer quality. However, within the industrialized countries, they conform quite well to an inverted "U-shaped" curve first hypothesized by Kuznets, with inequalities increasing in the early stages, and then gradually decreasing. With some exceptions, the experience of the developing countries thus far seems largely to confirm the first part of the hypothesis.[8]

By the mid-nineteenth century, income differentials between "early" and "late" industrializers had triggered yet another disparity: one in theorizing about and formulating

countries were largely nonindustrialized, so that "whether . . . development was concentrated in industry or in agriculture seems to imply no important difference as far as increases in standards of living were concerned" (Bairoch and Levy-Leboyer, *Disparities*, p. 9). W. Arthur Lewis spells out the implications of high agricultural productivity and wages in these countries for the concurrently widening North-South disparities in *The Evolution of the International Economic Order* (Princeton: Princeton University Press, 1977), esp. ch. 3.

6. Bairoch and Levy-Leboyer, *Disparities*, pp. 10—11.

7. *Ibid.*, p. 11, and table 1.5. Note also that the Gini coefficient for the developed countries dropped sharply between 1950 and 1975, from 0.302 to 0.131; Robert Summers, Irving B. Kravis, and Alan Heston, "Inequality among Nations: 1950 and 1975," in Bairoch and Levy-Leboyer, *Disparities*, ch. 2.

8. For an extensive cross-sectional test, see Montek S. Ahluwalia, "Inequality, Poverty and Development," *Journal of Development Economics* (1976), vol. 3. There exists no formula that predicts when the reversal commences. Examining the relationship between growth and poverty in twenty-four countries in the nineteenth century, Adelman and Morris found that "the early phases of economic growth appear to have worked systematically to reduce the levels of living of the very poor for periods from several decades to much longer." Irma Adelman and Cynthia Taft Morris, "Growth and Impoverishment in the Middle of the Nineteenth Century," *World Development* (March 1978), 6:258. In England and Belgium, two early industrializers, "more than a half a century elapsed before expansionary influences were sufficient to produce either a significant rise in average incomes of urban and agricultural workers or a marked reduction in the incidence of extreme poverty" (pp. 253—54).

policy responses to the effects of the international economy on differential rates of national development. The position of the front-runner was represented by David Ricardo, via his model of the free exchange of cloth for wine between England and Portugal in accordance with their comparative advantage.[9] At least as it is presented in chapter 7 of the *Principles of Political Economy and Taxation,* from which the received wisdom of orthodox trade theory derives, this specialization entailed no important dynamic implications for growth or development, but simply provided static gains from trade that made both parties better off than they would have been in its absence.[10] Indeed, Ricardo explicitly allowed for the possibility of a role reversal between the two countries, thereby suggesting that no qualitative or structural consequences attended the production of either good. A very different model was advanced by Friedrich List, who spoke for the later European developers, in particular for Germany.[11] List contrasted the "true or national political economy" from the purely hypothetical "cosmopolitical economy" of Smith and his followers. Political economy, as he used the term, "teaches how a given *nation* in the present state of the world and its own special national relations can maintain and improve its economical conditions," whereas cosmopolitical economy "teaches how the entire human race may attain prosperity" on the assumption "that all nations of the earth form but one society living in a per-

9. David Ricardo, *Works,* Piero Sraffa, ed. (Cambridge: Cambridge University Press, 1955).

10. However, Ronald Findlay has argued that the Ricardo of pure trade theory "is a pale shadow of the real one." Findlay maintains that the "real" Ricardo is seen more fully in the *Essay on the Influence of a Low Price of Corn upon the Profits of Stock,* where he urged repeal of the Corn Laws not so much for the sake of static gains from trade as dynamic "gains for growth." Findlay's reinterpretation of Ricardo is part of an excellent exposition and analysis of the literature on "Growth and Development in Trade Models," in Peter B. Kenen and R. W. Jones, eds., *Handbook of International Economics* (Amsterdam: North-Holland, forthcoming), from which I have benefited greatly.

11. Friedrich List, *The National System of Political Economy,* New Edition, Sampson S. Lloyd, trans. (London: Longmans, Green, 1904).

petual state of peace."[12] Political economy embodied a theory of productive powers, cosmopolitical economy only a theory of values of exchange. National development required development of national productive powers. For late industrializers, this necessitated deliberate state intervention domestically and the judicious use of external tariffs. To meet an industrially supreme Britain on the grounds of laissez faire and free trade, he concluded, would undermine any attempt to build up equally powerful economies by the other European nations, and would relegate them to the status of tributary economies.[13] However, as Europe as a whole came to specialize in the production of manufactures, the tropical areas, thanks to colonialism of which List approved, would be induced to supply the needed raw materials and agricultural products while serving as a market for manufactured goods. A complementary global division of labor would emerge but it would be hierarchical, because the production of manufactured goods offered increasing returns to scale that could not be reaped by the production of primary products.[14] In sum, where Ricardo saw only quantitative differences between the producers of cloth and wine that free exchange would mutually reward, List stressed qualitative differences that free exchange would exacerbate and that the state, therefore, had to overcome.[15]

12. These distinctions are elaborated in List, *National System*, ch. 11; citations at pp. 99, 97, 100; emphasis in original.

13. *Ibid.*, ch. 12.

14. *Ibid.*, ch. 22.

15. For a juxtaposition of the views of Ricardo and List that is unusually sympathetic to the latter by Anglo-American standards, see Marcello de Cecco, *Money and Empire* (Oxford: Basil Blackwell, 1974), ch. 1. Closer to the norm is the sole reference to List in my college Economics 1 text. It appears as part of a longer footnote and reads as follows: "Friedrich List, a German writer of around 1840, is typical of some aspects of romanticism; his arguments for tariffs have carried weight, and some of his nationalistic followers became apologists for fascist economics." Paul A. Samuelson, *Economics*, 5th ed. (New York: McGraw-Hill, 1961), p. 835. De Cecco takes pleasure in suggesting that the inattention paid to List in the Anglo-American literature is matched only by the near-universal adoption of his recipes by what today are the industrialized countries (pp. 12– 13).

As noted above, relative income similarity at relatively high levels has been achieved among the industrialized countries. But international as well as domestic income disparities persist between the industrialized and developing countries, and so do disagreements about the relationship between patterns of international interdependence and differential rates of national development. The conjunction of these three facts broadly circumscribes the range of our inquiry.

III

The post—World War II era has witnessed several institutional innovations in the international political economy. In the immediate postwar years, a major effort was undertaken to internationalize public authority in the monetary and trade fields, in the attempt to prevent a recurrence of the international economic disarticulation of the interwar period, and to provide for a stable and growing world economy. The regimes for money and trade that emerged initially made no special provisions for the developing countries. But insofar as the mandate of the International Bank for Reconstruction and Development included concessional lending of investment capital to developing countries, the concept of an international role in the development process was instituted as well. The adequacy and terms of those initial capital transfers became matters of great debate right from the start. Over the course of the next thirty-five years, this debate came not simply to involve questions of aid and investment, but to implicate the regimes for money and trade, and, indeed, ultimately to challenge the very structure of the world economy on the ground that it contributed to rather than alleviated income disparities between the industrialized and the developing countries.[16]

16. The evolution from the early SUNFED debates to the NIEO is briefly traced in Branislav Gosovic and John Gerard Ruggie, "The NIEO: Origins and Evolution of the Concept," *International Social Science Journal* (Autumn 1976), vol. 28.

At issue today are the character and scope of what we might call the world development regime.[17] That this concern is being addressed at all itself marks a discontinuity of some magnitude. But the question at the heart of this concern is simply the contemporary, North-South, variant of the same question that has always preoccupied the so-called late industrializers: how closely and on what terms should the developing countries seek to integrate themselves into the world economy in order to maximize their prospects for significant and sustainable welfare gains? Three major contending positions can be identified.

The first position prescribes "outward-oriented" or "export-led" development strategies. Among its advocates is the World Bank: "As a group, the successful [developing] countries have been those which have resisted or overcome the temptation to adopt inward-looking trade policies and to delay transition to greater export orientation."[18] This outward orientation is seen to account for the recent successes of three tiers of developing countries. At the forefront are the newly industrializing or "semi-industrial" countries of East Asia, such as Singapore and South Korea. From being low-income countries in the 1950s, they have transformed their economies to become major exporters of manufactures and are now among the wealthier middle-income countries. A later but similar reorientation of policy in several Latin American countries is said to have brought them to "the stage at which they can begin to shift into more demanding, skill- and technology-intensive areas of production."[19] Lastly, and still further down the rungs of the international division of labor, according to the Bank the outward orientation of certain primary producing countries, like the

17. I take up the notion of regimes more extensively in ch. 9. Simply to restate for the moment the, by now, standard definition, an international regime is a social institution around which actor expectations converge in any given domain of international relations. See Stephen D. Krasner's "Introduction" to the special issue on international regimes of *International Organization* (Spring 1982), vol. 36.

18. IRBD, *World Development Report, 1981*, p. 25.

19. *Ibid.*

Ivory Coast, has led to a deepening and broadening of their agricultural exports that now allows them to move into processing and industrial sectors.[20] The reasons advanced for the success of these strategies are simply that an outward orientation increases efficiency in the allocation of resources, competitiveness of goods produced, and flexibility to adapt to the ever-changing opportunities and constraints thrown up by the international economy—including rapid adjustment to the severe external shocks of the 1970s.[21] The pull of expanding industrial country markets is no longer thought to be as important to the successful middle-income countries as it was in the past; their own competitiveness, entrepreneurship, and exports to third markets all having increased substantially. Nevertheless, the industrial countries are assigned the responsibility of themselves adjusting to the imperatives of a changing international division of labor by avoiding protectionism and support for their declining industries. Lastly, since this dynamic is *not* expected to affect the low-income countries in the near future—even under the most favorable of assumptions, the Bank predicts both relative and absolute widening of income gaps between the richest and poorest countries, and between the middle-income and low-income countries[22]—augmented direct assistance to them targeted at the basic human needs of their populations is also called for.

The second position is embodied in the program of the New International Economic Order. Its components are well known and can be summarized briefly.[23] In general terms,

20. *Ibid.,* p. 26.

21. *Ibid.,* ch. 6, where it is argued that the experience of the 1970s suggests only a weak association between the magnitude of external shocks and subsequent growth rates, the mediating factor being economic policy. And whereas outward-oriented economics may be more vulnerable to external shocks, the Bank concludes that they also "managed to effect adjustment with only a temporary interruption in growth" (p. 75).

22. *Ibid.,* ch. 2, which contains ten-year forecasts.

23. A summary and analysis of the NIEO program and negotiating postures as of the time of the Seventh Special Session of the UN General Assembly may be found in Branislav Gosovic and John Gerard Ruggie, "On the Creation of a New

they include measures of a comprehensive, integrated, and regulatory character, designed to manipulate and direct international economic activities in such a way as to produce outcomes considered to be more favorable to the developing countries than those produced by current international market mechanisms. In the area of raw materials, commodity agreements with a Common Fund are intended to stabilize if not increase developing country export earnings and to diversify their export base. In trade, preferential and non-reciprocal measures are designed to obtain greater access to industrial-country markets. In industry, a greater share for developing countries in world production is the objective. The program also calls for international monetary reform and for a link between international liquidity creation via the SDR and development assistance. Easier access to credit and selective debt relief too are urged, as are greater quantities and automaticity of aid flows. Codes of conduct are proposed for technology transfer and for the governance of certain activities of transnational corporations. Lastly, the developing countries have sought greater influence over the decision-making process of the International Monetary Fund and the World Bank, as well as by the UN General Assembly over these and other institutions in the social and economic sectors of the UN system.

In sum, whereas the outward-oriented development strategies advocated by the World Bank would integrate the developing countries into the world economy on the basis of dynamic comparative advantage, the NIEO calls for their integration on a more planned basis, with redistributive principles directly guiding the allocation of resources.

The third position, that of the "de-linkers," does not seek the integration of the developing countries on *any* terms.

International Economic Order," *International Organization* (Spring 1976), vol. 30. Not a great deal has taken place by way of implementation, as the most recent UN document on the subject makes clear: Report of the Director-General for Development and International Economic Co-operation, *Towards the New International Economic Order* (New York: United Nations, 1982).

On the contrary, to achieve development they deem it necessary to pursue dissociation and self-reliance. There is, however, no dominant variant of this position. A relatively mild form, at this time still meant to be supplementary to the NIEO, is the program of "collective self-reliance" adopted by the Group of 77.[24] It would establish a system of trade preferences among developing countries, and encourage cooperation among LDC state trading organizations. It would move toward greater use of Third World payments and credit arrangements. It proposes industrial cooperation in the form of LDC multinational production enterprises. And it encourages the exchange of technical skills and technology among developing countries so as to build up a more appropriate and endogenous LDC technological capacity. More radical forms of dissociation have been practiced by individual countries, notably the Soviet Union in the 1930s, post-revolutionary China and Cuba, as well as Albania, Burma, Kampuchea, and, more questionably, North Korea. However, as a conscious and systematic development strategy, dissociation and self-reliance have flourished best in the province of the intelligentsia.[25] There, self-reliance is conceived

24. "Arusha Programme for Collective Self-Reliance and Framework for Negotiations," adopted at the Fourth Ministerial Meeting of the Group of 77, Arusha, February 12–16, 1969, reprinted in Karl P. Sauvant, *The Group of 77* (New York: Oceana, 1981), Annex II.

25. Some advocates of self-reliance would challenge this claim. Note, for one example, this assessment by Johan Galtung: "It should be emphasized from the very beginning that to talk about the politics of self-reliance is not to talk about a strategy of transition to something utopian, but to talk about a process very much alive that takes place in the world today for everybody to watch, talk about and participate in—or fight against, as many do and more will do as it gains momentum. Roughly speaking, it may already be a process that involves one billion human beings; *a quarter of humankind* in the active forerunner phase with the remaining three quarters on the sidelines, apathetic or talking about developmental processes of yesteryear." Galtung, "The Politics of Self-Reliance," in Galtung et al., eds., *Self-Reliance: A Strategy for Development* (London: Bogle-L'Ouverture, for the Institute of Development Studies, Geneva, 1980), p. 355, emphasis in original. Galtung includes in his count parts of China, former Indochina, India, Sri Lanka, North Korea, Tanzania, Madagascar, Somalia, Albania, and even the Nordic countries. Obviously, some difficult definitional problems have to be resolved before a definitive assessment is possible.

unequivocally as the "negation of dependency."[26] That, in turn, is assumed to entail nothing less than the negation of liberalism in its broad philosophical no less than specifically economic dimensions. The primary social unit becomes the group or community, serving a collective purpose.[27] Production for use value constitutes the norm of economic activity, the satisfaction of basic consumption goods its proximate objective.[28] Cooperation among like units forms the basis for the division of labor.[29] And the authenticity as well as generative capacity of endogenous thought and cultures are celebrated.[30]

Each of these positions draws upon a certain body of

26. Johan Galtung, "On the Technology of Self-Reliance," in Galtung et al., *Self-Reliance*, p. 227.

27. "Liberal capitalism values the *individualistic* concept of self-help. To help oneself, even when it is at the expense of others, was supposed to be good for the country and possibly the world. On the contrary, *collective* self-*reliance* is only compatible with a social cosmology which favours the group or community as opposed to the individual." Roy Preiswerk, "Introduction," in Galtung et al., *Self-Reliance*, p. 12, emphases in original.

28. "The basic economic principle, then, would be to use local factors and produce for local consumption. Before producing anything, however, the question only asked in a penetrating manner during times of crisis should *always* be asked: do we really need this product? The argument that it can be used for *exchange* even if we do not need it for any *use* presupposes that there are other communities not based on self-reliance — like capitalism assumes there will always be a periphery somewhere that can serve as a 'market.' " Johan Galtung, "Self-Reliance: Concepts, Practice and Rationale," in Galtung et al., *Self-Reliance*, p. 24, emphases in original.

29. "The point is not to cut out trade but to *redirect* it and *recompose* it by giving preference to cooperation with those in the same position, preferring the neighbour to the more distant possibility, cooperation to exchange, and intra-sector to inter-sector trade." Galtung, et al., *Self-Reliance*, p. 26. In the area of trade, the most important dynamic tendency to result from self-reliance, according to Galtung (p. 36), would be a marked decrease in trade "across genuine gaps in the level of processing." Galtung fails to mention and comment upon the fact that intra-sectoral as opposed to inter-sectoral specialization is, of course, the very basis of the international division of labor *among* the advanced capitalist countries. More of what this phenomenon signifies in chapter 9, below.

30. Kanyana Mutombo, "Self-Reliance and Authenticity: Two Components of a Single Problem," in Galtung et al., *Self-Reliance*. Roy Preiswerk, "Sources of Resistance to Self-Reliance," in Galtung et al., *Self-Reliance*, points out that self-reliance thus rejects the belief common to liberalism and Marxism, namely, that they comprise sets of universal truths and truly cosmopolitan cultures.

economic theory and holds to a certain premise about the international division of labor. The theoretical scaffolding of the outward-oriented development strategies derives from neoclassical trade theory. Its lineage traces back to the model of Ricardo, as amended by Heckscher, Ohlin, and Samuelson, to make trade not simply of mutual advantage but an instrument for reducing international disparities. Though it is now accepted that there exist numerous anomalies to and asymmetries in the rule of mutually beneficial exchange, not to mention equalization, these are treated as special and/or temporary cases. The fundamental premise remains welfare gains and declining income differentials through comparative advantage and market forces.[31] The NIEO program reflects the critique of conventional trade theory that was produced by Raul Prebisch and others at ECLA (UN Economic Commission for Latin America) in the late 1940s. The "ECLA theses" in turn have roots in List and Keynes, and to some extent Marx. They comprise a dynamic but asymmetrical model of center-periphery relations. The model presupposes inherent distortions in the international division of labor, stemming largely from the ability by the center to appropriate a disproportionate share of the benefits of productivity increases in both center and periphery, thus maintaining and even widening the gap between the two. But it takes these to be distortions that can be corrected by individual and collective governmental regulation of market forces and economic agents.[32] The advocacy of dissociation and self-reliance has at least two different roots, each of which reflects a different concern. One strand draws on dependency theory. This theory, or perspective, itself is an amalgam of the "ECLA theses" and the Marxist approach

31. Findlay, in Kenen and Jones, eds., *Handbook*, traces the evolution of this literature.

32. Fernando H. Cardoso, "The Originality of the Copy: CEPAL and the Idea of Development," *CEPAL Review* (second half of 1977); and Osvaldo Sunkel, "The Development of Development Thinking," in Jose J. Villamil, ed., *Transnational Capitalism and National Development* (Atlantic Highlands, N.J.: Humanities Press, 1979).

to imperialism and late development, which at best grants that the international division of labor can produce dependent and distorted capitalist development in the Third World, and at worst predicts continued underdevelopment and impoverishment due to the process of uneven and exploitative capital accumulation on a world scale.[33] Another intellectual root of dissociation is inspired by a concern with the viability of unconventional, basic-needs-oriented, domestic development strategies when these are exposed and subjected to hostile international economic forces embodying the social relations of generalized commodity production.[34]

It is our purpose in this volume to examine critically some of the claims and premises of these three positions. However, we do so not in abstract theoretical terms, but by examining actual strategies and policies of governments in concrete historical settings. We do not strive to formulate or even to "test" causal laws; the complexity and diversity of experiences forbid both at this juncture. Rather, our hope is to produce situationally valid generalizations, which will better equip both scholars and practitioners to resist the

33. For a sympathetic yet critical review of dependency theory, see Gabriel Palma, "Dependency: A Formal Theory of Underdevelopment or a Methodology for the Analysis of Concrete Situations of Under-Development?" *World Development* (July/August 1978), vol. 6; on the relationship between dependency theory and dissociation/self-reliance, see Galtung et al., *Self-Reliance,* and Ismail-Sabri Abdalla, ed., *Economic Integration and Third World Collective Self-Reliance,* Nyon, Switzerland, Third World Forum, Occasional Paper No. 4, 1979.

34. On the whole, this tends to be more a Northern rather than a Southern concern. See "What Now? Another Development," *Development Dialogue* (1975 #2); published by the Dag Hammarskjold Foundation, Uppsala, Sweden; and virtually any issue of the *Dossier* published by the International Foundation for Development Alternatives (IFDA), Nyon, Switzerland. Carlos F. Diaz-Alejandro is skeptical about some sources of Northern support for Southern dissociation and self-reliance, finding two in particular to be objectionable. The first is simply worried about Southern exports: "It is not surprising, then, that *Business Week* should refer to Samir Amin as one of the Third World's best economists and expound his views." The second he calls paternalistic progressives: "Some Northern academics, especially in Europe, who regard themselves as progressives and friends of the LDCs, appear to take the paternalistic view that if LDCs do not delink on their own, Northern progressives (those academics and their trade union allies) will do it for them." "Open Economy, Closed Polity?" *Millennium* (forthcoming).

temptation of axiomatic substitutes for thought and struggle, while, at the same time, providing some systematic basis for picking and choosing among plausible and possible
policy options.

We pay closest attention to the "associative" posture, as
we will call it for short, of an outward-oriented strategy designed to find a niche in the international economy based
on comparative advantage. We do so because it clearly represents the hegemonic position among the three at this
time. It is hegemonic in part for the obvious reason that it
reflects the principles of economic organization favored by
the dominant economic powers. But its hegemony is also
due to the fact that it is seen widely, and increasingly by the
developing countries themselves, to come closest to embodying those forces that actually produce change in national economies and upgrade their status in the international division of labor.[35] The newly found favor of this
strategy among the developing countries no doubt is inspired by the impressive rates of growth in output and the
extraordinary rates of growth in manufactured exports
achieved by the newly industrializing countries, especially
those in East Asia.

We also examine the alternative attempt to achieve
greater self-reliance by means of self-conscious arms-length
relationships vis-à-vis the international division of labor, or
what we call the "dissociative" posture. However, unless one
includes every invocation of infant industry arguments or
protectionist measures, the historical record of self-reliance, in the sense of the unconventional and autocentric

35. For example, during the negotiations for the Third United Nations Development Decade, the Group of 77 was clearly cross-pressured along liberalization-
NIEO lines. The result was that strong support for the NIEO was reiterated in the
final text, but, at the same time, "a system of trade based on a dynamic pattern
of comparative advantage reflecting a more effective international division of labor" was urged as "a fundamental objective of the international community." *Report of the Preparatory Committee for the New International Development Strategy* (New York: United Nations, 1981), p. 176; this document summarizes the
evolution of the negotiation positions.

strategy that its advocates take it to be, is not strong, and cases are sometimes hard to distinguish. Moreover, instances of voluntary pure dissociation are so rare as to be of interest mainly as anomalies.[36] The extensive degree of dissociation exhibited by several post-revolutionary socialist cases was a product of external exigency more than of choice. In addition, prior to the Sino-Soviet split, China received substantial assistance from the Soviet Union, and Cuba still does. Our focus, therefore, is on the even more difficult-to-identify middle ground of "selective dissociation."[37] And our analysis of it perforce is less exhaustive and more speculative in character than for the case of association. Nonetheless, examining this strategy can be justified on more than merely theoretical grounds. Given current conditions in the world economy, together with the problem posed by the fallacy of composition to subsequent tiers of newly industrializing countries,[38] there is every likelihood that the incidence of selective dissociation will increase in the future.

Lastly, we make brief reference to the third alternative

36. For a detailed look at one such anomaly, the case of Burma, see Kal J. Holsti, "From Diversification to Isolation: Burma, 1963–1967," in Holsti et al., *Why Nations Realign* (London: Allen & Unwin, 1982).

37. While there exists no universally agreed-upon definition of what is meant by selective dissociation, Carlos F. Diaz-Alejandro has presented a sketch of its general features. A government adopting this posture as part of an unconventional, self-reliant development strategy will, according to Diaz, participate in international markets, but on a limited basis in which the external links are an explicit complement to but not a substitute for indigenous development objectives and efforts. Diaz-Alejandro, "Delinking North and South," pp. 110–22. More specific definitions, appropriate to the individual contexts that they discuss, will be found in chapters 6 to 8, below.

38. Paul Bairoch illustrates the problem with simple arithmetic: "if the underdeveloped countries [excluding the socialist countries among them] had exported in 1970 as many manufactured goods per capita as Hong Kong did, these exports would have risen to $1040 billion, i.e., nineteen times more than the total Third World exports and over three times more than total world exports." *The Economic Development of the Third World Since 1900*, Lady Cynthia Postan, trans. (Berkeley: University of California Press, 1975), p. 100. Including the socialist developing countries, especially China, would of course raise the figure to utterly absurd levels.

strategy, the attempt to alter the world development regime through multilateral negotiations. The reference will be brief because, as we will show, this strategy can complement in limited fashion efforts at the national level, but cannot substitute for them.

The major generalizations suggested by our study, in highly stylized form, are these:

1. The effect of international economic interdependence on national welfare is ambivalent. Openness toward the international economy creates opportunities, but also produces dislocating consequences. This is so irrespective of the institutional form within which international economic interdependence is embedded. A successful associative posture therefore requires devising means to exploit the opportunities and to cushion the dislocations.

2. Any presumed identity between an outward-oriented development strategy and laissez-faire is fictitious, or, perhaps more accurately, ideological. Except for the most powerful economies, which have greater scope to externalize or absorb adjustment costs, and for the city-state of Hong Kong, domestic state intervention attending the successful deployment of an outward-looking strategy is as deep and systematic as that of its more inward-looking alternatives. The differences lie in the proximate ends of state intervention, the areas targeted for intervention, and the means selected. In general, governments pursuing an outward-looking strategy initially follow market signals in identifying their niche in the international division of labor, but then utilize a battery of interventionist techniques in the attempt to maintain and diversify the basis of their comparative advantage. This is true of the associators among the newly industrializing countries of the Third World as well as of the advanced industrial but small European states.

3. Devising domestic means to exploit the opportunities and control the adverse consequences of economic openness is not simply a question of devising optimal economic and social policies. To be sure, such policies are ab-

solutely crucial to the accomplishment of both purposes, and they can go some way toward compensating for small size and external dependence. However, the capacity fully to implement such policies itself reflects the prior existence of certain political conditions. In pure form, these conditions enable governing coalitions either to integrate the major sectional interests of society into the cooperative regulation of domestic distributional strife, or to insulate policy-making from their influence and to pursue state-defined national development objectives. History and contemporary experience offer variants of both and of their combination. But none exists in great abundance in the Third World at this time.

4. Generating the political infrastructure for a successful associative posture is not an impossible task. Countries that lack it at one time subsequently are found to possess it. The historical experience of Northern and Southern countries alike suggests, however, that these political arrangements rarely evolve smoothly simply as a by-product of association. Where they emerge at all, they are shaped at least in part by major crises, including depression, civil war, and international war. Although the point requires much more detailed analysis, it may be the case that the political requisites of successful (long-term) association emerge more smoothly from a (temporary) dissociative stance. The most successful among the current group of newly industrializing countries exhibit such "phases" in their strategies. Again excepting the singularity of Hong Kong, all of them laid the institutional bases for industrialization under regimes of import substitution. These institutional bases subsequently allowed those among them not disposing of a large home market to turn to export-led strategies.

5. Pursuing an outward-oriented development strategy in the absence of the requisite political conditions (or some functional equivalents thereto) will not necessarily retard rates of economic growth. Indeed, in some cases these may well increase, at least over the short term. Such a posture

will entail costs of a different sort, primarily by exacerbating domestic cleavages. What more will follow obviously depends on specific circumstances, including the depth, scope, and forms of association and of domestic cleavages, as well as the precise configuration of domestic state-society relations. In general, income inequalities almost surely will not be attenuated, and, on the contrary, are likely to increase. Beyond a higher threshold, disadvantaged social groups may experience greater marginalization and the domestic economy growing disarticulation. At the extreme, domestic political disintegration may ensue or be averted by extremist means. Our cases show that this array of possible consequences does not depict a uniquely Third World syndrome.

6. As was mentioned above, not the extent of state intervention but its proximate ends, the areas targeted, and the means selected differentiate dissociative from associative postures. In a dissociative posture, endogenously determined configurations of domestic sectoral objectives rather than whatever niche is offered up by the international economy comprise the proximate ends of state policy; the close monitoring and filtering of external links takes the place of liberalization; and the active encouragement, protection, exploitation, and integration of indigenous capacities and resources takes the place of domestic compensation for liberalization.

7. As with association, the success of a dissociative posture depends on more than devising optimal policy measures. Assuming the commitment of a government to selective dissociation as part of a more self-reliant development strategy, the process of implementation faces several additional sets of possible constraints. The most obvious is that social groups that benefited from association may resist dissociation. They are likely to have skills and resources that are scarce in most developing countries so that their involvement in the implementation of the strategy is at once desirable and problematical. A second constraint

is the heavy administrative burden imposed by this strategy, which may be beyond the capacity of many developing countries in the short term even though it might help develop such a capacity in the longer term. A third concerns the tendency in many developing countries to discount indigenous products and processes in favor of patterns prevailing in the advanced industrialized countries. This tendency is visible in the economic, cultural, and military realms, and it potentially undermines the efficacy of the very resources on which the strategy is designed to draw. A fourth constraint is posed by the centripetal pull exerted by the international system, above all by the forces embodied in the transnationalization of production, and in the dynamic of the global balance of power. The former may induce deviation from the dissociative course; the latter may preempt it altogether. Only in specific contexts can one say which of these, or still other, constraints comprise how serious a problem for attempts at dissociation. Our cases do suggest, however, that success or failure ultimately is determined more directly by domestic than by international factors, and that domestic factors, while influenced by the international situation, are not its mere reflection.

8. No simple generalization fully captures the complex issue of the respective welfare effects of the two strategies. In terms of reducing intercountry disparities, the historical experience of the West and the more recent cases of the newly industrializing countries of the Third World suggest that whether or not the appropriate political infrastructure exists for *either* strategy may be more important a factor than the strategies themselves. The question for future industrializers thus becomes, which set of political requisites appears more feasible for them to institute in light of international and domestic constraints? In terms of reducing domestic disparities, a similarly contingent conclusion is reached. There appears to exist no direct correlation, either positive or negative, between external posture and measures of human welfare. The critical intervening factor is the

distribution of assets and access to productive resources within a society. Favorable domestic distributive patterns together with *either* strategy have produced relatively high levels of human welfare in the past. The question for future industrializers thus becomes, which strategy is more likely to generate and sustain favorable domestic distributive patterns? Although there will of course be exceptions, it is our impression that when the answers to these questions are tallied for individual countries further down the rungs of the international division of labor, mimicry of the most recent phase of the East Asian NICs' strategy will not fare better on domestic welfare grounds for most of them, well into the medium term, than greater self-reliance requiring at least partial dissociation.

9. The current world economic situation and, more profoundly, the extent to which the laws of comparative advantage in the world economy are circumscribed by political, economic, and social considerations emanating from the advanced capitalist countries, point in the same direction. They suggest a far more limited absorptive capacity of the markets of the industrialized world for the exports of future industrializers than was the case during the 1960s and 1970s.

10. Lastly, the strategy of altering the terms of association for developing countries by means of multilateral negotiations is not viable as a distinct strategy. International rules and conventions for development are embedded within and constrained by broader international economic regimes. These regimes in turn reflect and serve the international and domestic needs of the regime-making states. The major mechanism of change in these regimes is the ability to project effective demand. The developing countries on several occasions have managed thereby to alter the functioning of existing regimes in modest ways. In general, however, any international strategy on the part of the developing countries at best can provide a facilitative framework

for change, which must rest, in the final analysis, on self-help measures.

In sum, we conclude that the hegemony of the outward-oriented development strategies advocated by mainstream economists and by the institutions that reflect their views is unwarranted. But we are also dubious about some of the claims advanced from the dependency perspective. We are skeptical of both for the identical reason: both overstate the determining impact of the international division of labor on national welfare, the one positively and the other negatively. This leads the mainstream to ignore the critical importance of, and many dependistas to discount the generative potential inherent in, domestic political structures. The political realm is not an autonomous realm, especially in weak and heavily penetrated developing countries. But no explanation of economic outcomes and no program of economic change can succeed that does not systematically incorporate its varying degrees of "relative autonomy."

Brief thematic summaries of the individual papers, which suggest these generalizations, follow below.

IV

A variety of experiences with associative development, historical and contemporary, Northern and Southern, is examined in chapters 1 through 5. This section of the book begins with Robert Keohane's analysis of the posture of the United States from independence to the Civil War, a period during which the United States was transformed, in Keohane's words, "from a postcolonial fragment to an important country undergoing self-sustaining economic growth."[39] This transformation was achieved, for the most part, by the

39. Keohane in this volume.

government remaining passive in the face of the forces of comparative advantage. There were two sets of exceptions to this rule, the dissociation effected during the period of 1808 to 1815 by the Embargo, its successor measures, and the War of 1812, as well as successive bouts with protective tariffs thereafter. However, neither was part of any conscious economic strategy, according to Keohane, and neither played a major role in stimulating long-term industrialization. In aggregate economic terms, this unmanaged associative posture was tremendously successful, especially in the period after 1820. Rates of growth in output and in per capita income were high, as were rates of capital accumulation, while foreign debt was relatively low and overall dependence on exports modest. Internal trade grew in importance relative to foreign trade, especially between the agricultural West and the increasingly industrialized Northeast, and intraregional trade grew still more rapidly. But the prevailing pattern of antebellum development in the United States also produced costly by-products. One of these was growing inequalities in income and wealth. Far more important was the fact that there emerged not one but two economies in the United States, and the central state was insufficiently strong to hold them together. The economy based on the interregional division of labor between the West and Northeast diversified and industrialized, and it became increasingly self-sustaining. The plantation economy of the South, based on slave labor and constituting the dominant supplier of cotton to the world market, did none of these things. The growing contradictions between the two, Keohane argues, through a complex interplay of factors—economic and political, domestic and international—ultimately resulted in the Civil War. Keohane concludes that, while close association with the world economy thus produced a variety of "negative externalities" for American society as a whole, the most costly of which was to entrench slavery in the South, it is doubtful that alternative policies would have been politically feasible given the structure of incentives prevailing at the time.

The long-term economic success of the United States was assured by the fact that, as Keohane puts it in his amendment of Louis Hartz's phrase, the United States not only was born free, it also was born lucky. Three-quarters of a century after the Civil War, the United States was the world's paramount economic power with which others had to learn to cope. Among those who learned well are the small capitalist states of Western Europe. These states have been the step-children of conventional international political studies, even while they appear to comprise the archetype of the small, open economy that is the basic building block of neoclassical trade theory. Peter Katzenstein, in chapter 2, shows that neither view is justified.[40] The experience of these countries in managing the effects of an external economic environment they cannot control sheds considerable light on the predicament faced by other countries both above and below them in the international economic hierarchy. At the same time, their manner of managing these effects incorporates but goes well beyond "free market" methods. By means of a characteristic mix of policies, Katzenstein argues, the small European states have managed to combine external dependence with domestic social cohesion, high levels of prosperity, and economic equality. They are a paradigmatic case of economic association that has worked by any measure. To what is their success due? Katzenstein depicts the post-World War II economic strategies of the small European states as systematically balancing a strong commitment to international liberalism with extensive domestic compensatory interventionism. Their commitment to international liberalism, in comparison with the larger industrial states, is seen in their early advocacy of the abolition of trade and monetary restrictions, their relatively lower tariff and

40. The seven countries that are the subject of his analysis are Austria, Belgium, Denmark, The Netherlands, Norway, Sweden, and Switzerland.

non-tariff barriers to trade, the fact that they adjust more readily to changes in international specialization while availing themselves less frequently of restrictive safeguarding measures, and in their strong support for the principles and institutions of economic multilateralism. On the domestic side, while the specific forms of interventionism vary, as a group these states uniformly exhibit extensive and active policies designed to achieve wage and price stability, and in return to provide generous social welfare benefits and adjustment assistance. Katzenstein contends that what makes this conjunction of international liberalism and domestic compensation possible as a strategy is that it rests on a particular fusion of state and society that he calls corporatist politics. By this he means the centralization of social power within peak organizations and, based on some shared notion of social partnership, the incorporation of business, labor, and the state into the decision-making arena. These structural arrangements minimize distributive friction and political stalemate, and thus facilitate the formulation and implementation of socially highly demanding sets of policies. Katzenstein explains that the social consensus on which these political structures rest emerged, after World War II, in reaction against the deep social dislocations that plagued all of these countries during the interwar years, ranging in intensity from labor strife everywhere to civil war in Austria, as well as the more general sense of vulnerability produced by the depression, fascism, and the war itself. And since the war, these structures have been reinforced by the requirements of international competitiveness in the world economy. Past success, of course, does not guarantee success in a future and less hospitable international economic environment, and the policy mix of one set of countries cannot simply be generalized beyond the mix of international and domestic situations that gave rise to it. Nevertheless, the adaptive capacity of the small European states appears to be higher than that of the larger and more powerful industrialized economies; and the balancing act on which this capacity hinges, even if not the specific balancing mechanisms, appears to express a more general requirement for small and dependent economies.

This last point is reflected in the experience of the newly industrializing countries of the Third World.[41] In comparison with the small European states, the newly industrializing countries have less diversified economies, and their import dependence and export concentration are higher. Moreover, where the small European economies can count on robust invisibles sectors to help offset their chronic balance of trade deficits, the newly industrializing countries are much more heavily dependent on external sources of financing. The domestic social and political structures of the two sets of states contrast still more sharply. But the shift toward an outward orientation in the newly industrializing countries has also been accompanied by "domestic compensation," involving a shift in the role and power of the state. Though no single pattern characterizes this shift, the fact of the shift, and one pattern, is illustrated by the case of South Korea, one of the most successful of the outward-oriented newly industrializing countries. In chapter 3, Stephan Haggard and Chung-in Moon briefly compare the "East Asian" and "Latin American" variants of the NIC industrialization strategies, and then focus on the state and export-led development in Korea.

With respect to economic strategies, perhaps the most significant difference between the Asian and Latin American NICs lies in their respective responses to the exhaustion of the so-called easy phase of import-substituting industrialization. The Latin American NICs, disposing of larger domestic markets, moved into a secondary phase of import substitution, coupling this with specific but limited forms of export promotion. The Asian NICs moved into "export substitution," as Haggard and Moon term it, to export those

41. In the lexicon of the OECD, the category of Third World NICs includes Hong Kong, Singapore, South Korea, and Taiwan in Asia, and Brazil and Mexico in Latin America. However, this ascription can be quite elastic, depending upon its source.

goods which, under import substitution, had come to be produced domestically, and they coupled this with a thoroughgoing reform of previous economic policies and institutional arrangements. South Korea's transformation at first glance resembles the textbook case. Exploiting its comparative advantage in low-wage labor, South Korea found a niche in the production for export of light manufactures. It liberalized its exchange rate, tariff, and investment regimes. International openness subsequently not only stimulated economic growth, but also helped to upgrade Korean exports into technologically more demanding and rewarding sectors. The economy has diversified both in terms of export products and trading partners. Wages have continued to rise, and income distribution is relatively egalitarian. However, behind this economic transformation stands a battery of state policies. They range in depth of intervention from the simple provision of certain public goods like market information and infrastructure, to a variety of incentives and disincentives for domestic and foreign-owned enterprises that bias economic activity in favor of designated exports, to state control over the allocation of credit with the same end in mind, and, most recently, to a direct state role in production in the heavy and chemical industries. Indeed, so active is the state in South Korea that Haggard and Moon characterize Korean industrialization as "state-led." The state, they argue, has managed to accumulate both the political power and the economic resources to insulate itself from social and political pressures, to control business and above all labor, and to keep the economy on its charted course—a course that close alliance with the United States helped to chart. This posture has had its costs. As Haggard and Moon caution, establishing causal links between outward-oriented development strategies and authoritarian politics is a very tricky business.[42] But, they suggest, an af-

42. For a comparative exploration of this relationship in the Latin American context, see David Collier, ed., *The New Authoritarianism in Latin America* (Princeton: Princeton University Press, 1979), and Diaz-Alejandro, "Open Economy, Closed Polity?"

finity between the two does exist in South Korea. Moreover, the state-led move to deepen industrialization has severely tested the adequacy of the Korean model, in both its external and domestic dimensions, to sustain the process of continued upgrading, and it has created an economic and political crisis from which the country has yet to recover. Lastly, the equitable distribution of wealth and income in South Korea, which has its origins in the destruction of the landed aristocracy achieved under Japanese colonial auspices, and which was subsequently reinforced by successive land reforms begun during the American occupation, has in fact deteriorated over time, at least in part as an inherent by-product of Korea's industrialization strategy.[43]

As noted in the previous section, by the reckoning of the IBRD, South Korea is in the top tier of developing countries successfully exploiting the opportunities offered by outward-oriented strategies. The rung below is occupied by a group of middle-income Latin American countries, which are said to be poised to shift into more skill- and technology-intensive areas of production. As an oil exporter, Venezuela is considered to be in a category apart from this group. But it resembles the group in its outward-oriented posture, and in its desire successfully to undertake the economic shift described by the Bank. Moreover, the case of Venezuela helps greatly to illuminate the complex interplay between external and domestic factors in determining patterns of economic outcomes in the Third World—an issue on which we have faulted both neoclassical and dependency views. Venezuela offers this opportunity because it already pos-

43. As a comparison with Taiwan makes clear, the problem is not simply one of openness, but of the structure of the domestic industrialization effort that is inserted into the international economy. No such deterioration appears to have occurred in Taiwan, which resembles South Korea in its initially advantageous distribution and which has pursued an equally outward-oriented strategy. One major difference between the two is the decentralized character of industrialization in Taiwan, which has helped to attenuate urban-rural disparities and the dislocating social effects that normally accompany them. On the Taiwanese case, see Gustav Ranis, "Equity with Growth in Taiwan: How 'Special' is the 'Special Case'?" *World Development* (March 1978), vol. 6.

sessed many of the economic and political attributes usually deemed necessary for economic development when the quadrupling of crude oil prices in 1973–74 suddenly removed a major external constraint.[44] In chapter 4, Jeffrey Hart focuses on this nexus in analyzing and explaining recent patterns of development in Venezuela.

Although less impressive than in the Asian NICs, the Venezuelan economy has also experienced high rates of growth. Diversification has taken place from its oil base into manufacturing production. Imports of consumer durables and especially capital goods have continued to be high, but have not resulted in chronic payments deficits. Agricultural production has lagged behind, and one result of the increased purchasing power made possible by petroleum revenues has been a rapid increase in agricultural imports. Industrial wages, led by the petroleum sector, have been relatively high by developing country standards; unemployment and inflation have both been moderate. The state in Venezuela plays an active role in aggregate terms, accounting for over 40 percent of GDP in 1977. The current state strategy of economic transformation is twofold. With the low-wage exports option being unavailable, the state has led the attempt to deepen industrialization by investing directly in basic industries and industrial infrastructure. The objective is to provide inputs into domestic private industries at a price that will enhance their internationally competitive position, thus diversifying Venezuela's exports. Second, even before 1973, the state has been active in the direct provisioning of basic services to the impoverished sections of the population. Hart assesses both efforts and concludes that success has been modest. Why, he asks, is this so, despite the combination of state commitment and the inflow of petrodollars that provides the financial means? One answer is temporal: the poor timing of certain state investments, given the in-

44. For the capital-deficit oil exporters, the category in which Venezuela falls, the net barter terms of trade improved by 120 percent as a result of these initial price increases. IBRD, *World Development Report, 1981*, p. 88.

ternational economic climate and growing surplus capacity in several of the industries concerned; and simply the length of time it takes to overcome patterns of inequality and poverty that go back to the plantation economy of the colonial era. But Hart also locates a more structural factor in the character of domestic policy networks in Venezuela. The governing coalition comprises the state and domestic business, in a truncated form of corporatism that excludes labor except for a relatively small contingent that is allied with the two major political parties, and which dominates all other social groups in the political process. This particular arrangement is a product of the import-substitution phase of Venezuelan industrialization, which commenced in 1958 and lasted into the early 1970s. In the present phase, failure to incorporate labor into the governing coalition makes it difficult to achieve wage restraints in the very industries on which the success of the state's strategy of industrial deepening and export diversification depends. However, the incorporation of labor would require more fundamental progress on the social welfare front, and this in turn is blocked by the dominant business groups allied with the state. In this context, the boon of increased petroleum revenues in fact has produced an ambivalent result. On the one hand, it has provided the means by which some progress has been achieved in the direction of both industrial deepening and diversification as well as providing for the needs of the poor. On the other hand, by virtue of doing so, it has reduced the pressure for change in the prevailing structure of coalitions and thereby has contributed to continued stalemate, which prevents moving more rapidly and fully in either direction. Hart concludes that only a substantial disruption of the status quo is likely to break this stalemate.

The third tier of successful outward-oriented developing countries, according to the World Bank, are those, like the Ivory Coast, in which a deepening and broadening of agricultural exports has brought them to the point of being able to move into processing and industrial sectors. The experience of the Ivory Coast as described by Lynn Mytelka in chapter 5 leads to a very different assessment of its prospects. The Ivory Coast, along with Kenya and Senegal, turned relatively early to export-oriented manufacturing. As recounted by Mytelka, import substitution had failed because it relied on inputs imported by multinationals to reproduce previously imported goods for a domestic elite market that was growing very slowly. As a result, the process offered few employment opportunities and created few linkage effects. It skewed domestic incentives and exacerbated balance of payments problems. The move to export-oriented manufacturing initially led to a rapid increase in African manufactured exports, but this was soon followed by stagnation and subsequent relative, and even absolute, declines. By examining in detail the textile industry in the Ivory Coast, and its relationship to the European Community with which it is closely tied, Mytelka seeks to discover the reasons for failure. It is precisely in this relationship that she locates the problem. In response to the global redeployment of manufacturing activity under way in the early 1970s, the EEC encouraged direct investment in African manufacturing and granted preferential access of its products to EEC markets. The Ivorian state did its part by providing a variety of inducements to foreign investors to reduce their risks and increase their rewards. These incentives were necessary to compete with Asian and Latin American production sites. However, according to Mytelka, the major consequence of the particular mix of incentives made available to multinational firms was a highly technology-intensive form of production, which offered limited local employment opportunities while increasing the need for expatriate personnel, vastly raised borrowing requirements and interest payments, and so skewed product and technology choices that the final goods produced were uncompetitive in any but the sheltered EEC market. Since the state guaranteed profits, the firms had no incentive to move toward more efficient production. The benefits of this pattern of industrialization predictably were few and highly concentrated. While per capita income in the Ivory Coast is second only to Gabon in sub-Saharan Africa, the rate of growth in per capita income from 1960 to 1979 ranks tenth in this group, and in terms of access to basic services and other measures of human welfare, the Ivory Coast falls at or well below the group average. In the end, not even this pattern of industrialization proved sustainable. Mytelka describes how the intensified pressure from non-African textile imports in the mid-1970s led the EEC to abandon its previous strategy of encouraging African manufacturing. Plans for further investment in the Ivorian industry were shelved. Instead, the EEC negotiated the second Lomé Convention, which was favorable to the expansion of primary production in Africa. The Ivory Coast, according to Mytelka, was thereby pushed back into the export-oriented agricultural sector. In sum, far from demonstrating the ability of an outward-oriented strategy to pull productive activity into more advanced sectors, the Ivorian case as described by Mytelka illustrates the inability of a small and weak economy to sustain *any* consistent pattern of economic development via close and unmediated external reliance. (The growing disarticulation of the Kenyan economy and the attendant social strife and political instability may be viewed in the same light.) With dependent import-substituting and export-oriented manufacturing both having failed, Mytelka concludes by recommending an autocentric, self-reliant development strategy for the Ivory Coast.

This brief survey of several types of experiences with outward-oriented strategies clearly shows the critical importance of the role of the state and of domestic social coalitions in mediating the effects of international interdependence on national welfare. At the same time, it is also true that "neglect of a minimum of old-fashioned microeconomic efficiency has thwarted the plans of more than one reformist or revolutionary [domestic] regime."[45] Moreover,

45. Diaz-Alejandro, "Delinking North and South," p. 118.

the cases suggest that there exists a sizable group of developing countries, of which the Ivory Coast is only one, for which an associative posture may not be appropriate because they lack the capacity to exploit the opportunities it offers and to compensate for the problems that are its by-products. What are these countries' prospects for success by means of a *dissociative* posture? Chapters 6 through 8 are designed to help answer this question, by focusing respectively: on what a strategy of selective dissociation looks like and what its political correlates of success appear to be; on an unconventional resource that is available to some developing countries to pursue this strategy but which is not normally considered as a component of economic policy; and on the constraints posed for dissociation by factors that link national economic choices to the international security system. In each case, the analysis is couched not in terms of what governments *should* do, according to the lights of some normative standard imposed by the authors, but what governments committed to self-reliant development via selective dissociation *have done* and *can do* in order to achieve their objective.

In chapter 6, Helge Hveem investigates patterns and consequences of selective dissociation in the technology sector. This sector is central to any national development strategy; at the same time, it is also central to the global strategies of multinational corporations. It therefore offers a unique vantage point from which to view the opportunities for and constraints upon selective dissociation. Hveem reviews the very different attempts by Algeria and India to achieve self-reliant industrialization via a selective dissociative posture in technology.

The Algerian case combines a pattern of extensive state ownership with a national development plan that seeks to establish mutually supportive linkages between domestic agriculture and industry, as well as among various industrial sectors, and ultimately between each of these and an indigenous science and technology capacity. In the long run, state investment in education, training, and research and development is expected to generate and sustain this capacity. In the short run, the state is attempting actively to acquire its foundation from foreign sources by means of state-mediated purchases, adaptation, and endogenization. Petrodollars make possible the financing of both sets of policies. Important progress has been achieved along a number of dimensions. Nevertheless, Hveem finds that the strain between short-term means and long-term objectives is increasing. The centripetal pull from the international economy that results from the former typically is stronger than the institutional capacity of the state to counteract it. As a result, the long-term objective of self-reliant and balanced industrialization is becoming increasingly elusive.

The situation in India is quite different. In terms of growth rates, India's economic performance does not excel. But India possesses a considerable industrial base, some products of which are internationally competitive, and it has the largest science and technology capacity of any developing country. India has accomplished both without extensive reliance on external sources, and indeed has deliberately guarded against it. A self-conscious dissociative posture vis-à-vis foreign capital is coupled with strong state support for the indigenous science and technology effort. At the same time, India also suffers from a pervasive dualism, and huge segments of its population live in abject poverty. In the realm of science and technology, this dualism is expressed in the distinction between "modern" and "traditional" sectors. According to Hveem, economic and social incentives in India are biased in favor of the former, even though it is weakly linked to the direct production and consumption needs of the vast majority of Indians. And the so-called traditional sector, even when supported by state subvention as in various areas of "appropriate" technology and small-scale or village industry, is kept marginalized from the dominant patterns of production. Hveem explains this bias as reflecting the imperatives of politico-strategic competition and the demands it makes for advanced technology in the military sector, class-based preferences to emulate production and consumption styles prevalent abroad, together with a deeper cultural denigration of local processes and products. And he maintains that this bias prevents India from exploiting fully its indigenous material and human resources. Hveem concludes his analysis by outlining the general features of an ideal type selective dissociation strategy in the technology sector, and by arguing that for many Third World countries the welfare effects of such a strategy compare favorably with those of an associative technology strategy.

The cultural factor, touched upon by Hveem, is taken up more directly by David Laitin in chapter 7. Laitin explains the reasons for continued linguistic association between newly independent states and former colonial powers. Metropolitan languages, he argues, are a means to acquire external expertise and resources, they provide a unifying element in culturally and linguistically heterogeneous societies, and they comprise a capital investment for the "organizational bourgeoisie" that is in charge of the state apparatus. Laitin goes on to explore the possibility that linguistic dissociation, or the promotion of national vernaculars, in certain circumstances may facilitate a broader dissociative posture, lead to greater self-reliance, and generate more equitable patterns of development. Laitin begins by pointing out that there is nothing *inherently* progressive in the promotion of national languages. Nevertheless, he reminds the reader of the role played by national vernaculars in the creation and emergence of the European states, and he argues that in contemporary Africa, the particular focus of his analysis, such a language policy would be advantageous on both autonomy and welfare grounds. Laitin draws on a variety of illustrative cases to explore five possible contributions of linguistic dissociation. He suggests that it may help African peoples to overcome the still-lingering psychological and cultural ties of dependence; become a source of innovation for indigenous processes and products; serve as a means to trigger social mobilization; increase state attention and responsiveness to the needs of domestic peripheral areas; and help to plug the brain drain. Laitin concludes by describing ongoing efforts at linguistic dissociation in Africa, and by assessing the pros and cons of the different types of language strategies that are available to the would-be linguistic dissociator.

Perhaps a self-evident but nonetheless an important inference to be drawn from the cases analyzed by Hveem and Laitin is that the more conventional and imitative a dissociative strategy remains, the less likely it is to succeed in its avowed aims. The successful dissociator manages to disembody the products and techniques that it needs to import from their broader economic, social, and cultural matrix and to incorporate them into its own matrix, which in turn it guards vigilantly and nurtures constantly. It follows that a moderate strategy of selective dissociation in the end may represent an unstable policy posture for many developing countries, in the sense of proving to be an inadequate means to buffer the adverse effects from centripetal forces exerted by the international economy and the models diffused by the metropoles. Where this is acknowledged to constitute a problem that requires a response, selective dissociation may yield to a more thoroughgoing dissociative posture. At that point, the analysis of economic policy and its consequences enters a very different realm. For, once down the road toward more complete dissociation, the dissociating state may encounter difficulties from the international security system. In chapter 8, Barry Buzan elaborates this scenario.

Buzan's chapter is based on the premise that, since substantial dissociation entails breaking existing patterns of center-periphery relations, it poses a threat to elements in both the center and the periphery countries concerned. He surveys a variety of actual and hypothetical cases to explore the conditions under which the very security of the periphery state may come to be at stake, leading, in the extreme case, to foreign intervention designed to snuff out the attempt to dissociate. He shows that the success of economic dissociation may be critically dependent upon success in devising an appropriate security policy, one that will forestall the security threat but do so in a manner that itself remains consistent with the self-reliance aims of dissociation. As Laitin did for the realm of language policy, so Buzan analyzes the pros and cons of alternative security policies that are available to the dissociating state in order to assess which best meets these desiderata. He examines the policies of appeasement, establishing an alternative associative relationship, attempting to purchase and ultimately to replicate the weapons systems of the advanced industrial countries, and developing what he calls unconventional military self-reliance, a strategy that is akin to Maoist defense doctrines. His conclusion is parallel to those reached by Hveem and Laitin: the more the security strategy exploits indigenous strengths rather than imitating internationally prevailing doctrines and weaponry, the better the chances that it will succeed in the security realm without at the same time undermining the broader economic, political, and social objectives that it is intended to support.

In sum, our review of cases finds no universally valid answer to the question, borrowing Keohane's felicitous phrase, of "whether 'tis better to associate or dissociate." While it is currently fashionable to aver, particularly in political circles but to some extent in the academy as well, that the invocation of contingency and complexity as descriptors of the real world is a sign of intellectual if not moral weakness, that nevertheless is precisely the conclusion we reach. We have sought to go further, however, than merely to say that the answer all depends; we have also tried to delineate some of the political factors that it depends upon. Moreover, ours has not been an imperial mission to drive out or dominate other explanations, but an attempt to gain a place under the political economy sun for factors that the prevailing explanations typically marginalize if they consider them at all.

The final paper in this volume is inspired by and draws upon the other contributions, but it takes off from them rather than seeking to synthesize their arguments. It is predicated on the proposition that, just as mainstream and some dependency views discount if not ignore altogether the mediating and even generative role of political factors in assessing the impact of the international economy on national welfare, so too do they offer only a partial understanding of the international economic order itself. The paper first defines the constituent parts of the international economic order: international economic regimes and the international division of labor. It then asks how much elasticity there is in either to accommodate the welfare demands of developing countries. In the attempt to answer this question, the paper reviews the evolution of the monetary and trade regimes over the course of the past thirty-five years, and then examines recent changes in patterns of world industrial production and trade. The focus of this review is on the impact of the changes that are discerned on the constraints and opportunities faced by the developing countries. The analysis shows that neither international economic regimes nor the international division of labor is as elastic as advocates of the NIEO and of outward-oriented development strategies, respectively, appear to assume. At the same time, neither is quite as rigid as detractors, including those who favor dissociation and self-reliance, are prone to maintain. And in both cases, the range of possibilities is circumscribed by the deeper political structure that gives shape to the international economic order. The paper concludes by outlining the contours of a model that relates international political structure to the international economic order, specifically to the prospects for present and future Third World industrializers.

PART I: MANAGING
ECONOMIC ASSOCIATION

1.

Associative American Development, 1776–1860: Economic Growth and Political Disintegration

ROBERT O. KEOHANE

THIS VOLUME DISCUSSES the effects on national political economies of international economic interdependence, and the responses of governments to the constraints and opportunities posed by the operation of the world system. We

Acknowledgements: Sylvia Maxfield volunteered her energy and her talents as a research assistant in the summer of 1980, when she helped me prepare the first draft of this essay. For comments on later drafts I am indebted to Walter Dean Burnham, Barry Buzan, William Domke, Alexander Field, Jeffrey Hart, Peter Hall, Terry Karl, Peter J. Katzenstein, David M. Kennedy, David D. Laitin, Patrick McGowan, John Gerard Ruggie, Aristide R. Zolberg, and the reviewer of this volume for Columbia University Press. Paul A. David, Morton Keller, Daniel Smith, and Ann Tickner provided me with valuable references. The Center for Advanced Study in the Behavioral Sciences made available its marvelous facilities during July 1982, when I completed the final major revision, on which Nannerl O. Keohane made helpful suggestions.

are particularly interested in the prospects for less developed countries (LDCs) in the capitalist world system. To what extent can these countries achieve sociopolitical as well as economic development by adopting policies of "association," which link them closely to the major capitalist centers through trade, capital flows, and the operations of multinational corporations? Or, on the contrary, is it necessary for them to "delink," following strategies of "dissociation," in order to achieve genuine development and to fulfill the basic human needs of their people?

Proponents of associative strategies emphasize the contribution of these policies to global welfare, as explained by Ricardo and generations of classical and neoclassical economists. In the absence of barriers to trade, countries (or regions) will specialize in areas where they have comparative advantages. Undistorted price signals will direct factors of production toward their most efficient uses. Advocates of dissociation, on the other hand, argue that the gains of pursuing comparative advantage are outweighed by economic, political, and social costs. In particular, countries may run the risk of becoming "enclave economies," specializing in one or two staple crops and failing to develop manufacturing capabilities or even diversified agriculture. The result may be a short-lived boom, followed by disastrous decline as a result of loss of demand for the staple. The country or region may stagnate, as technological advances and the benefits of "learning by doing" are captured by areas with more balanced economic structures. Furthermore, if staple production is carried on with plantation agriculture, social inequality and political authoritarianism are likely to result.

As the papers in this volume indicate, there is no general answer to the question of "whether 'tis better to associate or dissociate." Almost no one would advocate association with the world political economy regardless of the terms; but neither is total self-sufficiency, or autarky, widely regarded as a viable option. In practice, however, few countries *choose* between the ideal types of complete openness and autarky. Strategies emerge from sequences of decisions taken not merely on the basis of abstract principles but also in the light of specific historical conditions. As Hveem and Laitin indicate in their essays later in this volume, decisions often depend on the particular areas of activity considered: different policies may be followed on technology-transfer questions than on language issues. Choices are also affected by characteristics of the international political economy (such as patterns of comparative advantage) and by domestic social and political structures.

In keeping with the spirit of the book, this chapter will consider strategies of association and dissociation in an historically specific, rather than abstract, context. Rather than focusing on contemporary developing countries—not my own area of comparative advantage—I propose to shed some light on these issues by examining how the United States dealt with issues of association and dissociation between 1776 and 1860. Far from being the superpower of today, the United States was in the early part of this period a relatively weak, overwhelmingly agricultural country, whose economy and polity were strongly affected by the policies of the great powers of the day, particularly Britain and France. Students of the contemporary international political economy often fail sufficiently to recognize the extent to which—albeit under very different international and domestic conditions—the United States dealt with issues similar to those that face less-developed countries today.

Yet the United States was not merely an ordinary little country. It was already "imperial-sized—difficult to get at and heavily self-sufficient in fact (if not always in policy). At the time of the adoption of the Constitution, in fact, James Monroe referred to this as a frame of government for organizing an empire; and he was not alone."[1] Furthermore, the United States grew remarkably fast, so that by 1840 its per

1. This quotation is from a set of comments on an earlier draft of this paper, kindly sent to me by Professor Walter Dean Burnham of MIT.

capita income was almost the same as that of Britain, and by 1860 its population was larger than that of the United Kingdom.[2] Even within the period under review, therefore, its situation changed, from a postcolonial fragment to an important country undergoing self-sustaining economic growth. Furthermore, the American experience was distinctive in the magnitude of immigration. In the decade 1845–1854 alone, almost three million immigrants arrived—amounting to 14.5 percent of the population in 1845.[3]

These differences between the antebellum United States and contemporary Third World countries imply that one should be cautious about drawing conclusions about the present from America's historical experience. Lessons cannot be learned that easily. Yet it may be worthwhile to examine the experience of the United States—both its successes and its failures—in order to understand to what extent the problems facing less-developed countries today are the product of distinctive times and circumstances, and to what extent, on the contrary, they have recurred, for countries on the periphery of the world system, in other international systems at other times.[4]

2. Sidney Ratner, James H. Soltow, and Richard Scylla, *The Evolution of the American Economy* (New York: Basic Books, 1979), p. 240, provides the estimate on per capita income; data on population for the United States (slightly over 5 million in 1800 and over 31 million in 1860) are from Paul A. David, "The Growth of Real Product in the United States Before 1840: New Evidence, Controlled Conjectures," *Journal of Economic History* (June 1967), 27(2):165; data on population for Great Britain, including Ireland (over 15 million in 1801 and almost 29 million in 1861) come from *European Historical Statistics, 1981*, pp. 31, 34.

3. David M. Potter, *The Impending Crisis, 1848–1861*, Don E. Fehrenbacher, ed. (New York, Harper & Row, 1976), p. 241. Potter points out that the wave of immigration during this decade was greater, as a percentage of population, than the great immigration of 1905–1914. In private correspondence, Aristide R. Zolberg has pointed out to me that U.S. capitalists encouraged immigration, especially after 1830, in a conscious effort to increase their labor supply; and that this was seen by British investors in the United States as beneficial to them as well.

4. Twenty years ago Seymour Martin Lipset examined the early United States experience from the perspective of the literature on "political development" in the postcolonial areas of the world, in *The First New Nation: The United States in Historical and Comparative Perspective* (New York: Basic Books, 1963). In a general sense, the impetus behind my paper is similar, although my focus is specifically

The following discussion will be divided into three major sections. In the first, I will investigate the position of the United States in the international division of labor between 1776 and 1860. This period divides rather evenly into two: 1776–1815, when the focus of United States activity was on gaining and then consolidating national control over policy and opposing attempts by Britain and France to restrict and dominate American commerce; and 1815–1860, when the United States economy grew impressively, but the nation failed to avert the eruption of a deadly civil war. In the first period the United States desperately tried to protect its commerce, and its political autonomy, from the impact of the Napoleonic Wars, even to the point of declaring a general embargo on shipping. American policies, however, were divisive at home and ineffective abroad, although the basic self-sufficiency of an agricultural economy prevented economic collapse. After 1815, the northern and western sections of the country embarked on a path of self-sustaining growth, in which foreign trade became relatively less important. The South, however, experienced "growth without development" as an export economy. The uneven development of the United States—the growth of industrial capitalism in the Northeast, linked to homestead agriculture in the West and juxtaposed to a Southern plantation economy employing slave labor to produce cotton for export—contributed to the sectional conflict leading to the Civil War.

The second section of the essay asks in more detail about the economic and social effects of United States policies; or rather about the effects of the *absence* of coherent policies for most of the period under review. The tendency of the federal government to permit forces of comparative advantage to operate seems to have contributed to Ameri-

---

on the relationship of the United States to the world economy and on the effects of foreign economic policies on the failure to develop such policies. My analysis is also indebted, in its emphasis on policies and institutions, to the work of Douglass C. North. See particularly his *Structure and Change in Economic History* (New York: Norton, 1981).

can economic growth, although this growth was accompanied by increased social inequality. Dissociative policies were sporadic and provided minor benefits at best: the Embargo probably damaged more sectors of the economy than it assisted, and protective tariffs were on balance insignificant as stimulants to growth or industrialization. In narrowly economic terms, over the short run, association "worked."

Yet despite the benefits for economic welfare, pursuing the logic of the market had tragic effects in the long run. The economic impact on the South of growth without diversification or industrialization was harmful enough. Much more serious were the social and political results of making cotton king: slavery was entrenched and civil war became increasingly likely. The third section suggests that from a long-term political-economic standpoint it might have been worthwhile to limit cotton exports and thereby make slavery less profitable. Yet the economic interests and political importance of the South rendered any such policies politically unfeasible. Antebellum history therefore resembles a Greek tragedy: slavery, America's fatal flaw, was reinforced by the economic position of the South in the international division of labor and its political standing in the United States. Since this flaw could not be corrected by the exercise of choice, it led, despite sometimes desperate efforts to thwart Fate, to the disaster of the Civil War.

The conclusion returns to issues of Third World development that provide the common theme for this volume. It is difficult to draw from the world system of the nineteenth century lessons that apply to the late twentieth century. Nevertheless, the American experience is sobering, since it implies that countries with comparative advantages in the export of raw materials may be "doomed to association." Incentives to take advantage of export markets may be too attractive for even the most farsighted leadership to resist. Antebellum American foreign economic policy suggests that even where economic success beckons, the dangers of associative policies should not be underestimated.

THE UNITED STATES IN THE WORLD POLITICAL ECONOMY, 1776–1860

American economic growth, and American politics, were profoundly affected by the evolution of the world political economy throughout the period between the Declaration of Independence and the Civil War. The impact of external conditions on the political economy of the United States during this period can be conveniently discussed under three headings: 1) the struggle between 1776 and 1815 against European domination, whether in the form of overt political control or economic mercantilism and naval harassment; 2) the contribution of the world economy to American growth, particularly through cotton exports after 1815; and 3) the effects of the external demand for cotton on slavery, and ultimately on the collapse of the ties binding the North and South together, leading to the Civil War. Although the second and third topics both focus on the 1815–1860 period, the second is concerned with effects of external events on economic growth, the third with effects on political cohesion. If the former effects were benign, the latter most assuredly were not.

European Mercantilism and the American Reaction, 1776–1815

In a sense, British mercantilism, by stimulating a process of antagonistic imitation, brought the United States into being as a country. Especially after 1763, the British government sought to restrict competition from North America through a series of measures that affected American commerce and also increased the burden of taxation in the colonies.[5] Resistance to these measures was a major factor in the eventual movement for independence. One of the grievances expressed in the Declaration of Independence states that King

5. Curtis P. Nettels, "British Mercantilism and the Economic Development of the Thirteen Colonies," *Journal of Economic History* (1952), 12:105–14.

George III gave his consent to acts of "pretended legisla-tion" including actions "cutting off our trade with all parts of the world."

The constraints imposed on North American commerce did not end with the successful completion of the War of Independence. After the peace treaty was signed, the United States economy entered a difficult period of postwar depression. Having won its independence, the United States found that it had lost its special privileges in the British market, and that the British, Spanish, and Portuguese West Indies were closed to American ships.[6] As a result, although shipping was a major American industry, almost half of American foreign trade was carried in foreign vessels in 1789–90.[7] As Jefferson complained in December 1793, American shipping stood at the mercy of British whim:

> We can carry no article, not of our own production, to the British ports in Europe. Nor even our own produce to her Ameri-can possessions. Our ships, though purchased and navigated by their own subjects, are not permitted to be used, even in their trade with us. While the vessels of other nations are secured by standing laws, which cannot be altered but by the concurrent will of the three branches of the British Legislature, in carrying thither any produce or manufacture of the country to which they belong, which may be lawfully carried in any vessels, ours, with the same prohibition of what is foreign, are further prohibited by a standing law (12 Car. 2, 18, Sec. 3) from carrying thither all and any of our own domestic productions and manufactures. A subsequent act, indeed, has authorized their Executive to permit the carriage of our own productions in our own bottoms *at its sole discretion;* and the permission has been given, from year to year, by procla-mation, but subject every moment to being withdrawn *on that sin-gle will,* in which event our vessels, having anything on board, stand interdicted from entry of all British ports. . . .

6. Curtis P. Nettels, *The Emergence of a National Economy, 1775–1815* (New York: Holt, Rinehart & Winston, 1962), pp. 50–60; Douglass C. North, *The Eco-nomic Growth of the United States, 1790–1860* (Englewood Cliffs, N.J.: Prentice-Hall, 1961), p. 21.

7. North, p. 19.

The greater part of what they receive from us is reexported to other countries, under the useless charges of an intermediate deposite, and double voyage.[8]

In 1790, U.S. exports to Britain were less than those of the colonies at the beginning of the Revolution. As Douglass North comments:

The problem of United States foreign economic relationships in 1790 was that, in those goods and services where it enjoyed a distinct comparative advantage, the commercial policies of England and Europe effectively prevented U.S. competition. In other major exports, predominantly agricultural, the advantage was not sufficient to overcome high transport costs and assure an expanding market in a Europe at peace, still largely agricultural and self-sufficient in most primary products.[9]

To some extent, the disabilities imposed by other governments on the American economy reflected the weakness of the American government during the period of the Articles of Confederation and provided a major reason for the enactment of the Constitution and establishment of a federal government. In the monetary field, as well as in trade, the absence of strong national authority was debilitating. The postwar depression in the United States had its immediate causes in the outflow of specie, as a result of an uncontrolled surge in imports after the cessation of hostilities, and in export difficulties. Credit formerly offered by British firms could not be repaid; firms in both the United States and Britain failed, and a liquidity crisis resulted.[10]

The experience of the United States between 1783 and 1789 illustrates the severe costs of an uncontrolled associative policy in an international economy dominated by a great power following mercantilist policies. The United States in this period did not have a sufficiently strong government to

---

8. Quoted in *ibid.*, pp. 21– 22. See also Paul Varg, *Foreign Policies of the Founding Fathers* (Lansing: Michigan State University Press, 1963), p. 98.

9. North, *Economic Growth*, p. 20.

10. Nettels, *Emergence*, p. 64.

be able to devise dissociative policies, even if its leaders had wished to do so. British policy imposed dissociation in trade, but not in finance: the hegemonic power was able to be selective, but not the peripheral country. It is not clear that Britain was helped as a result; but the United States was certainly harmed.[11] Britain did not practice either benign or malign neglect toward her former colony, but rather a policy of active discrimination. Had the global political-economic situation remained indefinitely as it was in 1789, prospects for rapid United States commercial development would have been bleak indeed.

In 1793 the situation changed dramatically with the outbreak of warfare between Britain and France—a war that was to continue, except for intermittent periods of peace, until 1815. Until 1807 the economic effects of the Anglo-French war were extremely positive for the United States. War increased demand for American products and was even more important in promoting the re-export trade, in which American ships brought goods from the West Indian possessions of France and its allies to the United States, then re-exported them to the mother countries, thus exploiting a loophole in British blockade regulations.[12] Domestic exports doubled between 1790 and 1807, but re-exports increased two-hundredfold to constitute about 55 percent of

11. This experience recalls two later situations. Under the pre-1914 gold standard, Britain could draw gold from peripheral countries by raising interest rates. Cyclical fluctuations were therefore more severe on the periphery than in the center. See Alec G. Ford, *The Gold Standard, 1880–1914: Britain and Argentina* (Oxford: Clarendon Press, 1962); and Peter H. Lindert, *Key Currencies and Gold, 1900–1913*, Princeton Studies in International Finance, No. 24 (International Finance Section, Princeton University, 1969). The second case refers to American economic policy toward Europe after 1920. Like Britain in the 1780s, the United States imposed direct restrictions on trade but allowed financial flows to take place without corresponding restraints. As in the 1780s, the eventual consequence at the end of the 1920s was financial panic, when it became impossible to pay interest or repay principal on the loans that had been contracted to finance an unbalanced trade account. See Charles P. Kindleberger, *The World in Depression, 1929–1939* (Berkeley: University of California Press, 1974).

12. Varg, *Foreign Policies*, p. 175.

all exports. Furthermore, strong wartime demand increased commodity prices, so that the export price index for the United States more than doubled between 1793 and 1798– 99 and remained above its 1793 level throughout the Napoleonic Wars. Meanwhile, import prices increased much less so that U.S. terms of trade, after falling until 1794, remained well above the 1790 level throughout the 1795– 1807 period.[13] During this period, as in the colonial period, shipping and agriculture were the major industries. Agricultural products were sent to the West Indies, and manufactured goods were purchased principally from Britain. Although Alexander Hamilton produced his famous *Report on Manufactures* in 1791, it had little immediate effect on policy.[14]

These favorable international economic developments had positive effects in the economy as a whole, although they were not spectacular. The sharp improvement in U.S. terms of trade after 1793 led to modest increases in national income. Growth rates in per capita income appear to have been around 1 percent per year. "Improved trading conditions led to an increase in the per capita income growth rate of about a quarter of a percentage point."[15]

Politically, the effects of the Anglo-French wars were much less benign, since they brought the United States into military conflict with both belligerents and led to severe domestic partisan disputes. Early in the war, Great Britain began seizing American vessels; by March 1794, Britain held 250 American vessels in the West Indies alone. The Washington administration responded by ratifying a treaty negotiated with Britain in 1794 by John Jay; in so doing, the United States abandoned a strict interpretation of neutral-

13. North, *Economic Growth,* pp. 25, 221, 229.
14. F. W. Taussig, *The Tariff History of the United States* (New York: Putnam, first published, 1892; 8th ed., 1931), p. 16.
15. Claudia G. Goldin and Frank D. Lewis, "The Role of Exports in American Economic Growth during the Napoleonic Wars, 1793 to 1807," *Explorations in Economic History* (January 1980), 17:21– 22.

ity—that neutral ships could carry any goods they pleased, or that "free ships make free goods." This led not only to severe protests from the Republicans, led by Jefferson and Madison, but to the Quasi-War, an undeclared naval conflict with France, occasioned by French seizures of U.S. vessels. France claimed that the United States had agreed to a broad definition of contraband devised by the British and had therefore broken the "free ships-free goods" rule of the 1778 Franco-American Treaty of Commerce.[16] It was not until 1800 that the Convention of Mortefontaine was signed, bringing the Quasi-War to an end.

American-French hostilities and negotiations aggravated the bitter conflicts at home between Federalists, who tended to be pro-British and anti-French, and Republicans, whose sympathies were reversed. The French revolutionary government sought to exploit these differences with the activities of Citizen Genet and in the XYZ Affair. Party strife in the United States was perhaps more severe in the Adams administration (1797–1801) than ever before, or since, in the United States, reinforced as it was by ideological differences and, on both sides, suspicions that the other was engaged in treason.[17]

The resumption of Anglo-French hostilities in 1803 led to new and eventually more serious political troubles for the United States, this time focusing on Britain. Eventually, a series of events led to the War of 1812 between Britain and the United States. Once again, domestic political quarrels were linked closely to foreign relations, although in this case regional differences and differences of economic interest were more important than ideological affiliation. Neither Britain nor Napoleonic France had a particularly appealing political system from the American point of view, although

16. Varg, *Foreign Policies*, pp. 95–116; Alexander DeConde, *The Quasi-War* (New York: Scribners, 1966), p. 10.
17. For a discussion see DeConde, *The Quasi-War*. Not all strife in this period followed party lines: mutual suspicions and conflict also divided the Federalist cabinet of John Adams.

some Anglophilia remained among New England Federalists in particular. Pressures for war came principally from the South and West; representatives from New Jersey, New York, and New England voted heavily against the declaration of war. In general, agricultural interests favored war; mercantile sectors opposed it.[18]

The Anglo-American disputes of these years did not begin, however, with threats of war but with economic sanctions. In the years immediately before 1807, Britain and America were each other's best customers. Over 40 percent of American exports were to Britain; about one-third of British exports were shipped to the United States. Britain imported American foodstuffs and cotton; the United States imported British manufactured goods, particularly textiles. As the Anglo-French war continued, more and more of this trade was carried in American ships: the American merchant marine increased in tonnage by 80 percent between 1802 and 1810.[19]

Each side thought that the economic interdependence reflected in these figures was politically asymmetrical in its own favor—that a restriction of trade would damage the other country more than itself. British leaders believed that the United States, an upstart nation, could, and should, be subordinated to British policy. Americans, at the same time, thought that the British West Indies were at their mercy:

> The Americans believed that the West Indies need for food provided an obvious way of bringing pressure upon the entire empire. "If we shut up the export trade six months the Islands would be starved," a Republican commercial expert wrote in 1806; "the West India islands are dependent on it [the United States] for the necessaries of life, both for the white and black population."[20]

At the same time, Britain was suspected, with good reason, of using its war with France as an excuse to gain com-

18. Bradford Perkins, *Prologue to War: England and the United States, 1805–1812* (Berkeley: University of California Press, 1961), pp. 32–66, 409.

19. *Ibid.,* pp. 22–31.

20. *Ibid.,* p. 23.

mercial advantages over the United States. Henry Clay argued in 1811 that "the real cause of British aggression, was not to distress an enemy but to destroy a rival," and Perkins concludes that most British cabinets between 1805 and 1812 "sought not to foster trade but to monopolize it."[21]

The exigencies of war soon provided opportunities for the United States to test the belief of President Jefferson and his political allies that the United States could gain political advantage from economic sanctions. In 1805, in the *Essex* case, the British Admiralty ruled that Britain could legally seize American vessels carrying goods between the West Indies and France, or French allies, even if they stopped in the United States en route. This decision threatened the lucrative re-export trade. By January 1807, Napoleon had declared a blockade of the British Isles, and Britain had prohibited neutrals from engaging in coastwise trade in Napoleonic Europe. "For the first time the United States faced actual exclusion from carrying on any trade with the continent."[22]

Congress reacted to the *Essex* decision and high-handed British actions on the seas by passing the Nonimportation Act of 1806. This act, however, did not proscribe the importation of the most important American purchases from Britain—cottons, cheap woolens, iron, and steel—and was not enforced until the spring of 1808. In the meantime, Monroe and Pinckney negotiated a treaty with Britain in December 1806, which President Jefferson rejected on the grounds that it did not deal with the British practice of impressment—stopping American merchant vessels and forcing some members of their crews to join the British navy on the spot. When a British warship fired on the U.S.S. *Chesapeake* and forced it to turn over four of its crew members, some Americans urged a declaration of war. Jefferson sought to avoid this action. Responding to the British refusal to be conciliatory, he proclaimed a general embargo prohibiting Ameri-

21. *Ibid.*, pp. 21–22.
22. Varg, *Foreign Policies*, p. 193.

can ships from leaving port, securing its adoption by Congress within a few days.[23]

Jefferson signed the Embargo Act on December 22, 1807. Although the Embargo was enforced unevenly, it did reduce American exports by almost 80 percent between 1807 and 1808; imports (including those for re-export) fell by 60 percent and imports for consumption by almost 50 percent. The share of British exports taken by the United States shrank from one-third to one-seventh.[24]

As a political instrument, however, this remarkable measure of dissociation was ineffective. Britain found new markets in the Spanish Empire for its exports after the Iberian revolt against Napoleon in the spring of 1808. Although the British West Indies were damaged by the American action, and prices rose, the British government made successful efforts, as the British minister in Washington urged, to show "the People of this Country that the Threat to starve His Majesty's Islands in the West Indies, is as vain as it is illiberal and disgusting."[25] Britain had overimported cotton in 1807, and therefore had a stockpile to cushion the effects of the embargo on its textile mills. The price of wheat in England did rise, but not enough to force the government to ban distilling: for Britain, the Embargo was, in the end, only an inconvenience.

For the United States, however, the Embargo's effects were more severe. Shipping interests suffered greatly, but so did cotton planters, since cotton prices dropped by half. Wholesale prices of western produce in New Orleans were 15 percent lower in 1808 than in 1807.[26] Political conflict and even threats of disunion followed. In New England, courts often failed to convict those charged with violations of the Embargo; and a mob at Gloucester even destroyed a

23. Perkins, *Prologue to War*, pp. 153–56.
24. The figures on American exports and imports can be found in North, *Economic Growth*, pp. 221, 228. The information on the share of British exports taken by the United States appears in Perkins, *Prologue to War*, p. 168.
25. Perkins, p. 169.
26. *Ibid.*, p. 171.

revenue cutter. The Republican Joseph Story led opposition to the measures, which "had prostrated the whole commerce of America."[27] As opposition increased, Congress, at the end of February 1809, substituted a Nonintercourse Act for the hated Embargo. This act

repealed the Embargo, closed trade, both export and import, with the British Empire and the areas controlled by Napoleon; prohibited armed British and French ships from entering American ports; and authorized the President to reopen trade with a power that ceased to violate American maritime rights. Nobody seriously believed that England and France, able to stand up against the Embargo, would be effectively coerced by this lesser pressure. "We have trusted our most precious interests in this leaky vessel," scoffed John Randolph in one of those colorful metaphors that studded his speeches, "and now, by way of amendment, we are going to bore additional holes in this machine, which, like a cask, derives all its value, if it have any, from being water-tight."[28]

Once American ships were allowed to leave port, their eventual destinations could not be controlled: "in the first four months of the new administration seventy-nine ships sailed from New York in nominal search of a market in the Azores."[29]

The justification for replacement of the Embargo with the Nonintercourse Act was not that the latter would be more effective internationally, but that it was less offensive at home. John Quincy Adams claimed that "I was the efficient cause of the substitution of the Nonintercourse for the embargo, which I verily believe saved the country from a civil war."[30]

In 1809 Congress adopted Macon's Bill No. 2, which repealed the Nonintercourse Act and freed commerce with Britain. This admission of political defeat allowed exports to increase to 60 percent of the 1807 level, triple that of 1808.[31]

27. North, *Economic Growth,* p. 55.
28. Perkins, *Prologue to War,* pp. 231–32.
29. *Ibid.,* p. 232.
30. *Ibid.,* p. 179.
31. North, *Economic Growth,* p. 221; Perkins, *Prologue to War,* p. 244.

The bill also provided, however, that if one belligerent were to modify its edicts against American shipping, the United States would repeal measures against it and reapply the provisions of the Nonintercourse Act to the other. Napoleon took advantage of this provision, maneuvering the United States into a prohibition of all British imports in February 1811. In conjunction with numerous other grievances between the United States and Great Britain, as well as the desire of some Southerners and Westerners for war and British unwillingness to yield, this sequence of events led to the War of 1812 (1812– 15) between Britain and the United States.[32]

The United States was neither economically strong enough, nor sufficiently coherent politically, to impose an embargo successfully on Great Britain, even when Britain was involved in an arduous war against France. The strategy of dissociation could not insulate the United States from the ramifications of a European conflict amounting to an Atlantic, if not a world, war. Indeed, dissociation aggravated internal fissures in the American polity to the point that responsible political leaders worried about civil war. It led to a series of half-measures that not only failed to secure U.S. maritime objectives but that helped to drag the country into a military conflict that it could not win.

During the period between 1793 and 1815, as a whole, the United States was in a position quite unlike the situation faced by less-developed countries today. Economically, international developments at first favored the United States by stimulating demands for American shipping and American exports. Policies of close association with the European powers were therefore economically advantageous, at least in the short run. Politically, however, the United States was

---

32. Varg, *Foreign Policies*, pp. 244, 282. Madison, who had been the chief architect of the restrictions, sought to enforce them effectively during the War of 1812, but with indifferent success. See Donald R. Hickey, "American Trade Restrictions during the War of 1812," *Journal of American History* (December 1981), 68(3):517– 38.

severely threatened by the side effects of the Napoleonic Wars, and when the Embargo eventually took effect, it had a strong adverse impact on national income. Although numerous manufacturing industries developed between 1808 and 1815, they did not compensate for the loss of export and shipping revenue. It was not until about 1820 that U.S. per capita income once again reached the levels of 1807. The value of United States exports did not reach the 1807 level again until 1835, although apart from re-exports, the 1807 level was surpassed by 1816.[33] Politically, as we have seen, the Embargo and subsequent War of 1812 aroused severe resistance, especially in New England.

Yet at this time the United States was less dependent on the world economy than many LDCs are now, and this enabled it to weather the storm. In 1810 83 percent of the labor force was engaged in agriculture, much of it in the form of almost self-sufficient family farms. Domestic supplies of essential food and energy were abundant. Ratios of exports to GNP, although higher than subsequently, did not exceed the range of 14−20 percent.[34] Unlike many contemporary less-developed countries, the United States did not have to face choices between production of crops for export and provision of sufficient food to meet basic human needs at home, nor could it be cut off from supplies that were essential for the functioning of its agricultural economy.[35] Without the support of significant allies, the United States was treated harshly by the great powers of the period; the American government had little success in maneuvering between the superpowers. Yet its high degree of national economic self-sufficiency helped it to withstand foreign pressure and to overcome the effects of its own political fragmentation.

33. David, "Growth of Real Product," pp. 186−93; North, *Economic Growth*, pp. 58, 221, 233.

34. David, "Growth of Real Product," p. 191.

35. I am indebted for the elaboration of this point to comments by Professor Barry Buzan of Warwick University.

American Economic Growth: 1815—1860
The period between the end of the War of 1812 and the beginning of the Civil War was one of considerable economic growth: indeed, a recent economic history textbook characterizes it as the crucial period in which United States economic growth accelerated and began to be self-sustaining.[36] Real per capita income growth seems to have been around 1.3 percent per year for the period as a whole, while the total population and labor force grew at per annum rates of over 3 percent—higher than in any subsequent period of twenty years or more.[37]

Part of this strong performance can be accounted for by the expansion of cotton production during this period. The invention of the cotton gin made it commercially worthwhile to grow cotton throughout wide areas of the South, just as innovations in the textile industry, particularly in Britain, increased the demand. Cotton production rose from less than 200,000 bales in 1815 and 400,000 bales in 1820 to an average of over 4 million bales in the three years preceding 1860.[38] Although cotton prices fell by about 25 percent between 1820 and 1860, the value of cotton exports increased more than eight times over the same forty years. By 1860 cotton accounted for almost 60 percent of total U.S. exports, up from about 30 percent in 1820. Since import prices fell more than export prices, U.S. terms of trade sharply improved between 1820 and 1860, being especially strong in 1834—39 and 1847—60.[39]

During this period, international conditions were remarkably favorable for the cotton sector. The demand for cotton grew annually by 5 percent between 1830 and 1860.[40]

36. Ratner et al., *Evolution of the American Economy*, p. 240.
37. David, "Growth of Real Product," pp. 165, 183—88; Jeffrey G. Williamson and Peter H. Lindert, *American Inequality: A Macroeconomic History* (New York: Academic Press, 1980), p. 206.
38. Robert William Fogel and Stanley L. Engerman, *Time on the Cross: The Economics of American Negro Slavery* (Boston: Little, Brown, 1974), p. 90.
39. *Ibid.*, p. 91; North, *Economic Growth*, p. 233.
40. Gavin Wright, "Prosperity, Progress, and American Slavery," in Paul A. David, Herbert G. Gutman, Richard Sutch, Peter Temin, and Gavin Wright, *Reckoning with Slavery* (New York: Oxford University Press, 1976), p. 309.

Since the American South was the dominant supplier of the material to the world market, it possessed some degree of monopoly power.[41] Cotton supply was elastic to demand over a range of output that could be produced using available land suitable for cotton; but when demand outpaced available land (as in the 1830s and 1850s), prices rose rapidly, since there was a lag of about four years between increased land sales (stimulated by higher cotton prices) and increased cotton supply.[42]

Cotton was important for the North as well as the South: ports such as New York flourished, the American shipping industry grew, and Northern financiers provided credit for Southern planters. Cotton became the chief raw material for Northern industry. Nevertheless, it did not provide the major engine of growth for the economy of the North and West.[43] On the contrary, the most important stimulus for Northern and Western growth during this period was the construction of canals and railroads linking the Eastern Seaboard with areas across the Appalachian Mountains. This internal "transportation revolution" led to dramatic declines in costs: inland freight rates fell during the nineteenth century to one-fiftieth of their late eighteenth century values.[44] Interregional exports (among the Northeast, South, and West) increased from $109 million in 1839 to $480 million in 1860, compared to an increase in exports to other countries from $102 million to $316 million.[45] West-South trade was relatively small and did not grow rapidly; Northeast-West trade was both more dynamic and more important.[46] Intra-

41. David et al., "Time on the Cross and the Burden of Quantitative History," in David et al., *Reckoning with Slavery*, p. 352.

42. North, *Economic Growth*, pp. 72–73.

43. This is the thesis of North, *Economic Growth*.

44. Ratner et al., *Evolution of the American Economy*, pp. 121–22.

45. Albert Fishlow, "Antebellum Interregional Trade Reconsidered," *American Economic Review* (May 1964), 54(3):363.

46. *Ibid.*; Albert Fishlow, *American Railroads and the Transformation of the Ante-Bellum Economy* (Cambridge: Harvard University Press, 1965); William N. Parker, ed., *The Structure of the Cotton Economy of the Antebellum South* (Wash-

regional trade seems to have risen even faster, as improved transportation facilitated the widening and deepening of markets within sectors of the country—as New Yorkers, for example, traded with each other via the Erie Canal. Only the South, with its export orientation, failed to develop this pattern of intraregional trade.[47] Thus, as a result of internal transportation improvements, the ratio of exports to gross domestic product fell: Paul David estimates that between 1800–10 and the 1830s it dropped from about 14–20 percent to 8–9 percent.[48]

Growth led to changes in the structure of the economy, both in the Northeast and in the West. Cotton textiles were the initial leading sector: between 1815 and 1833, this sector expanded at a rate of 16 percent annually.[49] During the period between 1808 and 1815, numerous American manufacturing firms had been formed, especially in the cotton textile sector, but also to produce woolens, iron goods, and other products formerly imported from Britain or the European continent. These industries faced a postwar crisis when British products again could appear in American markets. A number of American manufacturers were driven into bankruptcy, but after the crisis had passed, American cotton-textile and woolen manufacturers were competitive in the home market, even without the tariff protection extended in 1816, 1824, and 1828.[50]

The growth of textile manufacturing was followed, especially during the 1840s, by a surge in the output of the Pennsylvania-based iron and steel industry, and by the development of a more diversified domestic manufacturing sector. Extraordinarily high rates of capital accumulation

ington: Agricultural History Society, 1970), originally the January 1970 issue of *Agricultural History*.

47. Ratner et al., *Evolution of the American Economy*, p. 224.
48. David, "Growth of Real Product," pp. 190–92.
49. Ratner et al., *Evolution of the American Economy*, p. 198.
50. Taussig, *Tariff History*, pp. 25–45; Paul A. David, "Learning by Doing and Tariff Protection: A Reconsideration of the Case of the Ante-Bellum United States Cotton Textile Industry," *Journal of Economic History* (1970), 30:521–601.

contributed to rapid rates of output growth in manufacturing: almost 10 percent annually in the 1840s and almost 6 percent annually during the 1850s.[51] Between 1820 and 1860, the proportion of the gainfully employed labor force occupied outside of agriculture increased from 21 to 47 percent.[52] Although total factor productivity growth in agriculture during the 1815–1860 period increased only by about .6 percent per year, in cotton textiles it rose by over 3 1/2 percent annually, and in transportation by over 4 1/2 percent.[53] Even before the Civil War, the Northeast was becoming industrialized.

As this was taking place, the West was expanding; the frontier moved beyond the Mississippi to the Great Plains. What is now the Middle West developed a diversified and market-oriented agricultural economy, replacing pioneer self-sufficiency. By 1860 the Northeast and West together had more railroad mileage per capita than any other region of the world, with the South not far behind.[54] The Northeast and West were becoming increasingly closely linked to one another, as intrasectoral ties were also being deepened.

The capital accumulation that propelled this growth came principally from Americans rather than from abroad. Domestic savings rates increased throughout the period, but particularly after 1835.[55] Net foreign capital invested in the United States did rise from $70 million to $380 million between 1790 and 1860, but this was a "trivial" amount compared with indigenous capital formation.[56] Nevertheless, at particular times external sources of capital were important: 1815–18, 1832–39, and 1850–57 were periods of especially large foreign borrowing. In particular, the boom of the 1830s was fueled by foreign investment and the consequent inflow of specie into the United States. As a result, in

---

51. Williamson and Lindert, *American Inequality*, pp. 162, 232.
52. David, "Growth of Real Product," p. 166.
53. Williamson and Lindert, *American Inequality*, pp. 170–71.
54. Fogel and Engerman, *Time on the Cross*, p. 256.
55. Williamson and Lindert, *American Inequality*, p. 256.
56. Ratner et al., *Evolution of the American Economy*, p. 218.

periods such as this one, the United States was in a classically dependent situation. Milton Esbitt argues, for instance, that "American economic growth in the 1830s depended on a healthy British economy, just as Europe's in the late 1940s and early 1950s did on that of the American economy."[57] When the Bank of England reacted to the effects of a poor domestic grain harvest by tightening its monetary policy in 1837, credit for cotton purchases was reduced, cotton prices collapsed, and specie was exported to Britain from the United States. The result in the United States was monetary contraction, financial distress for borrowers and their banks, and depression—the panic of 1837.[58]

Instability was fostered by loose lending practices and poor performance by borrowers. Land speculation in the West left many investors vulnerable to the price collapses in cotton that took place in 1837 and 1839. During this period, Nicholas Biddle of the United States Bank of Pennsylvania (formerly the Second Bank of the United States) attempted to maintain the price of cotton, in an early form of commodity price stabilization that predates Brazilian efforts in coffee as well as recent commodity agreements and demands for a Common Fund. The 1839 crash brought down Biddle's bank and led to widespread defaults on obligations to British creditors.

Public investors added to the difficulties. Much of American borrowing in the 1830s was carried on by public enterprises—creations of state and local governments—for transportation projects, particularly canals: 70 percent of the canals built in the United States during this period were constructed with public funds borrowed from private investors.[59] Many of these projects had been stimulated by the success of the Erie Canal and rivalry among cities for access

57. Milton Esbitt, *International Capital Flows and Domestic Economic Fluctuations* (New York: Arno Press, 1978), p. 361.

58. Leland H. Jenks, *The Migration of British Capital to 1875* (New York: Knopf, 1927), discusses both the crisis of 1837 and the crisis of 1857, precipitated by actions of the Bank of France. On the crisis of 1857, see also North, *Economic Growth*, pp. 212–14.

59. Ratner et al., *Evolution of the American Economy*, p. 115.

to the interior of the country; often they were ill-conceived and failed to generate sufficient revenue to repay the loans that had been contracted. This led in the 1840s to widespread defaults on state debts.[60]

As a result of the crash of the late 1830s, during the 1840s "there was no market in London for any American security." The contemporary counterpart to the International Monetary Fund, the House of Rothschild, apparently blacklisted the United States for a time. As Jenks reports it, " 'You may tell your government,' said the Paris Rothschild to Duff Green, 'that you have seen the man who is at the head of the finances of Europe, and that he has told you that they cannot borrow a dollar, not a dollar.' "[61] The U.S. Congress was asked by the creditors to assume the debts of the states, but failed to act after considering the issue in 1842.

Like contemporary developing countries, the United States was subject to temporary disciplinary actions by creditors, but these were not sustained over long periods of time. Unlike many contemporary developing countries, American debts were relatively small. Aggregate U.S. foreign indebtedness, which stayed below $100 million until 1833, with the brief exception of 1817, rose to $297 million by 1839, fell sharply during the 1840s, then rose to about $380 million in 1860. Interest and dividends on foreign indebtedness amounted to about 7 percent of export earnings in 1820, about 6 1/2 percent in 1830, over 9 1/2 percent in 1850, and about 7 1/2 percent in 1860.[62]

In contrast to the Northeast and the West, the South did not diversify its economy. Nor did it industrialize. Instead, it exploited its comparative advantage in cotton production by

60. Jenks, *Migration of British Capital,* pp. 78–106.

61. Both quotations are from Jenks, *Migration of British Capital;* they appear on pp. 99 and 106, respectively.

62. These debt service ratios are lower than recent ratios for "middle income" developing countries. World Bank figures indicate that in 1978 the debt service ratio of these countries averaged about 13.8 percent. *World Development Report, 1980,* pp. 134–35.

extending that production westward, using slave labor. Whether the economic success of plantation agriculture could have been maintained beyond 1860 is controversial. Fogel and Engerman claim that slavery could have continued to prosper as cotton production expanded.[63] Wright, on the contrary, has argued that even without the Civil War, the Southern economy would have declined after 1860.[64] Both sides agree that demand for cotton continued to increase after 1866, but only by 1.5 percent per year rather than 5 percent. The issue is whether to place more importance on the continued increase in demand or on the decline in the rate of increase.

In either case, the South before 1860 experienced what would now be called "growth without development":

The general prosperity of the late antebellum era of southern history, and its basis in the prosperity of plantation slavery, are facts beyond serious dispute. Their historical significance, however, is another matter. Consideration of the sources and of the nature of this movement suggests that the prosperity of the period was not only unprecedented but evanescent. The southern economy, at this time, was absorbing the benefits of strong and rapidly growing demands for raw cotton in international markets—demands connected with the process of industrialization elsewhere. Yet full advantage was not being taken of these fortuitous circumstances to lay more permanent foundations for prosperity—foundations that at a future date might have sustained a cumulative process of economic transformation and growth in the South itself.[65]

I will argue below that this pattern of southern growth had serious implications for the Union. Indeed, it could be argued that external economic conditions were too benign for the United States during the decades before 1860, since

63. Fogel and Engerman, *Time on the Cross*, pp. 96–97.
64. Wright, "Prosperity, Progress, and American Slavery," in David, *Reckoning with Slavery*, p. 309.
65. David et al., "Time on the Cross and the Burden of Quantitative History," in David et al., *Reckoning with Slavery*, p. 349.

strong demand for cotton, with a Europe at peace, created incentives for plantation agriculture to maintain itself and to spread. Yet it would have been difficult for contemporary economists (even armed with twentieth-century ideas) to object. American produce was in strong demand; funds could be borrowed for internal development without serious sanctions for default; and hard-working immigrants arrived in substantial numbers from Europe. From a strictly economic point of view, before 1860, association "worked."

The American South in the World Economy: Slavery and Civil War

Much of the historiography of the Civil War has revolved around the question of the importance of slavery in precipitating the conflict. The conventional view emphasizing the central role of slavery was challenged in the 1920s by Charles and Mary Beard, who emphasized that the war "had not been a contest over principles but a struggle for power— a clash of economic sections in which freedom did not necessarily combat slavery but industrialism most assuredly combated the planter interests."[66] The South was an agrarian economy, closely associated with Britain; its interests lay in low tariffs and competitive conditions in shipping and banking. Northeastern manufacturers, by contrast, sought a protective tariff, wishing to take advantage of Southern cotton for their textile mills.

Yet as Barrington Moore has pointed out, there is no inherent reason why capitalists and aristocratic planters cannot collaborate: the Bismarckian alliance between the capitalists of the Rhineland and the East Elbian Junkers illustrates this possibility. Moore asks the right *political* question raised by the economic determinist thesis: "Why did Northern capitalists have no need of Southern 'Junkers' in order to establish and strengthen industrial capitalism in the

66. David M. Potter, *The South and the Sectional Conflict* (Baton Rouge: Louisiana State University Press, 1968), p. 91.

United States?"[67] His answer, essentially, is that slavery made the southern planters an unattractive coalition partner. Western farmers feared the extension of slavery and were therefore unwilling to collaborate with the Southern agrarians, although both factions would have had similar interests in low tariffs and internal improvements. The collapse of the Democratic party in the 1850s indicates how slavery—particularly the issue of slavery in the territories—tore apart the Jacksonian coalition.[68] Northern industrialists were not only reluctant to become closely associated with the planters on ideological grounds (many of them were linked to abolitionists and free-soilers); they also had an attractive alternative partner, since the Western fear of slavery in the territories made free-state farmers more willing to align with industrialists against the South. Thus the Whig party—formerly the party of propertied men, North and South—collapsed even before the Jacksonians did; and a new Republican majority of North and West was formed. As Moore characterizes the realignment:

> The essence of the bargain was simple and direct: business was to support the farmers' demand for land, popular also in industrial working-class circles, in return for support for a higher tariff. "Vote yourself a farm—vote yourself a tariff" became Republican rallying cries in 1860. In this fashion there came to be constituted a "marriage of iron and rye"—to glance once more at the German combination of industry and Junkers—but with western family farmers, not landed aristocrats, and hence with diametrically opposite political consequences.[69]

67. Barrington Moore, Jr., *Social Origins of Dictatorship and Democracy: Lord and Peasant in the Making of the Modern World* (Boston: Beacon Press, 1966), p. 115. Professor Peter Katzenstein of Cornell and Professor Pat McGowan of Arizona State reminded me of Moore's brilliant chapter on the American Civil War.

68. Potter, *The Impending Crisis,* discusses this collapse, which took place despite the almost heroic efforts of Stephen A. Douglas to prevent it. In a sense, the failure of Douglas's efforts at compromise revealed that the Democratic party by 1860 no longer existed.

69. Moore, *Social Origins,* p. 130. The ideological opposition to slavery of Northern industrialists is crucial to this argument. Such opposition can be seen, following a recent discussion by David Laitin of British suppression of the slave

Only after slavery had been abolished, and a period of time had elapsed after the war, did the Southern planters once again become a candidate for a winning political coalition. This realignment took place in 1876, when the disputed Hayes-Tilden election was settled by bringing an end to Reconstruction and permitting Southern whites eventually to disenfranchise and dominate Southern blacks. As Moore argues:

When Southern "Junkers" were no longer slaveholders and had acquired a larger tincture of urban business and when northern capitalists faced radical rumblings, the classic conservative coalition was possible. So came Thermidor to liquidate the "Second American Revolution."[70]

Moore's argument suggests that it is futile to seek to disentangle slavery from "economic" or "political" causes of the Civil War. Moore explicitly recognizes this, although he views the economic causes as fundamental:

It is impossible to speak of purely economic factors as the main causes behind the war, just as it is impossible to speak of the war as mainly a consequence of moral differences over slavery. The moral issues arose from economic differences.[71]

David M. Potter makes a similar point, without Moore's emphasis on the primacy of economic forces. He acknowledges that even antislavery Northerners were generally racists by modern standards and did not have the interests of black people at heart. "The North did not hate slavery

---

trade, as an attempt to institutionalize a particular "moral order" in a manner that was consistent with Britain's own efforts to exert "ideological hegemony." Laitin comments: "If [Britain's acceptance of a hegemonic role] meant for the other states in the core the internationalization of free trade, it meant for the periphery the internationalization of a new moral order." Since the American North was in the core and the South in the periphery, it is not surprising that British hegemony had different meanings in these two sections of the United States. See David D. Laitin, "Capitalism and Hegemony: Yorubaland and the International Economy," *International Organization* (Autumn 1982), 36(4):711.

70. *Ibid.*, p. 149.
71. *Ibid.*, p. 123.

enough to go to war about it; slavery was too close to capitalism to justify the old antithesis of industrialism versus agrarianism; the conflict of economic interests was negotiable." Yet he goes on:

> Nevertheless, in every aspect, slavery was important. Economically, it was an immensely powerful property interest, somewhat inimical to the interests of free farming, because the independent farmer could not compete with the slave. Socially, it was the keystone of a static society of social hierarchy which challenged the dynamic, mobile, and equalitarian modes of life and labor that prevailed in the free states. Ideologically, it was a negative of the basic American principles of freedom and equality. It is futile to draw analytical distinctions between the slavery issue and (a) economic conflict of interest, (b) cultural incompatibilities, and (c) ideals as a social force. For the slavery issue was not, for explanatory purposes, an alternative to any of the others. It was part of the essence of all of them.[72]

If slavery is crucial to understanding the Civil War, an adequate analysis of the conflict must take into account changes in the world economy, since slavery was so intimately tied to the South's role in the international division of labor. Strong demand for cotton, particularly from Britain, led to exponential growth in production between 1820 and 1860. This led to the extension of cotton production to what was then the Southwest from the Old South; and to the movement of the center of gravity of slavery from Virginia and the Carolinas in 1790 to Georgia by 1860.[73] There seems to be general agreement now that slavery was profitable, both for plantations in the Old South (net "exporters" of slaves) and plantations in the better cotton-growing areas of the Southwest.[74] This profitability of slavery resulted from the suitability of the area for cotton cultivation, combined

72. Potter, *The South and the Sectional Conflict,* p. 118.
73. Fogel and Engerman, *Time on the Cross,* p. 45.
74. Fogel and Engerman make this a major part of their thesis; see also Moore, p. 118; David et al., p. 349; Ratner et al., *Evolution of the American Economy,* pp. 147–48.

with the lack of other available cotton-producing areas to supply the mills of Lancashire: "The American South was the dominant supplier of cotton to the world market at the time, and this conveyed some degree of monopoly power."[75]

As slavery became increasingly profitable, southern commitment to it increased. At the time of the Declaration of Independence, "both North and South had moved in unison to condemn slavery as an evil":

> Southern and northern congressmen alike had joined in voting to abolish the importation of slaves after the year 1808. Slavery was barred from the Old Northwest by the Ordinance of 1787; it was confined, even within the South, mostly to the limited areas of tobacco culture and rice culture, both of which were static. At this point, it seemed to many men in both sections only a question of time until the institution would wither and die.[76]

By the 1830s, however, the Southern mood had changed, and the South "had begun to formulate a doctrine that slavery was permanent, morally right, and socially desirable." By the 1850s, a Southern majority on the Supreme Court had ruled that Congress could not exclude slavery from the territories, and in his "House Divided" speech, Abraham Lincoln warned that the Court might, in the future, even go so far as to hold that "the Constitution of the United States does not permit a *state* to exclude slavery from its limits."[77] The profitability of slavery increased both Southern commitment to it and Northern fear of its extension.

British demand for cotton thus had fateful effects on the Union, by committing Southerners more strongly to slavery and giving Northerners more reason to fear it. From the Northern standpoint, extension of slavery would have created a country, not just a region, inhospitable to freedom and to individual economic opportunity. Moore even

75. David et al., "Time on the Cross," in David et al., *Reckoning with Slavery,* p. 352.

76. Potter, *The Impending Crisis,* p. 38.

77. The quotations in this paragraph are from Potter, *The Impending Crisis,* pp. 39 and 349, respectively.

argues that a Southern victory would have put the United States "in the position of some modernizing countries today, with a latifundia economy, a dominant antidemocratic aristocracy, and a weak and dependent commercial and industrial class unable and unwilling to push forward toward political democracy."[78] This puts in modern terms what many Northerners feared. From the standpoint of Southern elites, acceptance of restriction of slavery to states in which it already existed could have maintained the institution temporarily although any profits to be gained from exploiting new areas for plantation agriculture would have been sacrificed. But Southern planters would have had to remain citizens of a country in which they would have been increasingly despised. They would have had to worry more about slave revolts. Their position of political and military power in the United States would have steadily deteriorated, so a later contest would have been more one-sided. And they would have lived with the realization that their way of life was ultimately doomed to extinction.

In the preceding section of this paper, we saw that from a strictly economic point of view, the ante-bellum association of the United States with the world economy "worked." Understanding the effects of association on slavery and the sectional conflict, however, leads to a severe qualification of this conclusion. In the long run, growth without development might have proven to be an inadequate economic strategy for the South. This hypothetical economic danger is dwarfed, however, by the political reality. The effects of close association with the world economy—the entrenchment of slavery and (to a considerable degree) the Civil War—were almost disastrous for the Union and tragic for a large proportion of Americans. Although fewer than five million men voted in the election of 1860, 600,000 men died in the subsequent war.[79] Relative to population, the American Civil War was the bloodiest war in American history. In

78. Moore, *Social Origins,* p. 153.
79. Potter, *The Impending Crisis,* pp. 443, 583.

the absence of dissociative policies, the United States became the victim of forces in the world economy that—in conjunction with intersectional cultural differences and the impact of ideals—tore the Union apart.

UNITED STATES POLICIES

As we have seen, American economic development was strongly influenced by political and economic events abroad. Yet United States policies also played a role. Alexander Hamilton laid the basis for close transatlantic economic ties with his funding of foreign, domestic and state debts, and the establishment of the first Bank of the United States.[80] These measures were designed to enable the United States to borrow abroad and to begin the construction of an indigenous capital market.

Economic association between the United States and the Old World was promoted more, however, by lack of policy than by positive governmental action. For the most part, the government let forces of comparative advantage operate: it is difficult to find a consistent or self-conscious U.S. strategy of foreign economic policy in the antebellum years. Between 1793 and 1807 the United States allowed shipping and the export of agricultural produce to expand rapidly despite the vulnerability of these activities to wartime disruption and loss. No sustained program to promote manufacturing was undertaken, despite Hamilton's advice in the *Report on Manufactures.* After the War of 1812, the United States was content to let cotton exports rise, even though this pattern of development intensified conflict over slavery. Thus, despite serious negative externalities attached to associative development, public measures were not taken to alter these patterns of growth. On the whole, American pol-

---

80. Varg, *Foreign Policies,* pp. 77–82; North, *Economic Growth,* p. 46.

icy was passive and could be characterized as one of "un-managed association."

The most dramatic exception to this generalization is, of course, the period between 1808 and 1815 when Jefferson's Embargo, subsequent legislation, and then the War of 1812 cut the United States off from most of its foreign trade. Here a policy of virtually complete dissociation was tried, although not for economic reasons but in reaction to dire political circumstances. A more limited instance of dissociative policy is provided by U.S. protective tariff legislation, particularly between 1816 and 1833 and again between 1842 and 1846. High tariffs on textiles and iron, as well as other manufactured products, distorted patterns of comparative advantage. Henry Clay's "American System" expressed a widespread desire, at least in the 1820s, for a more self-sufficient national economy.

This section considers the brief but remarkably complete dissociation of the embargo period and the selective dissociation of the protective tariff. For each episode the reasons for deviating from the usual laissez-faire approach and the consequences of policies actually followed will be noted. Some observations on the implications of economic policies for political cohesion conclude the section.

Dissociation: The Embargo and the War of 1812
As indicated earlier, the period between 1808 and 1815 saw real income in the United States decline as established patterns of economic development were ruptured. This fact could be used to indicate that associative policies had been beneficial. However, all sudden changes in the structure of an economy involve adjustment costs, and temporary losses in national income could have been subsequently overshadowed by long-run gains. High immediate costs of dissociation therefore do not necessarily imply policy failure.

In the period between 1808 and 1815, American manufacturing industries did grow strongly, aided by the strong protection provided by the Embargo, its successors, and the War of 1812. Taussig comments:

> The embargo, the non-intercourse acts, and the war of 1812 rudely shook the country out of the grooves in which it was running, and brought about a state of confusion from which a new industrial system could emerge more easily than from a well-settled organization of industry. The restrictive period may indeed be considered to have been one of extreme protection. The stimulus which it gave to manufactures perhaps shows that the first steps in these were not taken without some artificial help.[81]

Nevertheless, the subsequent collapse of many industries begun during this period suggests that many of them had not become competitive, even after an initial period of learning and innovation. Manufacturing output in the Northeast was apparently lower in 1820, after the crisis for manufacturing of the previous five years, than it had been in 1810.[82] The iron industry was not competitive, even in the home market, until the 1840s. Only for cotton textiles and woolens, and perhaps for some smaller industries, could it be argued that the embargo and wartime period had economic benefits by encouraging "learning by doing," helping entrepreneurs to overcome imperfections of capital markets and providing sufficiently high profits that investment was carried out despite externalities associated with innovation that could not be captured by the manufacturer himself.[83] At best, it seems that the embargo period may have speeded up the process of innovation and the growth of manufacturing, although in an abrupt and economically costly fashion. Certainly it would be difficult to hold it up as an example of the economic benefits of a dissociative policy.

81. Taussig, *Tariff History,* pp. 62–63.
82. North, *Economic Growth,* p. 165.
83. Taussig, *Tariff History,* pp. 25–67; David, "Learning by Doing and Tariff Protection." David's article provides an excellent discussion of the conditions that must apply for the "learning by doing" or "infant industry" argument to be correct.

Partial Dissociation: The Protective Tariff

Before 1816, the United States maintained relatively low tariffs. The Tariff of 1789 was, according to Taussig, "protective in intention and spirit," with specific duties imposed on
certain items as a way of stimulating domestic production.[84]
Yet the general duty was only 5 percent *ad valorem;* and
even the specific duties were not high compared to what
was to come later. Until 1808 tariffs continued to be moderate, although they were raised occasionally to provide additional revenue.

In 1816 Congress reacted to the flood of goods that
entered the country after the War of 1812 by legislating a
higher tariff, both in order to pay the war debt and to protect infant industries such as cotton and woolen textiles, and
iron. Yet the highest rate of duty provided for in this tariff
was only 25 percent. In 1824, however, a full-fledged protective tariff was adopted, increasing rates of duty on cotton
and woolen goods to 33-1/3 percent. In 1828 the "tariff
of abominations" raised rates still further, although tariffs
were moderated in 1833. In 1842 the Whigs passed another
high-tariff measure, which was superseded in 1846 by a
low-tariff bill adopted by a Democratic Congress. In 1857
duties were further reduced.[85]

It is a striking feature of this tariff history that the United
States had no coherent international economic strategy of
which tariffs were a part. The South was consistently against
high tariffs; the Western and Mid-Atlantic states favored
them; and New England was divided. Regional differences
were compounded by party politics, with the Democrats
generally favoring lower tariffs than the Whigs. Furthermore, at crucial junctures personalities, and presidential
politics, entered into the equation. The 1820s were years of
intense domestic political competition, in which tariffs became the central focus. The tariff of 1828 was enacted as a

84. Taussig, *Tariff History,* p. 14.
85. *Ibid.,* pp. 68– 115.

result of maneuvering by Jackson's supporters in the Congress, who planned to embarrass their political opponents, supporters of John Quincy Adams:

> A high-tariff bill was to be laid before the House. It was to satisfy the protective demands of the western and middle states, and at the same time to be obnoxious to the New England members. The Jackson men of all shades, the protectionists from the North and the free-traders from the South, were to unite in preventing any amendments; that bill, and no other, was to be voted on. When the final vote came, the southern men were to turn around and vote against their own measure. The New England men, and the Adams men in general, would be unable to swallow it, and would also vote against it. Combined, they would prevent its passage, even though the Jackson men from the North voted for it. The result expected was that no tariff bill at all would be passed during the session, which was the object of the southern wing of the opposition. On the other hand, the obloquy of defeating it would be cast on the Adams party, which was the object of the Jacksonians of the North. The tariff bill would be defeated, and yet the Jackson men would be able to parade as the true "friends of domestic industry."[86]

Unfortunately for the inventors of this complex maneuver, the Adams supporters favored the bill in the House, and crucial senators, particularly Daniel Webster, supported it in the Senate for fear of the political consequences of opposition. After the legislation was adopted, John Randolph said, "The bill referred to manufactures of no sort or kind, except the manufacture of a President of the United States."[87]

American tariffs may have contributed to American economic development through their fiscal effects: they taxed consumption and contributed to a reduction of the national debt, which reduced interest rates.[88] But they did not play a major role in stimulating the industries—textiles and iron—

86. *Ibid.*, pp. 88–89.
87. *Ibid.*, pp. 101–2.
88. Ratner et al., *Evolution of the American Economy*, pp. 177–78.

toward which they were particularly directed. The iron tariffs of the 1820s were entirely unjustified, since as long as U.S. industry relied on charcoal, it could not be competitive with British iron (using coke) or Swedish and Russian iron (using cheaper labor). U.S. duties on iron placed a heavy burden on U.S. users, failed to stimulate or even retarded innovation in the domestic industry, and hindered U.S. economic growth. This was also true for the high iron tariffs of 1832 and 1842– 46.[89] Cotton-textile and woolen tariffs had greater justification—since the industries they protected were viable in the medium-to-long-run—but economic historians generally regard them as redundant. United States tariff policy toward the cotton textile industry, says one observer, should be viewed as "a means of redistributing income in favor of the cotton textile producers."[90] Taussig claims that the United States developed "a new arrangement of its productive forces" after the crisis of 1818– 19, with little assistance from protective legislation.[91]

In the American experience before 1860, therefore, little could be said for policies of dissociation on purely economic grounds. The dissociation of the embargo period was economically costly, and was imposed for noneconomic reasons. Tariff policies were also expensive. In the long run, the passivity of the government, which accepted associative development, seemed economically wise.

89. Taussig, *Tariff History*, pp. 55 ff., 134; Williamson and Lindert, *American Inequality*, p. 138.

90. David, "Learning by Doing and Tariff Protection," p. 600.

91. Taussig, *Tariff History*, pp. 62– 63. Christopher Chase-Dunn has recently published an article based on the hunch that the United States movement from a semiperipheral or peripheral status in the world economy, to a core position, might have been based on U.S. high-tariff policies in the antebellum period. The problem with such an analysis is that tariffs did not seem to make much difference in the development of U.S. manufactures in this period. Professor Chase-Dunn acknowledges this, but curiously persists in an enterprise premised on the opposite assumption. See Christopher Chase-Dunn, "The Development of Core Capitalism in the Ante-Bellum United States: Tariff Politics and Class Struggle in an Upwardly Mobile Semi-periphery," in Albert Bergesen, ed., *Studies of the Modern World System* (New York: Academic Press, 1980).

Economic Policies and Political Cohesion
Between 1776 and 1815, the United States government established control over its own policy and asserted its independence vis-à-vis Britain and France. It did not do so, however, as a unified government leading a united people.
Indeed, the internal divisions associated with the policy of
dependence reduction involved severe political conflicts and
even threats of secession. In the 1790s, the Alien and Se-
dition Acts were passed, and severe differences erupted over
the degree to which the United States should assert its independence of Britain. Likewise the years preceding the War
of 1812 were stormy ones, and in 1814 the Hartford Convention raised the threat of possible New England secession. As is often the case today, external relations for a dependent country led to internal political stress.

Associative economic development contributed, as we
have seen, to the political fragmentation that led to the
American Civil War. The direction that rapid economic growth
took was destabilizing for the Union. In the case of the
United States, as with contemporary developing countries,
it would be. myopic to evaluate economic policies on the
basis of their economic consequences alone.

The pattern of antebellum development had important
social consequences as well, although their political implications were overshadowed by the Civil War. Most striking
is the fact that income and wealth inequalities increased
sharply between 1820 and 1860. America during this period
is often seen as a Jacksonian democracy, in which every
white man (not yet, every person) was substantially equal.
Alexis de Tocqueville, writing in 1835, observed that "America exhibits in her social state an extraordinary phenomenon":

> Men are seen there on a greater equality in point of fortune
> and intellect, or in other words, more equal in their strength, than
> in any other country of the world, or in any age of which history
> has preserved the remembrance.[92]

92. Alexis de Tocqueville, *Democracy in America* (New York: Knopf, Vintage
Edition, 1957), 1:55. (Originally published in 1835.)

As a comparison with Europe, this may well have been correct, although it should also be recalled that Tocqueville warned about the dangers of a "manufacturing aristocracy."[93] But when changes over time are considered, it appears that "inequality in income and wealth rose sharply in America between 1820 and 1860." In 1860 the richest 1 percent of free-wealth-holders held 29 percent of total assets, up from an estimated 12.6 percent in 1774; the richest decile held 73 percent of assets compared to less than 50 percent in the earlier year. Williamson and Lindert argue that in "four short decades" between 1816 and 1856, "the American Northeast was transformed from the 'Jeffersonian ideal' to a society more typical of developing economies with very wide pay differentials and, presumably, marked inequality in the distribution of wage income." Capital accumulation led to mechanization and to a rise in the demand for skilled as opposed to unskilled labor.[94] It is not clear that increasing inequality can be attributed to associative policies; nevertheless, the conjunction between capital accumulation and inequality observed in the nineteenth century United States parallels similar patterns in the contemporary Third World, which have been criticized by advocates of more egalitarian policies entailing dissociation.

Despite the widening inequalities, Northeastern and Western development was successful from an aggregate standpoint: efficient economic patterns were established and real incomes rose. By 1840 United States per capita income "approached that of Great Britain and was somewhat greater than that of France."[95] The open frontier provided opportunities for many, under less comfortable but more egalitarian conditions than those available in metropolitan centers. Yet growth in the South was economically problematic and

93. Williamson and Lindert, *American Inequality,* p. 37.

94. For the source of these data, see Williamson and Lindert, *American Inequality.* The quotations appear on pp. 95 and 68, respectively. Asset data is to be found on p. 36 and the conclusion about capital accumulation on pp. 165 and 232. Williamson and Lindert criticize the thesis that there was a causal connection between accumulation and inequality (see ch. 12).

95. Ratner et al., *Evolution of the American Economy,* p. 239.

politically disastrous. As indicated earlier, the South experienced "growth without development." Its maintenance of slavery was reinforced by the openness of the United States to the world economy and the strong British demand for cotton. The economic success of associative policies cannot be celebrated without the sober realization that the export economy of the American South upheld slavery and that the ruling elites of the South eventually sought to secede from the Union at the cost of a long and bloody civil war.

WERE SUPERIOR STRATEGIES AVAILABLE?

In terms of economic growth alone, it is hard to object to associative American policies in the period between 1789 and 1860. The costs lay elsewhere: in the social and political patterns that this type of economic growth fostered. The major issues here are two:

1. Policies followed between 1793 and 1807 permitted, and even encouraged, the development of the U.S. shipping industry, despite the fact that an extensive shipping industry could be preyed upon by belligerents, which might lead to war, and despite the losses that would be incurred when shipping was cut off.
2. Policies followed after 1815 permitted the rapid expansion of the cotton economy, which increased the dependence of the United States on Europe, entrenched slavery by making it more profitable in a wider area of the South, and led to a sharp conflict of interest between the Northeast and West, on the one hand, and the South, on the other.

In both cases, associative policies led to the imposition of burdens on others that were not borne by the merchants and landowners who benefited from trade. Shipowners and shipbuilders did not, alone, pay the costs of increased defense expenditures or of the disruptions and losses of war; slaveholding planters were not morally outraged by slavery, nor did they bear the physical and moral costs of slavery inflicted on the slaves themselves. Eventually, their descendants (and the descendants of other Southerners, black and white), bore the costs of the Civil War and its aftermath, as well as the long-term costs of growth without diversification that the South had experienced; but these consequences were not anticipated by the planters of the 1830s, 1840s, and 1850s.

As shown earlier, the Embargo, the War of 1812, and later tariffs seem to have had negative economic effects on the United States. Nevertheless, a mildly dissociative international economic policy during the 1793–1807 period could have had some strategic benefits, even if it had been economically costly. The shock of the embargo would not have been so great; in particular, American shipping would not have grown so rapidly and would therefore not have been so vulnerable to restrictions on trade. New England's political reaction to federal government policies after 1807 might also, therefore, have been less extreme.

Such dissociative policies have become commonplace for countries preparing for, or trying to avoid, war. Nazi Germany is a prime example of the former.[96] More generally, many national policies in this century—including U.S. policies ranging from minerals stockpiling to oil import quotas—have been sincerely or hypocritically put forward as being justified by national security. Yet, given the weakness of the manufacturing sector before 1808, and the ferocity of party quarrels, it hardly seems likely that a conscious policy of protection for the sake of national defense could have been implemented. Nevertheless, something could have been said for it.

The associative policy of the post-1820 period was a great tragedy, insofar as it helped to entrench slavery and

96. Albert O. Hirschman, *National Power and the Structure of Foreign Trade* (Berkeley: University of California Press, 1945).

contributed to the Civil War. In retrospect, it would seem that the United States should have been willing to pay a considerable price to avoid that result. A path of economic development that would have made slavery uneconomic would certainly have had major benefits.

Once again, however, it is difficult to regard such a policy as politically feasible. Not only the South, but the Northeast and the West, gained from the cotton export trade. The cotton economy, resting on slavery, was not merely one sector among others but one of the most important and dynamic sectors, and a principal generator of foreign exchange. Even if Northern and Western interests had been willing to sacrifice their indirect gains from the slave-labor plantation system, legislation sufficient to stop the spread of slavery, even if it could have been enacted, might well have led to secession and civil war in the 1820s or 1830s. Discrimination against the cotton sector, for example, by imposing an export tax, was prohibited by the Constitution (Article I, section 9, paragraph 5), in a clause insisted upon by the Southerners at the constitutional convention in 1787.[97]

The constitutional prohibition against an export tax suggests, as David M. Kennedy has put it, that "in some serious sense it is not proper to speak about 'The United States' as an integrated economic or political entity in the early nineteenth century," or as Walter Dean Burnham wrote, "the chief distinguishing characteristic of the American political system before 1861 is that *there was no state.*"[98] In

97. I was reminded of this constitutional provision by both Professor Walter Dean Burnham of MIT and Professor David M. Kennedy of Stanford. In the short run, a cotton export tax (even if constitutional) might not have hurt the cotton industry sufficiently to discourage slavery, since the American South held a predominant export position in cotton before 1860. Furthermore, if Fogel and Engerman are correct, and slavery was profitable in urban areas as well as on cotton plantations, merely to have limited the cotton economy would not necessarily have been sufficient to halt the growth of slavery.

98. These quotations are from the communications of Professors Kennedy and Burnham to me with respect to an earlier draft of this paper.

the absence of a coherent state, North and South followed different economic strategies:

> The South *did* have a consistent and coherent associationist strategy, just as the North had a consistent and coherent dissociationist strategy in this period. The problem was that neither of them fully dominated the national political apparatus until after the Civil War decided things.[99]

In the absence of a strong state, the momentum of southern association, given the incentives working for it, was so great that it was impossible to stop. Even had the state been stronger and more coherent, extraordinary vision and political leadership would have been necessary to achieve such a result: people would have had to be more farsighted than they could reasonably be expected to be.

The U.S. experience therefore suggests that dissociative strategies should not be seen as simply a matter of choice. In the American experience, dissociation only occurred when it was forced onto the country by external events. For much of the period, associative strategies were so advantageous economically to dominant interests that they seem to have been virtually inevitable. The experience of Venezuela, as discussed by Jeffrey Hart in this volume, provides a relevant comparison. Despite their awareness of the dangers of external dependency, the Venezuelans have pursued an economic policy based on the export of petroleum: the ease with which oil produces large revenues makes this course of action virtually irresistible. Very poor or isolated countries have to be self-reliant, since they have little to sell and can only borrow with difficulty. Countries that can export on the world market under favorable terms of trade find that the lure of wealth prevents decisive moves toward dissociation: the United States between 1820 and 1860, Argentina around the turn of the century, and Mexico and Venezuela today, seem "doomed to association." The United States and Argentina might have managed associa-

99. David M. Kennedy's comments to the author.

tive strategies better than they did; it is to be hoped that Mexico and Venezuela will be more successful in this respect during the rest of the century. But for countries this fortunate in their resource bases, relative to prevailing patterns of demand in the world economy, it is difficult to envision dissociation as a viable long-term option. The efficiency benefits of tying themselves closely to the world economy—exporting, borrowing for infrastructural development, and using the funds (if leadership is farsighted) to diversify their industrial structure—will be too attractive for dominant elites to resist, even if they are unusually willing to forego the huge rents that can accrue to those who mediate between a wealthy export economy and the outside world.[100]

If dissociation becomes a viable option, it is unlikely to do so as a result of purely economic calculations. The major instance of dissociative American policy—the Embargo of 1807—constituted a desperate effort to preserve autonomy, honor, and peace simultaneously. This policy seemed to American leaders to be forced on them by foreign powers. It was hardly the result of a long-term strategy designed to reduce ties between the United States and the rest of the world.

CONCLUSIONS

It is impossible to draw simple parallels between the situation of the United States in the early nineteenth century and the less-developed countries in the world economy today. After 1820 the United States found itself in a peculiarly advantageous situation. Demand was strong for cotton, and capital was often available in Britain. Technological gaps

100. For this point I am indebted to the work of Terry Karl. See "The Political Economy of Petrodollars: Oil and Democracy in Venezuela" (Ph.D. diss., Stanford University, 1981).

between British and American industry were relatively small; trade barriers were low and declining; and the United States did not have to contend with highly organized multinational corporations, although it did have to deal with a small set of European bankers who communicated effectively with one another. Perhaps most important, the United States had a growing and prosperous agricultural sector outside of the Southern plantation economy. These farmers were not closely tied to the world economy, but they did generate demands for manufactured goods (many of which could be produced in the United States); and expectations of further agricultural expansion stimulated efforts to extend railroad and canal networks westward.[101] Westward expansion, facilitated by the transportation revolution of the antebellum era, stimulated growth.

It should not be inferred from this that the international economy of the nineteenth century was, in general, more favorable to growth by peripheral countries than the period since the end of World War II. By historical standards, LDC growth rates since the end of World War II have been much higher. For most countries on the periphery of the world economic system there was little *per capita* income growth before 1860.[102] As we have seen, U.S. gross domestic product per capita grew at about 1.3 percent annually in this period. Between 1960 and 1975 median per capita growth rates for non-oil less-developed countries were about 2 percent per year.[103] Northeastern and Western success in economic growth was not a matter of extraordinarily rapid development but rather of managing to cultivate virgin lands, assimilate millions of immigrants, and maintain substantial social mobility, while sustaining steady rates of growth in

101. Fishlow, *American Railroads and the Transformation of the Ante-Bellum Economy.*

102. W. Arthur Lewis, *Growth and Fluctuations, 1870–1913* (London: Allen & Unwin, 1978), p. 29.

103. Stephen D. Krasner, "North-South Economic Relations," in Kenneth Oye et al., *Eagle Entangled: U.S. Foreign Policy in a Complex World* (New York: Longman, 1979), p. 131.

per capita income. This performance was the result less of government policy than of the open frontier. Apart from the South, the United States was not only "born free," in Louis Hartz's phrase; it was "born lucky."

The United States experience suggests that the strengths and weaknesses of associationist development strategies are not unique to the contemporary world. The United States had, in effect, two economies: the export-oriented plantation economy of the South and the relatively self-sufficient, increasingly balanced economy of the Northeast and West. In the South, associative strategies led to growth without development and a reinforcement of inegalitarian social patterns that failed to meet the basic human needs of much of the population. Slavery denied the most basic rights to millions of individuals. In the Northeast and West, by contrast, maintenance of openness to the world economy had beneficial effects: after 1815 there was little danger of excessive dependence on external trade; and European funds helped pay for the transportation networks that bound West and North together.

The American experience helps to reinforce a generalization sometimes made about the contemporary world. Countries with relatively well-integrated political economies, which have prospects for indigenous balanced development, may be wise to follow relatively open policies toward the world economy, while countries with large plantation sectors producing for export need to be more cautious, lest they perpetuate patterns of dualism and great social inequalities. Countries such as the nineteenth-century United States, containing both types of regions, may find that close association with the world economy tends to accentuate interregional divisions.

Ironically, however, political and economic patterns appear to be somewhat at odds with one another. Dominant landed elites in export enclaves will have strong interests in associative policies, since they benefit so much from their comparative advantage on a world scale. Their class interests, especially in the short term, reinforce long-term dependence and dualism. Yet in more balanced economies, which may benefit from openness, sentiments for protectionism are likely to be fostered by the very strength of import-competing sectors. Thus, in the United States, the South stood for free trade, while much of the Northeast and West favored protection.

Early United States development suggests strongly what other essays in this volume argue or imply for the contemporary world: strategies of association or dissociation cannot be assessed in a vacuum, but only in the context of particular, historically given circumstances. It was the resources of the West, and the availability of capital and free labor to develop them, that made close association with the world economy tolerable for the United States. Without these resources, interregional and intraregional trade would not have grown so fast, and foreign trade ratios would have remained higher. A policy of openness toward Europe could have made a less well-endowed United States much more dependent than it in fact became.

American experience also suggests that dissociation may sometimes be chosen as a political means to establish control over one's own policy—to assert one's autonomy as in the Embargo—rather than as a strategy designed to achieve economic development. In the contemporary world, development rhetoric may be used to legitimize a strategy of autonomy, but this should not blind analysts to the real motivations of the policy.

A review of American foreign economic policy also makes it easier to understand why certain governments in the Third World—China being the most obvious example—have returned to more associative policies after a period of dissociation. The United States itself behaved in this way, cutting ties with Europe between 1808 and 1815, then reopening its economy to foreign trade and capital. Dissociation may be unattractive as a long-run policy for countries with large internal resources and the potential for economic development at relatively modest levels of dependence; but it may nevertheless be an appropriate short-term policy, as a way of establishing one's autonomy and thus creating the conditions under which a self-directed policy of association can be successfully undertaken.

Growth took place in the antebellum United States as a result of a conjunction of favorable internal and external conditions. The United States prospered without developing a coherent economic growth strategy, either of dissociation or managed association. Yet its economic successes were accompanied by the political failure of secession and civil war. Despite this mixed record, and the difficulties of generalizing from the American experience (or from myths about it) to contemporary less-developed countries, Americans characteristically view their own history as demonstrating the virtues of laissez-faire and economic openness. In this respect, American ideology reinforces the interest of the twentieth century United States in maintaining a liberal world economy. It is therefore difficult to persuade United States policymakers of the virtues of state-run strategies of "self-reliance" in the Third World. To a country that was born free and born lucky, the protective actions of the less free and the unlucky do not strike a responsive chord.

2.

The Small European States in the International Economy: Economic Dependence and Corporatist Politics

PETER J. KATZENSTEIN

"IN AN INTERDEPENDENT world the forms of managing interdependence differ, but not the fact of interdependence itself."[1] This statement is a truism which, for the small European states, contains only a partial truth. For the difficulty that Switzerland, the Netherlands, Sweden, Belgium, Austria, Denmark, and Norway face is not the management of interdependence but of dependence. For them "the neces-

This paper is drawn in part from a larger study of the position of the small European states in the international economy. I would like to thank the Rockefeller Foundation and the German Marshall Fund for supporting the project and the contributors to this volume for commenting on earlier drafts of this paper.

1. Robert A. Dahl and Edward R. Tufte, *Size and Democracy* (Stanford: Stanford University Press, 1973), p. 133.

sity to comply increasingly with the world economy . . . implies further restrictions in decisions and burdensome rationalization . . . in order to ensure national development. [However, the] efficient utilization of the international division of labor can increase the competitiveness and the capability of resistance of small countries in many fields and set up a system of economic interdependence the effects of which are useful weapons in the fight for preserving sovereignty."[2] Exposed to developments in international markets and dependent on actors beyond their reach, the small, advanced industrial states have, in fact, maintained both successful political strategies and coherent domestic structures since World War II. In the process, they have achieved standards of living that, if they do not constitute absolutely the highest, certainly are among the very highest achieved anywhere in the world.

Unfortunately, the experience of the small European states has not been studied in the traditional international relations literature. Hedley Bull, for one, muses that "however viable the small state might be in international politics, does it really present a viable subject of study?"[3] Others point to the importance of the economic dependence of the small, advanced industrial states without ever exploring the character, causes and consequences of the dependence. Thus "small states (besides their security problem) also have a problem of survival in their trade policy, which under most circumstances and during the longest periods seems far more important than their security problem."[4] One of the

2. Béla Kádár, *Small Countries in World Economy* (Budapest: Center for Afro-Asian Research of the Hungarian Academy of Sciences, 1970), p. 21.

3. Annette B. Fox, "The Small States in the International System, 1919–1969," *International Affairs* (1969), 24(4):751. For general reviews of the analysis of small states see Peter R. Baehr, "Small States: A Tool for Analysis?" *World Politics* (April 1975), 27(3):456–66; and Michael Stein, "Interim Report on the 'Small States' Project, Jerusalem Group for National Planning, Van Leer Jerusalem Foundation," 1975. Manuscript.

4. Ole K. Pedersen as quoted in Niels Amstrup, "The Perennial Problem of Small States: A Survey of Research Efforts," *Cooperation and Conflict* (1976), 3:173.

few studies of the economic dimension of the foreign policy of small states thus concludes that "the importance of economic factors in small-state foreign policy is demonstrated. The involvement of economic bureaucracies and the utilization of economic techniques of statecraft are more frequent in the foreign policy of small states than in that of large states."[5]

The small European states deserve analysis for their own sake. But their experience may also shed some light on the predicaments facing both the large, advanced industrial states (United States, Britain, West Germany, France, and Japan) and the less-developed countries. In the international division of labor, the small European states hold an intermediary position between the two. The dependence on world markets with which the small states must cope is more pressing than the dependence which characterizes the large, advanced industrial states. On the other hand, their dependence differs drastically from that of the less-developed countries, in that the small European states "somehow manage to be dependent in a more autonomous way than the countries of the Third World and . . . their dependence at least to some degree allows the state to steer its own course."[6] Their management of dependence results from distinctive forms of political strategies and structures. These strategies and structures may be of interest to those advanced industrial states whose position in the international division of labor is slipping, as well as to the newly industrializing states in the Third World who are attempting to sustain their recent rise.

Because, more than the large industrial states, the small European states are open and vulnerable to developments in the international economy, their political strategies for

5. Maurice A. East, "Size and Foreign Policy Behavior: A Test of Two Models," *World Politics* (July 1973), 25(4):576.

6. Samuel N. Eisenstadt, "Sociological Characteristics and Problems of Small States: A Research Note," *The Jerusalem Journal of International Relations* (Winter 1976–77), 2:39.

dealing with the international economy have necessarily differed. The United States and Britain champion the cause of economic interdependence and market institutions. They tend to deal with the adverse consequences of economic openness through selective protection, which temporarily shifts the costs of economic change to other states. Japan and France, on the other hand, espouse the cause of political autonomy through state institutions. These two countries deal with the consequences of openness primarily through selective protection of and intervention in their economies and seek to preempt the costs of economic change by strengthening promising sectors of production. The small European states (and Germany, which in this regard closely resembles them) have adopted the dual strategy of international liberalization and domestic compensation, based on corporatist political structures. It is my contention that corporatism has made possible the pursuit of strategies that differ from those either of liberalism or statism.

Taxonomic distinctions are useful for locating the strategy and structure of the small European states in comparison to those of the large industrial states. But why was corporatism a plausible political option for a number of small European states in the twentieth century? The answer to that question is both historical and functional. The Great Depression, fascism, and World War II created a perception of vulnerability widely shared throughout these European societies. The "historical compromise" between business and unions, which was struck in the 1930s and 1940s, thereafter was altered and reinforced during a generation of peace and prosperity by the requirement of international competitiveness in the world economy. A historical and a functional explanation thus converge in accounting for the prevalence of the corporatist politics of the small European states.

The first section of this paper argues that the position the small European states occupy in the international division of labor differs considerably from that of the large industrial states; small states are more open to and dependent on developments in international markets than large states. The second section examines two political strategies, international liberalization and domestic compensation, with which the small European states exploit the opportunities and cushion the adverse consequences of economic openness. The third section argues that economic openness and vulnerability have had a distinctive impact on the corporatist structures which distinguish the small European states from the liberal and statist forms of capitalism prevailing in the large industrial states. The conclusion briefly suggests how the experience of the small European states relates to the economic problems faced by other countries, especially the newly industrializing countries of the Third World.

ECONOMIC OPENNESS

Small domestic markets lead to a degree of economic openness in the small European states which for two reasons is much greater than in the large, advanced industrial countries. First, because they do not offer the necessary economies of scale to a number of industries absolutely critical to the functioning of a modern economy, the small European states must import a wide range of goods which the large, advanced industrial countries produce domestically. Secondly, small domestic markets lead the small European states to seek their specialization and economies of scale in export markets. Dependence on imports and the necessity to export make the economies of the small European states both more open and more specialized than those of the large industrial states.

A number of studies conducted since 1945 all point to the conclusion that the import dependence of the small Eu-

ropean states reflects the absence of critically important industries requiring large domestic markets. As a result, the
industrial structures of the small European states are less
diversified than those of the large, advanced industrial
countries.[7] This selectivity in their industrial structures leads
to an important dependence of the small European states,
which is much stronger in investment than in consumer
goods, and which encourages a degree of openness towards influences from the international economy far greater
than that of the large countries.[8] In the Netherlands, for example, in the late 1970s more than half of the total domestic demand for manufactures was supplied by foreign producers. This example concurs with the undisputed finding
of virtually all studies on the subject. One recent statistical
analysis concludes that small countries have high levels of
imports irrespective of their level of income while in the large
countries the propensity to import declines when income
levels rise. The exposure to foreign competition in the small
European states is, on average, more than three times as
large as in the large countries.[9]

7. United Nations, Department of Economic and Social Affairs, *A Study of Industrial Growth* (New York: United Nations, 1963); United Nations, Economic Commission for Europe, *Structure and Change in European Industry* (New York: United Nations, 1977); UNCTAD, *Restructuring of World Industry: New Dimensions for Trade Cooperation* (New York: United Nations, 1978); "Comparative Analysis of Economic Structures by Means of Input-Output Tables," *Economic Bulletin for Europe* (1971), 23(1):3, 17, 21; United Nations Industrial Development Organization, *World Industry Since 1960: Progress and Prospect. Special Issue of the Industrial Development Survey for the Third General Conference on UNIDO* (New York: United Nations, 1979), pp. 43–49, 331–65; and Bela Balassa, " 'Revealed' Comparative Advantage Revisited: An Analysis of Relative Export Shares of the Industrial Countries, 1953–1971," *The Manchester School of Economic and Social Studies* (December 1977), 45(4):337.

8. Hollis B. Chenery and Lance Taylor, "Development Patterns: Among Countries and Over Time," *The Review of Economics and Statistics* (November 1968), 50(4):399, 412–13; Kádár, *Small Countries in World Economy*, pp. 11, 15, table 5; and Alfred Maizels, *Industrial Growth and World Trade* (Cambridge: Cambridge University Press, 1963), pp. 266–67 and 135–36. The sample of countries included in Maizel's analysis differs from the group of states analyzed here. See also Peter J. Lloyd, *International Trade Problems of Small Nations* (Durham, N.C.: Duke University Press, 1968), p. 37.

9. L. B. M. Mennes, "Adjustment of the Industrial Structure of Developed Economies in Particular the Netherlands," paper prepared for the International

Swiss chemicals, Belgian steel, and Norwegian ship-building are three prominent examples of industries in the small European states that have sought their economies of scale in international markets. Furthermore, because of the necessity to export, the small European states, unlike the large countries, have traditionally sought a mixture of stan-dardized and high-value-added products to fill the market niches particularly well suited to their traditional economic strengths and resource endowments. During the last two decades, for example, Switzerland and Austria have bene-fited greatly from the production of ski clothes and equip-ment. Sweden is exploiting its traditional strength in wood and furniture products in the computer software market, through specialization in the exterior furnishings of mini-computers and in office design. And Denmark has devel-oped highly sophisticated marketing strategies in a wide range of consumer goods typified best by the phenomenal success of Lego toys. Furthermore, statistical studies have concluded that in the mid- and late 1960s the economies of the small European states were much more specialized in their exports than were the larger European countries.[10]

In expanding their export markets abroad, the small European states have a distinctive capacity in specific types

Symposium on Maritime Research and European Shipping and Shipbuilding, Rot-terdam, March 29–31, 1978, p. 3; Simon Kuznets, "Economic Growth of Small Nations," in E. A. G. Robinson, ed., *Economic Consequences of the Size of Na-tions: Proceedings of a Conference held by the International Economic Association* (London: Macmillan, 1960), pp. 14–32; Lloyd, *International Trade Problems,* pp. 28–29, 33–34; Nadim G. Khalaf, *Economic Implications of the Size of Nations: With Special Reference to Lebanon* (Leiden: Brill, 1971), pp. 99–122; Nadim G. Khalaf, "Country Size and Trade Concentration," *Journal of Development Studies* (October 1974), 11:81–85; Raimo Värynen, "The Position of Small Powers in the West European Network of Economic Relations," *European Journal of Political Re-search* (June 1974), 2(2):153; D. H. Macgregor, "Trade of Large and Small Coun-tries," *Economic Journal* (December 1925), 35:642–45; and Raoul Gross and Mi-chael Keating, "An Empirical Analysis of Competition in Export and Domestic Markets," *Occasional Studies, OECD Economic Outlook* (December 1970), p. 15.

10. United Nations, *Structure and Change in European Industry,* pp. 25–26. The sample of large countries excludes the United States and Japan but includes Italy. See also United Nations Industrial Development Organization, *World Industry Since 1960,* p. 48.

of industry. While numerous studies have differed slightly in their definition of what constitutes a "modern" as compared to a "traditional" industry, all of these studies suggest that, by and large, the small European states have developed their comparative advantage in the latter. This pattern of export specialization in the postwar era left the relative share of exports in GNP in the small European states twice as large as in the large countries.[11]

Dependence on the import of investment goods and the export of consumer goods creates, within the context of openness and vulnerability toward developments in international markets, tendencies that reinforce imbalances in the economic structures of the small European states. Their economic specialization leaves different sectors of the economy less integrated than those in the large countries. Throughout the postwar era, the large, advanced industrial countries have had a more diversified and integrated economic structure than have the small European states.[12] Openness to international markets, specialization, and imbalance give the economic structures of the small European states, to borrow a phrase from David Riesman, a propensity for being "other-directed." The small European states tend to develop two different economic sectors, one externally oriented and competitive, the other internally oriented and protected. Few would deny that "the structural differences between these two sectors are usually greater in small than larger societies."[13]

11. Fritz Breuss, "Die Makrostruktur der Österreichischen Wirtschaft im Vergleich mit den Europäischen Wirtschaftspartnern," in *Der Kleinstaat in der Europäischen Wirtschaftlichen Zusammenarbeit aus der Sicht Ungarns and Österreichs* (Vienna: Verlag für Geschichte und Politik, 1975), pp. 62–63; Peer Hull Kristensen and Jørn Levinsen, *Small Country Squeeze* (Roskilde, Denmark: Institute of Economics, Politics, and Administration, 1978), pp. 112, 117; Balassa, " 'Revealed' Comparative Advantage," pp. 334–36; Kádár, *Small Countries in World Economy,* pp. 11, 15, table 5; and United Nations, *Study of Industrial Growth,* pp. 9, 13–14.

12. Balassa, " 'Revealed' Comparative Advantage," p. 337.

13. Dieter Senghaas, *Weltwirtschaftsordnung und Entwicklungspolitik: Plä-*

A strong specialization in their export trade is apparently insufficient to offset fully the disadvantages which the small European states suffer from their great dependence on imports. Between 1938 and 1967 the value of their export trade grew by a factor of eight as compared to a tenfold increase in imports. Commodities which enjoyed a high growth rate in world trade between 1954 and 1969 increased by 14.2 percent in the five large industrial states but by only 9.1 percent in the small European states. Conversely, commodities with an average growth rate declined by .8 percent in the five large countries while they increased by 7.4 percent in the small European states.[14] It is thus not surprising that the import level of the small European states covered by gross international reserves is about a third lower than in the large countries.[15] Furthermore, the small European states tend to run consistently sizable deficits in their balance of foreign trade. While the large countries found themselves in surplus two-thirds of the time between 1960 and 1977, the small European states ran on average a deficit in their trade balance two years out of three.[16] Perhaps overstating his case, one observer, reflecting on the constraints which the small European states confront in their export trade, concluded that "small countries appeared to experience a comparative disadvantage in most manufacturing industries."[17]

---

doyer für Dissoziation (Frankfurt: Suhrkamp, 1977), pp. 34–35; and Kristensen and Levinsen, *Small Country Squeeze*, p. 112.

14. Kádár, *Small Countries in World Economy*, pp. 10–11, 23, and Kristensen and Levinsen, *Small Country Squeeze*, p. 114. Switzerland and Austria are not included in the figures for the small European states. Since they differ along a number of dimensions measuring the relative modernity of their industrial structures, their exclusion from these figures probably does not bias these findings.

15. *World Development Report, 1979* (Washington, D.C.: The World Bank, August 1979), table 15, p. 155. Switzerland has been excluded from the calculations.

16. Organization for Co-operation and Development, *Balance of Payments of OECD Countries 1960–1977* (Paris: OECD, 1979), my calculations.

17. Donald B. Keesing, "Population and Industrial Development: Some Evidence from Trade Patterns," *American Economic Review* (June 1968), 50(3/1):454–55.

One consequence of these structural trade deficits is the fact that the small European states generate a substantial surplus in their invisible trade, the export of services.[18] It is next to impossible to separate out the service component from merchandise trade, particularly in technologically advanced sectors where know-how, consulting, and service are all an integral part of one product package; but it is striking that the small European states offer an unusually broad range of services, including finance and insurance (Switzerland), commerce (Netherlands), shipping (Norway), and tourism (Austria).[19] In 1976 receipts from invisible trade amounted to 12 percent of the GNP of the small European states as compared to 5 percent for the large countries. Calculated on per capita basis this was a lead of about three to one in favor of the small states.[20]

A second consequence of their structural trade deficits has been a great reliance on the flow of foreign capital into the small European economies.[21] Compared to the flow of direct foreign investment into the large, industrial states, it increased from 11 percent in 1960 to about 30 percent a decade later before declining to about 25 percent in 1973–75. The proportion of factor income paid to the rest of the

18. Kristensen and Levinsen, *Small Country Squeeze*, p. 108.

19. Richard Blackhurst, Nicolas Marian, Jan Tumlir, *Trade Liberalization, Protectionism and Interdependence* (Geneva: General Agreement on Tariffs and Trade, 1977), p. 62, fn 10; Samuel N. Eisenstadt, "Sociological Characteristics and Problems of Small States," p. 39; and Levinsen and Kristensen, *Small Country Squeeze*, pp. 127, 135.

20. Committee on Invisible Exports, *World Invisible Trade*, pp. 15, 30, 32; my calculations.

21. Organization for Economic Co-operation and Development, *Policy Perspectives for International Trade and Economic Relations: Report by the High Level Group on Trade and Related Problems to the Secretary General of the OECD* (Paris: OECD, 1972), p. 158; and United Nations, *Transnational Corporations in World Development: A Re-Examination* (New York: U.N. Economic and Social Council, 1978), pp. 263–64. Preliminary figures for 1976 indicate a further decline. See also Volker Bornschier, *Wachstum, Konzentration und Multinationalisierung von Industrieunternehmen* (Frauenfeld: Huber, 1976).

world over national income increased between 1960 and 1968 by 5.9 percent per year in the small European states as compared to only 3.1 percent in the large industrial countries. In 1970 the ratio of investment over trade-inflow was 2.96 for the small European states as compared to 2.17 for the large industrial countries. This is in sharp contrast to the corresponding ratio of outward flow, which was 4.34 for the large countries and only 1.71 for the small ones. By the early 1970s the estimated share of manufacturing held by foreign enterprises was therefore much larger in the small European states than in the large countries. On the average, foreign firms control 26 percent of the sales and 18 percent of employment in the small European states as compared to 15 and 11 percent respectively in the large industrial countries. Together with the export of services, the inflow of long-term capital has been a second factor countering the persistent trade deficit of the small European states and bringing their basic balance of foreign transactions into equilibrium.

Compared to the large industrial states, the small European countries are unusually open to and dependent on a global economy which is beyond their control. The economic structure of the small European states is less diversified than that of the large states. Furthermore the small European states depend heavily on the import of investment goods and other products for which their small domestic markets simply do not offer large economies of scale. Instead they seek these economies of scale through a specialization in their exports especially in relatively "traditional" industries. This pattern of import dependence and export specialization leaves the small European economies with a structural trade deficit which narrows temporarily only in times of recession. The small European states rely on their service sectors as well as on the import of foreign capital in order to partly cover their perennial trade deficits.

POLITICAL STRATEGIES

Because of their economic openness, the small European states have adopted a political strategy that links international liberalization more tightly to domestic compensation than is true of the large, advanced industrial states. The commitment of the small European states to the principle of international liberalization is not mere rhetoric. Throughout the 1960s and 1970s, their tariff levels, on the whole, have been lower than those of the large, advanced industrial states. Furthermore the small European states have been more hesitant than their larger counterparts to protect declining industrial sectors faced with inexpensive imports from the advanced less-developed countries. Throughout the postwar years, the small European states have always welcomed the inflow of foreign capital as an ingredient essential rather than detrimental to their economic and political aspirations.

The small European states balance their strategy of international liberalization with a strategy of domestic compensation. While each of the small European states has developed a distinctive capacity for a particular set of policies, these countries are distinguished as a group by the range, adaptability, and innovativeness of their policies. The Netherlands and Norway, for example, are known for their economic planning policies, Sweden for its active labor market and industrial policies, Austria for its centralized incomes policy, and, with the exception of Switzerland, all of the small European states for a large public sector and generous social welfare expenditures. Compared with the other small European states, Austria's pursuit of a compensation strategy has been quite typical. Austria and the other small European states are thus clear exceptions to the generalization that liberalism in the international economy and interventionism in the domestic economy are incompatible.[22] The experience of the small European states suggests instead that political intervention in the domestic economy does not constrain but complements international liberalization. In the 1970s conspicuous deviations from the principle of free trade occurred primarily where well-designed, broad-ranging domestic policies were lacking.

International Liberalization

In confronting change, the economic openness of the small European states inspires a fear of economic retaliation which inhibits protectionist policies. The securing of a liberal international economy has been an overriding objective which the small European states pursue in the international economy. Since "in a 'bilateral' world the position of the small state is intrinsically weak," this group of states has a strong interest in lowering tariffs, in preventing the formation of economic blocs, and in strengthening the principle of multilateralism.[23] When, in 1954, the United Kingdom attempted, unsuccessfully as it turned out, to amend the General Agreement on Tariffs and Trade (GATT) by adding a new article permitting preferential trade links between a metropolitan country and her colonies—provided such links contributed substantially to the exclusive benefit of the dependent territory—the small European states were counted among the proposal's most vigorous opponents.[24] And for a variety of reasons the small European states were highly

22. Melvyn B. Krauss, *The New Protectionism: The Welfare State and International Trade* (New York: New York University Press, 1978). A more plausible argument, that the combination of international liberalization and domestic interventionism has constituted a regime norm throughout the postwar era, is developed by John Gerard Ruggie, "International Regimes, Transactions, and Change: Embedded Liberalism in the Postwar Economic Order," *International Organization* (Spring 1982), 36(2):379–416.

23. George A. Duncan, "The Small States and International Economic Equilibrium," *Economia Internazionale* (November 1950), 3(4):939.

24. Gardner C. Patterson, *Discrimination in International Trade: The Policy Issues 1945–1965* (Princeton: Princeton University Press, 1966), pp. 332–33.

critical of the European Steel and Coal Community (ECSC).

In 1958 these states welcomed the advent of free convertibility. By 1962 they had dropped all trade restrictions due to balance of payment difficulties. While Canada (1962), the United Kingdom (1964 and 1968), France (1968), and the United States (1971) invoked the GATT's balance of payments safeguard provision, of the seven small European states Denmark was alone in levying a temporary import surcharge in 1971 for balance of payments reasons. Quantitative import restrictions in the trade of nonagricultural commodities also illustrate the great commitment of the small European states to the principle of free trade. In the 1960s and 1970s, the five large industrial countries were much more likely to impose quantitative restrictions on trade than were the small European states.

The small European states have been active and enthusiastic supporters of successive rounds of tariff reductions culminating in the Tokyo Round Agreements of 1979. In the words of one knowledgeable observer, they "exercised a distinct influence of the tone of postwar international economic relations."[25] Although several methodological and statistical difficulties suggest caution, a comparison of nominal tariff levels provides one rough indicator of the degree of economic liberalism or protection of different countries. Generally speaking, during the last thirty years, the small European states have been distinguished by tariff rates which were much lower than those of the large, advanced industrial countries.[26]

25. Andrew Shonfield, "International Economic Relations of the Western World: An Overall View," in Andrew Shonfield, ed., *International Economic Relations of the Western World 1959–1971*, vol. I, *Politics and Trade* (London: Oxford University Press, 1976), p. 97.
26. Hans Mayrzedt, *Multilaterale Wirschaftsdiplomatie zwischen westlichen Industriestaaten als Instrument zur Stärkung der multilateralen und liberalen Handelspolitik* (Bern: Lang, 1979), p. 376; and Wilbur F. Monroe, *International Trade Policy in Transition* (Lexington, Mass.: Heath, 1975), p. 23. Since the European Economic Communities counted free-trade oriented Netherlands and Belgium along its members, the difference between the small European states and the large industrial states was probably larger.

But nominal tariff figures render only an incomplete picture of the "new protectionism." Various forms of invisible trade restrictions, including export support schemes and a variety of nontariff barriers impeding imports, are less easily measured. The evidence available suggests here as well that the small European states are much more liberal in their trade policies than the large industrial countries. A United Nations study concluded as early as the late 1950s that the most fully developed export credit guarantee schemes could be found in the large countries.[27] An analysis of expenditures for export promotion in 1972 yields similar results. West Germany, France, and Britain spent a total of $102.1 million on trade promotion as compared to a $37.7-million total for all of the small European states. The ratio of expenditures for export promotion in the small and large states was considerably smaller (18.5 percent) than either the ratio of population (29.6 percent) or of total export trade in 1972 (31.1 percent).[28] The spotty evidence on export cartels also suggests that these cartels are favored primarily by the large, rather than the small, states, even though the cartel legislation of the small European states is typically less restrictive than that in the large countries.[29]

With different forms of trade restrictions, both visible and invisible, spreading in the 1970s, the small European states counted among the persistent champions of a liberal international trade regime. The initiatives for a reordering of the international monetary system after 1971, and the implementation of sector-specific trade regimes in declining industries such as textiles, without fail have emanated

27. "A note on recent developments and problems of export-credit guarantees (with special reference to Western Europe)," *UN Economic Bulletin for Europe* (1960), 12(2):53.

28. *Botschaft des Bundesrates an die Bundesversammlung über einen Beitrag an die Schweizerische Zentrale für Handelsförderung,* February 26, 1975, pp. 11–13; and Kristensen and Levinsen, *Small Country Squeeze,* p. 71.

29. Organization for Economic Co-operation and Development, *Export Cartels: Report of the Committee of Experts on Restrictive Business Practices* (Paris: OECD, 1974), pp. 8, 24.

from the large countries. The small European states, by way of contrast, have pressed hard on every conceivable occasion for a reaffirmation of the principle of free trade. A liberal international economy is the preferred choice of the small European states, not because it eliminates dependence, but because it diffuses such dependence in a wider market rather than concentrating it on particular states.[30] The pursuit of economic liberalism is thus not based on disinterested notions of aggregate world welfare, but is rooted firmly in the awareness that the political autonomy and economic welfare of the small European states are best served by such a strategy.

For the small European states, with their open economies and fear of retaliation by other governments, exporting the costs of change through protectionist policies is simply not a viable political strategy. Since the end of World War II, economic openness and dependence have reinforced processes of economic growth and decline, as well as of industrial obsolescence and rejuvenation, which have occurred faster in the small European states than in the large ones. Political leaders in the open economies of the small European states are thus accustomed to accept as normal, rates of economic change and dislocation which elites in larger countries regard as intolerably high.

Domestic Compensation
Policies of domestic compensation are essential for facilitating international liberalization. This is illustrated clearly by the case of incomes policy, which is perhaps the best example of corporatist politics in the small European states. Control over wages and prices is particularly urgent in the small European states. Due to their open economies, these countries import inflation from world markets. In contrast to the large countries, inflation in the small states not only has indirect effects, through increasing demands for ex-

30. Patterson, *Discrimination in International Trade*, p. 303.

ports or through the balance of payments, but it also acts directly via price dissemination of imported goods and services. A mixture of wage restraint and price control is often a requirement of international competitiveness and of the need for relative (compared to other countries, especially larger ones) stability if an equilibrium in the balance of payments is to be achieved. In a preliminary analysis of ten episodes of incomes policy in the 1940s and 1950s, Peter Lange concluded that the logic of economic vulnerability prevailed over the logic of worker militancy in forcing political outcomes stressing consensual wage bargaining.[31] At least in the short run, for the small European states "the currency crisis thus furnishes an example of the civilizing influence of common adversity on communal behavior . . . social problems that do not yield to competitive pressures arising from individual activity should be tackled, not by the state alone, but by 'interest group activities' which may have caused them in the first place."[32]

The centralization of the industrial relations systems in most of the small European states is an important condition for the achievement of wage and price stability. Incomes policy and collective bargaining were intimately linked, for example, in both Sweden's "private" version of a central wage bargain and in the Netherland's "public" version of an official incomes policy in the 1950s and 1960s. In fact, with the sole exception of Switzerland, all of the small European states have highly centralized collective bargaining systems. Of these, only Belgium lacked a de facto or explicit incomes policy in the 1950s, 1960s, and 1970s; but even Belgium, since the convening of its Economic and Social Conference in 1970, has moved to peak-level bargaining and

---

31. Peter Lange, "The Conjunctural Condition for Consensual Wage Regulation: An Initial Examination of Some Hypotheses," paper prepared for presentation at the Annual Meeting of the American Political Science Association, New York, September 1981, pp. 62, 64.

32. Lloyd Ulman and Robert J. Flanagan, *Wage Restraint: A Study of Incomes Policies of Western Europe* (Berkeley: University of California Press, 1971), pp. 219, 222–23.

conflict resolution illustrated clearly by the government's economic recovery plan of 1980–1981. "In five of the six smallest and most-open, small European states—and in only one large economy, West Germany—powerful coordinated employers' federations face coordinated labor unions. On the other hand, in six of the seven large industrial states uncoordinated labor unions face uncoordinated employers organizations."[33]

This effort to stabilize wages and prices has been supported by the substantial degree of consensus through which economic openness and dependence have transformed the class struggle in the small European states. In his work on the political economy of strikes, Hibbs concluded that in contrast to the large industrial countries in the postwar era, a significant reduction of strike activity to negligible levels had occurred only in Denmark, the Netherlands, Norway, and Sweden. Had Austria and Switzerland been included in his study, they would have fallen in the same category. Only Belgium experienced a decline in strike activity that still allows today for sizable industrial disputes. By way of contrast, during the interwar years, and their much lower levels of economic openness, the small European states were much more strike prone than the large industrial countries. "The withering away of the strike is a rather limited phenomenon confined largely to small democracies."[34] Even short strikes today have large repercussions, both real and psychological, in small open economies. In sum, within the open economies of the small European states, postwar incomes policy and centralized collective bargaining have provided the cement by which the truce between the business community and the labor movement has been translated into a durable peace.

The small European states rely on their public sector as

33. Anne Romanis, "Cost Inflation and Incomes Policies in Industrial Countries," *IMF Staff Papers* (March 1967), 14(1):196.
34. Douglas A. Hibbs, Jr., "On the Political Economy of Long-Run Trends in Strike Activity," *British Journal of Political Science* (1978), 8:162.

a critically important instrument in supplementing their incomes policies and economic stabilization. Because stabilization is so important to the small European states, the influence of elections on variations in public spending—the so-called electoral business cycle—is less notable in them than in the large industrial countries.[35] The size and the rate of increase of the public economy has been unusually large in the small European states. Several studies suggest the conclusion that in these states governments of the right, center, and left have all tended to rely on the public economy to counter some of the harmful effects of an open economy.

The growing role of the government's tax and revenue policies in national attempts at constraining wage and price increases points to a more general development, which sets the strong corporatist structures of the small European states apart from the weak ones of the large industrial states. The most comprehensive recent analysis by the OECD of public expenditure trends shows, for example, that in the small European states more than in all other industrial countries, "the share of public expenditure in GNP has increased by two-thirds in the last twenty years, notably on account of a well-above-average growth in 'welfare' outlays."[36] This growth is due primarily to a substantial increase in transfer payments, primarily from government to households but also to producers, rather than to growth in government consumption itself. A number of studies support the conclusion that it was only in the 1950s and 1960s—i.e., during the time of international liberalization—that the public sector assumed such a prominent role in the small European states. OECD data, for example, show that in the 1950s the total public expenditure (as a percentage of GDP) of the large industrial countries exceeded slightly those of the small European states; from the mid-1960s on,

35. Dahl and Tufte, *Size and Democracy,* pp. 11–12.
36. Organization for Economic Co-operation and Development, *Public Expenditure Trends* (Paris: OECD, 1978), p. 12.

an increasingly rapid divergence occurred. By the mid-1970s, the average for the small European states was 45 percent of GDP as compared to only 38 percent for the large industrial countries.[37] In 1956–1957 the share of social security expenditures in national income was an identical 13 percent average in both the small European and the large industrial states; but by 1971, the small European states spent, on the average, 20.9 percent of their GNP on social security as compared to 14.3 percent for the large industrial states.[38] "The largest governments—size being measured by government expenditures as a percentage of national income—were to be found in the Federal Republic of Germany, France, and the United Kingdom in the 1950s, but in Denmark, the Netherlands, and Norway in the 1970s."[39] Between 1950 and the early 1970s the average annual increase in government expenditures as a percentage of national income varies for the small European states between a high of 1.84 percent for Sweden and a low of .62 percent for Switzerland as compared to a high of .55 percent for the United Kingdom and a low of .44 percent for France among the large industrial countries. Put slightly differently, during the postwar years the growth of public spending in "conservative" Switzerland exceeded the growth of spending in "socialist" Britain.[40] It remains still true, though, that among the small European states Switzerland defies the rule of a large public economy. But, unlike the other two "laggards" in the growth of a public economy among the large indus-

37. *Ibid.*, pp. 14–15.
38. Henry Aron, "Social Security: International Comparisons," in Otto Eckstein, ed., *Studies in the Economics of Income Maintenance* (Washington, D.C.: Brookings Institution, 1967), p. 47; Harold L. Wilensky, *The 'New Corporatism,' Centralization, and the Welfare State* (Beverly Hills: Sage, 1976); and Harold L. Wilensky, "Leftism, Catholicism, and Democratic Corporatism: The Role of Political Parties in Recent Welfare State Development," in Peter Flora and Arnold J. Heidenheimer, eds., *The Development of Welfare States in Europe and America* (New Brunswick: Transaction, 1981), pp. 345–82.
39. Warren G. Nutter, *Growth of Government in the West* (Washington, D.C.: American Enterprise Institute, 1978), p. 6.
40. *Ibid.*, p. 12.

trial countries, the United States and Canada, which share with Switzerland a high per capita income and a conservative political coloration, Switzerland's public economy grew much faster between 1967 and 1976 and experienced, in fact, the highest *relative* growth rate among all OECD members states.[41]

In the early and mid-1970s, the proportion of Gross National Income (GNI) devoted to nonmilitary public-sector spending was substantially greater in the small European states (41 percent) than in the large industrial states (32 percent).[42] With the exception of Switzerland, the public social welfare efforts of the small European states have been active and progressive in countries as divergent as the Netherlands, Sweden, and Denmark. Due to increases in pensions, which account for about two-thirds of all income maintenance programs, expenditure elasticities for income maintenance programs have been close to the OECD's maximum of 2 in the Netherlands, Sweden, Denmark and Norway.[43] Changes in the demographic composition of the population and an extension of eligibility to a higher proportion of older people have pushed pension costs upward in all countries irrespective of their size; but only three small European states—Switzerland, the Netherlands, and Norway—made concerted political efforts between 1962 and 1972 to increase benefits substantially.

Large and rapidly growing public expenditures in the small European states were, of course, accompanied by increasing tax burdens, which are now greater in the small European states than in any other part of the Western world. In 1955–1957 the average tax burden in the five large industrial countries exceeded by a percentage point the 26

41. OECD, *Public Expenditure Trends*, p. 12. This is due partly to the sharp contraction of the Swiss Gross Domestic Product in the mid-1970s.

42. John D. Stephens, *The Transition from Capitalism to Socialism* (London: Macmillan, 1979), pp. 96, 118.

43. Organization for Economic Co-operation and Development, *Public Expenditure on Income Maintenance Programmes* (Paris: OECD, 1976), pp. 7, 20, 35.

percent in the small European states. But from the early 1960s on, taxation began to rise sharply in the small European states. By the mid-1960s, their levels of taxation exceeded those of the five large countries, and by the mid-1970s the relative share of total taxes in GDP was 41 percent in the small European states as compared to 32 percent in the large countries, with the greatest difference occurring in the incidence of direct taxation.[44]

Political developments in the 1970s illustrate that this heavy tax burden is the major reason that the growth in public-sector spending has met more active resistance in the small European states than in the large industrial countries. Denmark is the most frequently cited example of "welfare backlash."[45] Between 1953 and 1973 public consumption, rather than transfer payments as in the Netherlands, grew more sharply in Denmark than in any other small European state. Since most of the revenues were raised through direct taxes, Danish citizens could not escape noting that they had become the most heavily taxed in the OECD. In 1970 the share of the Danish work force in the public sector exceeded the work force in manufacturing industry (10 vs. 17 percent).[46] The late 1970s illustrate clearly the deleterious consequences of these changes for Denmark's international competitiveness. The backlash against the welfare state has shattered the foundations of Denmark's party system. But despite high inflation, an unemployment of about 10 percent, and pressing balance of payments deficits in the late 1970s, the rebellion of the Danish voters does not appear to signify the attempt of any sizable segment of either the general public or of the political elite to dismantle the Danish welfare state. Sounding the theme

44. OECD, *Public Expenditure Trends*, p. 42.

45. Douglas A. Hibbs and Henrik Jess Madsen, "Public Reactions to the Growth of Taxation and Government Expenditure," *World Politics* (April 1981), 33(3):413–35.

46. Organization for Economic Co-operation and Development, *The Industrial Policies of 14 Member Countries* (Paris: OECD, 1971), p. 120. Nutter, *Growth of Government*, pp. 12, 20.

common among several studies two knowledgeable observers concluded rather that "reform and improvement of administrative procedures, concerns about costs and benefit,
these rather than radical alternatives are the issues that appeal to even proponents of the 'anti-system' parties . . .
The Scandinavian welfare state is alive and well."[47]

In sharp contrast to the large industrial countries, where
the effect of partisanship on the size of the public sector is
more pronounced, the great expansion in the public economy of both the Netherlands (governed through much of
the postwar era by coalition governments led by conserva-
tives or liberals) and of Sweden (ruled by Social Democrats)
illustrates that in the small European states "all governments—whether formed by leftists or nonleftist parties—
have been impelled by the exigencies of the open economy
to expand the role of the state. . . . the openness of the
economy is the best single predictor of the growth of public
revenues relative to the economic product of a nation."[48]
Another observer concludes similarly that "the association
between high spending and Social Democratic dominance
in government—characteristic of the Scandinavian countries but not of the Netherlands—appears mainly to stem
from the fact that both are the products of the same set of
structural factors, rather than implying a strong and direct
causal relation."[49]

The paradoxical convergence of international liberalization and domestic stabilization sets the parameters for the
public policies which the small European states pursue over
a wide range of issues. These countries have tried to re-

47. Eric S. Einhorn and John A. Logue, "Welfare States in Hard Times: Denmark and Sweden in the 1970s" (1979), pp. 1, 4. Manuscript.

48. David R. Cameron, "The Expansion of the Public Economy: A Comparative
Analysis," *American Political Science Review* (December 1978), 72(4):1253–54.
See also Francis G. Castles, "How Does Politics Matter? Structure or Agency in the
Determination of Public Policy Outcomes," *European Journal of Political Research*
(June 1981), 9(2):119–32.

49. Rudolf Klein, "Public Expenditures in an Inflationary World" (1978), p. 46.
Manuscript.

strain their wages and, occasionally, prices, either through a government-coordinated incomes policy (as in the Netherlands and Denmark), or through a centralized system of collective bargaining (as in Sweden and Norway), or through some combination of the two (as in Austria). That wage restraint has been linked to generous public spending. In the area of economic growth wage restraint typically coincided with a sizable expansion of publicly funded, rapidly increasing, income-supplementing payments. In the era of stagflation, Sweden has tried to create the conditions for wage restraint through a coordinated use of tax cuts to increase disposable incomes, while in the Netherlands the government has occasionally facilitated collective bargaining by adjusting social welfare premiums downward to induce employers to settle for higher wages than they might otherwise have agreed to. Whether by increased spending, or through a reduction in taxes or social security contributions, the results have been that in most of the small European states the distributional struggle has shifted away "from the private marketplace, where allocation takes place through collective bargaining and industrial conflict, to the public arena, where labor and capital compete through political negotiation and electoral mobilization."[50]

CORPORATIST STRUCTURES

International liberalization and domestic compensation emanate from distinct domestic structures. The small European states differ from the large industrial countries in their centralized and integrated corporatist structures, which fuse state and society. Corporatism reduces unnecessary friction and stalemate and thus facilitates the formulation and implementation of policy. In the area of economic policy, corporatism can be viewed as a response to openness

50. Douglas A. Hibbs, Jr., "On the Political Economy of Long-Run Trends in Strike Activity," p. 154.

to and dependence on the world economy. The incorporation of all of the major producer groups and political actors
creates a relatively dull and predictable kind of politics, including the ritualistic expression of ideological conflict, that
tends to conceal its costs. These concealed costs do, at
times, reinforce political challenges to which corporatist
structures in the small European states have been subjected
in the 1960s and 1970s. This is illustrated by the growing
importance of the referendum in Swiss politics, the slow im-
plantation of a Social Democratic regime in Austria, the trend
towards class politics in the reordering of Dutch political life,
the reappearance of militant ethnic politics in Belgium, and
the instabilities in Scandinavian party systems. To date,
however, these manifold political challenges have failed to
break the corporatist structures as a critically important political feature of the small European states.

Analyses of how the small European states cope with
economic openness and dependence typically emphasize
that these countries are small and international markets are
large. And because of their size the small European countries are often viewed as harmonious manifestations of Ba-
con's New Atlantis—endowed with coherence, agility, and
intelligence.[51] Simon Kuznets, for example, speculates that
the social homogeneity and consensus on the one hand,
and the quickness and effectiveness of political adjustments
on the other, must be the main reasons that small states
have been able to overcome the disadvantages associated
with their economic openness and dependence.[52] In a similar vein, a Hungarian economist, Kádár, points to a number
of characteristic features in the domestic politics of the small
European states which encourage political interventions in
the domestic economy and counterbalance a relative weakness in international markets.[53] Even Vital's pessimistic ap-

51. Kristensen and Levinsen, Small Country Squeeze, p. 132.
52. Kuznets, "Economic Growth," pp. 28–30. Simon Kuznets, Six Lectures
on Economic Growth (New York: Free Press, 1961), p. 95.
53. Kádár, Small Countries in World Economy, pp. 9, 14.

praisal of the viability of small states concludes on what, in light of the available evidence, should be an opening note, at least in the case of the small European states: "The crucial factor in almost every case is the human one . . . where the society coheres and is strongly led, very great obstacles can often be overcome."[54] In different ways these assessments concur in the notion that the small European states compensate for their economic openness and dependence on world markets through a distinctive politics. But it is necessary to replace assumptions about mystical forms of social coherence and common purpose with an analysis of how power is organized by domestic structures of the small European states.

"Corporatism," "neocorporatism," "liberal corporatism," and "societal corporatism" are among the concepts which recent studies of advanced industrial states have coined for a phenomenon whose existence is agreed on by most observers: the voluntary, cooperative regulation of conflicts over economic and social issues through highly structured and interpenetrated sets of political relationships by business, the unions, and the state, augmented at times by political parties. Different theoretical orientations will lead different authors to emphasize one or the other of the three different levels comprised by social coalitions, policy networks, and policy processes. But all authors appear to concur in the central political significance of this aspect of the politics of advanced industrial states.[55]

"Strong" corporatist structures have a pervasive ideology of social partnership shared by the leaders of business

54. David Vital, *The Inequality of States: A Study of Small Powers in International Relations* (Oxford: Clarendon Press, 1967), pp. 190–91.

55. Philippe C. Schmitter and Gerhard Lehmbruch, eds., *Trends Towards Corporatist Intermediation* (Beverly Hills: Sage, 1979); Suzanne D. Berger, ed., *Organizing Interests in Western Europe* (Cambridge: Cambridge University Press, 1981); Heinrich August Winkler, *Organisierter Kapitalismus* (Göttingen: Vandenhoeck and Ruprecht, 1974); Wilensky, *The 'New Corporatism'*; and Wilensky, "Leftism, Catholicism, and Democratic Corporatism" in Flora and Heidenheimer, *The Development of Welfare States*, pp. 345–82.

and the unions, rely on the cooperative efforts of relatively centralized institutions representing business, unions, and the state in key economic and social policies, and lack in worker militancy. "Weak" corporatist structures lack an ideology of social partnership, rely on the conflictual efforts of relatively decentralized institutions representing business, unions, and the state in key economic and social policies and display considerable worker militancy.[56] Even though they do not meet equally all stipulated criteria according to this definition, the small European states meet a sufficient number of them to warrant their characterization as strong corporatist structures.

The effect of economic openness and dependence on the corporatist structures of the small European states was perhaps never clearer than in the 1930s and 1940s. In many ways the domestic structures and political strategies which then emerged provided the guide for a generation of leaders who, until the 1960s, were in charge of economic reconstruction and expansion. Economic openness and dependence established a compelling need for consensus which, through complex and delicate political arrangements, have transformed the conflict among the main social forces in the small European states. The truce between the business community and the labor movement expressed, for example, in Norway's "Basic Agreement" of 1935, Switzerland's "Peace Agreement" of 1937, Sweden's "Saltsjöbaden Agreement" of 1938, and Belgium's "Social Solidarity Pact" of

56. How to define corporatism is a theoretically contentious issue. The definition I have adopted here from Manfred Schmidt has the advantage of touching on each of the three levels — social coalitions, policy networks, and policy process — at which an analysis of small states should be conducted. It incorporates as well the element of ideology which, due to their economic openness and dependence, is important for all of the small European states. See Manfred G. Schmidt, "Wohlfahrtsstaatliche Politik unter bürgerlichen und sozialdemokratischen Regierungen," Constance: University of Constance (1980), pp. 176–77. Manuscript. See also Manfred G. Schmidt, "Economic Crisis, Politics and Rates of Unemployment in Capitalist Democracies in the Seventies," paper prepared for the ECPR workshop, Unemployment and Selective Labor Market Policies of Advanced Industrial Societies, at the University of Lancaster, England, March 29–April 4, 1981.

1945 has been translated into a durable peace.[57] And in Austria the memories of the civil war of 1934 have encouraged similar developments. The political manifestations of that peace can be found in corporatist political practices and institutions which are more prevalent in the small European states than in the large industrial countries. In the small European states, political metaphors often recall and reinforce the historical memories of the 1930s and 1940s in emphasizing that all members of society sit in the same small boat, that the waves are high, and that all must pull on the same oar. Domestic quarrels are a luxury not tolerated in such adverse circumstances.

Corporatist patterns of politics and policy emerged on economic and social issues in the 1930s and 1940s and were reinforced by the pressures which an increasingly liberal international economy exerted on the open economies in the 1960s and 1970s. In some of the small European states, like Belgium, the Netherlands, Switzerland, and Austria, these corporatist patterns agreed with the accommodative politics which had emerged in the nineteenth and twentieth centuries in societies politically divided into different ethnic, linguistic, and religious camps. In the case of Belgium, for example, that compulsion existed already in the first hours of the new state. Belgium's "unionisme" refers to a coalition among Liberals and Catholics established during that country's secession in 1830. In the Netherlands, the "politics of accommodation"[58] over the hotly contested issue of religion and education were accelerated by the outbreak of World War I. The incorporation of the Swiss Socialist party in the federal cabinet in 1943 resulted from a convergence between Left and Right forced during the 1930s

57. Arend Lijphart, "Consociational Democracy," *World Politics* (October 1968), 21(1):217.

58. Arend Lijphart, *The Politics of Accommodation: Pluralism and Democracy in the Netherlands* (Berkeley: University of California Press, 1968); and Gerhard Lehmbruch, "Konkordanzdemokratien im internationalen System: Ein Paradigma für die Analyse von internen und externen Bedingungen politischer Systeme," *Politische Vierteljahresschrift* (1969), Sonderheft 1, 10:149–54.

and 1940s by fascism and war and strengthened by the long-standing tradition of proportional linguistic and geographic representation of different sectors of society. Confronting an occupation by the four Allies, as well as overwhelming economic odds, Austria established an all-party government in 1945. "Consociationalism," "Proporz Democracy," and "Amicable Agreement" are some of the concepts with which students of these small European states have summarized their descriptions of distinctive political structures and political practices in these societies.[59] In these small European states, groups are held together by the pragmatic bargains struck by a handful of political leaders at the summit. Political compromises across the main social cleavages assures political quiescence and, equally important, reinforces political control within each camp. The greater the degree of segmentation dividing these societies, the more pronounced are, typically, elite coalescence and consociational arrangements which defuse conflict.[60] In the Scandinavian countries, economic openness and vulnerability has produced a similar result. There "the coalescent style of deci-

59. Kenneth McRae, ed., *Consociational Democracy: Political Accommodation in Segmented Societies* (Toronto: McClelland and Stewart, 1974); Martin O. Heisler, ed., *Politics in Europe: Structures and Processes in some Postindustrial Democracies* (New York: McKay, 1974); Arend Lijphart, *Democracy in Plural Societies: A Comparative Exploration* (New Haven: Yale University Press, 1977); and Wilensky, *The 'New Corporatism.'* See also Jeffrey Obler, Jürg Steiner, and Guido Diericx, *Decision-Making in Smaller Democracies: The Consociational "Burden"* (Beverly Hills: Sage, 1977); Robert Dahl, ed., *Political Oppositions in Western Democracies* (New Haven: Yale University Press, 1966); Gerhard Lehmbruch, *Proporzdemokratie: Politisches System und Politische Kultur in der Schweiz und Österreich* (Tübingen: Mohr, 1967); Eric A. Nordlinger, *Conflict Regulation in Divided Societies* (Cambridge, Mass.: Harvard University, Center for International Affairs, 1972); David R. Cameron, "Consociation, Cleavage and Realignment: Postindustrialization and Partisan Change in Eight European Nations," paper prepared for delivery at the 1974 Annual Meeting of the American Political Science Association, Chicago, August 29– September 2, 1974; Brian Berry, "Political Accommodation and Consociational Democracy," *British Journal of Political Science* (October 1975), 5(4):490– 500; and Hans Daalder, "The Consociational Democracy Theme," *World Politics* (July 1974), 26(4):604– 22.

60. Jürg Steiner, "Major und Proporz," *Politische Vierteljahresschrift* (March 1970), 11:142– 44.

sion making has become quite pervasive. . . . probably more so than elsewhere in the Western World," at least in the field of economic and social policy.[61] The key purpose of these corporatist institutions and political practices—promulgated by political parties and interest groups—is to enhance political predictability and to ensure political stability. The politics and policy typical of the small European states are based on the principle of co-optation and compromise rather than competition and conflict.[62]

The small European states have in common corporatist structures which, compared to the large advanced industrial states, are tightly knit in centralizing political power. These structures minimize the difference between the public and the private realm. The maintenance of these institutional characteristics is facilitated by the small size of the country. "Other things being equal . . . the larger the country, the greater the number of organizations and subunits it will contain."[63] Looking at it from the perspective of the management of the economy, Peter Wiles has characterized aptly the situation in which the small European states find themselves: "So it is never difficult to put through an agreed new policy. This is the phenomenon of 'willy-nilly Frenchy planning' in small countries: the *economie* is informally *concertée*, whatever may be the official arrangements or lack of them. This is as much as to say, there can be no laissez faire in a rich small country with a market economy since the number of large enterprises is too small, and the intermarriage of elite families is inevitable, where the elite contains both enterprise directors and senior civil servants. Give

61. Lijphart, *Democracy in Plural Societies,* p. 111.

62. Eisenstadt, "Sociological Characteristics and Problems of Small States," p. 44; and Gerhard Lehmbruch, "Consociational Democracy in the International System," *European Journal of Political Research* (December 1975), 3(4):378–79.

63. Dahl and Tufte, *Size and Democracy,* p. 40. See also Jane J. Mansbridge, *Beyond Adversary Democracy* (New York: Basic Books, 1980), pp. 278–89; and Margret Sieber, *Die Abhängigkeit der Schweiz von ihrer internationalen Umwelt: Konzepte und Indikatoren* (Frauenfeld: Huber, 1981), pp. 372–74.

a cocktail party, and you have to invite them all."[64] The functional substitute for the differentiation of organizations and the specialization of functions in larger states is the "structural polyvalence" of organizations in small states which perform manifold, specialized, differentiated functions.[65] "Organizations in small societies find it especially profitable to keep themselves very open and available for possible alliances with many other organizations."[66] Selectivity in problem definition, personalization of interorganizational relations, and versatility in response are some of the typical institutional reactions in the small European states. But this fluidity of relationships within the policy networks of small states coincides with strong oligarchic tendencies. Political power is concentrated in the hands of few decision-makers and rests with strong parties or strong interest groups.[67]

A number of recent studies confirm the existence of a striking correlation between the economic openness and dependence of the small European states on the one hand, and the incidence of corporatist structures on the other. A recent, important paper by Philippe Schmitter has a direct bearing on the argument presented here. Table 2.1 gives the rank ordering of the small European states and the large industrial countries along different dimensions of corporatism: societal corporatism (a measure of the organizational centralization and the associational monopoly of labor organizations); citizen acquiescence (a measure of citizen-ini-

64. Peter Wiles, "The Importance of Country Size" (n.d.), pp. 9– 10. Manuscript.

65. Hans Geser and Francois Höpflinger, "Problems of Structural Differentiation in Small Societies: A Sociological Contribution to the Theory of Small States and Federalism," *Bulletin of the Sociological Institute of the University of Zurich* (July 1975), 31:59.

66. *Ibid.*, pp. 64, 87.

67. Eisenstadt, "Sociological Characteristics," p. 40; and Gabriel Sheffer, "Public Mood, Policy Making Elites and Surprise Attacks on Some Small States," Cornell University, 1975, pp. 17– 28. Manuscript.

TABLE 2.1: Corporatism, Openness, and Dependence in Small and Large Industrial States

	Small States[a]	Large States[b]
A. *Corporatism*[c]		
1. Corporatism (average rank)	4.1	9.3
2. Citizen acquiescence (average rank)	4.1	9.3
3. Fiscal effectiveness (average rank)	4.3	9.0
B. *Openness*		
4. Exports of goods/GNP, 1955 (%)	24.4	11.3
Exports of goods/GNP, 1975 (%)	30.4	15.5
5. Exports of goods and services/GNP, 1955 (%)	31.0	13.8
Exports of goods and services/GNP, 1975 (%)	37.7	18.8
6. Foreign letters/Total letters, 1955 (%)	13.6	6.0
Foreign letters/Total letters, 1975 (%)	12.2	6.1
7. Foreign patents/Total patents, 1965 (%)	82.5	39.8
Foreign patents/Total patents, 1975 (%)	84.9	49.9
C. *Dependence*		
8. Balance of trade in goods as % of imports, 1955	−16.6	0.3
Balance of trade in goods as % of imports, 1975	−10.2	−0.1
9. Balance of trade in goods and services as % of imports, 1960	−0.7	8.7
Balance of trade in goods and services as % of imports, 1973	−2.2	3.6
10. Direct foreign investment/GNP, 1967 (%)	4.4	3.1
Direct foreign investment/GNP, 1973 (%)	4.9	3.0
11. Energy imports/Energy consumption, 1960 (%)	62.0	24.2
Energy imports/Energy consumption, 1975 (%)	50.3	53.7

SOURCE: *Rows 1–3:* Philippe C. Schmitter, "Interest Intermediation and Regime Governability in Contemporary Western Europe and North America," in Suzanne D. Berger, ed., *Organizing Interests in Western Europe: Pluralism, Corporatism, and the Transformation of Politics* (Cambridge: Cambridge University Press, 1981), pp. 294, 304–5, 310. *Rows 4–11:* Margret Sieber, *Dimensionen Kleinstaatlicher Auslandabhaengigkeit,* Kleine Studien zur Politischen Wissenschaft, No. 206–7 (Zurich: University of Zurich, Forschungsstelle für Politische Wissenschaft, 1981), pp. 156–59.

[a] Unweighted average for Austria, Switzerland, Sweden, Norway, Denmark, Netherlands, Belgium.

[b] Unweighted average for the United States, Britain, West Germany, France, and Japan.

[c] The terminology in Rows 1–3 is mine, not Schmitter's. The rank orderings in rows 2 and 3 are inverted from those Schmitter provides. For further descriptions of concepts and indicators see Schmitter's essay. Japan is not included in rows 1–3.

tiated protest or resistance, based on different statistical indicators of collective protest, internal war, and strike); and fiscal effectiveness (a measure based on different indicators of the government's fiscal strength). And table 2.1 also offers different measures of the economic openness and dependence of small and large states. Excepting Japan, for which Schmitter does not provide any data, table 2.1 points to a strong correlation between openness and dependence on the one hand, and corporatism on the other. On Schmitter's three dimensions of corporatism, for example, there exist only four exceptions to a rank ordering which separates the seven small European states consistently out from the four large industrial countries: West Germany ranks ahead of Switzerland on the dimension of societal corporatism, of Belgium on the dimension of citizen acquiescence, and, together with France, of Belgium on the dimension of fiscal effectiveness. Only four of the eighty-four possible pair-wise comparisons (of each of the seven small states with each of the four large ones along three dimensions of corporatism), or about 5 percent, do not support the argument of a strong correlation between economic openness and dependence on the one hand and corporatist structures on the other.

Corporatist structures are facilitated by and encourage a degree of organizational centralization and institutional penetration of society which is much greater in the small European states than in the large industrial countries. David Cameron has tested statistically the argument that economic openness encourages distinctive domestic structures. He argues that in the small European states economic openness is associated with a high degree of industrial concentration, a small number of peak associations of business, and few but effective union federations.[68] Comparative data on union membership illustrate the point. Among the large industrial states only Britain approaches

68. Cameron, "Expansion of the Public Economy." Schmidt offers a critique and an extension in his manuscript "Wohlfahrtsstaatliche Politik," pp. 25–28.

the unionization rates common in the small European states.[69] Unfortunately no systematic statistical measures of the "organization of capitalists" are currently available. But what evidence we have suggests that the structural preconditions for the institutional penetration of the business community are much more favorable in the small European states than in the large ones. The small size of domestic markets correlates highly with different measures of industrial concentration. Based on data originally collected by Pryor, Stephens classifies all of the seven small European states as having a high degree of economic monopolization, and all of the large industrial states as having a low degree of monopolization.[70] It would of course be risky to infer from a centralized economic structure to a centralized institutional structure of the business community. But a brief descriptive survey of different business associations in a number of these countries lends some support to the notion that in this instance economic structure shapes institutional forms.[71] Finally, in the absence of reliable cross-national data, the entire literature on corporatist politics has, to date, been based on the assumption, plausible only as a first approximation, of a symmetry in the degree of centralization of the unions on the one hand, and of business on the other. In measuring directly the former, it is argued that we are also measuring indirectly the latter. Summarizing his comparative analysis of industrial states, Stephens concludes that the countries "fall neatly into two categories, the

69. John P. Windmuller, "Concentration Trends in Union Structure: An International Comparison," *Industrial and Labor Relations Review,* 35(1):43–57; and Stephens, *Transition from Capitalism to Socialism,* p. 118. Due to the exodus of foreign workers, the unionization rate of the Swiss work force has increased sharply in the 1970s and is now about 38 percent rather than the 27 percent reported by Stephens who relied on estimates from the early 1970s.

70. Stephens, *Transition from Capitalism to Socialism,* pp. 91–93, 110, 118–19. Japan is not included in this study.

71. Werner Melis, "Aufgaben und Bedeutung der Handelskammern im Ausland," Johannes Koren and Manfred Ebner, eds., *Österreich auf einem Weg: Handelskammern und Sozialpartnerschaft im Wandel der Zeiten* (Graz: Stocker, 1974), pp. 11–26.

small democracies and the larger democracies with a large gap between them."[72]

Other comparative studies indirectly support the argument that economic openness is the main determinant of corporatist structures by showing that variables other than economic openness are less successful in distinguishing between the strong corporatist structures in the small European states on the one hand, and the weak corporatist structures in the large industrial countries on the other. For example, these two groups of states, Schmitter concludes, do not differ systematically in their political instability (measured by changes in governments and major ministries, the decrease in the electoral margin of the governing party and the fractionalization of the party system). By these measures Denmark, Norway, and Britain are very unstable and Austria, Switzerland, and the United States are very stable.[73] Corporatism is thus not strongly associated with political stability. Similarly, strong corporatist arrangements, Wilensky concludes, occur in the presence of both strong socialist parties and strong Catholic parties or of the coincidence of both.[74] Corporatism is thus not strongly associated with the domination of a particular party and ideology. The data on working-class mobilization (as measured by the percentage of workers unionized and of the electoral strength of leftist parties) which Esping-Andersen and Korpi have collected show that the working-class mobilization in Britain's weak corporatism is too high and the Netherlands' and Switzerland's strong corporatism too low.[75] Corporatism is thus not strongly associated with the mobilization of the working class. In line with the argument developed here, Cameron

72. Stephens, *Transition from Capitalism to Socialism*, p. 117.

73. Schmitter, "Interest Intermediation," pp. 304–5, table 10.2, p. 307, figure 10.2.

74. Wilensky, "Leftism, Catholicism, and Democratic Corporatism," p. 359 and passim.

75. Gösta Esping-Andersen and Walter Korpi, "From Poor Relief to Institutional Welfare States: The Development of Scandinavian Social Policy." Stockholm, Swedish Institute for Social Research, September 1981, table 1. Manuscript.

concludes that the openness of the economy has a stronger effect on the growth of the public economy than does the partisanship of the government. For that growth, "leftist domination was not a necessary condition, since several nations experienced large increases in spite of the absence of a strong leftist representation in government. Included in this latter group are the Netherlands and Belgium . . . which share at least one common trait: their economies are relatively open."[76]

Lower levels of labor organization, shorter periods of socialist rule, and the breakdown of Dutch incomes policy since the late 1960s make the Netherlands an anomaly for those comparative studies of corporatist politics which focus on the strength of the Left as the prime determinant. Stephens, for example, calls the Netherlands a "deviant case" of corporatist politics. "It may be that the Dutch system of bargaining centralization owes more to the combination of very heavy export dependency and the 'politics of accommodation' than to the political and economic strength of the labor movement."[77] Lacking an incomes policy, a centralized system of collective bargaining, and a strong Left, Switzerland further accentuates those features toward which Dutch politics in the 1970s has moved. But Switzerland has a centralized business community, accords business a critically important role in foreign economic policy, and exhibits an ideology of social partnership shared by both business and labor leaders on key questions of economic and social policy. These are some of the features which lead Kriesi to conclude in the most comprehensive study published on the subject to date, that Switzerland has a quasi-corporatist pattern of politics and policy, which differs from the neocorporatism of Austria and the Scandinavian countries, but retains essential aspects of the collaborative arrangements and institutional centralization and interpene-

76. Cameron, "Expansion of the Public Economy," p. 1253.
77. Stephens, *Transition from Capitalism to Socialism,* p. 124.

tration which define the concept of corporatism.[78] Confronted with the cleavage between externally oriented and domestically oriented economic sectors, Switzerland and the other small European states have developed corporatist structures which enhance political predictability through facilitating cooperation and compromise. External pressures force domestic accommodation even in societies like Switzerland, which feature less-centralized political institutions and practices: "people forfeit opposition policies because they know, in the end, that their security and their wealth depend on the confidence they inspire elsewhere."[79]

CONCLUSION

This paper has argued that in the postwar era, the small European states have maintained successful political strategies and coherent domestic structures. They have accomplished this feat by adjusting to the constraints and opportunities of their economic openness and vulnerability. Strategies of international liberalization and domestic compensation have, to date, succeeded in matching the necessities of economic openness with the requirements of domestic politics. And corporatist domestic structures distinguish the small European states from the liberal and statist variants of capitalism in the large industrial states.

In seeking to understand how dependence, successful strategies, and coherent domestic structures are brought into a viable balance by the small European states, this paper disagrees with the view held by Barrington Moore and many others, which emphasizes the simplicity of their polit-

78. Hauspeter Kriesi, *Entscheidungsstrukturen und Entscheidungsprozesse in der Schweizer Politik* (Frankfurt: Campus, 1980), pp. 377–78, 689–90.

79. Jane Kramer, "A Reporter in Zurich," *The New Yorker,* December 15, 1980, p. 134.

ical circumstances and the uniqueness of their political experience. "The fact that the smaller western countries depend economically and politically on big and powerful ones
means that the decisive causes of their politics lie outside
their own boundaries. It also means that their political problems are not really comparable to those of larger countries."[80] Although they hold a specific position in the international division of labor, the experience of the small
European states, far from being unique, illuminates those
of other states. Like Switzerland and the Netherlands, the
United States, West Germany, and Japan hold a favorable
position in the international economy due to their particular
configurations of power. And the experience of some countries in Southern Europe and Eastern Europe, as well as of
some of the advanced less-developed countries, bears some
resemblance to the experience of Austria, Denmark, and
Norway, which stems from their position of relative inferiority in the international division of labor.

Similarly, the domestic structures of the small European states, far from being unique, can aid in the analysis
of the domestic structures of other states. The corporatism
of the small European states, for example, could be viewed
as a halfway house between the statist domestic structures
of Japan and France, and the liberal domestic structures of
the United States and Britain. Alternatively, corporatism may
be viewed as a particular institutional mechanism concentrating power in the attempt to manage dependence. In
other settings, such a concentration of power has occurred
in Leninist parties or in state bureaucracies backed by particular social sectors.[81]

80. Barrington Moore, Jr., *Social Origins of Dictatorships and Democracy: Lord and Peasant in the Making of the Modern World* (Boston: Beacon, 1967), p. xiii. Philosophically different in tone but similar in conclusion is E. F. Schumacher's *Small Is Beautiful: Economics As If People Mattered* (New York: Harper & Row, 1973).

81. Kenneth Jowitt, *The Leninist Response to National Dependency* (University of California, Berkeley: Institute of International Studies, 1978), pp. 74–79; and David Laitin, "A Classification of Strategies Designed to Overcome Depen-

If the small European states are not unique, they are, however, different. In comparison with the developing countries, the insertion of the small European states in the world economy occurred at an earlier date. The geographic and commodity concentration of foreign trade, the imbalance between the import of manufactured products and the export of raw materials, as well as between the export of "traditional" vs. "modern" manufactured products, are all greater in the small European states than in the large industrialized states, but they are smaller than in the developing countries. The small European states have in their service sectors a valuable set of economic activities which narrow significantly the perpetual trade deficit imposed by the structure of their economies. And, although the small European states depend heavily on foreign investments both for a continuous modernization of their economies and for further reducing the deficit in their trade balance, this dependence is not reflected in "dependency."[82] In the developing countries, in place of the corporatism characteristic of the small European states, there frequently emerges an alliance between the state bureaucracy, the military, and segments of the business community—authoritarian structures which exclude labor and which in times of crisis may adopt repressive measures directed against labor. None of this has occurred in the small European states since 1945.

In view of these differences, the experience of the small European states cannot simply be translated into action programs for Third World countries. The small European states have generated a particular set of political structures and strategies that are appropriate to their location in the international division of labor and feasible given their domestic situations. However, the analysis of their structures

dency and Economic Backwardness," paper presented at the Mexico City meeting of the study group that led to the present volume.

82. This distinction, by now standard in the literature, is elaborated by James A. Caporaso, "Introduction: Dependence and Dependency in the Global System," *International Organization* (Winter 1978), vol. 32.

and strategies in comparison with those of the larger industrialized states on the one hand, and the newly industrializing countries of the Third World on the other, should shed light on the more general political correlates of successful economic strategies. The international economy both offers opportunities and produces dislocating consequences for national economies. The historical and comparative study of ways to exploit the one while coping with the other is helpful in distinguishing between genuine insights and mere faddishness in the perennial debate on development strategies.

3.

The South Korean State in the International Economy: Liberal, Dependent, or Mercantile?

STEPHAN HAGGARD and CHUNG-IN MOON

TO MANY ECONOMISTS, South Korea represents the paradigmatic case of a developing country realizing high levels of growth through specialization and close integration into the international division of labor. Unlike the majority of LDCs which have continued to pursue inward-looking, import-substituting growth strategies, South Korea "took off" following a liberalization of tariffs and the exchange rate re-

This paper is a revision of one given at the International Studies Association Conference in Cincinnati, March 1982. We have benefited from the comments of Vinnie Aggarwal, Tun-jen Cheng, Jeff Frieden, Jeff Hart, Peter Katzenstein, Robert Keohane, Stephen Krasner, Charles Lipson, John Odell, Joe Oppenheimer, John Ruggie and John Zysman, and from the assistance of Tim Shorrock of the Nautilus Pacific Action Research Center in securing materials. Research was facilitated by a grant from the Institute for the Study of World Politics.

gime and increased incentives toward foreign direct investment and borrowing. Realizing an initial comparative advantage in low-wage labor, the South Korean economy has
continued to undergo structural transformation which would
seem to vindicate theories of the product cycle and international comparative advantage. With growth initially led by
exports of light manufactures such as textiles, the diffusion
of technology through multinationals and learning by Korean firms has resulted in a gradual upgrading of South Korea's exports. The dimensions of the "miracle" have been
widely documented: average annual growth of GNP over the
seventies of 9.7 percent, manufacturing growth averaging
18 percent and annual export growth over 20 percent.[1]

As a result of these successes, Korea has been catego-
rized as one of the newly industrializing countries, or NICs.
The boundaries of this category are as much political as an-
alytic. The NICs have emerged as an object of attention primarily due to their domination of the rapidly growing LDC
trade in manufactures. By 1975, seven countries—Hong
Kong, Taiwan, Singapore, and South Korea, the Asian "Gang
of Four," and Brazil, Mexico, and Argentina—accounted for
over 60 percent of all LDC exports of manufactures.[2] While
the share of total OECD imports coming from the NICs
reamins low, about 9 percent in 1979, the NICs have placed
pressure on a number of sectors in the advanced industrial
states, including not only textiles, but steel and shipbuilding as well.[3]

Several other characteristics of the NICs international

1. Korea Exchange Bank, *Monthly Review,* January 1980. For an economist's
reivew of the process of structural change, see Paul Kuznets, *Economic Growth
and Structural Change in the Republic of Korea* (New Haven: Yale University Press,
1977).

2. Donald Keesing, "World Output and Trade in Manufactures: Structural Trends
and Developing Country Exports," World Bank Staff Working Paper, no. 316 (January 1979).

3. The figure of 8.9 percent is based on an expanded set of NICs which includes the above list minus Argentina and plus Yugoslavia, Greece, Portugal, and
Spain. From OECD, "The Impact of the NICs: Updating of Selected Tables from the
1979 Report" (Paris: OECD, 1981). The major studies of the NICs include OECD,
The Impact of the Newly Industrializing Countries on Production and Trade in

position distinguish them from the rest of the developing world. The NICs are large borrowers, major recipients of foreign direct investment and, as is sometimes forgotten, large importers of capital and intermediate goods, raw materials, and energy. Despite their impressive export performances, the NICs run a large collective deficit on current account.

What separates the NICs most starkly from other developing countries however is their relatively high level of industrialization and continued industrial growth. A recent UNIDO study notes that ten countries, excluding Taiwan, accounted for 73 percent of all manufacturing growth in the developing world between 1963 and 1975.[4] Thus the emergence of the NICs is not only symptomatic of a changing division of labor between North and South, but of a profound differentiation within the developing world as well.

A closer examination of the NICs reveals important differences among them in development sequencing and strategy, which bring into question the concept of a relatively homogenous semi-periphery advocated by proponents of a world-systems perspective.[5] These differences may be outlined by contrasting two ideal-typical patterns of NIC industrialization. On the one hand are the small, relatively open Asian countries, such as Taiwan and South Korea.[6] On the other are the large Latin American NICs, particularly Brazil and Mexico.

Both the Latin American and Asian NICs began their

Manufactures (Paris: OECD, 1979); Louis Turner et al., *Living with the Newly Industrializing Countries* (London: Royal Institute of International Affairs); and Bela Balassa, *The Newly Industrializing Countries in the World Economy* (Oxford: Pergamon Press, 1981).

4. UNIDO, *World Industry since 1960: Progress and Prospects* (New York: United Nations, 1979), p. 42.

5. On the world-systems perspective, see Richard Rubinson, ed., *Dynamics of World Development* (Beverly Hills: Sage, 1981) and Albert Bergesen, ed., *Studies of the Modern World System* (New York: Academic Press, 1980). On the concept of the semi-periphery, see Immanuel Wallerstein "Semi-Peripheral Countries in the Contemporary World Crisis," *Theory and Society* (1973), no. 3.

6. As city-states and entrepots lacking any significant agricultural sector, Hong Kong and Singapore represent a different type of development.

contact with the modern international economy as primary product exporters, a "strategy," if we may call it that, dictated by external political dominance. The primary sector produced both the domestic food supply and an exportable surplus, which permitted the import of consumer goods. The commodity content of exports and rural social structures differed in important ways. In Latin America, latifundia and plantation organization of agricultural production coexisted with mineral extraction demanding large-scale infrastructural investments. In East Asia, sugar and rice exports were organized around different tenancy patterns. In Mexico and Brazil, the early phases of industrialization date to the late nineteenth century. In Korea and Taiwan, significant industrialization had occurred under Japanese auspices, though its form was limited by imperial objectives. The "newly" industrializing countries thus entered the postwar period already possessing the beginnings of modern industrial sectors.

In both the Asian and Latin American NICs, as in most developing countries, industrialization began by primary import-substituting industrialization (ISI). In Latin America, this initial ISI phase was given a push by the depression, while in East Asia, reconstruction efforts and the severance of previous export markets to Japan and China in the late 1940s dictated market closure. In all cases, persistent balance-of-payments problems forced the limiting of imports and encouragement of domestic production.

The ISI policy package included a mix of exchange controls, import licensing, protective tariffs, and multiple exchange rates, generally combined with deficit financing, inflation, and an overvalued currency. This should not be taken to mean that ISI was "autarchic" in other than a formal economic sense. In Latin America, primary product exports financed the import of producer goods and intermediates which formed the basis of light industries serving the local market. In Taiwan and South Korea, American aid played a critical role in financing imports, cementing a strong reliance on the United States.

Important differences are visible among the countries in this first stage. The first concerns the nature of the agricultural sector. In South Korea, the United States occupation forces supported the redistribution of Japanese land holdings in a effort to create a centrist peasantry as an option to what were seen as left and right extremes. These reforms were continued under the first postindependence government. While agriculture was subsequently ignored by the regime, the reforms had several important social and political consequences. First, they eliminated the possibility that the countryside would become the base for a leftist challenge to the regime, a possibility which had already been greatly reduced by the American-backed suppression of peasant revolts in 1947.[7] Second, the reforms also greatly reduced the political strength of the potentially anti-urban, anti-industrial landlord class. A similar outcome is seen in Taiwan and in Mexico. Intersectoral conflict between landed and industrial elites was low in Taiwan because of a Kuomintang land reform and in Mexico as a result of reforms undertaken during the thirties under Cardenas. Argentina and Brazil offer interesting contrasts. Import substitution in these countries was carried out under a populist coalition of national business, labor, and the state, which had as a major raison d'etre opposition to landed agro-export elites. Korea had no such populist coalition.

Finally, the land reforms served to equalize assets and undoubtedly contributed to the relative income equality in South Korea. In Taiwan, where the land reforms were actively supported by complementary investments, rural productivity and incomes were even higher and the agricultural sector served as an important source of funds for industrialization. In Mexico, land reforms have not been continuously supported, resulting in reconcentration of landholdings and worsening inequality. The process has only been accelerated by the continued reliance on agricultural exports as a source of foreign exchange earnings. Brazil, where there

7. On the American occupation, see the excellent study by Bruce Cumings, *The Origins of the Korean War* (Princeton: Princeton University Press, 1981).

have been no land reforms and where agricultural exports are also important, also has a highly skewed pattern of income distribution.

The other crucial difference between the Latin American and Asian NICs was in the rate of domestic protection. Latin American tariffs were extremely high, even redundant. As Gustav Ranis summarizes, ISI demands a delicate balance:

As traditional, land-based entrepreneurs are converted into industrial entrepreneurs, the level of protection and of profit transfer needs to be high enough for infant industry reasons, but not so high or persistent as to discourage entrepreneurial maturation.[8]

In Latin America, the high tariff strategy produced an industrial sector with strong economic and political interests in maintaining protection.

There is some debate over the inevitability and character of the "exhaustion" of ISI.[9] At some point, certain industries do reach market saturation and continued growth comes not from "horizontal" market expansion, but from the forging of backward linkages and vertical integration. The response to this particular crisis of ISI distinguishes the Latin American and Asian NICs.

In East Asia, policy moved toward primary-export substitution, ie., the export of those goods which had previously been substituted. This shift was accomplished primarily through a reform of the structure of incentives, including a lowering of protection and liberalization of the exchange rate regime. These policy reforms encouraged integration into the international economy on the basis of the export of labor-intensive manufactures. Selective import substitution

8. Gustav Ranis, "Challenges and Opportunities Posed by Asia's Superexporters: Implications for Manufactured Exports for Latin America," in Malcolm Gillis and Werner Baer, eds., *Export Diversification and the New Protectionism* (Champaign: University of Illinois, 1981), p. 208; and Barend A. de Vries, "Export Promotion Policies," World Bank Staff Working Paper, no. 313 (January 1979).

9. Albert Hirschman, "The Political Economy of Import-Substituting Industrialization in Latin America," in *A Bias for Hope* (New Haven: Yale University Press, 1971).

continued, but growth has been led by the export sector.

In the Latin American cases, by contrast, the primary phase of ISI was followed directly by a secondary phase, in part because of the potential offered by large domestic markets. To accomplish this, the protective instruments of the first phase have been continually expanded and rationalized.

At different times and to importantly different degrees, both Mexico and Brazil moved to augment import substitution with selective export-promotion policies. Unlike Korea, however, these reforms did not constitute a wholesale reform of the incentive system in the direction of the acceptance of comparative advantage.[10] As large countries, the contribution of the external sector to GNP has remained small. Subsidies play a critical role in forcing exports out of protected sectors, even in Brazil where the outward turn, particularly after 1968, is dramatic. Growth continues to be led by successive rounds of import substitution in which the state's role both in inducing backward linkages and in direct production has increased rapidly.

The purpose of this paper is to explore the political economy of export-led industrialization in South Korea as a way of clarifying a number of interrelated debates on strategies of association and dissociation in the international political economy. These include the domestic political prerequisites of export-led growth and the range of international maneuverability open to small trading states. Finally, we seek to address some of the theoretical problems raised by both liberal and dependency analyses of peripheral industrialization. The following arguments will be made.

The turning point in South Korean growth came with a series of liberalizing policy reforms taken between 1963 and 1965. An analysis of these reforms suggests that liberalization has important domestic political prerequisites ignored

10. The exception is the Mexican border industrialization program, which resembles the export processing zones of the Far East and accounts for a significant portion of Mexican exports.

by liberal economists. First, the state must be strong enough to impose stabilization and resist pressures from domestic business and other groups favored by closure. This proves not to be a once-and-for-all task. Despite the purported benefits of export-led growth, the South Korean government has been faced with continuing political opposition to its economic policies. Second, the state must possess adequate resources and the ability to channel them selectively to ease the reorientation of the economy in an outward direction. "Liberalization" does not correspond with domestic laissez-faire. Indeed, state control of business through credit allocation policies is one hallmark of the Korean model. Finally, the shift would never have occurred without the ascendence of a new reformist leadership which saw economic reform in its long-term *political* interest. In South Korea, this leadership was provided by the military following the coup of 1961.

South Korea has faced a series of external constraints including protectionism, competitive pressures, and the transmission of various international economic disturbances, which also tend to be ignored by advocates of export-led growth. These international pressures have generated countervailing strategies which demonstrate the precarious range of maneuver open to small trading-states.

South Korea's strategy toward existing regimes such as the GATT, and to international reform efforts such as the NIEO, differ somewhat from those of the large, more inward-oriented NICs. With their large external sectors, the small trading NICs are particularly vulnerable to political pressure to participate in the trade regime as equal partners. As major beneficiaries of the liberal trading order, their long-term interest is in sustaining the openness of the trading system and in strengthening those regime mechanisms which will protect them from the arbitrary actions of their larger trading partners. This remains a long-term goal, however. Pursuing effective bilateral bargaining strategies has gained in importance as increasing amounts of NIC trade are managed under "exceptionalist" trade arrangements.

Geographic diversification of external economic ties, a classic risk-reduction strategy, has become a key component of South Korea's foreign economic policy. Diversification has not only occurred as a firm level response to market opportunities, but has been facilitated, prompted, and controlled by the state. The interest of the NICs in market diversification suggests that they are likely to be in the forefront of the construction of new South-South ties.

Export product diversification has been one of the major challenges to the export-oriented NICs over the course of the seventies. As labor costs have risen, comparative advantage in light manufactures has eroded. South Korea's aggressive effort to break its previous pattern of international specialization proved politically and economically disastrous at least in the short run. The crisis provoked a rethinking of strategy and has raised important questions on the limits of industrial deepening in small, open economies.

A final, more theoretical, theme of this paper stems from the observation that export-led growth has been accompanied by a somewhat different pattern of social and political control and external dependency than the pattern in the large Latin American NICs. This suggests that modifications are required if models of bureaucratic authoritarianism and dependency developed in the Latin American context are to be extended to East Asia.[11] These models stress the determinacy of underlying economic forces, both domestic and in-

11. On bureaucratic authoritarianism, see the work of Guillermo O'Donnell, particularly *Modernization and Bureaucratic Authoritarianism* (Berkeley: Institute of International Studies, 1973); and the slightly different argument in "Reflections on the Patterns of Change in the Bureaucratic Authoritarian State," *Latin American Research Review* (Winter 1978), vol. 12 no. 1. A debate on O'Donnell's work has appeared, edited by David Collier, *The New Authoritarianism in Latin America* (Princeton: Princeton University Press, 1979). The concept of dependent development, the most sophisticated form of the dependency argument, was developed by Fernando Cardoso, "Associated Dependent Development: Theoretical and Practical Implications," In Alfred Stepan, ed., *Authoritarian Brazil* (New Haven: Yale University Press, 1973) and has been developed in Peter Evans, *Dependent Development: The Alliance of Multinational, State and Local Capital in Brazil* (Princeton: Princeton University Press, 1979).

ternational, on state policy. We argue, however, that Korean development is best understood in terms of a statist model, in which the state is conceived as having relative autonomy in its ability to define developmental goals and the power to build the social coalitions to support them. Such an approach appears suited to South Korean development which has been led by a state that is relatively strong vis-à-vis social actors. If we look at some of the other NICs however—particularly Brazil, Mexico, Taiwan, and Singapore—they seem to differ from other developing countries precisely in the existence of relatively strong states. Indeed, much of their economic success appears attributable to such state strength.

As a trading nation, South Korea's economic "dependency" is as much a function of external market relations, international macroeconomic conditions, and changes in international comparative advantage as it is of the penetration of foreign firms. Foreign investment has played a different role in industrialization and trade in Korea than in the Latin American NICs. This is in part due to the trade-oriented strategy itself, in part because the South Korean leadership has self-consciously fostered an internationally oriented and competitive domestic bourgeoisie. In general, it appears that dependency theorists have overestimated the effects of multinational corporations on national development, while paying inadequate attention to the constraints transmitted through external market relations. Dependency is often treated as a rigid, determinate international structure, rather than as a set of shifting constraints within which states seek to maneuver. A country's position in the international division of labor is not pre-given, but is in part determined by state industrialization and development strategies. While significantly constrained by both external market and corporate pressures, the South Korean state has sought to use both for the purpose of expanding its power and flexibility both domestically and internationally. In this sense, South Korea's foreign economic policy and industrial strategy are best understood as mercantile rather than either liberal or dependent.

THE POLITICAL PREREQUISITES OF EXPORT-LED GROWTH

The consensus on the value of manufactured exports to LDC industrialization is surprisingly wide. From the Brandt Commission to the IMF, from UNCTAD to the World Bank, a group of otherwise querulous economists seem to agree that export promotion pays off in efficiency, employment, and growth. The domestic political bases of the policy shift toward export-led growth remain largely unexamined, however. The South Korean case suggests several likely prerequisites for such policy reform that are not likely to be found widely in the developing world.

Strong State

The first prerequisite for liberalization is a strong state.[12] The relative strength of the state can be measured along two dimensions, what may be called "autonomy" and "capacity." First, the state may be considered strong to the extent that decision-making elites are capable of organizationally insulating themselves from societal pressures by controlling channels of interest representation and autonomously defining "national" tasks. Second, state strength can be measured by the capacity to extract resources and to implement policies which change the behavior of private actors and that ultimately may lead to changes in the social structure itself.[13]

12. This follows Stephen Krasner, *Defending the National Interest* (Princeton University Press, 1978), particularly ch. 3. See also Theda Skocpol, *States and Social Revolutions* (Cambridge: Cambridge University Press, 1979).
13. The distinction between strong and weak states should not be confused with differences in regime type. Democratic states exhibit varying degrees of au-

Korea achieved independence with a strong-state apparatus already in place. The Japanese had developed the colonial bureaucracy to realize their interests in the country. Rather than reforming it, the American occupation forces strengthened the state still further as a bulwark against the Left. Syngman Rhee's autocratic course continued the centralizing tradition, though his lack of interest in economic development resulted in an incoherent strategy.

One result of the military coup of 1961 was the further centralization of political power. All existing political organizations were disbanded, as was the National Assembly. The labor union structure, already weakened by its close ties to Rhee's Liberal party, was reorganized, with the government having a hand in selecting the new leadership. The National Agricultural Cooperatives Federation was tightly integrated into the central bureaucracy. New business organizations such as traders' and manufacturers' associations were formed under government auspices. Perhaps the most powerful instrument of social and political control was the Korean Central Intelligence Agency, created in 1961. Responsible only to the executive, the KCIA's significance in all matters—ranging from intelligence gathering and secret police functions to the implementation of economic policy and interbureaucratic coordination—cannot be overestimated.

At the same time the military restructured and strengthened the economic policymaking machinery into an Economic Planning Board having wide responsibilities including control of the budget. Even more important was the organization of the Presidential Secretariat within the presidential mansion or Blue House. This extremely insulated policymaking unit concentrated decision-making authority closely around Park Chung-hee. These organizational reforms were to survive the transition to civilian rule in 1964.

---

tonomy (the United States vs. Japan, for example), while authoritarian regimes may be penetrated by dominant social classes, or weak in their ability to implement policy.

The National Assembly's power vis-à-vis the executive was to remain small, while interest groups were to have few channels of access not controlled directly by the government. Even Park's own party was only a weak source of policy initiative. This political insulation and institutional centralization was to prove important in initiating and sustaining the outward-looking course.

First, export promotion demanded financial stabilization. After an initially inflationary course, the military imposed stabilizing measures which compressed real wages, restricted credit to domestic firms, and raised the prices of inputs to domestic farmers. One needs only to look to the two previous South Korean governments for contrasts: stabilization efforts, undertaken at the insistence of the Americans, contributed to the downfall of both the Rhee and Chang Myon governments.

Equally important was the need to resist pressure from domestic entrepreneurs privileged under the old, import-substituting regime. As a U.S. Congressional investigative team noted in 1960:

Any manufacturer can make a profit if the exchange rate for the materials and the machinery he imports is favorable. If he can buy raw materials at 650 hwan per $1 and sell his finished product at hwan prices reflecting 1200 hwan per $1 rate, he is completely insulated against the forces of world competition.[14]

Under Rhee, close links had developed between the U.S. aid program, the governing Liberal party, and the state and domestic entrepreneurs.[15] The bureaucracy, which controlled import licenses and foreign exchange allocation could funnel money and goods to supporters of the regime in re-

14. Report of the Staff Survey Team on Economic Assistance to Korea . . . , U.S. Foreign Affairs Committee, House of Representatives (Washington, D.C.: GPO, 1960) p. 11.
15. See K. Kim, "Political Factors in the Formation of the Entrepreneurial Elite in South Korea," *Asian Survey*, vol. 16, no. 5, and Leroy Jones and Il Sakong, *Government, Business and Entrepreneurship in Economic Development: The Korean Case* (Cambridge: Harvard University Press, 1980).

turn for kickbacks or simply to retain a base of political support. Domestic business could either process these goods, realizing high rates of return due to the level of protection, or simply profit through pure arbitrage. This system was attacked by the military's campaign against "illicitly accumulated wealth." Many of these entrepreneurs were not heavily penalized and were finally co-opted into the planning efforts of the new regime. Corrupt relations between government and business continued to be a political issue over the 1960s and 1970s. Nonetheless, the entrepreneurial context was dictated by a new policy orientation which severely restricted the potential for zero-sum arbitrage.

The strong state has continued to be of importance in maintaining an outward orientation even after the initial policy reforms. Over the course of the 1960s, Park pursued a high-growth, inflationary course, heavily biased in favor of industrialization. This strategy had disruptive consequences for a number of social groups, providing the political base for the opposition. Agriculture was ignored, leading to a relative decline in rural incomes. Despite growing urban employment, rapid internal migrations produced a large class of urban marginals and squatters. Labor continued to be tightly controlled. At the same time, a visibly wealthy business class with close relations with the state had emerged, providing a target for critics of the regime. The tight centralization of political power around Park and the atrophy of democratic institutions served as the rallying point for the opposition. While its economic program remained inchoate, the imbalanced export-led growth strategy was held accountable for many of the country's problems. Ineffective in the 1967 election, which came at the height of the economic successes of the sixties, the opposition New Democratic party (NDP) launched a vigorous campaign in 1971, losing the presidential election narrowly amid charges of election fraud.

Park's declaration of emergency in December 1971 and the institution of the authoritarian Yushin Constitution in the following year further consolidated executive authority. In the name of national security—the state interest par excellence—Park placed new controls on labor, student, and dissident activity. The "New Village Movement," launched in 1970, sought to tie the countryside closer to the regime, while reversing the perception of rural neglect. The state's role in settling labor disputes was enhanced. Direct repression became an increasingly important tool of government control.

This consolidation of state power in the name of national security had the consequence of destroying the political bases for the articulation of alternative development strategies. It is far from clear that the opposition could have abandoned export-led growth. Nonetheless, there has been a continuity in opposition programs since the sixties, emphasizing balanced growth, redistributive and welfare policies, expansion of the domestic market, and a reduction of the degree of reliance on exports and foreign capital. Since the late seventies, some opposition analysis has become increasingly leftist, emphasizing the connections between export-led capitalist industrialization, external dependency, exploitation of workers and peasants and authoritarianism.[16]

The position of the state vis-à-vis labor deserves further comment. In Brazil and Argentina, the installation of bureaucratic authoritarian regimes was partially a response to the radical mobilization of labor. The protectionist strategy

16. On the character of the opposition, see Sunjoo Han, *The Failure of Democracy in South Korea* (Berkeley: University of California Press, 1974) for the Chang Myon period; on the 1967 NDP platform, see John Kie-Chang Oh, *Korea: Democracy on Trial* (Ithaca: Cornell University Press, 1968). One of the big issues of the 1971 campaign was "Dae-jung economics." While Park argued for growth first, with redistribution to follow, opposition leader Kim Dae-jung argued for redistribution with growth. A leaflet widely distributed at a student demonstration in Seoul in December 1980 argues that "facism is a cover for state monopoly capitalism," and develops the links between export-led growth and domestic political repression. For recent critical analysis in Korean, see Pyun Hyung-yun *Reflections on the Korean Economy* (Seoul: Pak Young Sa, 1981); and Kim Yun-whan and H. Y. Pyun, eds., *Theses on the Korean Economy* (Seoul: Yoopung Chulpanso, 1981).

made it possible to grant concessions to labor because international competitiveness was not at issue. As import substitution slowed and distributive issues surfaced within the populist coalition, labor became increasingly militant in its demands. The military interventions in the Southern Cone of Latin America were partly motivated by labor's left turn.

The South Korean case differs somewhat. Korean labor had traditionally been weak. The American occupation had weakened the militant elements of Korean labor in the forties. Rhee built quasi-corporatist ties between his Liberal party and the unions in the fifties which facilitated top-down control. Import substitution was not carried out under the auspices of a populist coalition linking a mobilized working class and domestic business against rural elites. The labor unions grew in membership *after* the policy reforms of 1964 and 1965 as labor was pulled out of the countryside into the cities.

The shift to export-led growth was premised on an international comparative advantage in low-wage labor. The government could not prevent wages from rising beginning in the late sixties in response to labor scarcity and inflation. The government *could,* however, control and actively repress efforts on the part of labor to increase its political voice and organizational strength, thus maintaining a relatively free market in labor. There has been, for example, no effective minimum-wage legislation in Korea. By the end of the seventies, membership in Korean unions was only 24.4 percent of the total organizable work force.[17] The close relationship between export-led growth and control of labor was seen most clearly in the special labor law enacted in January 1970. Following lengthy labor disputes with two export-oriented American firms, this law placed special restrictions on labor organization and collective action in foreign invested firms. Following the declaration of the state of emergency these provisions were extended to workers in all en-

17. Economic Planning Board, *Economic Survey* (Seoul, 1980), p. 61.

terprises.[18] There has clearly been an "elective affinity" between state controls on labor and export-led growth.

The strong state proved important for the pursuit of outward oriented growth for several reasons. Previous regimes had proved politically incapable of imposing domestic stabilization. In addition, policy reform demanded a reoritation and internationalization of domestic firms and control of labor, even if these changes did not motivate the coup and subsequent consolidation of state power. Finally, the closure of the political realm and control of the opposition limited the political base from which a more inward-looking strategy could be articulated. Accomplishing all of these goals was facilitated by state control over finance and the generation of new resources, both domestic and foreign.

State Control Over Economic Resources

Undoubtedly, the growth of Korean manufactured exports can be partly explained in neoclassical terms.[19] A realistic

18. There is no formal wage control machinery in Korea. In the late seventies nominal wages grew rapidly, outstripping both the consumer price index and productivity. Economic Planning Board, *Economic Survey* (Seoul, 1980). The aggregate statistics hide the large pockets of low-wage labor that exist precisely in many export industries such as textiles and apparel. See Kim Chong Soo, "Marginalization, Development and the Korean Workers' Movement," in *AMPO*, vol. 9, no. 3. See also Park Young-Ki, "Labour and the Business Environment in Korea" (Seoul: Sogang University, n.d.), mimeo. The regime has consistently tied the control of labor to national security. Unlike the Latin American coups, the authoritarian installation of 1972 is difficult to trace directly to labor unrest, though labor had shown new signs of activism. The domestic opposition was not based primarily on labor radicalism or socialist ideology, however, but included students and others in a diffuse democratic opposition. See D. Valence, "Opposition in South Korea," *New Left Review* (January-February 1973); and Sunjoo Han, "Student Activism: A Comparison Between the 1960 Uprising and the 1971 Protest Movement," in Chong Lim Kim, ed., *Political Participation in Korea: Democracy, Mobilization and Stability* (Santa Barbara, Calif.: Clio Books, 1980).

19. The major studies are Gilbert Brown, *Korean Pricing Policies and Economic Development in the 1960's* (Baltimore: Johns Hopkins University Press, 1973); Charles Frank, Kwang Suk Kim, and Larry Westphal, *Foreign Trade Regimes and Economic Development: South Korea* (New York: National Bureau of Economic Re-

exchange rate signaled firms about their international comparative advantage. Exporters were exempted from numerous import restrictions and enjoyed access to inputs at world market prices. The government also provided certain public goods, such as market information and infrastructure, which enhanced profitability.

But the government also promoted exports by indirect subsidies channeled through the financial system in the form of highly differential interest rates. Subsidized credit helped finance exports, imported inputs, and new investment in export-related industries. The military had seized the outstanding private shares of the commercial banking system as part of its campaign against illegally accumulated wealth. Even more important, the military drafted new legislation to govern the Bank of Korea, giving the executive wide discretionary power over any decisions taken by its governing board.[20] Initially, export incentives were granted with little attention given to sectoral composition or domestic value-added. The state "followed the market" allowing firm-level initiative to determine the allocation of resources and supporting those industries demonstrating success. As early as 1964, however, the Bank of Korea was granted the authority to designate sectors to receive special attention. Financial institutions were required to concentrate their portfolios in those sectors. State control over credit thus came to play three mutually supportive functions. First, it provided a powerful tool of microeconomic control. Second, it subsidized the initial entry of firms into foreign markets. Finally,

---

search, 1975); Wontack Hong, *Trade, Distortions and Growth in Korea* (Seoul: Korea Development Institute, 1979); and Anne Krueger, *The Development Role of the Foreign Sector and Aid* (Cambridge: Harvard University Press, 1979).

20. Kwangsam Kim, "Report on the Bank of Korea," *Wolgang Choong Ana,* March 1978, p. 147 (in Korean). This greatly increased government discretion in manipulating banking funds, including for political purposes. Some stories are only now emerging. For example, in 1962, members of the junta forced the board of governors of the Bank of Korea to authorize a loan totaling 10 percent of all money then in circulation to cover up a stock market scandal. *Hankuk Ilbo,* February 24, 1982.

it built the political support of domestic business, cementing a close business-state alliance, though one in which the government held powerful levers of control.[21]

Financial resources were also required to achieve the final unification of the exchange rate in March 1965. Funds contracted with the IMF and the First National City Bank of New York allowed the government to deter speculative fluctuations in the foreign exchange market.

That export-led growth can be import-intensive is often overlooked. Korea is singularly unendowed with natural resources, importing large quantities of raw materials and energy. The ratio of imported inputs to total export value is high. The establishment of new export industries demands capital goods imports. Foreign exchange was needed to cover the deficits in the current account created by the surging imports which accompanied liberalization.

For these reasons—to ease the transition to foreign markets, to deter foreign exchange speculation, and to finance imports—adequate financial resources and the ability to channel them selectively appear to be critical to liberalization. These resources were generated in part through domestic interest rate reforms and the expanded capacity of the state to extract tax revenues. But while national savings increased from 7 percent of GNP in 1964 to 13.3 percent in 1968, foreign savings increased from 7.1 percent to 11.6 percent over the same period.[22] While this ratio was to steadily decline in favor of national savings, foreign capital, in the form of direct investment, borrowing, and multilateral aid, became an increasingly important component of Korea's strategy. The outward turn in trade went hand in hand with the increased use of foreign capital.

21. For more on business-government relations see Jones and Sakong, *Government, Business and Entrepreneurship.*
22. On these reforms see David Cole and Princeton Lyman, *Korean Development* (Cambridge: Harvard University Press, 1971) which remains one of the best overall studies of the country; and Ronald McKinnon, *Money and Capital in Economic Development* (Washington, D.C.: The Brookings Institution, 1974).

The Park government recognized on coming to power that foreign capital would be an important part of Korea's development strategy. The United States had signaled its intention to reduce the aid which was the financial mainstay of the Rhee regime. This forced the politically unpopular reconciliation with the Japanese, a process launched secretly in 1962 and which the United States had long avocated for strategic reasons.[23] The Property Claims Agreement, concluded in June 1965, provided up to $800 million in tied Japanese credits, $300 million in grant form. The quid pro quo came in part through expanded cooperation between Korea and Japan on matters of Japanese direct investment. One of Japan's industrial adjustment strategies has been to expand overseas investment in declining, low-wage sectors. This scheme was partly realized in the creation of the Masan Free Export Zone viewed by many critics as the epitome of Korea's relations with foreign capital.[24] The zone, the first of three, allowed 100 percent foreign ownership and attractive tax and capital repatriation concessions, while permitting duty-free import and export. The zone was a pure enclave, with the only Korean input being inexpensive labor.

The zones were by no means typical of Korea's relations with foreign capital, however. First, the zones account for only a small portion of total foreign capital entering the country, probably about 10 percent by 1975.[25] Export-oriented investments in textiles, light manufactures, and last-stage assembly tend to be small, often as little as $100,000. While much investment by Japanese firms tends to be trade related, American firms have continued to invest in import-substituting industries, such as chemicals and oil refining.

23. See Kim Kwan-bong, *The Korea-Japan Treaty Crisis and the Instability of the Korean Political System*, (New York: Praeger, 1971).

24. This argument is made in Tsuchiya Takeo, "South Korea: Masan-Epitome of the Japan-ROK Relationship," in *AMPO, Free Trade Zones and Industrialization in Asia*, special issue, 1977. The opening to Japan was also probably motivated by the quest for political funding for the DRP.

25. Estimate from *ibid.* and data supplied by the Economic Planning Board.

A recent study shows that from 1962 through 1974, 61 percent of Japan's direct investment was export oriented, i.e., in firms exporting more than 50 percent of their product, while only 10 percent of U.S. investment was. This still means, however, that 65 percent of all investment was domestically oriented.[26] The Japanese were motivated by an interest in exporting heavy, pollution-intensive industries as well as low-wage industries.

Second, direct investment has accounted for a relatively small portion of net capital inflow, only 3.7 percent between 1967 and 1971 and 7.9 percent between 1972 and 1976. This compares with 33.8 percent and 22.9 percent for Brazil in the comparable periods.[27] The government's control over foreign borrowing through the issue of loan guarantees gave it a powerful instrument it could use in guiding investment and building national firms. The government positively encouraged foreign borrowing, with interest rates on dollar denominated loans as low as half that for domestic credit.[28] Outstanding debt jumped from about $300 million in 1965 to over $13 billion by 1979, though it is a testament to Korea's export performance that the debt service ratio remained relatively constant over the entire period.

The Foreign Capital Inducement Law of 1965 and its revisions extended numerous incentives to foreign investors. The government has also acted to control foreign investment in a number of ways, however. Export requirements have limited foreign firms' access to the domestic market while local content requirements in certain sectors have forced domestic linkages. The prior screening process, which is highly discretionary, has explicitly sought to limit foreign investment in sectors where Korean firms can be internationally competitive. Except in the zones, the gov-

26. Chung H. Lee, "U.S. and Japanese Direct Investment in Korea: A Comparative Study," *Hitotsubishi Journal of Economics* (February 1980), vol. 20, no. 2.
27. Larry Westphal, "Korean Industrial Competence: Where it Came From," World Bank Staff Working Paper, no. 409 (July 1981), p. 23.
28. Anne Krueger, *Development Role of Foreign Sector and Aid*, p. 144.

ernment has favored joint ventures over 100 percent ownership. While proving flexible in making exceptions where a
project is deemed in the national interest, through the end
of 1978, 61.8 percent of all manufacturing direct investment had at least 50 percent Korean participation, while only
25.5 percent was 100 percent foreign owned.[29] The state
has clearly sought to orchestrate complementarity between
domestic and foreign firms.

This combination of policies toward foreign capital—
forced exports, the preference for debt over foreign investment, and controls over investment—has had an obvious
impact on the strength of national firms. The pursuit of an
externally oriented strategy had the unintended consequence of reducing the "denationalizing" competition between foreign and domestic firms in the local market, a long-
standing problem in the Latin American NICs. Through
protection and the promotion of joint ventures, the state has
fostered large, internationally competitive, groups, often
exercising monopoly power in the domestic market. In short,
the South Korean state has been instrumental in strengthening a national capitalist class. Similar developments are
clearly visible in Brazil and Taiwan. While domestic capital
has been highly dependent on, and controlled by, the state,
such a relationship may not prove inevitable, particularly as
the economic power of national firms continues to grow.

Reformist Leadership
The third prerequisite for liberalization is a reformist leadership. Within the policymaking apparatus, there must be
planners, indigenous or foreign, who can articulate a liberal
course in such a way that it corresponds with the interests
of political elites. Economic ideologies and political interests matter: one only needs to look at the influence of Pre-

29. Korea Exchange Bank, *Monthly Review,* November 1980. For the evolution of rules governing foreign investment, the best source is *Business Asia,* various issues.

bisch's ECLA on the inward-looking industrialization strategies chosen by so many Latin American states in the fifties.
In Korea, a significant influence was exercised by the U.S.
Agency for International Development, a fact which would
appear to underline Korea's external dependence. An examination of the political forces behind liberalization demonstrates, however, that it was motivated by the quest for
increased *autonomy* from the United States on the one
hand, and domestic political consolidation on the other.

Initially, the military showed little interest in pursuing
economic stabilization. The expansion of manufactured exports was not seen as the primary vehicle for promoting
growth, but rather as a measure for increasing self-reliance
by generating new sources of foreign exchange. The military's exchange rate policy even increased the gap between
the official and effective rate. The ambitious First Five-Year
Plan, unveiled hastily in 1961, stressed the building of a
heavy industrial base under a form of "guided capitalism,"
with little attention to the inflationary consequences. Primary exports were to be expanded to finance imports, implying a very different position in the international division
of labor than that which developed.

This economic strategy put the military government at
cross-purposes with its American donors, who protested the
mismanagement of the economy and the tendency to inflation throughout the fifties. Park tried to get around AID objections and maintain the elements of the plan by obtaining
private credits, but lack of experience in international borrowing quickly led to overextension.[30] A number of factors
pushed toward reconciliation with the Americans and the
emergence of a reformist consensus within the state.

The first was the political consolidation within the military of senior officers favoring a more "managerial" as opposed to "revolutionary" approach to economic policy. These
"managerial" forces came to be centered in the executive

30. *Far Eastern Economic Review,* August 8, 1963.

and the cabinet, forming a tacit alliance with the younger technocrats given wider recognition following a purge of the bureaucracy. The more radical junior officers, favoring a more nationalist economic posture, had developed their base of support in the military-created Democratic Republican party, which never fulfilled the vanguard role some of the colonels had envisioned.[31]

Second was the condition of the economy itself, particularly the inflation which had resulted from government spending, rapid increases in the money supply, and an abortive currency reform in 1962. A major justification for the coup had been the need to foster rapid economic development. The military was reformist from the beginning. The question was: what kind of reforms would work? As Park was forced to admit publicly, the military's expansionist course had not. Scandals in certain industries and the stock market had tarnished the military's image. In addition, the Americans had taken advantage of the rice crisis of 1963 to push both economic and political reforms, in particular, a return to democracy. Park, who was to run as a civilian, was thus open to ideas which would provide legitimation by improving economic performance. After his election, Park turned increasingly to civilian technocrats for economic advice, giving them the full political backing required to implement reforms.

While the role of the United States in pushing reforms is undeniable, it must be recognized that from Park's perspective, policy reform held out the promise of sustained growth and foreign exchange to replace declining aid commitments, both conducive to his broader national security and developmental aims. As with the liberalized posture toward foreign capital, the liberalization efforts became a way

31. Cole and Lyman, *Korean Development*, ch. 2; Hahn Been Lee, *Time, Change, and Administration,* (Honolulu: East-West Center, 1968). Lee shows the shifting character of the military alliance with the technocrats, and its domination by military interests. On the military-technocratic alliance in Latin America, see O'Donnell, works cited in fn. 11.

of *strengthening* the government's position, both domestically and internationally, a point overlooked by theorists of dependency and imperialism who tend to see the penetration of corporate and market forces as *weakening* the state.

South Korea thus seemed to possess important domestic political preconditions for external liberalization, particularly a strong state with flexible control of finance and a reformist leadership. The reforms of 1964, which unified the exchange rate and dismantled numerous trade controls, should not be equated with either domestic or external laissez-faire, however. As noted, the state wielded a powerful discretionary instrument through control of credit allocation. An analysis of South Korea's strategy for managing external interdependencies shows that the state's use of "liberal" policy-instruments has been highly selective. It also demonstrates that the state has recognized interdependence as a liability and has aggressively sought to reduce the costs associated with it.

INTERNATIONAL CONSTRAINTS
AND STATE RESPONSES

As a small trading nation, South Korea has been exposed to a number of pressures emanating from the international system. While some of these may be attributed to size and resource endowment, or lack of it, many are a function of the particular development strategy South Korea has pursued. States pursuing ISI have faced different external constraints than those pursuing export-led growth. This point is routinely overlooked by theorists of dependency. The precise character of a country's external economic relations is not reducible to backwardness or "structural position" in the international system alone. The relationship between the "international system" and the domestic political economy is established by state policies concerning tariff levels, exchange rate, foreign investment, borrowing, and industrialization. Similarly, economists advocating openness tend to downplay both the political and economic dilemmas of interdependence, stressing the gains in efficiency and output to be had through specialization. The concepts of dependence, sensitivity, and reliance allow us to avoid the rigid determinism of structuralist models of dependency while illustrating some of the political and adjustment costs of market integration overlooked by economists.

The first constraint South Korea has faced is dyadic dependence. The classic formulation of the political power generated through such inequality remains Albert Hirschman's *National Power and the Structure of International Trade*. Focusing on the economic concept of "gains from trade," Hirschman argued that a trade, financial, or investment relation which is more important for a small country than for a large one gives the larger partner a basis for influence by creating bilateral dependencies. By 1970 this had become a clearly recognized problem for the political leadership. In that year, 46 percent of South Korea's exports were going to the United States with another 28 percent going to Japan. On the import side, dependence on Japan was extremely large, creating trade imbalances which have become a standing political issue between the two countries. While Hirschman was concerned with the overt manipulation of bilateral ties, a possibility which obviously worried the Koreans during the Carter administration, this has not been the only concern. Bilateral dependence also tied South Korea to the economic performance of the United States and Japan.

This increased economic sensitivity, a second international constraint. Sensitivity is the extent to which domestic economic performance is determined by the performance of and trends in the international economy. There are of course numerous channels through which international disturbances may be transmitted to the domestic economy, including capital markets, the prices and quantities of traded goods, and so on. One rough indicator of South Korea's sensitivity and the openness of the economy may be seen in the ratio of exports plus imports to GDP. While in 1960, two-way trade was 16 percent of GDP, it had risen to 24 percent by 1965, 38 percent by 1970 and 64 percent by 1975.[32] During times of turbulence, small open economies experience shocks more dramatically, and, of course, the seventies was just such a period. In rapid succession, the 1970s saw the breakdown of the Bretton Woods regime, which immediately upset the *won*-dollar exchange rate, the rise in raw material prices, the oil crises, the deep recession and weak recovery, and massive increases in worldwide inflation.[33] These external shocks demanded major macroeconomic adjustments.

Equally troubling was the long-run trend in South Korea's international competitive position. South Korean export growth had been built around a fairly narrow range of products. In 1970 almost 60 percent of exports were accounted for by textiles, apparel, plywood, and wigs. This mix was vulnerable for a number of reasons. Real wages in the other Asian NICs had risen much more slowly than those in South Korea over the late 1960s. New low-wage entrants were seeking to replicate East Asia's success in the export of light manufactures. In 1971 the United States and South Korea initialed their first bilateral trade-restraint agreement in textiles, ushering in the era of protection. Export-led growth not only produced a general vulnerability to macroeconomic disturbances, but had placed pressure at the microeconomic, sectoral level as well.

32. Calculated from IMF, *Financial Statistics Yearbook,* various issues.
33. The concept of sensitivity is from Robert Keohane and Joseph Nye, *Power and Interdependence* (Boston: Little, Brown, 1978). It remains an interesting counterintuitive that the small open economies appeared to adjust more quickly to the oil shock than the large, more inward-looking NICs. See Bela Balassa, "The Newly Industrializing Countries after the Oil Crisis," World Bank Staff Working Paper, no. 437 (October 1980). Balassa's judgment came before the problems of 1980, however.

A third constraint associated with outward-looking growth may be called reliance. Reliance refers to the need for external inputs—capital, technology, raw materials, energy—to pursue a given development strategy. While all developing countries rely on external inputs and savings, South Korea's export-led growth has proved import and debt intensive. External reliance not only establishes the balance of payments as a constraint on growth, but poses what may be called an economic security dilemma by making the success of a given development strategy contingent on resources held by foreign actors: it is in part this contingency which has given rise to the Third World's call for increased self-reliance. While the costs of economic autarchy are high in terms of efficiency, the costs of interdependence are high in terms of security, vulnerability, and political autonomy. The political problems of external reliance are highly visible in those conflicts between host governments and multinational firms that have been detailed by writers in the dependency tradition. But the need for capital and technology from MNCs is not the only form of external reliance. Korean policymakers have become increasingly concerned by "resource nationalism," the increasing politicization of, and competition over, access to raw materials and energy, inflation in the cost of various intermediate inputs, and soaring interest rates.

In a highly militarized, national-security state, such as Korea, external reliance is closely related to the traditional security dilemma was well.[34] An examination of Park's writ-

34. The question of national security is a very sensitive issue in Korean politics. It is clear that Park manipulated the issue for domestic political purposes, contributing to tensions on the penninsula. Following the Yushin Constitution, stories of infiltration and spy rings became common ways of justifying attacks on the opposition and the need for political closure. Regardless of its origins, there can be little doubt that there is a security dilemma on the peninsula. North Korea maintains a huge army and has been militarily provocative on numerous occasions. On the military balance, see Stephen Gilbert, *Northeast Asia in U.S. Foreign Policy,* Washington Papers No. 71 (Beverly Hills: Sage, 1979); and *Far Eastern Economic Review,* March 5, 1982 for a somewhat alarmist view of the North's capabilities. For a comprehensive radical perspective which links the military and eco-

ings and speeches reveals the close links he drew between economic development, national security, and anti-Communism.[35] Park's calls for an independent and self-sufficient economy seem ludicrous in light of Korea's openness and specialization. The reassessment of America's position in the Pacific under Nixon, the troop withdrawal that followed, the debacle of Vietnam, and the apparent moves toward further disengagement under Carter, all posed the question of vulnerability in stark form and motivated the quest for increased self-reliance, particularly in defense-related industries.

Some of these international constraints are endemic to export-led growth. Sensitivity and external reliance are probably unavoidable for small countries, regardless of their level of development. Our interest here, however, is not the effect of these external relations on various domestic economic outcomes, such as rates of growth and inequality. This has been the purview of traditional economic writing and has become the focus of a growing body of literature purporting to test dependency theories.[36] Our interest is rather on the strategies that states pursue to manage these constraints. Three will be explored here. The first is political action within existing multilateral regimes, or political action aimed at changing them. The second is the effort to build alternative, diversified bilateral relations. The third is "self-help," in this case the effort to adjust the domestic industrial structure to enhance its international position in the face of competitive pressures. It has been found that South Korea's foreign economic and industrial policy over the seventies were dictated by two overriding concerns: the need

nomic issues, see Jon Halliday, "Capitalism and Socialism in East Asia," *New Left Review* (November–December 1980), no. 124.

35. See Park's *The Country, the Revolution and I* (Seoul: Hollym, 1970); and *Our Nation's Path* (Seoul: Hollym, 1970).

36. For a recent review of these efforts, see Volker Bornschier, "Dependent Industrialization in the World Economy," *Journal of Conflict Resolution* (September 1981), vol. 25, no. 3.

for markets and the need to remain internationally competitive. In responding to both of these external constraints, the state played a decisive role.

The NICs and the Trading Regime

Korea's position between North and South was reflected in the Tokyo Round negotiations and in its position toward the New International Economic Order agenda. Generally, the LDCs reaction to the outcome of the Tokyo Round was negative. The NICs found themselves in an ambiguous position. Their high levels of trade gave them an interest both in the tariff concessions and in strengthening those provisions of the regime that would protect them against arbitrary and discriminatory trade actions. In this sense, they could play the part of "principled liberals." They have also benefited—more than other LDCs—from preferential treatment, however, and thus have an equal interest in third-worldist reforms. This ambivalence toward the regime has been heightened by the steadily increasing amount of NIC trade governed by bilateral agreements or exceptionalist regimes such as the Multifibre Agreement. The growing importance of these exceptionalist arrangements has meant that bilateral bargaining strategies assume equal or greater importance than negotiations undertaken within the multilateral framework. A similar perception has guided NIC strategy toward the NIEO. While participating, and in the cases of Brazil and Mexico, even providing leadership in NIEO fora, the NICs continue to forge bilateral relations with other developing countries and seek preferential ties with select northern partners where possible.

South Korea continues to identify itself as a developing country. As such, Korea benefits both from the "negative" preferences which exempt LDCs from the obligations of full contracting parties as well as the "positive" preferences, such as the GSP which bestow special advantages. While Korea's tariff levels are low by developing country standards, import liberalization has always been highly selective. On coming to power, the military relied heavily on domestic entrepreneurs to perform the economic miracles which were to become the touchstone of Park's legitimacy. This business-state alliance has proscribed thoroughgoing liberalization. Though exporters have access to needed raw materials, inputs and capital goods, protection has remained in place not only in those sectors in which import substitution continues, but in precisely those sectors in which Korea enjoys a comparative advantage as well. Until the late 1970s, the converging interests of the state and domestic firms triumphed over efforts by some planners, trading partners, and international organizations to push further liberalization efforts.

In the late seventies, the government once again came under pressure to liberalize imports. The Americans and Europeans wanted Korea to open its markets. Some within the government thought that trade liberalization would increase Korea's leverage against the unilateral imposition of nontariff barriers. Liberals within the Economic Planning Board saw expanded exports as an antidote to the monopolistic structure of many domestic industries and increasing inflationary pressures. Domestic firms routinely used the protected domestic market to subsidize exports. A 14-inch black-and-white television sold for export at $42 brought $180 domestically.[37] In May 1978, following a positive trade balance in 1977, the Economic Planning Board announced a large-scale liberalization effort. Liberalization was to be carefully phased to allow domestic producers to adjust to anticipated competition. The announcement immediately triggered political opposition, as threatened business associations moved to protect themselves. The balance of payments shock of the second oil crisis no doubt contributed to the rethinking of the liberalization strategy. But the failure of the executive to intervene forcefully to save the pack-

37. Park Byung-yun, "Checking Import Liberalization," *Shin Dong Ah,* September 1978.

age resulted in a bureaucratic compromise which indicated the continued willingness to protect.[38]

Besides their continued protection of domestic industries, the NICs enjoy "positive" privileges through their identity as developing countries. Perhaps the most dramatic is their monopolization of the benefits of the Generalized System of Preferences. It has been amply demonstrated that a handful of developing countries receive the majority of benefits under the GSP. South Korea was the third-largest beneficiary of the American GSP in 1980, with 63 percent of Korean exports entering the United States duty free.[39]

While continuing to claim developing-country status, the NICs are obvious beneficiaries of the liberal trading regime itself. As both the tariff-cutting and nontariff-barrier negotiations showed, their status as large traders is making it increasingly difficult to avoid reciprocity.

Under Article XXXVI of the GATT, which specifies nonreciprocity, most developing countries do not feel required to participate in the multilateral tariff negotiations. Developed countries have been unwilling to let major LDC trading partners free-ride however, and the NICs, with the important exception of Mexico, are members and participants in the GATT. The perception of Korean negotiators was that the Europeans, but particularly the Americans, were heavy-handed in forcing concessions from developing countries, even if their subsequent implementation has been slowed with U.S. acquiesence.[40]

Many of South Korea's major export products were not even discussed during the Tokyo Round, including certain types of steel, televisions, textiles and apparel, and shoes. Nevertheless, the bilaterals signed with the Europeans, and Americans did provide for concessions in other areas. Several studies have also shown the predictable: the NICS stand

38. On the politics of the liberalization, see *ibid.*, and *Dong Ah Ilbo*, May 26, 1978.
39. Data supplied by the Office of the Special Trade Representative.
40. Interviews, Ministry of Foreign Affairs, and U.S. Embassy, Seoul, May 1981.

poised to be the major LDC beneficiaries of the Tokyo Round, in part because of their proven flexibility in responding to new opportunities, in part because their industrial structures are coming increasingly to resemble those of their northern trading partners.[41]

The NICs' strong position in the trading system, their advantages under the GSP system and their continued use of protective instruments and subsidies posed distinct problems in negotiating legal reforms in the GATT Framework Group. The text finally negotiated legally enshrines preferential treatment under the GSP, establishing a formally two-tiered system. The cost of the various legal reforms, the impact of which is still uncertain, was the inclusion of the concept of "graduation" in the Framework text. Pushed by the United States, graduation implies that the advanced LDCs are expected to gradually assume the full responsibilities of contracting parties. The concept was vigorously rejected by the Group of 77 as a "unilateral and arbitrary manner of discrimination among the developing countries."[42]

The "catch 22" facing the NICs was underlined in the various codes on nontariff barriers. There can be little doubt that South Korea has suffered from protectionist measures. By 1979, approximately $4 billion of Korea's exports were governed by restrictive measures, almost 40 percent of the total.[43] The NICs thus faced a combination of carrot and stick in signing the codes. All of the codes allow preferential treatment for the LDCs. To benefit, however, countries must become signatories. Becoming a signatory often means abandoning the very practices which the codes are designed to protect. For example, the subsidies code, which Korea signed, exempts LDCs from the ban on export subsi-

41. See GATT, *The Tokyo Round of Multilateral Trade Negotiations* (Geneva, 1979).

42. Decision of the Group of 77 on the Multilateral Trade Negotiations adopted at UNCTAD V.

43. Data supplied by the Ministry of Commerce and Industry. See also IMF, *The Rise in Protectionism* (Washington, D.C.: IMF, 1978) which details the protective actions against Korea through 1977.

dies unless they cause demonstrable injury. But the LDC signatories are expected to develop timetables to phase out such subsidies, a demand likely to be pushed vigorously in the case of the "graduating" NICs. The government procurement code allows LDCs to negotiate exceptions in line with their industrialization strategies, but in spite of three offers to the Americans on procurement, an agreement was never reached and South Korea remains outside the code. It should also be noted that no agreement was reached on the most salient nontariff barrier issue for the NICs, the right of countries to impose selective safeguards to protect domestic industries. Meanwhile, both the EEC and the United States are revising their GSP to include graduation provisions.

The small, trade-oriented NICs face several political dilemmas in the trading regime. Their industrial strategies, balance-of-payments problems and political structures argue against wholesale liberalization. Nonetheless, as trading nations, they are under external political pressure to participate and have their own interests in doing so as well. First, by remaining outside the institutional framework of world trade, they diminish their influence in the regime at a time when the GATT is a potential source of their protection. In his address to the GATT in 1980, the South Korean delegate cited the strengthening of the dispute settlement mechanism under the codes as one of South Korea's top priorities "in order to avoid the many ambiguities in the codes which invite arbitrary interpretation."[44] By participating, the NICs can attempt to bring pressure to bear to reverse the erosion of the regime at the edges. Second, unless they sign, they lose the material benefits of participation. In the case of tariff cutting, they have simply become too large not to participate. South Korea has of necessity become the defender of a liberalism which makes its own preferential treatment subject to attack.

The ambiguity toward reform can be seen in Korea's

44. Statement of H. E. Sangjin Chun, head of Korean Delegation, 36th Session of the Contracting Parties, Seoul, Ministry of Foreign Affairs, November 1980.

posture toward the NIEO debates. For the most part, Korea has shown little interest in them, supporting the Group of 77 as part of its general quest for Third World allies. South Korea's strategy is to focus on those issues which are of immediate interest, rather than to participate actively in the infighting within the Group of 77 or in the multilateral negotiations themselves. For example, as a large borrower, Korea strongly supports the South's proposals to increase the compensatory financing facilities of the IMF and international liquidity in general. On the other hand, as a large importer of raw materials, Korea is concerned that stabilization schemes might lead to restrictions on supply and rising prices. Commodity measures are supported only to the extent that they would stabilize prices and supplies. One writer's comments on Korea's pragmatic and selective interest in the NIEO could probably be extended to the GATT as well:

many people both inside and outside the government think that the NIEO issues are relatively less important for the current and future Korean economy than domestic economic policies and bilateral economic negotiations with certain countries.[45]

One relfection of this preference for bilateralism can be seen in the intensive push to diversify all forms of Korea's external economic relations.

Market Diversification
The motivations for market diversification are clear. Diversification lessens dependence directly. Between 1970 and 1979 South Korea expanded its exports to the EEC from 3 percent of total exports to almost 16 percent, while exports to other LDCs jumped from about 13 percent to over 25 percent.[46] The result was a correspondingly dramatic de-

45. Soo-yung Kim, "The New International Order and Korea," *Korea and World Affairs* (1981), vol. 5, no. 1.

46. Calculated from the IMF, *Direction of Trade Annual,* various issues.

crease in the degree of dependence on the American and Japanese markets. Diversification also reduces the effect of external shocks. A recent study has shown that export promotion and diversification helped insulate South Korea from the severe recession of its major trading partners, enabling the economy to grow at a respectable level during 1974 and 1975.[47] Finally, diversification is driven by the need to secure access to inputs, while it balances trade with those countries on which Korea is reliant. Korea has actively sought raw materials in Southeast Asia, oil in the Middle East and capital and technology in Europe.

A wide variety of instruments have been used in achieving South Korea's market diversification. These initiatives represent a conscious effort to build an alternative "international trade infrastructure." One of the common complaints of developing countries has been the lack of international ties among them. Relationships of dependence on northern partners are sustained and reproduced by networks and institutions—banks, buyers and suppliers, shipping and insurance companies, multinational corporations, trade associations, and diplomatic channels. To reduce dependence demands the creation of new networks, alliances, and institutions where none previously existed.

The most obvious effort has been exerted through diplomatic channels. In 1972 the government permitted trade with "nonhostile" Communist countries, while formal diplomatic relations with Africa, Latin America, and the Middle East continued to be strengthened. Embassies are given export targets, which they are expected to meet through trade promotion conferences. Although these instruments differ little from those of other states, the level of coordination between business and state is unusually high in South Korea. The distinction between public and private interests, between "high" politics and "low" is not clearly drawn.

47. Hee Yhon Song, "Economic Miracles in Korea," in Lawrence Krause and Sueo Sekiguchi, *Economic Interaction in the Pacific Basin* (Washington, D.C.: The Brookings Institution, 1980).

One example is the creation of the General Trading Companies as legal entities in 1975. The Japanese trading houses, on which the Korean GTCs were directly modeled, had long dominated Korean trade. In the early 1970s Korean traders started to pressure the government to back the country's own trading houses. Incentives to export had led to a proliferation of medium-size trading companies, inefficiencies, and lack of specialization. Small firms in particular would benefit from the existence of large firms that would serve as "windows" to international markets. The GTCs were ultimately to be conduits for raw materials and high technology as well. By bolstering the position of the largest trading groups, all of which were already tied to dominant industrial groups, South Korea could expand its markets and respond more flexibly to protection and the recession.

The inducements offered to the GTCs are examples of the use of state instruments to change firm behavior in line with national interests. Qualifying as a GTC led to numerous privileges, mostly financial: guaranteed letters of credit, loosened foreign exchange regulations, and further liberalization of import duties. The criteria for being designated as a GTC included overall capital and export requirements, that separated the ten or twelve largest firms from smaller traders. But some requirements demanded market exploration. GTCs had to export at least $10 million worth of goods to at least ten markets and had to have ten, then 15, then 20 foreign branches. By 1977, the GTCs were to have two branches each in Africa, South America, and the Middle East. Not surprisingly, the GTCs led Korea's expansion into new markets in the late 1970s.[48]

Two other institutional innovations have been the formation of an Ex-Im Bank and the granting of permission to Korean firms to invest abroad. The formation of the Ex-Im Bank in 1976 was a direct outgrowth of the need to finance

48. Korea Exchange Bank, *Monthly Review,* March 1979; Korean Traders Association, "Background to the GTC System," (in Korean); and *Far Eastern Economic Review,* November 19, 1976.

the export of heavy industrial goods, particularly ships and whole industrial plants. Through 1978, over 50 percent of the Ex-Im's financing went to Africa, South America, and Asia.[49] A second noteworthy development is the granting of foreign exchange clearance to Korean firms to allow investment abroad. The most extensive supports have been granted to overseas investments in raw materials, including coal, timber, and minerals. One of the largest of these investments was the $68 million by the state-owned Pohang Iron and Steel Corporation in the Tanoma, Pennsylvania, coalfield. Investments are also increasing in manufacturing, both in the developed countries to get around quotas, and in other LDCs, particularly in Southeast Asia, both for re-export and to service local markets.[50]

The best known of South Korea's diversification efforts has been the sustained push into Middle East construction. Korean construction firms first went abroad following Park's decision to participate in the Vietnam War. Korean contractors benefited from the generous financial support agreement signed with the Americans.[51] Following the oil crises, the Middle East was seen as a lucrative market for the expansion of Korean construction firms. A unique set of economic and political complementarities existed. South Korea was seeking to recoup large bilateral deficits caused by the surge in oil prices. Labor-poor Saudi Arabia, itself interested in diversification, had formulated ambitious development plans which called for extensive construction. South Korea would gain not only from the contracts themselves, and from workers' remittances, but from export of materials as well. Construction contracts and trade with the region

49. *IMF Survey,* November 26 and December 10, 1979; and Korean Ex-Im Bank, *Ex-Im Bulletin,* various issues.

50. Korea Exchange Bank, *Monthly Review,* September 1980; *Far Eastern Economic Review,* August 31, 1979; *Overseas Resources Development Promotion Act* (Seoul: Ministry of Energy and Natural Resources, 1979).

51. Frank Baldwin, "America's Rented Troops: South Koreans in Vietnam," *Bulletin of Concerned Asian Scholars* (1975), vol. 7, no. 4.

jumped from nil in 1972 to $9.8 billion and $3.2 billion respectively in 1981.[52]

The government has exercised extremely strict controls on entry into the Middle East. All overseas construction contracts, foreign exchange transactions, and dispatch of manpower are tightly controlled. These controls are, typically, balanced by substantial supports, which range from the guarantee of the large performance bonds required to operate in the Middle East to Korea's diplomatic tilt toward the PLO.

Korean efforts in Europe demonstrate the way the state can act directly to diversify trade and investment relations. Europe has been one region with which Korea has run a consistent trade surplus. Over the seventies, the EEC has put Korea on notice that persistent surpluses would not be tolerated. In 1981, two high-level missions were dispatched to Europe, each accompanied by an entourage of prominent business leaders. The government ministers brought shopping lists related to the Fifth Five-Year Plan.[53] In 1980 a similar move had been made to cement relations with France through the award of important contracts to two French firms in connection with the construction of two nuclear power plants. This switch, after a long nuclear relationship with Westinghouse, was clearly based on perceptions of the costs of continued dependence on the United States. The Carter administration's policy on nonproliferation had created significant uncertainty in Seoul. French policy toward technology and fuel transfer was liberal. South Korea was able to link the sale to the lifting of some barriers on light manufactured exports. In addition, Seoul saw closer ties with France as a way of gaining better access to Africa. The French and the Koreans are now participating in a joint venture to mine uranium in Gabon. The French Minister for

52. Data provided by the Ministry of Construction and the Korean Traders Association.

53. *Korea Herald*, August 27 and September 13, 1981.

Foreign Trade has even suggested the possibility that France could play a role in facilitating South Korea's ties with Mainland China.[54]

A final area of expansion of external ties has been Southeast Asia. ASEAN has been the target of South Korea's increasingly aggressive raw materials policy. Knowing that self-reliance would be impossible, the government has sought to develop long-term contracts through the "development/import" formula. South Korean firms, both private and parastatal, invest in overseas resource development in return for supply contracts. Recognizing Korea's comparative weakness vis-à-vis large international companies, one Korean study notes that "Korea must highlight the empathy which exists between developing countries and make every effort to contribute to the well-being of the host country in terms of providing infrastructure development and employment."[55] An example may be seen in a state-to-state joint venture with Indonesia's Pertamina. In return for a stable supply of crude from the project, Korea would provide 50 percent of the capital for exploration and sweeten the deal by extending technical assistance to rural electrification projects through the state-owned Korea Electric Company.[56] South Korea's increased profile in the region was signalled by Chun's ASEAN tour of 1981.[57]

Diversification does not provide a panacea for managing external constraints, and it probably has important limits. Diversification may have the effect of widening the geographical scope of protection by placing pressure on new markets. This has apparently been the case in textiles, where protection spread from U.S. bilaterals to a global regime, as Asian manufacturers sought to diversify both markets and

54. *Korea Herald*, November 9, 1980. On ties with Africa through France, see *World Business Weekly*, July 14, 1981; and *Machinery Korea*, June 1981.
55. Korea Exchange Bank, *Monthly Review*, September 1980.
56. *Korea Newsreview*, February 7, 1981; *Korea Herald*, October 9, 1981.
57. *Far Eastern Economic Review*, June 26 and July 2, 1981.

products.[58] The very size of the American and Japanese markets make them natural trading partners. In 1981, over 40 percent of South Korea's exports went to those two countries. The rate of reduction of dependence on these two markets has slowed and may have reached a stable bottom limit.

The limits of market diversification make bilateral bargaining a critical component of NIC trade strategy. There is a range of bargaining strategies small states may pursue *within* the context of continued bilateral dependence to extract increased gains.[59] Korea has sought to gain leverage with both Japan and the United States by directly linking economic issues to South Korea's strategic importance as a military ally. This linkage was made by Chun in his 1981 meeting with Reagan, and was clearly specified in the request to Japan for $6 billion in aid and loans during the Fifth Five-Year Plan period. Yoffie and Odell have shown that under certain conditions, other strategies and tactics can be effective as well. These include the forging of transnational coalitions, negotiating for ambiguity and flexibility in bilateral trade deals and bargaining for long-run gains.[60]

South-South ties are clearly increasing. As growth poles, the NICs are likely to lead the process. Their level of industrialization has resulted in new economic complementarities between developing countries. Several caveats are in order, however. There is no reason to believe that some of the conflicts which currently exist in the relations between North and South will not be reproduced in the NICs' rela-

58. Vinod Aggarwal, "Hanging by a Thread: International Regime Change in the Textile/Apparel System, 1950–1979" (Ph.D. diss., Stanford University, 1981).

59. John Odell, "Latin American Trade Negotiations with the United States," *International Organization* (Spring 1980). Odell shows how specific bargaining tactics can overcome power differences.

60. David Yoffie, "The Newly Industrializing Countries and the Political Economy of Protectionism," *International Studies Quarterly* (December 1981), vol. 25, no. 4; and "The Advantages of Adversity: Weak States and the Political Economy of Trade" (Ph.D. diss., Stanford University, 1981).

tionships with other LDCs. Other LDCs seeking to emulate the NICs are protecting their own infant industries and may see no particular benefit in South Korean, as opposed to Japanese or American, foreign investment. The Koreans already worry about their future in the Middle East. The Saudis are themselves instituting protectionist measures—local content requirements and indigenization policies under a "Saudization Plan." South Korea's moves into Latin America have been limited by the similarities in industrial structures. Ironically, Korea's moves into ASEAN may be frustrated by the nature of that South-South integration effort itself. Korean ties with Africa have been limited by the shallowness of markets and the low level of financial development.

The Korean case suggests that the building of stronger South-South ties heralded by some as the basis for "collective self-reliance" is most likely to emerge from concrete bilateral, economic complementarities rather than multilateral organizations and negotiations. Market diversification is a highly politicized form of competition for markets. Korea has been relatively successful precisely because of the close relations which exist between state and business and because of the high priority diversification has been given as a "national interest" by political elites.

Industrial Deepening in International Context
A third, and perhaps the most important, response to international vulnerability and reliance has been Korea's effort to upgrade and deepen its industrial structure. The defining characteristic of Korean industrial policy over the seventies was the rapid, state-led push into heavy and chemical industries. This strategy demonstrates three of the contradictory features of Korea's development: the relative strength of the Korean state in mobilizing resources and directing their allocation; the ultimate limitations, both international and domestic, on the effort to break patterns of international specialization; and the continuing inability of Park to

legitimate his authoritarian rule, particularly in the face of deteriorating economic conditions.

The Second Five-Year Plan (1967– 71) had initiated feasibility studies for a petrochemical plant and an integrated steel mill, both with direct state involvement and assistance from the Japanese. After the success of these projects, the Third Five-Year Plan (1972– 76) and particularly the Fourth Five-Year Plan (1977– 81) stated that heavy and chemical industries were to become a priority.[61] Perhaps the key statement of the government's intentions, however, came in the 1973 Heavy and Chemical Industry Development Plan, designed to serve as a master plan to guide the development of these industries over the course of the decade. The plan was the direct result of executive initiative. Prepared by a special committee around Park, the plan bypassed the formal planning machinery in the Economic Planning Board, where it was later to meet heavy criticism from economists wary of its ambition.

The plan had several justifications. Economically, Korea needed to find a new niche in the evolving international division of labor.

Considering the problems of advanced countries, such as pollution, high wages, and the general leisure trend, [sic] and also the prospective participation of less-developed countries in light industries, the promotion of heavy and chemical industries is justified on the principle of the international division of labor.[62]

The plan would also silence the regime's critics by overcoming some of the problems in Korean industrialization which had become evident over the course of the 1960s. The plan was the first major economic initiative following the Yushin Constitution. As one government description states:

61. Heavy and chemical industries were defined to include iron and steel, nonferrous metals, shipbuilding, machinery, electronics, fertilizers, chemical pulp, oil refining, and cement.
62. *Heavy and Chemical Industry Development Plan* (Seoul: 1973).

Concentrated development of these industries will settle one of the persistent problems facing the country in the field of industry; low competitiveness on the world market both in terms of price and product quality caused by the limited domestic market, sub-marginal scale of most existing enterprises, flimsy capital structure and backwardness in industrial technology.[63]

Finally, the plan was motivated by the quest for increased military self-reliance. North Korea continued to be perceived as a threat, while U.S. defense commitments often seemed uncertain. The giant Changwon industry complex was to house key defense-related industries.

The plan established both a general orientation for investment and designated specific projects demanding direct state involvement. In electronics and machinery, the government was to build large industrial estates to house new industries, relying on private response to the generous financial incentives extended under the plan. For the larger projects, the government was not to rely as it had in the past on arms-length instruments and the financial system alone, but was to greatly expand its direct role in production. In this, South Korea resembled the Latin American NICs. In both Brazil and Mexico, state involvement in production increased dramatically as development entered the phase of industrial deepening. State involvement was justified by the low profitability, technological complexity, and high risk of the projects.[64]

To finance this accelerated development, the government established a massive National Investment Fund, managed by the state-controlled commercial and special banks, which mobilized public employee pensions and a fixed portion of all bank deposits. The plan also called for massive increases in foreign savings as well. During the Fourth Five-Year Plan, 70 percent of financing of govern-

63. Korea Overseas Information Service, *Heavy and Chemical Industry* (Seoul, 1974), p. 30.
64. Leroy Jones, *Public Enterprises and Economic Development: The Case of Korea* (Seoul: Korean Development Institute, 1976).

ment identified projects, such as the petrochemical facilities, steel mill expansion, and oil refineries, was to come from foreign loans, while 60 percent of total heavy and chemical investment was to be financed by foreign loans and direct investment in joint ventures.[65] The plan thus demanded a continued, if not expanded, reliance on foreign capital.

There have undoubtedly been successes under the plans, such as the highly efficient state-owned Pohang Iron and Steel Company (POSCO), possibly the most efficient integrated steelmaking facility in the world.[66] There were, however, a number of serious problems with the plan, which demonstrate the difficulties of an aggressive adjustment strategy for a small trade-oriented economy. Over the course of 1977 and 1978, these difficulties generated a new critique of Park's overall management style within the government. The triumph of a new liberal consensus was evident in the wide-ranging stabilization plan of April 1979. This plan was too late to forestall broader political developments. High inflation, triggered in large part by the heavy industry plan, strengthened the opposition and contributed to the domestic violence which finally toppled Park. What had gone wrong?

The major problem was the inflationary impact of state investments in heavy and chemical industries which were covered not by budget balances, but by creation of credit through the state-controlled banks and by simply printing money. Inflation had long been a characteristic of Park's strategy of imbalanced and rapid growth. The willingness to pursue aggressive adjustment strategies regardless of the inflationary consequences was evident in the Korean response to the world recession of 1974. Rather than maintaining a fixed exchange rate, compressing imports, and

65. Economic Planning Board, internal documents.
66. On steel, see Korean Development Institute, *Long Term Prospect for Economic and Social Development 1977–1991* (Seoul, 1978); and *Far Eastern Economic Review*, March 10, 1978 and July 17, 1981.

deflating, as Taiwan did, South Korea devalued and launched a massive export drive.[67] While successful in the short run, this strategy contributed to an inflation which was only accelerated by the heavy industry investments of the 1977–79 period and the rapid inflows of foreign exchange from the Middle East. Motivated by the fear that Carter would resume U.S. troop withdrawals, investments were speeded in the defense-related heavy industries so that 97 percent of all investment planned over the 1977–81 period was made in the first three years.

Investments were also duplicative. The preferential schemes in the machinery sector were designed in part to foster the concentration and consolidation of the largest Korean firms. The large groups moved quickly to take advantage of the incentives offered, resulting in surplus capacity in key industry segments. The overall operation ratio in the machinery sector dropped from 74 percent in late 1977 to 35 percent in late 1980.[68]

Of more importance was the effect of the heavy industry drive on South Korea's international competitiveness. From the beginning there had been some confusion in the successive plans between industrial *deepening* and upgrading *exports.* The plans reflected the belief that heavy and chemical industries would improve South Korea's international position by moving into an emerging niche in the world market for relatively standardized, heavy industrial goods. The strategy demanded that economies of scale be supported by an expansion of export markets, though foreign demand was in fact treated as a residual.

The results revealed the inherent limitations on such a strategy. First, most of the technology demanded by the plan was to be imported. High royalty payments raised production costs without improving the technological capabilities

67. Han Sheng Cheng, "Alternative Balance of Payments Adjustment Experiences; Korea and Taiwan, 1973–1977," Federal Reserve Bank of San Francisco, *Economic Review* (Summer 1978).

68. Korea Exchange Bank, *Monthly Review,* December 1980.

of the participating firms, at least in the short run. Of the total investment in heavy and chemical industries between 1973 and 1979, only 5.5 percent went into research and development and human resource development, though these were absolutely essential if the effort was to be self-sustaining.[69] The new industries demanded skilled, not unskilled, labor, for example, placing pressures on those segments of the labor market which were already tight.

Second, the reliance on debt, both domestic and foreign, had resulted in a weakening of the financial structure of many firms. By 1979, firms were forced to resort to borrowing to repay principal and interest during a time when the government was seeking to slow inflation by tightening credit. This problem was faced not only by the large firms in the heavy and chemical sectors, but by the large trading houses as well, as the controversial collapse of the Yulsan Group demonstrated in 1979. Yulsan had overextended itself by aggressively pursuing and manipulating state-subsidized credits.[70] Smaller firms not favored by the strategy faced tightening credit as finance was drained into the heavy and chemical sectors, and into those large firms having close connections with the financial system. Business failures soared in 1979.

The bias toward heavy industries not only discriminated on the basis of size, but went hand in hand with a relative neglect of those light manufacturing industries which continued to be internationally competitive. There can be little doubt that the plans produced rapid changes in South Korea's industrial structure. Heavy and chemical industries accounted for about 50 percent of manufacturing output in 1979, while the ratio of heavy and chemical exports to the total had jumped from 15 percent to 38 percent between

69. Korean Development Institute, *Collection of Materials on Economic Stabilization Measures* (Seoul: KDI, 1981) p. 1276 (in Korean). This contains an extensive review of the performance of the plan and the "liberal" critique.

70. *Asian Wall Street Journal*, April 19, May 25, and June 9, 1979. This incident was important in pushing toward financial reforms.

1971 and 1979. As late as 1979, textiles, apparel, and shoes still accounted for 35 percent of South Korea's exports, and many exports classified as heavy and chemical were in fact products such as light electronics in which low-wage labor remained a key component of advantage. But between 1975 and 1980, over 75 percent of all manufacturing investment was channeled into heavy and chemical industries, though such investment was not increasing productivity substantially.[71] As one government report noted in late 1980, "labor-intensive manufacturing industry, which even today remains the backbone of the national economy, has been left to fend for itself.[72]

In 1979 export growth slowed dramatically, while the oil shock, liberalization efforts, and shortages of domestic credit led to surges in imports. In 1980 despite a 20 percent devaluation, South Korea experienced negative growth of 5 percent. The miracle had collapsed.

The lesson to many within the government had been clear for a long time. As one official in the Economic Planning Board put it:

In the 1970s, the most successful adjustments to new changes in the international economic environment came when the incentive structure was based on market principles and the initiatives of entrepreneurs. The least successful adaptations occurred when the market principles and law of comparative advantage were ignored.[73]

The economic debate which had emerged over the late seventies went to the heart of the relationship which had developed between state, society, and economy under Park. While the tight state control of the economy and the ambitious heavy and chemical industry drive was blamed for the

---

71. KDI, *Collection.*

72. Korea Exchange Bank, *Monthly Review,* December 1980.

73. K. W. Kim, "Industrial Restructuring in an Open Economy: The Case of Korea," paper presented at the UNIDO Conference on International Restructuring, Lisbon, October 1980.

economic problems, the political bases of the strategy were equally unstable.

In the National Assembly elections of December 1978, the opposition New Democratic party had captured a majority of the openly contested seats though Park continued to control the Assembly through direct executive appointments. The NDP directly challenged Park's continued hold on power, waging the campaign in large part around economic mismanagement and particularly, the high rates of inflation. Church leaders, students, and dissidents had continued to protest the Yushin Constitution over the course of the decade despite the harsh repressive measures against them. Christian organizations were active among the peasantry and workers. The NDP's protest of the "YH incident," in which a woman worker was killed in a demonstration over a plant closing, appeared to link the opposition party to labor issues. This would have provided the basis for the formation of the very "horizontal" alliances which Park's strategy of corporatist control and repression had sought to prevent. With the attempt to eject the opposition leader from the Assembly for remarks he had made to the *New York Times*, rioting erupted in several major cities. Disagreements within the leadership on how to respond were probably responsible for Park's assassination.

It is beyond the scope of this paper to assess the complicated set of political maneuvers through which Chun Doohwan consolidated political power over the course of 1980. The growth in political opposition which triggered the political collapse of 1979 is largely explicable in terms of Park's high growth strategy, however. Numerous sectors of the population saw themselves disfavored under Park's course. Students, intellectuals, politicians, and journalists pressed political demands. Organized labor and consumers were hurt by inflation. Many small- and medium-size businesses, particularly at the provincial level, failed under the drain of credit to heavy industries and the belated stabilization efforts of 1979. While the government was capable of insulating itself from social pressures and implementing development plans, it failed to build a legitimating consensus that would provide political stability.

The numerous reforms undertaken beginning in April 1979, and particularly with the Fifth plan, have had a dual purpose. On the one hand, liberal voices within the government have pushed a restructuring of the style of economic management, a loosening of state controls and a move back toward the acceptance of comparative advantage. On the other hand, Chun has sought to publicize a new emphasis on welfare as a way of appealing to wider segments of the population.

Export-led growth is to remain the heart of the strategy, but "liberalization" has become the watchword in Seoul. Import liberalization has moved forward, though at a slowed pace, and with the government retaining highly discretionary instruments, such as variable tariffs, with which it can control imports quickly and flexibly. Plans have been launched to liberalize and deepen the financial structure by returning banks to private hands, expanding their decision-making autonomy, and through numerous reforms of the capital and security markets, including increased foreign participation.

The Fifth Five-Year Plan contains a number of open criticisms of Park's strategy.[74] The plan states, for example, that growth in the seventies favored the upper classes and urban areas, with a subsequent worsening of income distribution. More attention is to be paid to upgrading light manufacturing, with small- and medium-size industries to receive new supports. The continued importance of heavy industry has not been directly challenged, but "problem sectors" have been consolidated. In addition, Chun's rhetoric has openly stressed welfare-statist goals: increased education, health and social expenditures, and distributive policies. While in-

74. *Summary Draft of the Fifth Five Year Social and Economic Development Plan* (Seoul, 1981).

tentions must be weighed against outcomes, it is politically interesting that Chun is willing to raise social expectations which if frustrated could be turned against the regime.

Chun has acted to forestall such an eventuality, however. The change in the style of economic management and the substance of South Korea's strategy are not to be accompanied by significant political reforms or expanded channels of political access. Direct state controls of labor have been dramatically tightened. The government's intention to directly suppress the opposition was signalled by the arrest of key opposition figures in April 1980 and the bloody suppression of the uprising in Kwangju which followed.

It is too early to assess the reforms. The most critical, such as the reform of the banking sector and import liberalization, will prove on-going battles. Two additional reforms of interest—the liberalization of direct investment rules and the restructuring of the heavy and chemical industries—are indicative of the new course, while demonstrating that the state continues to be strong in resisting domestic business interests and implementing desired reforms.

One component of the strategy to upgrade the technological capabilities of Korean firms has been to liberalize foreign investment. Studies by the Korean Traders Association and the Korean Chamber of Commerce and Industry had derided the heavy industry push for neglecting quality control and improvement of the intermediate and parts industries in which small and medium-size firms played a larger role.[75] The government's response, however, was to announce in late 1980 its intention to substantially liberalize foreign investment rules. One report noted that the "excessive emphasis on retaining control in the hands of Korean enterprises has served as a disincentive for foreign investors to utilize their most up-to-date manufacturing processes," and that strict discretionary regulations were only

75. KTA, "Policy Reccommendations to Restructure the Linkage between Trade Policy and Industrial Policy," November 1980; and KCCI, "Present Status of our Industrial Technology," 1981 (both in Korean).

a prerogative when the economy was expanding.[76] The new rules permit 100 percent foreign ownership in a large range of product categories. Over the course of 1981, after lengthy battles over which sectors to open, the discretionary control over foreign investment was eased, first by the announcement of a list of open industries, then in late 1981 by the move to an even more liberal negative list system.[77] In addition, the minimum investment amount was lowered significantly, from $500,000 to $100,000, a move which met strong opposition from small and medium firms.

Prospects for direct investment are not contingent upon screening procedures alone: the recession, stagnant economy, wage pressures, and profit levels, which have been dropping in Korea, will determine the level of incoming capital as well. The case is interesting because state perceptions of the importance of technical tie-ups and capital inducement dominated the interests of many local firms in avoiding increased foreign competition. The parallels to the earlier liberalization are clear.

The efforts to restructure certain heavy and chemical industries demonstrate that within a context of technological reliance, the state can develop a significant range of maneuver from both domestic and international firms.[78] Six sectors falling under the heavy and chemical industry plans, prominently including automobiles and power generating equipment, faced serious problems of surplus capacity. Power generating equipment attracted considerable attention from Korean firms, since the expansion of nuclear power and the energy needs of the economy would guarantee state purchases. Hyundai International was given a

76. Korea Exchange Bank, *Monthly Review*, December 1980.

77. *Ibid.*

78. The "problem six" were power generating equipment, automobiles, heavy electrical equipment, electronic switching systems, diesel engines, and copper smelting. In addition to interviews, the following draws on Korea Exchange Bank, *Monthly Review*, December 1980; K. W. Kim, "Restructuring"; "Korean Industry: Made to Order," *Insight* (February 1981); and *Asian Wall Street Journal* and *Business Asia*, various issues.

government guarantee of sufficient orders to ensure operation and began construction of a large, integrated machinery plant at the Changwon industrial complex. Daewoo and
Hyundai Construction joined the field by securing orders
from the state-owned Korea Electric Company (KECO). A
fourth firm, Samsung, also expressed interest. Each of the
four Korean groups had secured technical tie-ups and in
some cases capital commitments, from foreign counterparts. By 1977, the threat of surplus capacity was already
clear and in 1979, the government ordered mergers which
would have consolidated the two Hyundai's on the one hand,
and Daewoo and Samsung on the other. Conflicting corporate interests ruined the plan. Following Chun's ascension
to power, he issued a sweeping reorganization plan in which
Daewoo would be given control of the Hyundai International
plant at Changwon as the sole producer. The other firms
were paid off by giving them portions of other restructured
industries. Daewoo soon realized the difficult situation the
Changwon facility was in and announced that $1 billion, with
$300 million called for in the first year, was needed to fix
the situation. While the government initially appeared to
agree, the final restructuring left the government holding
the company through KECO and the Korean Development
Bank, which has often played this receivership role. Daewoo
got nothing.

The incident demonstrates the character of the state-
business alliance. Performance criteria determined the limits of government tolerance toward domestic business. Although indulgent in its dealings with the large groups, support was based on the quid pro quo of economic efficiency.

The government immediately sought foreign investors
not only to normalize the operation but to complete the remaining plants. While remaining heavily reliant on foreign
capital and technology to complete the project, the government was in a position to use privileged market access to
bargain with competing foreign firms. The Federation of
Korean Industries, representing the largest Korean firms,

quickly became the defenders of the national interest. FKI attacked the government joint ventures on a number of grounds, including the lack of linkages with the domestic economy and the problems of marketing potential exports through firms with conflicting global interests. The FKI criticisms were rebuffed with some cynicism, however, since the government believed that the Korean groups had their opportunity and missed it.

Several conclusions can be drawn from the heavy industry drive and subsequent restructuring. Small trading nations face powerful constraints in the form of shifts in the international division of labor. They have thus come to resemble the advanced industrial states in their need for industrial-adjustment, as well as industrial-development, policies. There are limits in pursuing an aggressive state-led adjustment strategy, however, which cannot be overlooked. South Korea's success hinged on a careful industrial sequencing which permitted the realization of dynamic comparative advantage. To the extent that policy departed too radically from comparative advantage, as it did in the big push of the late seventies when a number of new industries were promoted simultaneously, countervailing market forces acted to reduce competitiveness.

It is likely, however, that the move from light manufactures to a more integrated industrial structure could not be accomplished without direct state intervention. This poses a powerful dilemma. Staying put as a producer of light manufactures is neither ideologically nor economically feasible. Trusting solely in market signals, foreign investment, and firm-level initiative is equally risky. As with the Latin American NICS, industrial deepening has involved the state more directly in the economy. Recent policy in Singapore and Taiwan also would seem to confirm this.

The cases of the liberalization of direct investment and industrial restructuring again demonstrate the importance of a strong state in outward-looking growth, even if only to undo the damage it had previously caused. Reestablishing the "balanced" course demanded making openings to foreign investors and forcing firm-level competitiveness in ways reminiscent of the early 1960s. It also involved renewed controls on labor, which have been increasingly harsh under Chun, and the continued repression of those political interests urging an alternative strategy.

CONCLUSION

Despite its intellectual and prescriptive appeal, the strategy of radical dissociation from the international system is not an option for most developing countries. Even China and Tanzania, much heralded cases of self-reliance, have hardly pursued autarchic courses.[79] The questions then become, what kind of association? Under what conditions? And with what effects?

We have argued that association is a function of the broader strategies of development and industrialization, and that these, in turn, are rooted in domestic political processes and structures. We must ask not only what policies are good, but under what conditions certain policies are likely to emerge and prove feasible. One particularly close form of association—export-led growth—appears to have been facilitated in South Korea by a set of important political prerequisites, which may not be easily transferrable to other cases: a strong reformist state wielding highly discretionary financial instruments and pressure from a powerful ally.

We have attempted to show some of the limitations on either liberal or dependency interpretations of Korean development. Korean growth has been, above all, state-led.

79. See A. Doak Barnett, *China's Economy in Global Perspective* (Washington, D.C.: The Brookings Institution, 1981); and Thomas Biersteker, "Self-Reliance in Theory and Practice in Tanzanian Trade Relations," *International Organization* (Spring 1980), vol. 34.

The Korean state, and the state in other NICs as well, has substantial power in designing and implementing development policy and in controlling the economy. More importantly, however, the state appears to have substantial power in insulating itself from social and political pressures, and in controlling the classes and interests—including domestic and foreign business as well as labor—which serve as the bases for export-led growth.

We have also attempted to show that *association* has a number of discreet dimensions and must be disaggregated. External vulnerabilities are not reducible to the relationship with foreign capital or a dominant military partner. They also include a set of market vulnerabilities which have dictated and constrained South Korea's foreign economic and industrial policies. The Korean state has sought to neutralize the costs of association, though not always with complete success. Though under growing pressure to "graduate," South Korea, to date, has been selective in its liberalism, controlling direct investment and using trade and financial instruments to develop a domestic business class. South Korea has sought with some success to diversify its external trade relations and has bargained successfully to increase market access under conditions of growing protection. Finally, the state has acted to force industrial development. Although proving a short-term disaster, this policy may be seen in the future as having produced important gains.

The advocacy of close association via export-led growth may involve a fallacy of composition which has not been adequately recognized, however. The East Asian NICs entered the export game at an historically auspicious moment. Rapid world growth facilitated Korea's entry into the world trading system. By the time protectionist pressures and slowed macroeconomic conditions manifested themselves, Korea had developed a flexible state policy apparatus and a set of domestic firms seasoned to international competition. New entrants face a different set of prospects. The smooth absorption of LDCs into the international division of labor is now hindered by slowed world growth and the political and economic rigidities in the advanced industrial states which prohibit rapid industrial adjustment. Successful "association" is partly a function of timing.

Finally, we must ask what effect export-led growth has had on welfare and equity. A major contention of dependency analysis has been that close association and integration are associated with political exclusion and social marginalization and polarization. Indeed, explaining these social-structural distortions has been a major aim of dependency thinking. Korea, however, has often been cited as an example of the benefits to be gained by close integration into the international economy and the possibilities for redistribution with growth. Several caveats are in order on both sides.

First, Korea's rapid growth has been accompanied by rising incomes, expanded employment and the virtual elimination of the levels of poverty of the forties and fifties. These rising incomes have largely been generated in the urban industrial sector: agriculture has been "pulled" by industrial expansion, rather than leading it.[80]

Second, by any standards, Korea has a relatively egalitarian distribution of income.[81] This is partly attributable to export-led growth, based on labor-intensive manufactures, and expanding employment, which is beneficial to distribution. By keeping wages low, disparities between rural and urban incomes and within the urban working class were narrowed. Most seem to agree, however, that land reforms and the Korean War itself were the critical factors in redistributing assets. These events have little to do with export-

80. See Sung Hwan Ban, Pal Yung Moon, and Dwight Perkins, *Studies in the Modernization of the Republic of Korea 1945–1975: Rural Development* (Cambridge: Harvard University Press, 1980).

81. See Joel Bergsman, "Growth and Equity in Semi-Industrializing Countries," World Bank Staff Working Paper, no. 351 (August 1979); and Edward Mason et al., *The Economic and Social Modernization of Korea* (Cambridge: Harvard University Press, 1980). The Mason volume summarizes the findings of the multivolume Harvard study.

led growth; indeed, they preceded it. As we have argued, the reforms may have been a critical political precondition for any rapid industrialization.

The relative neglect of agriculture over the 1950s and 1960s resulted in some reconcentration of holdings and a deterioration of the rural-urban terms of trade as rates of productivity in the two sectors diverged.[82] Critics of the Korean model have argued that neglect of the rural sector was a conscious state policy aimed at creating a large pool of low-wage labor. As Taiwan shows, however, rural neglect is not intrinsic to export-led growth itself. Moreover, rural decline elsewhere has been identified with ISI strategies as well. Rather, political choices about the countryside appear as important as industrialization strategies per se. The ratio of rural to urban household incomes had sunk to 63 percent in 1968. To reverse the perception of rural decline, Park instituted several policies aimed at maintaining rural political support, including a change in rice pricing policy and the launching of the New Village movement. By 1975, rural and urban income levels had reached rough parity.[83]

As the Fifth plan itself admits, there has been a significant erosion of income equality over the seventies. Recent work has also demonstrated that the earlier picture of overall levels of equality has probably been distorted by the failure to adequately include the very wealthy in income statistics used in distribution studies.[84] A number of indicators, such as automobile ownership and tax data, suggest that incomes among the upper class have been increasing rapidly. At the same time, rapid growth resulted in large internal migrations and the creation of a significant squatter and marginal class in the cities. However, over the seventies, Korean growth has also produced a new urban middle class

82. For the World Bank's analysis, see Parvez Hasan, *Korea: Problems and Issues in a Rapidly Growing Economy* (Baltimore: Johns Hopkins University Press for the World Bank, 1976).

83. D. C. Rao, "Economic Growth and Equity in the Republic of Korea," *World Development* (1978), vol. 6, no. 3.

84. Mason, *Economic and Social Modernization of Korea*, ch. 12.

so that erosion in the overall level of income equality should not be interpreted as implying a general polarization of society.

As anyone familiar with Korea is aware, growth has been accompanied by authoritarian controls and the sometimes violent repression of political opposition. Making causal links between political structure and development strategy is not as easy as it might appear. Authoritarian controls predate the turn to export-led growth and have a history not only in the American and Japanese occupations, but in the traditional structure of Korean politics and society. Developing states pursuing different development strategies, including dissociationist ones, also have authoritarian regimes.

Given these caveats, we have argued that there have been some affinities between Korea's associationist strategy and authoritarianism. The first concerns labor. While not always successful in controlling wages directly, the state has acted to strictly control labor organization and political activity. The second affinity is a broader one, and concerns the leadership's capacity to autonomously define and implement a particular development orientation. Whatever its *motivation*, the government's political strategy has had the effect of fragmenting the opposition and limiting the channels through which popular demands could be articulated. It was in part this autonomy which permitted the government to pursue a strategy based on the rapid accumulation of capital and close integration into the international economy.

4.

The Constraints on Associative Development in a Privileged Developing Country: The Case of Venezuela

JEFFREY A. HART

VENEZUELA IS A developing country with many characteristics which, according to mainstream economists, should be conducive to economic development.[1] Newly industrializing

Financial support for travel and research assistance was provided by the Princeton University Committee on Research in the Humanities and Social Sciences. The Center of International Studies at Princeton and the Department of Political Science at Indiana provided typing assistance. I would like to acknowledge the research assistance of Narses Colmenares and the helpful advice of Robert Bond, Mercedes Pulido de Briceno, Barry Buzan, Alberto Fuenmayor, Henry Gomez, Eva Josko de Gueron, Howard Handelman, Terry Karl, Gerd Junne, Peter Katzenstein, Janet Kelly, David Laitin, Raul Osuna, Ramon Pinango, John Ruggie, Alida de Sulbaran, and Enrique ter Horst. I owe a special debt to Gene Bigler for his comments on an earlier draft and for sharing so generously his encyclopedic knowledge of Venezuela.

1. Economic development will be defined to be sustained economic growth which benefits even the lowest-income groups in society.

countries like Brazil, Mexico, Taiwan, and South Korea face strong external constraints to their development, whether in the form of high-energy import bills or in barriers to trade erected by the industrialized countries. For Venezuela, on the other hand, the post-1973 energy terms of trade have reduced international constraints on economic development and have made a sizable pool of capital available for investment. Moreover, Venezuela has substantial deposits of iron and aluminum ores as well as untapped sources of coal and hydroelectric power. It has a growing core of skilled personnel in both the private sector and in the state bureaucracies. It has an excellent credit rating on international financial markets and an ample supply of foreign exchange. Venezuela also has many of the political characteristics deemed necessary, by a variety of scholars, for economic development: an electoral form of government,[2] a strong state,[3] a mixture of developmentalist and distributionist economic philosophies,[4] a commitment to reducing dependence on foreign countries and corporations,[5] and a set of governmental programs designed to assure all members of society at least a minimum standard of living.[6]

And yet Venezuela still faces very important obstacles to development. Poverty, inadequate housing, and malnu-

2. Seymour Martin Lipset, *Political Man* (Garden City, N.Y.: Anchor Books, 1963), ch. 2. Lipset is usually interpreted as arguing that economic development begets democratic government, but his studies also have been used to make the argument that democracy is a prerequisite for development.

3. Alexander Gerschenkron, *Economic Backwardness in Historical Perspective* (Cambridge: Harvard Univeristy Press, Belknap Press, 1962).

4. Albert O. Hirschman, "The Turn to Authoritarianism in Latin America and the Search for its Economic Determinants," Princeton University, Institute for Advanced Studies, May 1977. Manuscript.

5. Carlos Diaz Alejandro, "Delinking North and South: Unshackled or Unhinged?," in Albert Fishlow et al., *Rich and Poor Nations in the World Economy* (New York: McGraw Hill, 1978).

6. For an example of a "developmentalist" analysis of the Venezuelan economy, see Pedro-Pablo Kuczynski, "The Economic Development of Venezuela: A Summary View as of 1975–1976," in Robert D. Bond, ed., *Contemporary Venezuela and Its Role in International Affairs* (New York: New York University Press, 1977).

trition are still the lot of many Venezuelans despite the influx of petrodollars. The degree of dualism in the Venezuelan economy is high. Agriculture remains a weak spot in the Venezuelan economy, which directly constrains growth through the resulting need to import larger and larger quantities of food products. There is an alarming level of corruption which drains away resources into unproductive activities. Finally, Venezuela remains highly dependent on petroleum revenues, and therefore, on the international economy, to fuel its economic development.

Why, despite the many favorable conditions that Venezuela enjoys, has it not made greater strides to deepen industrialization and to better the standard of living for the majority of its people? The reason, I suggest, are the rigidities in economic and social structure which are the consequence of Venezuela's history of "associated, dependent development."[7] This form of development comprises more than a set of external linkages between the developing country and the international economy. The case of Venezuela shows that even where these linkages are altered to the benefit of the developing country, and the constraints

7. This term is taken from the work of Fernando Henrique Cardoso, especially "Associated Dependent Development: Theoretical and Practical Implications," in Alfred Stepan, ed., *Authoritarian Brazil.* Associated dependent development can take place in the larger South American countries, according to Cardoso, because of the growth of state entrepreneurship and the slow increase in the power of popular sectors, especially the urban proletariat, in the face of industrialization. New social groups emerge that create the possibility of nationalist coalitions, which can counter the influence of foreign or international interests in a dependent economy. Such nationalist coalitions are weak or nonexistent in enclave economies because of the absence of a national entrepreneurial elite. In *Dependency and Development in Latin America,* Cardoso and Enzo Faletto argue that Venezuela has some characteristics of an enclave economy, but with some potential for industrialization because of the investment of foreign capital outside of the petroleum sector. See pp. 89–91 of *Dependencia y Desarrollo en America Latina* (Mexico: Siglo XXI, 1972). Below, I will argue that the increased role of the state in the Venezuelan economy, following the nationalization of both the petroleum and iron and steel industries, makes it much more credible to assert that Venezuela has a nationally oriented entrepreneurial elite, an elite which is inextricably tied to state policies.

they impose are attenuated, domestic social and institutional structures that were initially shaped by the external linkages can remain in place and continue to affect the character of economic policy and limit the possibility of fundamental change.

In the case of South Korea, as discussed in this volume by Stephan Haggard and Chung-in Moon, substantial domestic change triggered by the restructuring of social groups and institutions after World War II preceded the adoption of an outward-oriented strategy based on exporting manufactured goods with a high labor component. The external constraints to Korean development were attenuated slightly, thanks to the timing of this strategy, by the importance of South Korea in the security calculations of the United States. The relative success of this exporting strategy continued as long as Korea did not attempt to diversify its industrial production in the direction of heavier capital goods and basic industries such as steel and petrochemicals. When the Korean government did make a move to deepen its industrial base, it was confronted with a new set of external and domestic constraints which created an economic and political crisis from which that country has not yet recovered.

The key differences between the Korean and Venezuelan cases, therefore, are that (1) Korea chose an export-led rather than a secondary phase of import-substituting industrialization, and (2) the choice of this new strategy was clearly the result of major changes in domestic social and institutional structures, changes which did not occur during this same period in Venezuela. Venezuela never had the option of adopting an export-led growth strategy because of the relatively high wages paid to workers there, itself a consequence of the export of petroleum. And Korea, like most of the other newly industrializing countries, never had the option of financing its growth on the basis of the export of a raw material with a highly favorable international price.

The key similarities in the two cases center around the common desire to diversify the domestic economy so as to reduce external constraints to development. In both cases, a point is reached where the initial phase of industrialization ends and an attempt is made to create a base for a "deepening" of the industrial economy; that is, an effort is made to create a capacity for producing the basic inputs for industry—iron and steel, capital goods, and heavy industrial infrastructure. In both countries, it is the state which takes the lead in this effort, and in both countries, a major adjustment in social arrangements is necessary to pursue a deepening strategy. It is not clear yet whether either will be successful.

It may be helpful also to contrast the Venezuelan case with that of three other petroleum-exporting countries: Algeria, Iran, and Saudi Arabia. All of these countries benefited from the rapid increase in oil prices in the mid- and late 1970s. Of the four, Algeria and Venezuela have been the most ambitious in attempting to create a diversified industrial economy out of their petroleum revenues. Iran spent a large proportion of its revenues on military equipment and nuclear power plants with little left over for a major push toward a diversified industrial base. Saudi Arabia has also spent sizable sums on military equipment, and because of a very large surplus of revenues over current expenditures and an initially very-limited industrial base, has tended to use its revenues for economic investments in infrastructure—the purchase of turnkey plants for such products as petrochemicals and cement—while placing the remainder of its funds in various overseas investments.

Thus, the oil-exporting country most like Venezuela in attempting to use the temporary advantage of high oil prices to industrialize is Algeria. The Algerian strategy suffers from internal contradictions, as Hveem shows in his paper later in this volume. Moreover, Algeria's petroleum reserves were already declining rapidly in 1974–75. Total revenues, therefore, could not expand as rapidly as had been projected in 1973. After 1975, Algeria was stuck with the problem of readjusting its very ambitious plans to the realities of declining revenues. While Venezuela also had to face such a readjustment in 1977– 78, it had enjoyed a longer period of high revenues and, in general, its government had chosen more realistic targets and projects than had the Algerian government.

Venezuela is, therefore, a prime choice for studying the effects of a sudden and persisting attenuation of external constraints on economic development in a dependent country. It is an important case because some theories of dependency suggest that attenuation of these constraints is the key to development, while others place a stronger emphasis on the necessity for changes in domestic coalitions and strategies.[8] Mainstream economic approaches are concerned with external constraints primarily as they affect economic options through balance-of-payments deficits, shortages of foreign currency, exchange rates, and the like. Mainstream economists do not assert that a reduction in external constraints without correct domestic policies will necessarily result in improved economic performance. Nevertheless, they are likely to be puzzled by a country which, in the face of "sensible" policies *and* reduced external constraints, fails to grow and develop faster. Venezuela thus provides evidence for the failure of both some varieties of dependency theory and some mainstream economic approaches adequately to consider the effects of domestic social systems.

My discussion is organized as follows. I first show that despite the existence of a number of problems and cyclical

8. The work of Fernando Cardoso, as discussed in the previous note, leaves room for a variety of domestic political and social factors in explaining patterns of development in dependent Latin American countries. The work of Andre Gunder Frank, e.g., *Capitalism and Underdevelopment in Latin America* (New York: Monthly Review Press, 1969), puts a heavier emphasis on the nature of international linkages as the main factor inhibiting economic development in the Third World. Both authors accept the historical observation that development was accelerated during the world wars because of attenuation of linkages with the world economy, but Cardoso seems inclined to pay more attention to the nature of domestic social coalitions and the effect of these coalitions on policy choices in explaining economic outcomes.

downturns, in relative terms, the macroeconomic performance of Venezuela appears vigorous—external constraints have been attenuated and the state has become a more significant actor in the economy. I then go on to examine the performance of the Venezuelan economy from the point of view of the living standards of the majority of people. Here it is seen that, even with increased state intervention, the record remains modest. Third, I will explain this discrepancy in terms of the domestic social and institutional legacy of dependent development, which continues to shape the fundamental character of socio-economic policy in Venezuela today. Finally, I conclude with some general observations about the relevance of this case for the issues raised in this volume.

THE VENEZUELAN ECONOMY:
1958 TO THE PRESENT
IN TERMS OF MACROECONOMIC INDICATORS

The Venezuelan economy experienced high rates of growth in gross domestic product (GDP) and in GDP per capita during this period. The average annual rate of growth of GDP in constant prices was 5.4 percent from 1958 to 1979 (see table 4.1). Per capita GDP increased from $817 in 1958 to $3616 in 1979 at an average annual growth rate of 5.5 percent. Growth was not always steady. There were recessions of various intensities during four periods: 1959–61, 1965–67, 1970–72, and 1979–80. The most rapid rises in per capital GDP occurred between 1973 and 1974 and between 1978 and 1979, the years of the increases in petroleum prices.

Until 1973 Venezuela had not experienced major problems with inflation. Consumer prices actually declined during the recession of 1959–61. From 1973 to 1980, consumer prices increased at an annual average rate of 11.1

TABLE 4.1: Growth in GDP, Real GDP, and GDP Per Capita, 1958 to 1979

Year	GDP in Current Prices ($ million)	GDP in Constant Prices of 1975 ($ million)	Growth in Real GDP (%)	GDP Per Capita ($)
1958	5716	11537		817
1959	5944	12465	8.0	821
1960	5947	12963	4.0	794
1961	6279	13600	4.9	811
1962	6867	14842	9.1	858
1963	7486	15877	7.0	919
1964	8288	17407	9.6	984
1965	8821	18460	6.1	1013
1966	9191	18919	2.5	1020
1967	9681	19642	3.8	1040
1968	10460	20602	4.9	1087
1969	10940	21521	4.5	1100
1970	12091	23051	7.1	1177
1971	13256	23819	3.3	1249
1972	14721	24542	3.0	1346
1973	17698	26181	6.7	1569
1974	29707	27712	5.8	2554
1975	29151	29151	5.2	2431
1976	30947	31312	7.4	2503
1977	35766	33441	6.8	2626
1978	39758	35046	4.8	3030
1979	48888	34696	−1.0	3616

SOURCES: International Monetary Fund, *International Financial Statistics,* Annual Supplement (May 1978), pp. 406–07; *International Financial Statistics, Yearbook* (1981), pp. 250–51; Banco Central de Venezuela, *Informe Economico* (1980 and previous years).

Note: All GDP figures are expressed in dollars at the current exchange rate of 4.3 bolivars to the dollars. GDP per capita is calculated by dividing GDP in current dollars by annual population estimates.

percent. This new inflationary trend was discouraging to many Venezuelans because it signaled an inability of domestic production to keep up with the increase in aggregate demand. Nevertheless, production did increase rapidly in a variety of sectors, as will be shown in the next section.

Changes in the rate of unemployment mirrored changes in aggregate growth rates. Unemployment declined from a period high of 14.7 percent at the end of the 1959–61 recession to a period low of 4.3 percent in 1978. The rate of unemployment after 1973 remained lower than the average rate during the 1958–72 period, even during the 1979–80 downturn in the economy.

The Main Sectors of the Economy
The petroleum sector has dominated Venezuela's economy since the 1930s. There were signs after 1973, however, that the economy was becoming more diversified and that the manufacturing sector was increasingly taking over the role of petroleum as the generator of overall growth. The continued dominance of the petroleum sector could best be seen in the very close relationship between changes in the value of petroleum exports (which accounted for a nearly constant 90 percent of total export revenues during this period) and changes in real GDP.[9] The production of crude petroleum and natural gas accounted for 28 percent of GDP in 1958; it was still over 16 percent in 1977. The average rate of growth of the petroleum sector was only .03 percent from 1958 to 1977 (see table 4.2). The sector experienced an overall negative rate of growth between 1973 and 1977 despite the oil price increases. The reason for this was the drastic decline in the production of crude oil which occurred in the 1970s. Production reached a peak of 3.7 million barrels per day in 1970, dropping to 2.1 million barrels per day by 1980.

Manufacturing production grew at an average annual rate of 7 percent between 1958 and 1980. Between 1973 and 1976, annual growth rates were 10 percent or more. The manufacturing sector accounted for around 13 percent

9. I performed a simple regression analysis using the following equation: DELGDP = a DELPEX + b + u.

DELGDP is the change in gross domestic production; DELPEX is the change in the value of petroleum exports; a and b are constants; and u is the error term.

The least-square estimate of this equation explains 93 percent of the variance in DELGDP. For every increase of one bolivar in petroleum revenues, GDP increased by 1.74 bolivars. I used first differences in order to compensate for serial correlation. The Durbin-Watson statistic for the estimated equation was 1.35.

TABLE 4.2: Real Growth Rates by Sector, 1958–59 to 1979–80, in Percentages

Period	Petro.	Agr.	Mining	Mfg.	Util.	Cnstrct.	Transpt.	Retail/Whlsle.	Other
1958–59	6.6	4.2	10.8	15.0	19.6	5.5	8.8	5.3	8.6
1959–60	2.4	21.0	10.2	−2.1	10.4	−3.5	−7.2	−0.7	8.1
1960–61	2.3	0.6	−22.7	6.0	13.7	−10.7	−1.5	−4.1	11.0
1961–62	9.6	5.2	−7.0	9.0	18.7	−3.5	0.0	6.3	19.9
1962–63	1.5	5.6	−15.3	7.2	17.8	−5.6	4.9	6.5	14.5
1963–64	4.8	8.0	38.3	17.3	12.4	11.6	13.0	14.3	14.1
1964–65	2.1	6.2	9.0	3.7	11.3	3.3	7.3	26.4	9.5
1965–66	−3.1	4.2	0.5	1.0	9.5	6.7	3.1	4.4	5.7
1966–67	5.1	5.5	−3.7	5.4	10.6	8.9	4.9	3.7	4.2
1967–68	2.0	5.0	−10.9	5.7	16.4	21.3	6.6	7.4	2.7
1968–69	−0.6	9.9	24.0	4.1	10.2	−3.2	0.4	2.5	4.2
1969–70	9.0	2.1	44.3	10.0	13.5	−1.6	16.8	7.2	6.8
1970–71	−1.6	5.0	−11.2	6.4	10.5	16.0	5.6	4.8	7.8
1971–72	−7.9	−3.3	−5.6	8.3	7.6	26.8	10.8	0.4	6.3
1972–73	6.5	5.3	29.3	5.8	10.9	12.6	3.3	5.2	6.6
1973–74	−12.0	6.1	15.0	10.2	12.8	−1.5	10.2	10.4	10.4
1974–75	−22.3	8.1	−4.1	11.3	17.1	18.0	10.1	12.8	8.0
1975–76	−1.7	−3.6	−17.4	11.9	6.2	20.7	9.7	7.2	9.3
1976–77	−2.7	7.8	−9.5	4.3	7.2	24.4	12.3	4.3	6.8
1977–78	−3.2	6.3	1.6	4.9	5.0	11.0	7.3	0.2	2.9
1978–79	10.6	3.7	7.9	5.1	12.2	−9.7	−4.4	−5.3	−0.3
1979–80	−7.8	2.9	1.6	3.8	3.8	−15.3	−0.5	−15.5	2.2
Average 1958–80	−0.02	5.3	3.9	7.0	10.7	5.5	5.5	4.7	7.7
Standard Deviation	7.7	4.8	17.8	4.4	5.3	12.0	6.0	8.0	4.6
% of GDP in 1980	16.5	8.7	0.4	16.5	1.7	8.3	14.6	11.8	38.0

SOURCES: Banco Central de Venezuela, *La Economia Venezolana en los Ultimos Treinta Anos;* Banco Central de Venezuela, *Informe Economica,* 1980 and previous years.

of GDP from 1958 to 1973. Despite relatively rapid growth in the manufacturing sector from 1958 to 1980, it still accounted for only 16.5 percent of GDP in 1980. Between 15 and 20 percent of the employed labor force had jobs in the sector, as compared to the approximately 1 percent in the petroleum sector.[10] While the petroleum sector was almost

10. Oficina Central de Estadistica e Informatica, *Encuesta de Hogares por Muestreo* (Caracas: First Semester of 1977), pp. 40–45.

completely state-owned and managed after 1975, [11] albeit through the nationalized subsidiaries of multinational oil firms, the manufacturing sector had a mixture of firms ranging from completely state-run to wholly private concerns. Foreign investors dominated some branches of manufacturing, but most were predominantly national. Since the manufacturing sector was seen as the main hope for the Venezuelan economy in the petroleum-scarce future, the state promoted both private and public investments in manufacturing, especially after 1973, and sometimes at the expense of other sectors, including agriculture. [12]

Agriculture in Venezuela grew at the respectable rate of 5.3 percent per annum from 1958 to 1980. But Venezuelan agricultural production was subject to wide fluctuations; torrential rains resulted in massive crop failures in 1975–76, for example. The agricultural sector employed 18 percent of the employed working force in 1977 [13] and accounted for between 6 and 7 percent of GDP. Rural population declined rapidly and steadily. In 1950, 46 percent of the population lived in rural areas; by 1976, only 17.4 percent lived in rural areas. [14] There was a tendency for the size of landholdings to increase. In 1961, 49 percent of all farms had an area of less than five hectares; in 1971, only 37.8 percent had less than five hectares. [15] The productivity of agriculture in terms of per capita output increased substantially, yet agricultural productivity was lower in strictly monetary terms than any other sector of the economy. [16]

Venezuelan agriculture was oriented primarily toward the domestic market. Bananas, beans, corn, rice, yucca,

11. Franklin Tugwell, "Venezuela's Oil Nationalization: The Politics of Aftermath," in Bond, ed., *Contemporary Venezuela.*

12. Instituto Nacional de Nutricion, *Consideraciones Sobre la Situacion Nutricional Venezuela* (Caracas: February 1978), pp. 15–19.

13. *Ibid.*, p. 1.

14. *Ibid.*

15. Julio Paez Celis, "Aspectos Democraficos del Marginalismo en Venezuela," *Estadistica Venezolana* (January 1978), no. 11, p. 54.

16. This statement is based on the author's calculations of output per capita in different sectors of the economy.

fruit, cotton, and sesame accounted for over 80 percent of the area of land under cultivation. Coffee was the main agricultural export crop, but only 15 percent of the area under cultivation was devoted to coffee in 1976.[17] A great increase in the domestic demand for food was one of the results of the increases in purchasing power made possible by the increases in petroleum revenues in 1973−74. This combined with crop failures in 1975 produced a rapid rise in imports of agricultural products from 211 million dollars in 1973 to 560 million in 1976.[18] Agricultural imports included raw materials for agricultural production, such as fertilizers and cattle feed, as well as unprocessed food products. The imports of processed food rose as high as 814 million dollars in 1976, or around 9 percent of total export revenues.[19] In general, the agricultural sector did not develop as rapidly or as smoothly as the Venezuelan government desired.

To summarize, agriculture was one of the least dynamic sectors of the Venezuelan economy; manufacturing, along with utilities and services, was the most dynamic. Venezuela was being transformed gradually into an industrialized country, but there were some aspects of petroleum-based industrialization which were not present in other industrializing countries: 1) the economy was still dominated by petroleum (although to a lesser degree than before); 2) the proportion of the GDP and of the work force in the tertiary sectors was larger than normal in the early stages of industrialization; and 3) agriculture was unable to expand production rapidly enough to meet the increased food demand which resulted from the increases in petroleum revenues after 1973.

17. Banco Central de Vanezuela, *Informe Economico 1976* (Caracas: 1976), p. A154.
18. Federacion Venezolana de Camaras y Asociaciones de Comercio y Produccion (FEDECAMARAS), *XXXIII Asamblea Naual, Informe Final* (Caracas: 1977), p. 442.
19. *Latin America Special Report, Venezuela* (London: Latin American Newsletters, January 1978), p. 10.

External Constraints: Trade and the Balance of Payments
The main question raised by any account of the external
sector of the Venezuelan economy is whether this sector imposed a constraint on development. The external sector had
been a major constraining factor in the past. When Venezuela was still a coffee-exporting country, its growth was
highly constrained by the growth of demand for that product. Indeed, much of the legacy of poverty in Venezuela
stems from its earlier status as an agricultural exporter. Even
during the period after the restoration of electoral government in 1958, when Venezuela was the largest exporter of
crude petroleum in the world, the diversion of exploration
and production by the multinational oil companies away
from Venezuela and toward the Middle East created difficulties for the pursuit of even a relatively limited import substitution policy.

The value of Venezuelan exports took a large jump in
1973 and 1974 after a long period of stagnation, due to the
increase in petroleum prices. Export receipts dropped again
in 1975 when world demand for petroleum declined and the
need to conserve Venezuela's limited reserves imposed a
cutback in production. Despite its temporary nature, the
surge in export revenues produced by the 1973 price increases was sufficient to produce a seven-billion-dollar trade
surplus in 1974. By 1977 the trade surplus had been whit-
tled away by rising imports to less than 1.5 billion dollars.
There was a trade deficit in 1978. The price increases of
1978–79 restored the surplus once again. The speed with
which a massive surplus was turned into a deficit was disconcerting to many Venezuelans. Nevertheless, by 1976
Venezuela had accumulated over nine billion dollars in international reserves, which made it feasible to begin to borrow money at favorable rates on international financial markets. External debt, helped along considerably by massive
government spending prior to the election campaign of
1978, increased rapidly from 1975 on.

Exports were dominated, of course, by petroleum. The second largest source of export revenues was iron ore, followed by coffee and aluminum. The United States was Venezuela's largest export market. There was a rapid increase in nontraditional exports, but Venezuela was by no means an "export platform." The wages of Venezuelan workers, while low in terms of developed-country standards, were high relative to countries which chose to export goods produced with labor-intensive technologies. Venezuela expected eventually to become an exporter of high-grade metal products (even such sophisticated products as six-cylinder automobile engines), but that remained a distant prospect.[20]

Imports of raw materials, food, consumer durables, capital goods, and machinery accounted for most of Venezuela's imports. While food imports increased rapidly after 1973, raw material and machinery imports increased even faster. The attempt to build up basic industries and heavier manufacturing industries resulted in unprecedented levels of imports of capital goods which would diminish in the next few years.

The main constraint imposed by the external sector on Venezuelan development between 1958 and the present was the need to gear programs to the projected level of petroleum-export revenues. Venezuela did not face the usual problems of trade and balance-of-payments deficits and high ratios of debt-servicing to exports. Its constraints were more relative than absolute: that is, some years were better than others but none were disastrous.

The external sector may become a greater constraint in the future, however, if Venezuelan petroleum revenues begin to diminish at a faster rate than projected, because there are relatively few export products which can replace petroleum as major sources of income. Aluminum and steel

20. Fernando Coronil and Julie Skurski, "Reproducing Dependency: Auto Industry Policy and Petrodollar Circulation in Venezuela," *International Organization* (Winter 1982), 36:61–94.

products from Venezuela will have to compete on the world market with the products of highly industrialized countries as well as those of the low-wage industrializing countries. Perhaps Venezuela will have an edge because of the relatively lower cost of its raw materials and its proximity to major markets. If not, Venezuela will surely confront a balance-of-payments constraint on its future industrial development. Such external constraints could lead some future Venezuelan government to alter the current policy of keeping Venezuela relatively open to the international economy while industrializing.

The Dominant Role of the State in the Economy
The strength of the Venezuelan state was enhanced considerably by the oil-price increase of 1973. The jump in revenues made it possible for the government to carry out internationally accepted nationalizations of the iron ore industry in 1974 and the petroleum industry in 1975. The state accounted for 40.7 percent of the GDP in 1977.[21] The largest state firms were in petroleum (Petroven), iron ore (Ferrominera), steel (SIDOR), and the public utilities (Edelca and Cadafe). The Corporacion Venezolana de Guayana (CVG) had extensive powers over a variety of projects in the Guayana region, including joint ventures in bauxite mining and aluminum (Venalum and Alcasa), as well as the existing plants for steel production and hydroelectric power. By the end of the 1970s, there were over 300 firms or agencies in various sectors of the economy which were partially or wholly controlled by the state.[22]

The size of public investments could be gauged from

21. Banco Central de Venezuela, *Informe Economico 1977* (Caracas: 1977), p. 241.
22. Charles Taylor and Michael Hudson, *World Handbook of Political and Social Indicators,* 2d ed. (New Haven: Yale University Press, 1972), p. 11. The Venezuelan newsweekly *Resumen* (August 9, 1977), contains an incomplete list of enterprises over which the state has at least partial control. This list comes from a study done by the planning ministry in conjunction with a United Nations team.

TABLE 4.3: Estimated Investments in Major Projects, 1976–1980

Title	Nature of Project	Investments ($ billion)
SIDOR Plan IV	steel in Guayana	3.53
Venalum	aluminum	.60
Interalumina	aluminum	.56
IV Petroquimica	petrochemicals	.70
Zulia coal	coal mining	.07
Zulia steel	steel in Zulia	.51
Edelca	hydroelectric	1.91
Cadafe	utilities	2.21
Ferroviario	railroads	2.33
Caracas metro	rapid transit	.51
	communications	2.40
	infrastructure	5.72
	others	3.21
Total		24.26

SOURCE: *V Plan de la Nacion,* published in *Gaceta Oficial* (March 11, 1976), no. 1860. Recent studies suggest that the estimates are too low, especially for petrochemicals, Zulia steel, and the Caracas metro.

the estimates of the Fifth Plan of the Nation of the total projected outlays for various projects over the 1976–80 period (see table 4.3). While the plan projected a total outlay of around 24 billion dollars over a five-year period, more recent estimates put the figure at about 37 billion, assuming that all the projects would be carried out. The statistics on government expenditures showed that the percentage of government expenditures allocated to capital investments increased from 31 percent in 1973 to 56 percent in 1974. While the percentage of government expenditures allocated to capital investment declined to 35 percent again in 1977, it must be remembered that this was 35 percent of a much higher absolute expenditure.

The percentage of national income going for remuneration of capital (as opposed to labor) increased from 55 percent in 1973 to 64 percent in 1974. Most of the increase was the result of higher levels of state investment. In 1975, the level of gross fixed-capital formation was 46 percent higher than in the previous year, the largest increase in fixed capital during the entire period. The ratio of fixed capital to GDP was 31 percent in 1976, comparable to the level of fixed investment in Japan in 1965.[23]

The strategy behind state investments was clearly to limit state control to "basic" industries, such as petroleum, petrochemicals, iron and steel, and aluminum, and to industrial infrastructure, particularly electrical-power production. While some of these industries were supposed to produce goods for direct consumption or export, most were to provide inputs to domestic private enterprises. The metal-producing industries were particularly important in this regard. Steel was to be used in further exploitation of Venezuela's petroleum reserves, as well as in construction, automobiles, and railroads. Aluminum was to be used primarily in automobile production, especially in the production of lighter engines for fuel-efficient cars. The petrochemical industry had been remarkable for its inefficiency prior to 1973, and no major change occurred during the period studied here. Nevertheless, the goal for the state-controlled petrochemical industry, like that for steel and aluminum, was to provide inputs to domestic private industries at a coat which would make those industries internationally competitive.[24]

It is too early to evaluate the success of this strategy of state investments. The worldwide steel and aluminum industries are both suffering from overcapacity in the global recession which followed the 1979 oil price increases. New steel and aluminum capacity came on line only in the early 1980s. The true test of the success of the strategy will come when domestic and international demand for these metals and their by-products picks up again. Some cautious observations about the Venezuelan strategy can be made, however.

23. Taylor and Hudson, *World Handbook*, p. 341.

24. Michael Rediske, "State Policy and Industrial Development in Venezuela since 1974," discussion paper, University of Konstanz, F.R. Germany, Department of Political Science, 1978.

One important fault in the approach may be its reliance on the private entrepreneurs in Venezuela to capitalize on the lower input costs to produce internationally competitive goods. The structure of domestic private enterprise in Venezuela is strongly oligopolistic, with a small number of industrial groups dominating production in most products.[25] In a few industries, such as automobiles, markets are dominated by foreign multinationals which may or may not decide to increase production in Venezuela. In any case, the strategy depends on the ability of state-controlled basic industries to deliver industrial inputs at low cost, which in turn depends on the ability of the state to assure competent management and to limit wage increases in those industries. The pressure on state enterprises to increase profits may mitigate against delivering low-cost inputs to downstream private entrepreneurs.[26]

The state gambled on the future of aluminum and steel, and related industries, in its largest investments after 1973. The size of this gamble was such that if future leaders of the country wished to reorient radically the direction of state investments, they would have to face the writing off of very large sunken costs. They would also risk alienating the private interests which grew up around the new manufacturing industries. In this sense, the pattern of large-scale capital investments of the years after 1973 placed important constraints on the actions of future governments. Nevertheless, the state had become a central actor in the Venezuelan economy and was likely to remain so for a long time to come.

---

25. Meir Merhav, "El Informe Merhav (The Merhav Report)," *Resumen* (in several parts beginning on September 21, 1980). The report was done originally for the government but was not made public until published in *Resumen* because of its highly critical tone. The part which deals with the oligopolistic and concentrated nature of industrial structure begins on p. 22 of the October 5, 1980, issue.

26. Cf. Rediske, "State Policy and Industrial Development."

Summary

Despite the numerous problems mentioned above, the Venezuelan economy is in a vigorous phase of expansion. Industrialization is advancing, although perhaps not as rapidly as hoped, on a sound base of higher levels of capital investment and relatively inexpensive local inputs. There are potential problems in the tendency toward stagnating exports and higher imports, a weak agricultural sector, inflation, and increasing levels of external debt. Unless there are major external shocks, however, these problems are likely to remain potential rather than actual for the next ten years or so. It is impossible to determine from the macroeconomic data alone, however, whether the dynamic growth of the past twenty years translated into better or worse conditions for the majority of the population of Venezuela. In the next section the available information on that question will be examined.

BASIC HUMAN NEEDS

One would expect with the strides made in the macroeconomic performance of the Venezuelan economy that there would be a marked improvement in the living conditions of the majority of Venezuelans. Unfortunately, this does not appear to be the case. While in most respects the majority of Venezuelans are at least as well off as they were prior to 1973, the improvements in the condition of the least well-off have been very modest. In a few key areas, conditions have actually deteriorated. This has occurred despite increased state involvement in the delivery of services to low-income groups.

The historical legacy of poverty in Venezuela is a deep one. Malnutrition, illiteracy, poor housing and healthcare, and an extremely skewed income distribution have their origins in the plantation economy of the colonial era. The shift to petroleum as the major export good in the 1920s and 1930s has created a larger middle-income group and reduced the size of the marginalized sector. There is still a long way to go, however, before Venezuela comes to resemble the richer industrialized countries in the living conditions available to the poorest inhabitants.

What is the evidence concerning improvement in the standard of living for Venezuelans since 1958, especially those with the lowest income levels? The discussion will be organized in the following order: 1) food and nutrition, 2) health, 3) housing, 4) education, and 5) employment. The first three subjects may be considered to refer to "core" basic needs, needs which if not fulfilled can kill or physically harm the person. The next two subjects are also basic needs, in the sense that individuals living in industrializing capitalist economies cannot assure for themselves the fulfillment of core needs on a sustainable basis without them. Changes in the distribution of income and wealth will be discussed, and a review of government policies designed to deal with problems in basic needs provision will be given.[27]

Food and Nutrition
Malnutrition in Venezuela is a major problem primarily for small children and infants of low-income families. The main nutritional problem is an insufficient daily intake of calories

27. Throughout this section, I will be referring frequently to a book published by Michel Chossudovsky entitled *La Miseria en Venezuela* (Valencia, Venezuela: Vadell Hermanos, 1977). Chossudovsky is a Chilean sociologist who was commissioned by the planning ministry, CORDIPLAN, to conduct a study of socio-economic conditions among poor people. There he wrote a report which was too controversial for publication as a CORDIPLAN document, so it was published independently as a book. Needless to say, Chossudovsky was very critical of the policies of the Venezuelan government. Although some of his statistics are now out of date, his information, from a wide variety of sources, is more extensive than any previous author on this subject has assembled. "The Merhav Report" updated some of Chossudovsky's statistics and will also be cited frequently below.

(protein intake is less of a problem). The primary determinant of malnutrition seems to be family income. As income decreases, the gap between actual consumption and minimum requirements increases. Nevertheless, there is some evidence that educational programs can have a positive effective on nutrition among low-income groups.

Various studies suggest that about half the children less than five years old suffer from some form of malnutrition; about 1 percent have severe forms and 10−15 percent moderate forms of malnutrition.[28] The frequency of malnutrition stays about the same for elementary school children, but begins to decrease as children reach adolescence. The mortality rate for children less than five years old where death is attributed to malnutrition remained approximately constant from 1946 to 1976.[29] Malnutrition is a major cause of high death rates among small children, suggesting that prenatal nutritional programs are needed to attack this problem. Such a program was initiated in the late 1970s by the Perez government. Severe malnutrition results in mental retardation, affects the physical size of children, and reduces the ability of the individual to be physically active. Some employers complain that a large proportion of their workers suffer from malnutrition.[30]

Thus, it can be concluded that while Venezuelans are probably better off on the whole in the 1970s than they were in previous decades, the needs of the society have changed in such a way as to focus more attention on the problem of malnutrition. In order to pursue the goal of industrial deepening, it will be necessary to make greater progress in eliminating malnutrition, if only to assure the productivity of the labor force.

28. Merhav, "Merhav Report," *Resumen,* September 21, 1980, p. 18, gives higher estimates of the incidence of malnutrition among small children based on physiological data.

29. FEDECAMARAS, *XXXIII Asamblea.,* table 13.

30. Merhav, "Merhav Report," *Resumen,* September 21, 1980, p. 19.

Health

Health problems are highly related to nutrition in Venezuela because of the connection between infant mortality and malnutrition. In terms of adult health problems, Venezuela resembles developed countries more than other developing countries in the relative frequency of traffic accidents, heart attacks, and so on in the list of primary causes of death. Nevertheless, there are severe inequities in the delivery of health-care services to the Venezuelan population. Predictably, the lowest-income groups receive the least care; quantity and quality improves as one goes up the income ladder.

Private care is beyond the means of the majority of the population. Working-class families and middle-class families can subscribe to the Venezuelan Institute for Social Security (IVSS). The number of subscribers has increased rapidly since 1968, and especially since 1973.[31] Those who are not covered by this system depend on the services of the Ministry of Health and Social Aid. Only between 5 and 8 percent of the population can afford private medical care, and only about 25 *percent* are covered by the IVSS.[32] This leaves around two-thirds of the population dependent on the Ministry of Health. The facilities of the Ministry of Health are notoriously deficient in terms of number of medical personnel, hospital beds, medicines, and equipment. Despite the rapid rate of population growth in Venezuela, the number of public hospital beds has remained almost constant since 1958. When new hospitals are constructed, rooms are too expensive for middle- or lower-income groups. A large number of small private clinics, with adequate staff and facilities, have been built in recent years. Doctors usually shirk their practices in public hospitals in favor of highly remunerative private practices.[33]

In rural areas and in urban settlements, health care is very inadequate. Here the main problem is one of getting

31. Ministerio del Trabajo, *Memoria y Cuenta 1977*, ch. 5, p. 8.
32. *Ibid.*
33. See Chossudovsky, *La Miseria*, ch. 4.

health facilities located near the areas of greatest need. There also seems to be a tendency toward overspecialization. In 1070, for example, of the 2920 doctors employed in IVSS, only 776 were general practitioners while 2144 were specialists.[34] Despite these very difficult problems of health-care delivery, indicators of infant mortality and life expectancy showed modest gains during the years since 1958. Thus, while health care has improved for most Venezuelans over the past few decades, there is considerable room for improvement in health care for the impoverished.

Housing

One-third of the population of Venezuela lives in urban settlements called *barrios marginales* (marginal districts). The modal form of housing in these districts is the *rancho,* the Venezuelan word for a very simple dwelling, originally made of cardboard, corrugated iron, wood, or whatever, but now increasingly made of bricks or cinder blocks with metal instead of straw roofs. According to the official statistics, the percentage of dwellings which are classified as *ranchos* declined from 60.9 percent in 1941 to 22.1 percent in 1976. The number of units with straw roofs, earth floors, and no electricity, running water, or toilet has decreased markedly over the same period.[35] Nevertheless, there still remains a core of very poor urban settlements in every metropolitan area.

There are two polar types of urban settlements: those with improved *ranchos* located on stable soils and those with recently and poorly constructed *ranchos* placed precariously on unstable soils in the most unfavorable locations. About a quarter of the dwellings in poorest urban settlements in Venezuela fall in the latter category. There are fewer of them in provincial cities than in Caracas.[36]

34. *Ibid.,* p. 114.

35. See Paez Celis, in Bond, ed., *Contemporary Venezuela,* p. 70.

36. Fundacion para el Desarrollo de la Communidad y Fomento Municipal (FUNDACOMUN), *La Vivienda en las Areas Marginales Urbanas* (Caracas: June 1978), p. 11.

The people who live in the poorest urban settlements are people who migrated from the rural interior of the country in the hope of finding better economic opportunities. There has been a "push" factor in the declining returns to farming of certain export crops like beef and coffee. Population pressures in rural areas also make urban migration more attractive. In general, Venezuelan agriculture has become more capital-intensive and landholdings have increased in average size. Whether this is the cause or the result of massive urban migration is not clear, but the result is that the percentage of population living in towns of 1000 or more increased from 39 percent in 1941 to 76 percent in 1971.[37]

In recent years, illegal immigrants from neighboring countries like Colombia and Trinidad have come to occupy some of the newer and less-desirable settlements. There already is a "ghetto-like" flavor to some of these settlements. Their inhabitants suffer from high rates of unemployment, illiteracy, crime, mortality, illegitimacy, malnutrition, and all the other ills of urban poverty. High rates of inflation in housing prices after 1973, especially in urban centers, have been particularly costly to the poorest. It is not unknown for the most primitive *ranchos* to be sold for thousands of dollars.

Even though housing conditions appear to have improved somewhat for the poorest people in Venezuela, relatively permanent pockets of urban poverty are developing in all of Venezuela's major cities. The inhabitants of these districts are "marginal" in both the economic and the political sense. Urban marginalization in Venezuela is more a consequence of the inability of the existing economic system more rapidly to reverse the legacy of extreme poverty inherited from the prepetroleum past, than of a progressive deterioration in preexisting conditions. A more important

37. Oficina Central de Estadistica e Informatica, *Encuesta,* p. 40–45.

form of marginalization is taking place in the educational system.

Education

The most severe problems for Venezuela in the area of basic needs exist in the area of education. While the rate of illiteracy decreased markedly from 49 percent in 1950 to under 20 percent in 1977,[38] the Venezuelan population remained largely undereducated, given its requirements for skilled or semi-skilled workers. Of the literate population in 1975, more than half had attended only primary school.[39] Many became literate only after they left school. There was a serious shortage of teachers at all levels. Vocational and technical schools were understaffed and used outdated curricula. Colleges and universities tended to underproduce in the managerial, technical, and scientific fields (with the possible exception of petroleum engineering).

In 1975, 56.1 percent of the population were under twenty years of age. The medium age was seventeen. The age structure of Venezuela was highly skewed toward youth. Recent baby booms exacerbated this situation, creating heavy demands for expansion of primary and secondary schools. Despite increased demand, the percentage of school-age children who entered preschools or primary schools increased from 62.3 percent in 1973 to 70.5 percent in 1976.[40] The figures were slightly higher for urban areas and much lower for rural areas. Only half of the students who entered primary school were promoted to the sixth grade in the normal period of time. Dropout rates were highest in the primary schools and decreased as students progressed to secondary and university levels. As in other countries, the structure of school attendance was linked with

38. Paez Celis, p. 32.
39. *Ibid.*, p. 33.
40. Banco Central de Venezuela, *Informe Economico 1976*, p. A217.

the distribution of income and wealth. The level of education of individuals in Venezuela not only affected wages and income levels, but also the likelihood of employment.

In sum, the poorest Venezuelans are only marginally better off than they have been in previous decades. They face an educational system which, for the most part, has no room for them. The rigidity of the educational structure is likely to be a major impediment to the industrial-deepening strategy, as it guarantees a shortage of skilled workers. By limiting social mobility, it also serves to protect the less-than-perfectly competitive nature of private enterprise in Venezuela.

Employment

The statistics on employment and unemployment, unreliable as they may be for certain periods, indicate that Venezuela suffered very high levels of unemployment during the recessions of the 1960s but was able to reduce the level of unemployment rapidly after 1973. The rate of unemployment was around 5 percent in 1977,[41] giving rise to the claim on the part of the incumbent party that the government had attained "full employment." There was still a high level of "underemployment" in the Venezuelan economy, however, at least in the sense that a large proportion of the working force (around 20 percent) earned less than the legally mandated minimum wage.

Rural employment decreased steadily over this period. Employment in petroleum, mining, and utilities also decreased, but at a slower rate than in agriculture. The major

41. Statistics on employment and unemployment can be found in the following sources: Banco Central de Venezuela, *La Economia Venezolana en los Ultimos Treinta Anos;* Oficina Central de Estadistica e Informatica, *Encuesta de Hogares por Muestreo;* International Labour Organization, *Yearbook of Labour Statistics;* and Banco Central de Venezuela, *Informe Economico.* Recent estimates of unemployment depend on calculations by the author of unemployment based on estimates of the size of the labor force (x), the number of people employed (y), and the formula for the unemployment rate: $100\,(1-y/x)$.

sources of dynamism in employment were the manufacturing, construction, and transportation sectors. After 1973 there was a rapid increase in employment in the iron and steel industry. The service sectors expanded more rapidly than all the others, however, which raised questions about the sustainability of low unemployment rates in the face of declining oil revenues. A number of the industries which accounted for the rapid rise in employment in recent years (e.g., textiles, shoes, metalworking, and printing) experienced high rates of turnover in their labor forces.

There is no question that most Venezuelans are better off now than they were in previous decades in terms of opportunities for employment. However, problems in nutrition and education mean that the jobs available to Venezuelans are not as well paying as they might have been had there been a better fed and educated labor force.

The Distribution of Income
Although there are several competent studies of income distribution in Venezuela, most do not address the question of whether the post-1973 petrodollar bonanza and/or government policies have reduced income inequalities. They do indicate, however, that the distribution of income in Venezuela is very unequal. The World Bank reported that the wealthiest 10 percent of the households in Venezuela earned 41.2 percent of the total income in 1962, while the wealthiest 10 percent of the economically active population earned 51.2 percent of total income in 1971. On the basis of this, and three other surveys, the World Bank concluded that inequality increased between 1962 and 1971.[42] Eva Josko de Gueron, in a study of regional inequality found no change or a decrease in inequality in the distribution of income

42. Shail Jain, *Size Distribution of Income* (Washington, D.C.: World Bank, 1975), p. 118; Lourdes Urdaneta, *Distribucion del Ingreso: Analisis del Caso Venezolano* (Caracas: Banco Central, 1977), p. 337. Urdaneta found some evidence for a decline in inequality.

across regions; but within regions, rural/urban inequality increased markedly.[43] After 1974 the degree of sectorial inequality decreased as other economic sectors caught up with petroleum.[44]

Recent statistics on the monthly income levels of non-agricultural workers, collected in a semi-annual survey, showed that increases in the real incomes of the poorest employed people had increased since 1974.[45] Nevertheless, despite these increases, it has been estimated that as many as two thirds of the labor force do not earn enough to pay for a diet which would meet minimal nutritional standards.[46] Thus, Venezuelans are probably not much better off in terms of income distribution than they were before the oil price increases.

The State and Basic Needs
Between 1958 and 1978, but especially after 1973, the Venezuelan government adopted a number of measures which were designed to supplement large-scale, capital-intensive industrialization in meeting the basic needs of the population: 1) an ambitious land-reform program, 2) subsidies for consumers and price guarantees for producers of basic food items, 3) special subsidized-low-interest loans for small and medium-size industries, 4) New methods for delivering governmental services to poor people in "marginal districts," and 5) a scholarship program to increase the supply of skilled personnel through attendance of foreign universities.

Soon after the elections in 1958, a land-reform program was adopted. The land reform of the Betancourt administration was partly a way of paying back the peasants who had supported the AD party in the 1958 elections. But it was

43. Personal communication.
44. Calculations based on Central Bank statistics.
45. Oficina Central de Estadistica e Informatica, *Encuesta de Hogares por Muestreo,* various volumes (1975 through 1977).
46. Merhav, "Merhav Report," *Resumen,* September 21, 1980, p. 21.

also a response to the urgent need to deal with rural-urban migration and rapidly rising imports of food. Prior to 1958 the ownership of land was highly concentrated in large landholdings. Nearly 80 percent of the land was accounted for by approximately 5,000 large landholdings.

Agrarian reform, it was hoped, would keep more *campesinos* (peasants) back on the farm where they could at least be producing food for themselves rather than merely consuming . . . a basic principle of the reform was that productive agricultural units would generally not be affected.[47]

In order to accomplish these aims, the government distributed public lands and lands which were owned privately but had not been under cultivation. Even though about 140,000 families eventually received small plots of land, another 300,000 families or more might have benefited from land ownership. Title to the land distributed was withheld in many cases, leaving the new owners in a precarious legal position. Given the quality of land distributed, the size of the holdings, the absence of technical aid or adequate finances, it could be argued that the land reform increased the duality of the agricultural sector. Still, at great expense to the public treasury, a large number of *compesinos* were better off than they had been before 1958.

Under the Agricultural Debt Relief Law of 1974, farmers were exonerated of all debts owed to government agencies. Private debts were consolidated through state loans at 3 percent interest with up to 30 years to pay. A tax reform decree issued in 1974 exempted farmers and food processors from all income taxes. Banks were freed from paying taxes on profits from low-interest loans to the agricultural inputs, and placed price controls on raw materials needed for farming. The Agriculture-Livestock Credit Institute (ICAP) and the Agricultural Development Bank (BANDAGRO) ad-

47. Howard Handelman, *Scarcity Amidst Plenty: Food Problems in Oil-Rich Venezuela*, Report No. 42 (Hanover, N.H.: American University Field Staff, 1978), p. 3.

ministered a special fund created by the president in June
1974. ICAP made loans to small and medium-sized farmers, BANDAGRO to large landowners. Both offered loans at
substantially lower rates than commercial banks, but ICAP
rates were lower than BANDAGRO's.[48]

In 1973 the government established an agricultural
marketing corporation (called CORPOMERCADEO) in order
to set minimum prices for agricultural producers while at
the same time selling food products at fixed prices on the
retail market. Thus, CORPOMERCADEO was designed to
guarantee a high level of return to farmers at the same time
as it subsidized the food consumption of poorer urban
dwellers. When domestic producers could not produce
enough to meet demand, CORPOMERCADEO was authorized to purchase the necessary items abroad. A major portion of CORPOMERCADEO's budget for food subsidies in
1979 (71 percent of 181 million dollars) went for the purchase of milk products on international markets used in a
special program to reduce malnutrition in newborns and
young children. The total budget of CORPOMERCADEO was
over $1200 million in 1978, having approximately doubled
every year since 1974.[49]

The Corporation for the Development of Small and Medium-Sized Industry (CORPOINDUSTRIA) loaned funds at low
interest rates to a variety of smaller businesses. In 1977
CORPOINDUSTRIA made over two thousand loans to small
businessmen, mostly artisans, totaling only 6.3 million dollars. Loans to small manufacturing conerns totaled 125 million dollars.[50] These loans, although quite small compared
to those made by giant public financial organizations like
the Central Bank, the Venezuelan Industrial Bank, and the
Venezuelan Investment Fund, had a direct effect on the
quality of life of some low-income Venezuelans. One exam-

48. *Ibid.*, pp. 7–8.
49. *Ibid.*, p. 9.
50. Banco Central de Venezuela, *Informe Economico 1977* (Caracas: 1977),
p. 201.

ple is the rapid increase in the number of owner-operated minibuses (called *por puestos*) which carry around approximately fifteen people on assigned routes for a fixed price of one bolivar (22 cents) per person. CORPOINDUSTRIA also helped to finance a number of new firms in the machining and metalworking industries.

One of the ironies of the attempt to subsidize food consumption was that poor people often had to ride a bus for many miles to reach one of the markets set up by CORPO-MERCADEO. As a consequence, some of the poorest people in Venezuela had to rely on corner grocery stores to supply them with food at higher prices than those paid by the wealthy in their fancy supermarkets. The Perez administration established the Foundation for the Development of the Community and for Municipal Promotion (FUNDACOMUN) in 1974 to improve the delivery of essential services to the urban settlements.[51] The main channel for this was the *modulo de servico* (service module). Around 1800 service modules were to be placed in urban districts of approximately 40,000 inhabitants. Each module was to provide the following services: 1) health and social assistance; 2) markets for basic food items; 3) police protection; 4) day-care centers; 5) preschools; 6) libraries; 7) cultural and recreational activities; and 8) technical assistance for those wishing to establish small businesses. The government placed a high priority on the program, as indicated in budgeting and staffing. In the first year of its operation, FUNDACOMUN spent around 90 million dollars on the *modulos*. The director of FUNDA-COMUN until 1978 was Sonia Perez Rodriguez, daughter of the President.[52]

51. The legal basis for FUNDACOMUN was established by a presidential decree (No. 332) issued on August 13, 1974. The text of the decree can be found in the *Gaceta Oficial*, no. 30, p. 471. An instructive, number 29 of February 10, 1977, names FUNDACOMUN as the agency responsible for carrying out the tasks outlined in Decree No. 332 (see *Gaceta Oficial*, no. 31, p. 172). President Perez was widely criticized for the excessive use of presidential decrees.

52. FUNDACOMUN, *Los Modulos de Servicios: Un programa para los Asentamientos Marginales Urbanos* (Caracas: October 1977); interview materials.

To some extent, FUNDACOMUN was a bureaucrat's nightmare. Existing state agencies were supposed to provide services at the modules: e.g., the Ministry of Health was to provide health care, CORPOMERCADEO merchandise for the food stores, etc. It was not clear how FUNDACOMUN was going to handle the tricky jurisdictional problems raised by this arrangement or to coordinate the activities of all those disparate agencies. As of 1978, however, most of the modules only supplied police protection and day-care facilities. The best equipped modules tended predictably to be in districts where the governing party had the strongest support.

Besides the inevitable jurisdictional disputes and clientelism, FUNDACOMUN suffered from a more fundamental problem: the tendency of the Venezuelan government to adopt paternalistic patterns of interaction with poor people. Relatively little effort had been made to coordinate FUNDACOMUN programs with the local leadership and the citizens of the barrios. The prevailing image was one of extending the beneficent arm of the presidency (and the presidential party) into the barrios without undue interference from local leaders.[53]

While the policies discussed above were clearly aimed at meeting the basic needs of Venezuelans, especially the marginalized population, some basic needs were being sadly neglected. After 1975, for example, the rate of construction of public housing units dropped considerably, despite an urgent need for more housing. The National Institute of Housing (INAVI) tended to build units for middle-class occupants rather than for lower-income families. In comparison with the housing program of a poorer country like Colombia, Venezuelan public housing policy was sorely lacking in a basic needs orientation.[54]

After 1973 the Venezuelan government attempted to

53. Interview materials.
54. Howard Handelman, *High Rises and Shantytowns: Housing the Poor in Bogota and Caracas,* Report No. 9 (Hanover, N.H.: American Universities Field Staff, 1979).

deal with the problem of restricted access to higher education through the building of new colleges and universities
within Venezuela and through a scholarship program for attendance at foreign universities (the Gran Mariscal de Ayacucho Program). The Gran Mariscal de Ayacucho Program had
two main goals: (1) to increase the supply of skilled personnel, and (2) to reverse the pattern of privileged access to
higher education.[55] In pursuing the second aim, the program was instructed to choose a certain proportion of students from lower- and middle-income groups, leading some
Venezuelans to criticize it for not choosing the "best" students. It was not clear how the program would avoid the
usual problems of brain drain, maldistribution of occupa-
tional training, and posteducational placement that plagued
other developing countries' foreign scholarship programs.
It was an indication, however, of rigidities in the Venezuelan
educational system and social structure that the government was forced to resort to such a program to attack the
problem of privileged access.

While overall there was an acceptance of the basic human-needs philosophy within important parts of the Venezuelan state, it tended to be a paternalistic version of that
philosophy. The Venezuelan government gave a higher
priority to large-scale, capital-intensive industrialization than
to basic needs. The basic-needs programs it did support
were grossly inadequate in two areas crucial to the continued industrialization of the country, housing and education.
To explain why this was so the relations between the Venezuelan state and other major social actors need to be examined more closely.

Summary
The initial stages of industrialization in Venezuela produced
hardships for the poorest people, as evidenced by the rapid

55. *La Fundacion "Gran Mariscal de Ayacucho"* (Caracas: Ministerio de Edu-
cacion, 1977), p. 241.

rate of migration to the cities and increases in unemployment during periods of industrial growth. The legacy of the past, in terms of high rates of illiteracy and income inequality, poor schools and unequal delivery of social services, created tremendous potential obstacles to the sustained economic development of the country. With the great influx of petroleum revenues after 1973, however, modest improvements in nutrition, health care, housing, employment opportunities, and incomes occurred. Educational opportunities remained severely restricted, however, and the sustainability of other social gains was still in question despite a major increase in government activities to provide basic needs. The question this raises, given the attenuation of external constraints on Venezuelan development, is: What were the domestic social and economic constraints which prevented the post-1973 petroleum gains from being translated more rapidly into improved welfare for the poorest Venezuelans?

VENEZUELA'S POLICY NETWORK

Since 1958, the Venezuelan political system has been predicated on the existence of a "policy network" in which the state and the private business sector dominate all other social groups. Because the party in power controls the state, the two parties which have been in power, Accion Democratica (AD) and the Christian Democratic party (COPEI), must also be included in a description of Venezuela's policy network. While peasants figured early in the rise of AD to electoral power, as did workers in the petroleum industry, the rest of the labor force plays only a minor role in party politics, and is therefore excluded from the dominant coalition. Further industrialization of the country will call this arrangement into question.

The Power of the State
It has already been demonstrated that the government and the semi-autonomous state enterprises account for a very large percentage of national production and investment. Since 1973 the state has become involved much more extensively in the provision of basic necessities as well. The main pillar of state power, beginning with the initial concessions of the 1920s and lasting at least until the enactment of a progressive income tax in the late 1970s, was its ability to control a portion of the revenues from petroleum exploitation. The state's power increased between the 1920s and 1973 because it was able to extract a larger share of those revenues, mainly through increased taxes. The activism of the Venezuelan state in helping to found and strengthen the Organization of Petroleum Exporting Countries (beginning in the early 1960s) paid off in 1973 when OPEC agreed to quadruple the price of petroleum on world markets. The nationalization of the petroleum industry in 1975 was a turning point. After that point, further increments in state power would have to come largely from measures taken outside the sphere of petroleum politics.

After 1973 the state pushed for a diversification of the economy and for a broadening of its own tax base through the passage of a progressive income tax for individuals and businesses. The urgency of this diversification was increased by the widespread perception of the beginning of the end of cheap extraction of petroleum from existing reserves. But it would have occurred anyway, given the elite consensus on the need to replace the petroleum economy with a more diversified industrial economy, or, as the slogan went, to "sow the petroleum."

The international political strategy that went along with this domestic program was one of strong advocacy of reforms in the international economic order. Venezuela, in the person of Manuel Perez Guerrero, was one of the most important leaders of the group of moderate countries in the

Group of 77 which were pushing for agreements on specific proposals: an integrated program for commodities; a common fund to finance commodity agreements; inproved access to the markets of developed countries for the exports of developing countries; renegotiation and rescheduling of debt payments; less-expensive methods for transferring technology; and increased power of LDC-dominated institutions within the UN system (just to name the more important proposals).[56] Venezuela also pushed for changes in the regional and subregional trade regimes which would allow it to have access to larger markets in promoting its industrial exports.[57]

Venezuela's position on these questions was conditioned by its desire to defend the favorable terms of trade in petroleum while making it possible to export nontraditional exports in the future. Since Venezuela is not a low-wage country, relative to the rest of the developing world, it had to base its strategy on the feasibility of converting low resource-costs into comparative advantages through heavy state investments in basic industries and utilities. That these investments were highly capital intensive and involved long payback times was inconvenient politically because it militated against rapid improvements in the living conditions of the poorest people. Nevertheless, given Venezuela's wage structure—another legacy of the petroleum era—its resource base, and its integration into the world economy, there were few alternatives to such a strategy.

The most curious aspect of the post-1973 strategy is the state's careful avoidance of direct involvement in the development of manufacturing industries that would benefit from the state's development of basic industries and utilities. To understand this choice, it is necessary to have a

56. See Jeffrey Hart, *The New International Economic Order* (New York: St. Martin's Press, 1983), chs. 2 and 4.

57. Robert D. Bond, *Business Associations and Interest Politics in Venezuela: The FEDECAMARAS and the Determination of National Economic Policies* (Ph.D. diss., Vanderbilt University, 1975).

better description of the role of private business in the Venezuelan policy network.

The Power of Business

While the power of the state grew, the power of domestic private business groups also increased. Foreign private firms were responsible for developing and managing the petroleum industry, the most important single industry in the country, from the 1920s until (and some would say after) the nationalization in 1975. The adoption of an import-substitution policy in 1958 led not only to the growth of a more diversified set of domestic businesses, but also to an influx of new foreign capital in manufacturing. Gradually, the balance of power in the business community shifted away from the foreign and traditional domestic firms to the more dynamic and nontraditional domestic manufacturing firms. Conincident with this shift in power within the business community was a greater tendency of the state to co-opt new business groups through the use of contracts and selective reductions of import duties.

The main organizational expression of private business interests in Venezuela is FEDECAMARAS (the Federation of Chambers of Commerce). This organization was founded in 1943, more out of the fear of an expanding state than by a perceived need to confront a growing labor movement.[58] FEDECAMARAS played a key role in opposing the AD-dominated experiment in democracy between 1945 and 1948, despite efforts to co-opt the business group on a variety of decision-making bodies, because the business community considered the AD party to be too radical and antibusiness. The lesson was learned, and when the military government of Perez Jimenez ended in 1958, the three main parties (AD, COPEI, and URD) agreed not only to govern by coalition, but to align with all domestic groups (including business and the military) whose support was needed to maintain a dem-

58. *Ibid.*, p. 60.

ocratic government and to adopt an import-substitution strategy for industrialization.[59]

The political cost of the alignment with business and the military was the alienation of the left wing of AD and, along with the recession of the early 1960s, the encouragement of radical elements in Venezuela to emulate the Cuban revolution by forming small guerrilla groups. Although the guerrilla struggle persisted late into the 1960s, there was little prospect of a revolutionary takeover. Almost no major group in Venezuelan society (including the peasantry) had a stake in undermining the new regime. They correctly saw the alternative to be a return to military dictatorship.

Within FEDECAMARAS there was increased conflict between commercial and industrial interests over import substitution. The interests of the former dictated opposition to new tariff barriers, while the interests of the latter dictated strong support. The government attempted to increase support for import substitution by participating in the formation of Asociacion Pro-Venezuela, an organization which included representatives of private business, the military, and the Church. Pro-Venezuela, while very influential with respect to government policies during the Betancourt administration, never replaced FEDECAMARAS as the main articulator of business interests. By the time of the election of a COPEI President in 1969, Pro-Venezuela was on the decline.[60]

Governmental encouragement of import-substituting industries began to have an effect on industrial structure in the mid- and late 1960s. Industries with 100 or more employees increased from 196 in 1961 to 325 in 1966. Foreign investment accounted for 22 percent of total investment in manufacturing in 1966.[61] Foreign investors tended

59. David Eugene Blank, *Politics in Venezuela* (Boston: Little, Brown, 1973), pp. 26–28; Daniel Levine, *Conflict and Political Change in Venezuela* (Princeton: Princeton University Press, 1973), pp. 43–49.

60. Bond, *Business Associations*, pp. 74 and 84–90.

61. *Ibid.*, p. 90.

to concentrate on dynamic and high-technology industries: petrochemicals, aluminum, automotive equipment, etc. Domestic investors maintained control of traditional industries as well as a growing number of more sophisticated ones, such as agricultural machinery and the metalworking industries. Manufacturing production was concentrated in a relatively small number of large firms: the 325 firms with 100 or more employees in 1966 accounted for 66 percent of production. The number of organizations designed to represent the interests of industrial firms increased sharply, as did the representation of these firms within FEDECAMARAS.

By the end of the 1960s, Venezuela was reaching the end of the easy phase of import-substituting industralization. There was excess capacity in the consumer goods industries and an erosion of the dynamism of the early 1960s. Major industries tended to have an oligopolistic market structure. Some large private groups owned a very diversified set of concerns, which had two main effects: (1) it reduced the effective size of the Venezuelan entrepreneurial elite; and (2) it created incentives for greater unity across industries and sectors.[62] With few exceptions, neither the price nor the quality of many Venezuelan products could compete with that of goods produced elsewhere.

Petroleum revenues declined in the mid-1960s because of reduced capital investments and competition from Middle East production. In 1966, the Leoni administration tried to counter the effects of the decline in petroleum revenues by increasing yet again the government's share of the profits from oil exploitation. Its error however was to combine this with an attempt to reform the income tax laws. The result, predictably, was an alliance between the foreign oil companies and FEDECAMARAS. FEDECAMARAS had not been completely independent of the oil firms previously. The oil companies contributed both funds and personnel to the or-

62. James A. Hanson, "Cycles of Economic Growth and Structural Changes Since 1950," in John Martz and David Myers, eds., *Venezuela: The Democratic Experience* (New York: Praeger, 1977), p. 76.

ganization from time to time. In 1966, however, a major campaign to publicize the concerns of business was financed jointly with unprecedentedly large contributions from the oil companies.[63]

When the Leoni government negotiated a separate compromise agreement with the oil companies with respect to back taxes, the latter abandoned their opposition to the tax reform. Although FEDECAMARAS managed to get most of the concessions they wanted from the government, they naturally felt unhappy about the behavior of the oil companies in this matter. After 1966, FEDECAMARAS became much more the representative of nationalist business concerns and less an agent of foreign business interests.[64]

The events of 1966 also underlined the importance of Venezuelan private business groups of maintaining a unified and confident stance in confrontations with the government. The next major conflict between business and state involved the adherence of Venezuela to the Andean Pact, a subregional integration accord which arose out of dissatisfaction with earlier regional integration schemes like LAFTA (the Latin American Free Trade Association). Because of the vulnerability of Venezuelan industry to increased trade with the relatively lower-wage and more efficient economies of the Andean Group, FEDECAMARAS took a strong position against adherence to the Pact as originally drafted. The Leoni administration, which began the debate in 1968, did not feel

63. Bond, *Business Associations*, pp. 187–89.
64. See Franklin Tugwell, *The Politics of Oil in Venezuela* (Stanford: Stanford University Press, 1975), pp. 86–95. Fred Jongkind has written a series of unpublished papers on the relative strength of foreign and national firms in the Venezuelan economy. See his "Venezuelan Industrial Development: Dependent or Autonomous?" (Amsterdam: Center for Latin American Research and Documentation, October 1978). Jongkind argues that national firms are strong relative to foreign firms in Venezuela, but his survey design does not allow one to gauge the importance or dynamism of national versus foreign firms. Some evidence that foreign firms use more modern management techniques can be found in his "Modern management methods in Venezuelan industry," paper presented to the workshop on Comparative Research on Organizations and Society in Brussels on March 13–15, 1978.

strong enough to push the issue prior to the elections of that year. The Caldera administration delayed action and then more or less adopted the FEDECAMARAS position on renegotiating the accord. The result was that the other Andean Pact countries rejected the Venezuelan application for membership. The Caldera administration was then roundly criticized by the opposition parties, led by AD, for being too closely associated with FEDECAMARAS. Caldera responded by attempting to generate broader political support for membership in the Andean Group. But in the end, when Venezuela finally joined in 1973, most of FEDECAMARAS' goals had been integrated into the government's program.[65]

The victory of FEDECAMARAS in these two disputes was strong evidence of the independence and the strength of the private domestic business sector within the Venezuelan policy network. It was also evidence of the increasing power of manufacturing interests relative to that of commercial and agricultural interests within the business sector. Whereas FEDECAMARAS had initially opposed the entry of Venezuela into the Andean Group altogether, it came later to modify that stance by making entry conditional on protection of certain key industries. The more internationalist perspective of the major manufacturing interests within FEDECAMARAS prevailed over the more nationalistic perspective of commercial and agricultural interests.

After 1973, a number of important changes in the Venezuelan "policy network" followed the rapid rise in petroleum revenues. Although the state now had greater resources than ever before at its disposal, it became even more dependent on the good will of the private business sector than it had been previously. The parties remained dependent on business to provide the massive sums required to pursue a successful electoral campaign. The previous attempts to build up a domestic, and basically nationalistic, entrepreneurial sector had succeeded to such an

65. Bond, *Business Associations,* pp. 232–61.

extent that important economic policies could not be pursued without the approval of that sector. The inability of the government to obtain a relatively moderate income-tax reform without prior business approval, strong and effective business opposition to the price controls used by the government to combat growing inflation rates after 1973, and resistance to implementation of the Auto Policy Law of 1975 were all examples of the growing power of private domestic business.[66] The state attempted to create new levers of control over private business. The Perez administration used its powers to grant exemptions from import duties to specific firms to reward those entrepreneurs who supported it politically. The owners of firms in the metalworking industry and their bankers were especially favored in this way. The alliance between the state and this particular group of private businessmen was likely, given the latter's dependence on state policies with repect to the publicly owned basic metals industries.

Thus, the simultaneous growth of power of the state and domestic business created a situation of mutual dependence. This mutual dependence explains in part the post-1973 strategy of combining state control over basic industries and utilities with private domestic control over downstream industries. The state, while more powerful than it had ever been before, found itself in the late 1970s to be more dependent on the private business sector than it had been since the 1920s.

Labor: Excluded from the Network
In 1947 the government organized the Worker's Confederation of Venezuela (CTV), which remained the largest and most powerful labor organization in the country, despite its suppression during the 1948–58 dictatorship. It is worth noting that the state and the governing party were the main

---

66. Coronil and Skurski, "Reproducing Dependency."

forces behind the formation of the CTV. AD had gained strength among labor groups during the military dictatorships prior to 1945, especially in the oil fields of Maracaibo. In a way, the formation of the CTV was a way of giving greater cohesion and formal status to the already existing AD-oriented unions. It was also an attempt on the part of the state and AD to preempt independent labor organizations by continuing the semi-corporatistic modes of interaction with labor which had been adopted previously by the military regimes of Lopez Contreras and Medina Angarita.

A state which promoted a diversified economy in alliance with private business was likely to confront an increasingly strong and militant labor movement. There were several reasons why this should be so. First, and most obvious, a promoter state would be less likely to ally itself with state- or party-organized labor unions against private business in labor disputes, thus losing support for those unions among the rank and file.

Evidence that this had already begun to occur could be found in the speech by President Perez to the annual assembly of FEDECAMARAS in 1977:

Already we have observed how certain extremist radical sectors that do not obey any of the legalized parties are infiltrating themselves into the company unions, taking away the authority and importance of the Confederation of Venezuelan Workers (CTV) and giving it to the unions organized to provoke anarchical situations that create permanent conflict between capital and labor. The government fulfills its responsibilities by confronting this situation; the CTV by combating these anarchoid movements; the national business sector by satisfying the just requirements of the labor sector in Venezuela, in order thus to give strength to the democratic sindical movement.[67]

One response of the government to the challenges of growing labor militancy was to seek new laws guaranteeing the rights of unions to engage in collective bargaining. The

---

67. FEDECAMARAS, *XXXIII Asamblea Anual,* p. 87.

number of contracts and workers affected by contracts increased dramatically over the 1958—76 period, but many strikes remained classified as illegal work stoppages. Another government policy aimed at fostering peaceful labor relations was the promulgation of new laws for minimum wages and for guaranteed severance pay. These laws were strongly criticized by representatives of the business sector. For example, businessmen claimed that the new law for severance pay encouraged high rates of turnover. Thus, when the government of the ruling party tried to win support from labor by granting new concessions, they risked alienating their allies in the private business sector.

Another response to growing labor power, supported by both busingss and government, was to attempt to institutionalize a form of tripartite "concertation" in the setting of major economic policies. During the Perez administration (1973—78) a presidential commission was established in which the president, the head of FEDECAMARAS, and the head of CTV could get together every month to discuss economic policy. There were also local and regional concertation arrangements with the same sort of tripartite representation. One important result of concertation during the Perez administration was an agreement to import 20,000 skilled workers from abroad to work in the new industries in the Guayana region. Government and business were worried that labor would oppose this method of dealing with short-term labor shortages, but a package deal was negotiated which was satisfactory to all.

The main problem with concertation was that it did not allow for representation of any unions which were not allied with the two main political parties, AD and COPEI. The CTV was originally organized by AD, but during the presidency of Rafael Caldera (the leader of COPEI) the CTV came to be less dominated by AD party activists.[68] The reasons for this

68. Cecilia Valente, *The Political, Economic and Labor Climate in Venezuela* (Philadelphia: Wharton School Industrial Research Unit, 1979), p. 188. See also John Martz, "The Growth and Democratization of the Venezuelan Labor Movement," *Inter-American Economic Affairs* (Autumn 1963), 17:3—18.

were straightforward. The CTV needed the support of the state to win major concessions from business, and the state was controlled by COPEI. Thus, party competition in Venezuela helped to foster the growth of bipartisanism in the CTV, but the strength of the state ensured that the CTV would never be fully independent from the two major parties.

The subordination of the CTV to the state and the two parties made it impossible for that organization to adopt a militant posture in certain key industries, thus creating a vacuum which was filled by the unions organized by left-wing parties. An important example of this occurred in the 1977–78 period when leftist parties came to dominate the steelworkers' unions in the Guayana region. SIDOR, the state enterprise for producing steel in Guayana, had been allocated substantial portions of the new state investments designated by the Fifth Plan for the 1976–80 period. Steel and aluminum were to be the basis for a deepening of Venezuelan industrialization; export revenues generated from these two industries were to reduce Venezuela's dependence on the petroleum industry. Yet in the mid- and late 1970s, the wage demands of leftist-oriented unions in the steel industry in Guayana were threatening this vision of the future, at least for steel. The government eventually acceded to the demands of these unions, forcing a reevaluation of the prospects for the growth of exports of steel products and of the availability of domestically produced steel at competitive prices.

The unanticipated result of adopting a policy of state-led industrialization in basic metals, itself partly a consequence of a policy network which incorporated both a strong state and an increasingly powerful private domestic business sector but excluded labor, was to give certain unions an increased bargaining power which could, if the policy network was sufficiently flexible, lead eventually to the incorporation of labor. But the incorporation of labor into the policy network would require a major reorientation in social welfare policies, and in particular a direct attack on problems of education and housing—problems which have not been dealt with effectively in the past. In addition, it would probably result in a major falling out between the state and private business interests which would prefer to maintain the existing policy network. In the absence of such changes, it would be less likely that the deepening of industrialization could proceed or that a less-paternalistic approach to the provision of basic needs could be adopted by the state.

The pattern of successive incorporation of new social groups into the political system since 1958 provides a generally positive perspective on the outlook for the future.[69] However, it is one thing to incorporate new, but basically unchallenging, groups like the peasantry into an electoral system, another to assure that urban industrial workers are represented in a policy network that has previously been dominated by the state and private business. That previous domination was mainly the result of the earlier pattern of linkages between Venezuela and the world economy, especially its dependence on petroleum as the major source of export and government revenues.

CONCLUSIONS

This chapter has examined the nature of the domestic political constraints on industrialization and the meeting of basic human needs in a developing country which has been blessed with relatively lower external constraints than most. The Venezuelan case illustrates how even dependent countries with highly dualistic economies can evolve toward industrialization and begin to develop strategies for addressing human needs. But it also illustrates how even the most fortunate developing countries may come to grief over rigidities in their domestic social systems (their "policy net-

69. For an elaboration of this theme, see Daniel Levine, "Venezuelan Politics: Past and Future," in Bond, ed., *Contemporary Venezuela.*

works") while remaining subject to the vicissitudes of the international economy.

The argument pursued above may be summarized in the following manner. The early development of the petroleum industry in Venezuela made it possible for that country to grow on the basis of capturing increasing shares of the income from petroleum exports. This permitted a strong state to emerge, and, thanks to the adoption of an import substitution strategy in the late 1950s (for primarily political reasons), permitted a politically autonomous and diversified private domestic business sector to displace the foreign petroleum and manufacturing interests in their ability to influence state policies. Import substitution was the only available strategy for industrializing in the 1950s, given the high wages of Venezuelan workers relative to those in other developing countries. A policy network in which the state and private domestic business dominated came to exist as a result.

When the benefits of import substitution diminished and the potential for industrial deepening appeared to increase after the oil price increases of 1973, the state took upon itself the task of developing basic metals and other industrial inputs while delegating to private business the development of downstream industries. While nothing definite can be said yet about the feasibility of this approach, it appears to be stumbling over certain difficulties created by earlier social arrangements.

First, the attempt to shift the structure of production away from petroleum and toward industries dependent on basic metals increases the necessity for accepting a greater role for organized labor in policy networks. Second, it requires a greater investment in human capital than was traditional under the old arrangements. In the absence of a stronger role for organized labor in Venezuela's policy network, state policies toward marginalized groups are likely to continue to be paternalistic and only modestly effective in raising living conditions.

No simple answer to the problem of development in capitalist developing countries emerges from this analysis. A "strong state" alone is not the answer, since a strong state actually may inhibit the growth of an autonomous labor movement. A general commitment to redistributive policies on the part of key elites is not sufficient to overcome the specific constraints imposed by the extant social structure, which excludes those who can represent the workers and the poor. And an awareness of the need to reduce dependence does not suffice actually to accomplish that end, especially if industrialization remains heavily dependent on the development of export markets for manufactured goods.

The developed countries can do a great deal to reduce the external constraints on development in the Third World. They cannot, except at the risk of interventionism, alter the sensitive relationships which slowly evolve among major social forces like the state, private business, labor, the political parties, the military, and other groups. There is often a great deal of dynamism in these relationships. Yet some changes are more likely to be difficult than others. The pursuit of industrialization provides its own dynamic, even in dependent capitalist countries, but it will not lead to more than a token effort to meet the basic needs of the marginalized unless governmental commitment is combined with the organized might of the workers and the poor.

5.

The Limits of Export-Led Development: The Ivory Coast's Experience with Manufactures

LYNN KRIEGER MYTELKA

WITH THE GROWTH of Third World manufacturing activity, it became commonplace to argue that the colonial phase of center-periphery relations characterized by the export of raw materials in exchange for imports of manufactures from the industrialized countries had definitively ended. As Helge Hveem puts it, "[t]he belief that center capital would never permit the periphery to industrialize has turned out to be incorrect."[1]

Increased export-oriented manufacturing in a number of Asian and Latin American countries, moreover, led some to see in periphery industrialization a dynamic process

1. Helge Hveem, in this volume.

moving these countries, at last, along the development path traveled earlier by such late industrializers as Germany and Japan. In contrast, skeptics such as Samir Amin argue that this new phase of industrialization "in no way constitutes a 'step' towards the creation of a self-reliant (autocentric) economy . . . [rather] it prolongs the first extraverted phase."[2] The analysis of African industrialization presented here tends to support Amin's position, and thereby provides evidence for those advocating a need for selective delinking of African economies from the present international economic system.

While the existence of some industrial activity in Africa is not challenged, this paper does question the *nature* of the industrialization process currently underway there. It does so by situating the move towards export-led manufacturing in Africa in both the historical context of African development, and in terms of the changing relationship of Europe to Africa. The first and second sections of this paper deal with these themes. The third section focuses on the limitations of export-led manufacturing as these emerged by the end of the 1970s in countries, such as the Ivory Coast, which were among the first in Africa to embark upon an articulated strategy of export-oriented manufacturing. The final section, then explores the way in which Europe's changing requirements have combined with the failure of export-led manufacturing to cast Africa, once again, into the role of a primary producer within the international division of labor.

FROM IMPORT REPRODUCTION
TO EXPORT-LED MANUFACTURING

As Latin American countries were gaining their independence in the nineteenth century, Africa was first being col-

2. Samir Amin, "Développement autocentre, autonomie collective et nouvel ordre economique international-quelques reflexions," in Samir Amin, Alexandre

onized. For it was only when local African rulers could no longer ensure an adequate and stable supply of those raw materials for which European industrial demand was burgeoning that direct political rule became necessary.[3] During the next 100 years, African political economies were reshaped to supply these raw materials, either by coercion— direct colonial rule, taxation policies, labor conscription, military or police action—or by the penetration of international market-price relations.[4] Africa was, thus, cast into an essentially extractive role in a European-imposed division of labor.

By the 1950s many Latin American countries were experiencing growth problems resulting from, among other factors, declining terms of trade for their primary exports and an inability to capture the gains from technological change. Critics attributed these difficulties to the primary producing role which these political economies had been induced to assume. Under the impetus of economists such as Ragnar Nurkse, Albert Hirschman, Raul Prebisch, and W. Arthur Lewis, a new development strategy based on import-substituting industrialization was promoted.[5] This development strategy coincided with, and indeed helped, to induce a considerable expansion of direct foreign investment in manufacturing after 1950.

Faire, and Daniel Malkin, eds., *L'Avenir Industriel de l'Afrique* (Paris: l'Harmattan-ACCT, 1980), pp. 13–39.

3. Philip Ehrensaft, "The Political Economy of Informal Empire in Pre-Colonial Nigeria," *Canadian Journal of African Studies* (1972), 6(3):451–90; and A. G. Hopkins, *An Economic History of West Africa* (London: Longman, 1973), esp. chs. 4 and 5.

4. For details of this process see Colin Leys, *Underdevelopment in Kenya* (London: Heinemann, 1975); Samir Amin, *Le Developpement du Capitalisme en Cote d'Ivoire* (Paris: Minuit, 1967); and Rhoda Howard, *Colonialism and Underdevelopment in Ghana* (United Kingdom: Croom Helm, 1978).

5. For brief summaries of their ideas, see Paul Streeten, "Development Ideas in Historical Perspective," in *Toward a New Strategy for Development* (New York: Pergamon, 1979), pp. 21–52; and Fernando Henrique Cardoso, "The Originality of the Copy: The Economic Commission for Latin America and the Idea of Development," *ibid.*, pp. 53–72.

At independence in the 1960s, sub-Saharan Africa was disadvantaged relative to most of Asia and Latin America with respect to basic industrial infrastructure (transportation, telecommunications, electricity) as well as skilled manpower. Moreover, average literacy levels lagged far behind those of other "late" industrializers at that moment in their history when independence, unification, or domestic regime-change made possible the nationalist tariff, credit, and monetary policies which spurred their industrialization processes. Major postwar changes in the relationship of science and technology to industry, the scale of industrial efficiency, the size of firms and their geographical scope marked this period as one in which the newcomer would face difficulties not encountered by their nineteenth-century predecessors.

It was in this context that many postindependence regimes in Africa attempted to pursue import-substituting industrialization policies. However, as in Latin America,[6] the shortcomings of this strategy as it took shape under the direction of multinational corporations (MNCs) soon became apparent.[7] Africa's new industries did not substitute locally made goods based on domestic inputs for the foreign goods previously imported. Instead, they reproduced imported goods for which tastes had been developed among elites, and they did so by relying heavily upon a continuous stream of imported skills, know-how, capital-goods, and intermediates. By relying upon imported inputs and engendering a considerable outflow of capital in the form of profits, management, and other fees, as well as interest payments on the foreign borrowing undertaken to finance a large part of this industrialization effort, multinational subsidiaries in Af-

6. See, for example, Albert Hirschman, "The Political Economy of Import Substituting Industrialization in Latin America," in his A Bias for Hope (New Haven: Yale University Press, 1971), pp. 85–123.

7. For a detailed critique see Steven Langdon and Lynn K. Mytelka, "Africa in the Changing World Economy," in C. Legum, I. W. Zartman, S. Langdon, and L. K. Mytelka, Africa in the 1980s: A Continent in Crisis (New York: McGraw-Hill, 1979), pp. 165–77.

rica contributed to the growing balance-of-payments problems experienced by these countries during the 1960s and 1970s. The import-reproduction process, moreover, took place in a context in which high levels of industrial protection were demanded by multinational firms in order to secure the domestic market against competition and permit the translation of high production costs into high local prices. Heavy industrial protection and high prices in turn skewed domestic incentives against the agricultural sector, from which most export earnings still came, thus contributing to domestic imbalances and further exaggerating external-payments deficits and indebtedness problems for many African countries.

Recent evidence has shown that economic growth was restricted by the extreme inefficiency of much of this new industrial production.[8] Domestic distributional patterns were skewed by the limited employment and linkage effects of the capital-intensive techniques adopted and by the reliance on imported inputs. A diversion of scarce capital and skill resources also resulted from the decision to provide lucrative incentives in order to attract foreign firms into final-stage manufacturing activities.[9]

In the latter half of the 1960s and early 1970s, a powerful assault against import-substituting industrialization was

8. An interesting aggregate analysis of foreign investment flows and stocks, and their relationship to economic growth, measured as national savings and log GDP per capita showed that "direct foreign investment is *cumulatively* related to decreases in the relative rate of economic growth of countries . . . however, . . . in the short term, investment is positively associated, at virtually the same magnitude, with increasing rates of economic growth." Michael B. Dolan and Brian W. Tomlin, "First World-Third World Linkages: External Relations and Economic Development," *International Organization* (Winter 1980), 34(1):41–63.

9. S. W. Langdon, *Multinational Corporations in the Political Economy of Kenya* (London: Macmillan, 1981); Thomas Biersteker, *Distortion or Development? Contending Perspectives on the Multinational Corporation* (Cambridge: MIT, 1978); Bonnie Campbell, "Neo-Colonialism, Economic Dependence and Political Change: Cotton Textile Production in the Ivory Coast," *Review of African Political Economy* (1975), no. 2, pp. 36–53; and Justinian Rweyemamu, *Underdevelopment and Industrialization in Tanzania: A Study of Perverse Capitalist Industrial Development* (New York: Oxford University Press, 1974).

launched in a series of OECD-sponsored studies and spurred on by economists close to the World Bank.[10] These critics pointed to the contribution which export-led manufacturing was making to rapid growth in such countries as Taiwan, South Korea, Hong Kong, and Brazil in this period. Such a strategy, they contended, would promote industrial efficiency, solve foreign exchange problems, and provide more employment because it would focus on precisely those industrial sectors in which Third World countries had a clear comparative advantage in their cheaper labor costs. Some of these analysts not only supported the new export-orientation, but they argued that MNCs, by subcontracting to local firms and then organizing the marketing of finished products, were a vital component of the success of this new strategy.[11] As a recent OECD study concluded:

. . . the impressive overall export performance of several NICs (Newly Industrializing Countries) has resulted from a combination of strong comparative advantage and of export promotion policies aimed at exploiting the openings offered by trade liberalisation while overcoming or bypassing continuing or newly created trade barriers.[12]

Third World countries have increasingly been urged to adopt an export-oriented manufacturing strategy and to rely

10. See I. M. D. Little, T. Scitovsky, and M. Scott, *Industry and Trade in Some Developing Countries* (London: Oxford University Press, 1970); Bela Balassa, "Growth Strategies in Semi-Industrial Countries," *Quarterly Journal of Economics* (1970), 74:24−47; and Helen Hughes, *Prospects for Partnership: Industrialization and Trade Policies in the 1960s* (Baltimore: John Hopkins University Press, 1973).

11. See, for example, J. de la Torre, "Foreign Investment and Export Dependency," *Economic Development and Cultural Change* (1974), 23(1):133−50; and M. Sharpston, "International Sub-contracting," *World Development* (April 1976), 4:330−37.

12. OECD, *The Impact of the Newly Industrialising Countries on Production and Trade in Manufactures* (Paris: OECD, 1979), p. 11. Aggregate studies of trade flows from these newly industrializing countries to the advanced, industrial countries by Balassa and by Donges and J. Riedel make similar points. See J. B. Donges and J. Riedel, "The Expression of Manufactured Exports in Developing Countries: An Empirical Assessment of Supply and Demand Issues," in *Weltwirtschaftliches Archiv,* Bank 113, Heft 1 (1977), pp. 58−87; and B. Belassa, *The Changing Inter-*

TABLE 5.1: Third World Share of World Exports of Manufactures,
1963–1976

	1963 (%)	1976 (%)
Brazil	0.05	0.41
Mexico	0.17	0.51
Hong Kong	0.76	1.15
Korea	0.05	1.20
Taiwan	0.16	1.23
Singapore	0.38	0.52
India	0.85	0.49
Argentina	0.01	0.17
Total	2.43	5.68
Other Third World*	2.24	1.49
Grand Total	4.67	7.17

SOURCE: Calculated from OECD, *The Impact of the Newly Industrialising Countries on Production and Trade in Manufactures* (Paris: OECD, 1979), p. 19, table 2.

*Includes Yugoslavia with .40 percent of world exports of manufactures in 1963 and .60 percent in 1976.

on multinational firms as leading actors to implement it.[13] Such a strategy has been proposed especially for the smaller Third World countries, and it was a feature of the first Lomé Convention,[14] which bound African, Caribbean, and Pacific (ACP) former colonies to the European Economic Community (EEC).

Yet the newly industrializing countries (NICs) to which these proponents refer are, and have remained, few in number. As table 5.1 illustrates, while their share of world exports of manufactures rose from 2.43 percent in 1963 to 5.68 percent in 1976, the share of other Third World countries fell from 2.24 percent to 1.49 percent over the corre-

national Division of Labor in Manufactured Goods, World Bank Staff Working Paper, no. 329 (Washington, D.C.: IBRD, May 1979).

13. This was indeed the case of Kenya, and Langdon reports other examples. See Steven Langdon, "Industrial Dependence and Export Manufacturing in Kenya," paper prepared for an International Seminar on Alternative Futures for Africa (Halifax: Dalhousie University, May 1981).

14. The Lomé Conventions will be discussed in the second section.

sponding period. In most of these newly industrializing countries, moreover, domestic capital—private or state, rather than foreign, capital—dominated the industrialization process.[15] This casts doubts on the role that proponents of export-oriented manufacturing have assigned to the multinational corporation. Finally, as Steven Langdon has pointed out:

> . . . it is not at all clear that MNC's are broadly flexible in where they are prepared to undertake significant export manufacturing. There is considerable competition in the world economy in this context—with established South East Asian economies, Eastern European options, Mediterranean sources and well-advanced Latin American possibilities all competing for export MNC's. Countries outside this circle may well be marginalized in the changing international division of labor.[16]

How has Africa fared in this competition? The 1970s were a critical decade for African industrial development. It was in this period that the limitations of import reproduction became highly visible, yet political difficulties thwarted the implementation of income redistribution and regional integration strategies designed to widen domestic markets.[17] Export-oriented manufacturing, thus, appeared to provide an alternative, and was indeed seized upon by governments in Africa and Europe as they sought to reorient European-African economic relations during the 1970s. If at first this stimulated the move toward export-oriented manufacturing in Africa, the changing requirements of European industry subsequently led to a reexamination of the benefits to be gained from continuing this strategy.

15. B. I. Cohen, *Multinational Firms and Asian Exports* (New Haven: Yale University Press, 1975); and D. Nayyar, "Transnational Corporations and Manufactured Exports from Poor Countries," *The Economic Journal* (1978), vol. 88.

16. Langdon, "Industrial Dependence and Export Manufacturing in Kenya," p. 8.

17. Langdon and Mytelka, "Africa in the Changing World Economy," pp. 177–91.

AFRICAN TRADE AND INVESTMENT RELATIONS WITH EUROPE

To a large extent the advances and reversals of Africa's relationship with Europe, still overwhelmingly its major economic partner, can be charted through the two Lomé Conventions signed during the 1970s.[18] The first of these, negotiated in the early part of that decade and signed in February 1975, was designed to accomplish several objectives. On the one hand, it preserved certain elements of Africa's classical extractive role. This goal was pursued through STABEX, the European Communities' (EC) system for the stabilization of African export earnings from eleven and later twenty-seven traditional agricultural products and one mineral resource.[19] Unlike the Common Fund discussed at Nairobi during UNCTAD IV, STABEX does not stabilize the *price* of commodities nor the *incomes* to producers. It merely compensates for *shortfalls* in export earnings due to price fluctuations. Only unprocessed commodities on the STABEX list qualify,[20] and only when export earnings fall below a fixed percentage of the average for the preceding four years. Thus the STABEX system provides an incentive to maintain present levels of production in these commodities

18. Since the decision by Angola and Mozambique to participate in negotiations on Lomé III, the Lomé Convention currently counts all sub-Saharan African countries among the African, Caribbean, and Pacific associates with the exception of Namibia, and the Republic of South Africa. Relations with the Maghrebian countries of Algeria, Morocco, and Tunisia are governed by separate accords.

19. The Lomé I Convention included groundnuts, cocoa, coffee, cotton, coconuts and oil, palm nuts and oil, hides and skins, logs and sawn wood, bananas, tea and sisal on its STABEX list, along with iron ore. "ACP-EEC Convention of Lomé," complete text, printed in *The Courier* (March 1975), no. 31, title II, ch. 1. Sixteen agricultural commodities were added in Lomé II. These included vanilla, cloves, pepper, gum arabic, pyrethrum, essential oils, cotton seeds, sesame seed, cashew nuts, peas, beans, lentils, shrimp, squid, wool and mohair, and rubber. "The Second ACP-EEC Convention signed in Lomé on 31 October 1979," complete text, printed in *The Courier* (November 1979), no. 58, title II, ch. 1.

20. If an ACP country processes these commodities, thereby lowering actual exports, it is ineligible to receive STABEX funds.

and constitutes a disincentive to diversify commercial agricultural production, process raw materials locally, or develop domestic food production—all activities which would promote domestic economic linkages and bring the structures of demand and production within Africa more into line with one another.

On the other hand, Lomé I also promoted structural changes in Europe and Africa which were compatible with the global redeployment of manufacturing activity then underway. To accomplish this latter goal, a series of measures were introduced to encourage EC direct investment in African manufacturing, to guarantee preferential rights of establishment for EC firms vis-à-vis their Japanese or American multinational rivals, and to regulate access to the EC market for African manufactures produced by these new affiliates.[21]

This evolution in EC-African economic relations, I have argued elsewhere,[22] reflected above all a French need to adapt its industrial structure to a number of important changes in the world economy, notably:

1. growing American and Japanese direct investment in Third World manufacturing and the consequent ability to source worldwide and thus reduce production costs;[23]
2. Dutch and German industrial adjustment policies

21. In her report on the results of Lomé I, Katharina Focke, for example, noted that the convention laid down as its two top priorities, "the promotion of EC-ACP trade" and "the industrialization of the ACP." K. Focke, *From Lomé 1 towards Lomé 2* (Texts of the Report and Resolution adopted on September 26, 1980 by the ACP-EEC Consultative Assembly, Doc. No. ACP-EEC/19/80).

22. L. K. Mytelka and M. Dolan, "The EEC and the ACP Countries," in D. Seers and C. Vaitsos, eds., *Integration and Unequal Development* (London: Macmillan, 1980), pp. 237–60; and also L. K. Mytelka, "In Search of a Partner: The State and the Textile Industry in France," in Steven Cohen and Peter Gourevitch, eds., *France in a Troubled World Economy* (Sevenoaks, Kent: Butterworth, 1982), pp. 132–50.

23. Worldwide sourcing is the segmentation and geographical dispersion of a production process in order to take advantage of cheaper or more accessible inputs (labor, raw materials) in the manufacture of components and the assembly of finished products sold in third-party markets.

which emphasized modernization and rationalization through the use of outward processing in the more labor-intensive segments of such industrial production processes as textiles—a process which rendered German textiles and clothing competitive within the community and put the French textile and clothing industry under added pressures; and

3. the buoyant economies of certain newly industrializing countries—Mexico, Brazil, Korea, and India—which made them important markets for exports of machinery and equipment.

For traditional industries in France, the protected environment of the Lomé Convention provided the necessary space for industrial adjustment. But France was relatively alone among EC countries in promoting such an industrial strategy and, indeed, France's EC partners were reluctant to maintain a privileged relationship with Africa if to do so reduced their ability to develop closer economic ties with the more dynamic economies of Asia and Latin America. Interestingly enough, this was a sentiment shared by industrialists in the more technologically intensive industries in France as well. It is no surprise, therefore, that much of the new, direct foreign investment from France, Germany, the Netherlands, and the United Kingdom to the Third World during the 1970s was directed towards non-African areas.[24] Indeed, as table 5.2 shows, insofar as direct foreign investment from all advanced industrial countries was concerned, Africa was not a favored Third World area in the 1970s. From an African perspective, however, looking specifically at the principal sub-Saharan recipients of direct foreign investment from the OECD countries, it is apparent that European investors remain dominant in all but Liberia and Nigeria where Japanese and American investors have risen to prominence.

The 1970s, moreover, marked a period of slow growth throughout sub-Saharan Africa. This was particularly nota-

24. Mytelka and Dolan, "EEC and ACP Countries," pp. 246–51.

TABLE 5.2: Private Flows of Capital from DAC Countries to the Third
World and to Africa

Total	Net Direct Foreign Investment from DAC Members	Total Net Private Flows from DAC Members (US $ million)
Avg. 1970–72	2404.4	5139.4
Avg. 1973–75	5574.1	11348.2
1977	4130.1	17471.9
1978	6934.6	28379.0
Africa		
Avg. 1970–72	444.1	1004.5
Avg. 1973–75	111.3	1884.9
1977	373.6	5026.8
1978	414.7	6791.2

Principal[a] African Recipients of Direct Foreign Investment from DAC Countries	Net Direct Investment from DAC	Total Net Pvt. Flows from DAC	Total Net Pvt. Flows from EC	EC/DAC %
Cameroon				
Avg. 1970–72	0.3	1.2	–	–
Avg. 1973–75	3.7	14.1	14.1	100.0
1977	−0.3	116.7	87.2	74.7
1978	−1.8	77.0	79.7	104.0
Gabon				
Avg. 1970–72	0.2	10.0	–	–
Avg. 1973–75	23.6	78.5	62.4	79.4
1977	25.6	248.2	241.37	97.3
1978	9.1	54.0	51.70	95.7
Ivory Coast				
Avg. 1970–72	−1.4	27.8	–	–
Avg. 1973–75	3.7	42.3	35.35	83.6
1977	7.8	336.8	268.23	79.6
1978	5.5	345.1	340.23	98.6
Kenya				
Avg. 1970–72	7.3	13.2	–	–
Avg. 1973–75	13.1	17.1	13.96	81.6
1977	6.1	298.8	234.96	78.6
1978	−0.6	64.4	39.17	60.8

ble with respect to per capita Gross National Product (GNP) which had risen on average by 1.7 percent per annum in the period 1960−70 but increased by only .2 percent per year during the 1970s.[25] Although industrial production ini-

25. Banque Mondiale (IBRD), *Rapport Annuel* (1980), p. 16.

Principal[a] African Recipients of Direct Foreign Investment from DAC Countries	New Direct Investment from DAC	Total Net Pvt. Flows from DAC	Total Net Pvt. Flows from EC	EC/DAC %
Liberia				
Avg. 1970–72	14.6	63.7	38.69	60.7[b]
Avg. 1973–75	104.3	357.6	198.69	55.6
1977	170.4	678.5	282.87	41.7
1978	146.6	671.7	60.32	9.0
Nigeria				
Avg. 1970–72	119.4	125.9	—	—
Avg. 1973–75	51.3	95.5	121.4	127.1[c]
1977	32.2	83.3	104.41	125.3
1978	−14.3	377.4	332.48	88.1
Zaire				
Avg. 1970–72	7.5	89.7	—	—
Avg. 1973–75	26.3	260.5	168.76	64.8
1977	16.4	99.7	102.37	102.7
1978	93.8	203.8	110.28	54.1
Zambia				
Avg. 1970–72	13.2	19.4	—	—
Avg. 1973–75	21.2	106.0	96.82	91.3
1977	2.8	7.5	15.24	203.2
1978	0.9	47.9	55.97	116.8

SOURCE: *ACP Statistical Yearbook 1972–1978* (Eurostat 1980).

NOTE: DAC, the Development Assistance Committee of the OECD, is composed of the industrialized countries of Western Europe, North America, and Japan.

[a] "Principal" is defined as net DFI of greater than $10 million for at least one of the designated time periods. North African countries, Rhodesia, South Africa, Somalia, and Niger, which meet these criteria are not included here.

[b] To Liberia:

Total Net Pvt. Flows from (avg.)	1973–75	1977	1978
U.S.	58.0	26.0	−63.0
Japan	101.9	337.0	669.62

[c] To Nigeria:

Total Net Pvt. Flows from U.S.	1973	1974	1975	1976	1977	1978
	−257.0	−220.0	+332.0	−194.0	−12.0	53.0

tially grew rapidly from a very low base in the 1960s, Africa's share of world manufacturing value added stagnated at .7 percent during the period 1960– 1972, rose to .8 percent in 1973, and remained at that level for the rest of the decade.[26] Relative to its share of world population and in comparison to other Third World areas, African industrial output remained small, and its rate of growth stayed below that of other regions. Thus, table 5.3 reveals that although Africa's share of world population rose from 9.3 percent in 1966 to 10.2 percent in 1976, its share of world manufacturing output, as measured by ten major manufactured products, rose from 1.7 percent to only 2.3 percent over the same period. Taking its share of world industrial output as a ratio of the share of world population accounted for by Africa shows that Africa's net improvement over the years 1966 to 1976 amounted to a change of only 5 percentage points, whereas the corresponding improvement for Latin America was 13 percentage points over this ten year period (see row D, table 5.3).

Countries like the Ivory Coast, Kenya, and Senegal, which had moved rapidly into import substitution after independence, were now among the first to experience the limitations of that development model.[27] Particularly because African domestic markets were growing far slower than had been anticipated during the "development decade" of the 1960s, advisers from France and from the World Bank now proposed export-oriented manufacturing as a solution. At their suggestion, generous financial and fiscal incentives were offered to foreign firms willing to locate export-oriented affiliates in Africa.[28]

During the first half of the 1970s, production for export in traditional industries such as textiles and wood manufacturing rose, and the European Community absorbed an increasing proportion of these exported manufactured products.[29] Despite predictions to the contrary, however, exports

26. UNIDO, *World Industry Since 1960: Progress and Prospects* (New York: United Nations, 1979), p. 37.
27. These difficulties were temporarily avoided in Nigeria where oil production generated new revenues.
28. Including, as in Senegal, the creation of duty-free zones.
29. Mytelka and Dolan, "EEC and ACP Countries," pp. 238–46.

TABLE 5.3: Growth of Industrial Production in Africa, Latin America, and the World in 1966 and 1976

	World		Africa				Latin America			
			1966		1976		1966		1976	
	1966	1976	Amt.	%[a]	Amt.	%[a]	Amt.	%[a]	Amt.	%[a]
A. Population (millions)	3554	4044	311	9.3	412	10.2	170	5.1	224	5.5
B. Manufacturing										
Sugar (M.T.)[b]	64	87	4.0	6.3	6.0	6.9	7.4	11.6	13.0	14.9
Beer (HL)	523	805	9.2	1.8	31.8	4.0	24.7	4.7	40.4	5.0
Cigarettes ('000M)[c]	2374	3252	70.8	3.0	131.4	4.0	125.	5.3	207.	6.4
Noncellulosic continuous filaments ('000 tons)	1335	4194	4.3	0.3	25.6	0.06	31.2	2.3	162.9	3.9
-discontinuous fibers ('000T)	1135	4455	0.4	0.03	9.1	0.02	13.0	1.1	117.0	2.6
Sawnwood (m^3)	373	425	3.2	0.8	5.0	1.2	10.5	2.8	12.5	2.9
Paper (M.T.)	86	129	0.6	0.7	1.0	0.8	1.7	2.0	3.5	2.7
Nitrogenous fertilizer (M.T.)	21	46	0.2	1.0	0.7	1.5	0.3	1.4	0.5	1.1
Cement (M.T.)	464	729	12.1	2.6	24.	3.3	17.3	3.7	34.8	4.8
Crude steel (M.T.)	476	675	3.6	0.8	8.2	1.2	6.4	1.3	13.1	1.9
C. Average % share of world manufacturing production			1.7		2.3		3.6		4.6	
D. Share of world manufacturing in terms of share of world population (C/A × 100)			18.		23.		71.		84.	

SOURCE: *United Nations Statistical Yearbook* (1970), pp. 23, 24; (1977), pp. 3, 4.
[a] Percentage of world totals.
[b] Millions of tons.
[c] Thousand million.

TABLE 5.4: Change in African Export Performance Compared with Other Third World Regions or Country Groups from 1970–1971 to 1973–1976 (current U.S. $ million f.o.b.)

Exporting Area	Textiles	Clothing	Chemicals	Nonferrous Metals	Iron/Steel	Machinery/ Transport Equipment	Other Manufactures	Total
Africa	-127.0	–	-43.6	-2179.6	–	-31.1	-460.4	-2841.7
Latin America	212.0	201.1	532.2	-1366.8	-75.0	715.1	249.4	468.0
Asian Middle East	16.7	–	417.1	–	–	358.9	380.0	1172.7
Asia, other	372.8	2576.6	297.8	18.0	288.6	3461.9	3147.0	10062.7
OPEC countries	-76.9	–	439.6	–	–	-152.5	-15.8	194.4
Centrally planned Asia	129.5	243.8	21.5	48.0	-12.7	-2.2	159.3	268.2

SOURCES: UN, *Monthly Bulletin of Statistics* (August 1976), vol. 30, no. 8; (May 1977), vol. 31, no. 5; and (June 1978), vol. 32, no. 6, as reprinted in UNIDO, *Recent Industrial Development in Africa*, doc. no. UNIDO/ICIS, 117 (Vienna, August 6, 1979), p. 17, table 7.

of manufactures from Africa soon peaked and the African share in world exports of manufactures declined from an average of 1.12 percent in 1970–71 to .6 percent in 1975–76.[30] Worse yet, as table 5.4 illustrates, African exports of manufactures not only declined in relative terms, but in absolute terms as well. Textile exports, for example, fell by $127 million from 1970–71 to 1973–76. As to Africa's exports of manufactures to Europe, data through 1977 show that as a percentage of total Third World manufactured exports, they declined from 24 percent in 1974 to 13 percent in 1977.[31]

How can this failure of export-oriented manufacturing in Africa be explained? One way is to examine in detail a single industry. Textiles are generally considered to be a prime candidate for transfer to the Third World because of the labor intensity of its production processes and the local availability of a key raw material, cotton, so that it serves our purposes well. In addition, one might focus on a single country which is assumed to be particularly well situated to take advantage of this industrializing possibility. In the sub-Saharan African context, the Ivory Coast is widely regarded as a model for capitalist development. Thus, by looking closely at the experience of the Ivorian textile industry, the contradictions of export-led manufacturing as it has emerged in Africa can be better appreciated.[32]

30. UNIDO, "Recent Industrial Development in Africa" (Vienna: Doc. No. ICIS.117, August 6, 1979), p. 17.

31. Mytelka and Dolan, "EEC and ACP Countries," p. 243. Manufactured goods as a percentage of total ACP exports to the EEC have also decreased from nearly 20 percent in 1974 to barely 12 percent in 1977.

32. With the exception of Algeria, Angola, and Mozambique, foreign capital has deep roots and continues to influence the pattern of industrialization in all African countries. As the papers presented at the Conference on the African Bourgeoisie: "The Development of Capitalism in Nigeria, Kenya and the Ivory Coast" (Dakar, Senegal: December 2–4, 1980) indicate, much of the analysis presented here may be generalized to include other African countries as well.

MNC'S AND EXPORT-ORIENTED MANUFACTURING

Three generations of Ivorian textile firms are represented in table 5.5, and in each, foreign capital plays a predominant role. Of these firms, Gonfreville is the most diversified. Established in 1921 by a colonial official, it was later taken over by a French commercial company, Optorg, the engineering division of a large French textile company, Texunion, and a set of foreign banks. This combination of foreign commercial companies, technology suppliers, and banking capital became the typical ownership pattern in the Ivorian textile industry.

Second-generation firms, represented by ICODI, SO-TEXI, UNIWAX, and SOCITAS, were primarily import-substituting ventures, induced into the Ivorian market by a favorable investment climate created by the state and established by commercial firms anxious to maintain their share of the Ivorian market. These commercial companies recruited the technology suppliers who were also responsible for managing the new subsidiary. ICODI, for example, was founded by three large commercial companies—SCOA, CFAO, AND CFCI (Unilever)—Schaeffer, the engineering division of a major French textile company, and a number of private banks and national aid agencies. Subsequently, Riegel, the American manufacturer of Wrangler's blue jeans, also became a partner. Third-generation textile firms, COTIVO, UTEXI, and the Gonfreville "Grand Ensemble," are export-oriented, with COTIVO, for example, designed to produce denim for an upstream export-oriented, blue-jeans manufacturing firm (Blue Bell) established by Riegel Textiles and UTEXI and the Gonfreville Grand Ensemble intended to export mass-market textiles, such as bedsheets, to Europe.

Because the Ivory Coast seeks to attract foreign investors,[33] the state has not remained aloof from the industrial-

33. On the Ivorian development strategy and some reasons for it, see Bonnie Campbell, "Ivory Coast," in J. Dunn, ed., *West African States: Failure and Promise* (Cambridge: Cambridge University Press, 1978), pp. 66–116; and L. K. Mytelka,

TABLE 5.5: Factors in the Status of Ivorian Textile Firms in 1977–1978

Company	Year Established	Ownership Structure (by %) State	Private Ivorian	Foreign	Turnover (m F CFA)	Profitability[a]	Employment Total	% Ivorian	Activities
Gonfreville	1921	33.0	21.8	33.0	11,700	6.1	3268	92.0[b]	S,W,P,C,
Socitas[c]	1966	56.6	7.0	36.5	2,956	11.0	228	92.0	S,W,
Icodi	1962	31.8	—	68.2	6,100	12.3	378	90.0	P
Cotivo[c]	1973	28.6	—	71.4	4,631	(losses)	n.d.	n.d.	S,W,
Sotexi	1966	35.0	—	68.0	8,000	0.6	464	83.0	P
Utexi[c]	1972	20.3	—	79.7	4,316	-6.4	1529	96.9	S,W,
Uniwax	1966	—	15.0	85.0	7,000	9.0[d]	666	97.0	P
Sivoitex	1971	—	7.2	92.8	600	-24.7[e]	106	90.6	W,P,

SOURCE: Government and company interviews.

NOTE: S = spinning; W = weaving; P = printing; C = clothing.

[a] Profitability is measured as the average "net result" as a percentage of turnover in 1973–77.

[b] The remaining employees are primarily expatriates in the skilled-worker, supervisory, and management categories. Few non-Ivorian Africans are employed in the textile industry.

[c] Indented firms are affiliates of the firm preceding. Gonfreville owns 32 percent of SOCITAS and ICODI owns 90 percent of COTIVO.

[d] Declared after-tax profits as a percentage of turnover.

[e] Few of the firms in this survey were subject to corporate profits taxes. SIVOITEX, however, was and this might have led to a deflation of "gross results" in order to reduce taxable income.

ization process. Traditionally the state provided guarantees for loans from local banks. More recently, as foreign firms were reluctant to bring in new capital,[34] the state has invested in new firms alongside foreign capital. State intervention in the industrialization process has thus been designed to reduce the risks to foreign investors, but such policies also cheapen the cost of capital to foreign partners. While this made expansion into export-oriented activities more attractive, it also increased the tendency for technology suppliers, who were minority shareholders and managers of the firm, to choose capital-intensive technology and to overbuild these plants. This occurred both because funds were readily available and because the technology suppliers, although they were shareholders, received a commission on the sale of technology that was generally a function of total investment costs.

Choice of sophisticated production technology limited the growth of Ivorian industrial employment and inflated the wage bill because of the need to employ expatriate personnel. Heavy borrowing to meet this inflated investment program, moreover, led to high interest payments. These two factors have contributed to the relatively higher costs of production in each of the Ivorian textile firms, as compared with their Asian competitors. Yet by guaranteeing the profitability of these investments through the provisions of the Investment Code,[35] the tariff structure and the process of

---

"Direct Foreign Investment and Technological Choice in the Ivorian Textile and Wood Industries," in Dieter Ernst, ed., *Vierteljahresberichte der Entwicklungs-Landerforschung* (March 1981), pp. 61–79.

34. For balance-of-payments reasons, the French treasury in the early 1970s had restricted the outflow of capital and encouraged French firms to borrow abroad to finance their investments.

35. The Investment Code of September 3, 1959 (Loi No. 59–134) was adopted prior to independence. It provided for numerous fiscal incentives to foreign firms locating in the Ivory Coast. In addition, it permitted the duty-free import of raw materials, intermediates, and machinery used in the production process. These incentives were accorded to firms which received "priority status" under the code. SIVOITEX, a small-scale, Lebanese-owned and -managed firm, producing dish

price harmonization practiced with respect to textiles,[36] the state diminished the incentive in these firms to move towards more efficient production. As relatively inefficient producers, the output of these European affiliates needed the margin of protection provided by the Lomé Convention as against the General System of Preferences (GSP). These firms, thus, became vulnerable to even small shifts in demand or in the level of competition within the West European market to which the bulk of their output was directed. ICODI-COTIVO is a case in point.[37]

Technology suppliers in the Ivory Coast generally capitalized their technology and held up to 10 percent of the equity shares in these textile companies. Their major sources of income, however, were not dividends but commissions on the sale of capital goods whose purchase they organized, salaries to managerial and technical personnel, and technical assistance payments. Schaeffer, for example, receives a 3 percent commission on total investment costs and is paid 2.5 percent of turnover annually for technical assistance.[38] In 1964 and again in 1970, 1974, and 1976, Schaeffer chose the most sophisticated printing machinery for ICODI, as it later would do for COTIVO. The capital in-

---

towels, cleaning cloths, and other simple products made from recycled cotton wastes did not receive priority status. Normally priority status was awarded for a ten-year period and served to guarantee the profitability of the firm.

36. In effect, this amounted to price fixing by the textile firms in conjunction with the state. Within the context of a protected market, the textile oligopoly was thus able to transfer its high costs of production to the domestic consumer.

37. For detailed discussion of the Gonfreville and the Sotexi-Utexi cases see Mytelka, "Direct Foreign Investment and Technological Choice in the Ivorian Textile and Wood Industries." Similar findings with respect to the Kenyan textile industry and its crisis are reported in Langdon, "Industrial Dependence and Export Manufacturing in Kenya." Ivory Coast, therefore, is not an isolated case.

38. Data on ICODI-COTIVO were obtained through interviews with M. Knoph, Director, Schaeffer Impression (Vieux Thann, France: December 13, 1978); M. Hubert, Director, ICODI (Abidjan: January 31, 1979); and M. Boremans, Director, COTIVO (Agboville: February 12, 1979); and from Republique de Cote d'Ivoire, *Le Centrale des Bilans, 1977* (Abidjan: 1978); and *Memorandum Textile Pour la Communaute Economique Europeenne* (Abidjan: Ministere de l'Economie, des Finances et du Plan, Decembre 1978).

tensity of production in ICODI, measured as net fixed assets per employee, thus rose from 5,134 F CFA in 1974 to 9,025 F CFA by 1977.

In 1970 Mohamed Diawara, then Minister of Plan, approached ICODI with a view to persuading its owners to integrate backwards towards spinning and weaving, in keeping with the newly adopted export-oriented growth strategy. As ICODI's "priority status" was soon to expire and the firm would no longer be permitted to import the graycloth it printed free of customs duties, backward integration was now in its interest. The state agreed to grant the new firm, COTIVO, priority status under the Investment Code and it took an equity share of 28.6 percent. Schaeffer, which managed ICODI, would manage the new spinning and weaving plant and would assume all responsibility for the choice of technology. COTIVO, established in 1973, was designed to produce greycloth for both UNIWAX and ICODI's printing and finishing plant, thus ensuring that the spinning and weaving operations would be able to take advantage of economies of scale.[39] It was also intended to produce denim for Riegel's new blue jeans subsidiary in the Ivory Coast. COTIVO received a 1500 million F CFA loan from the European Investment Bank and additional long-term loans amounting to some 1700 million F CFA from the Ivorian Industrial Development Bank (BIDI), the German Aid Agency, DEG (also a partner in ICODI/COTIVO), and other national and international public lending agencies. In addition, COTIVO has a medium-term loan amounting to 3,200 million F CFA from a banking consortium led by the Banque Nationale de Paris' Ivorian affiliate, the BICICI. Loans constituted 67.2 percent of the capital invested and financial charges ran at 15 percent of turnover.

Not only is COTIVO heavily in debt and thus vulnerable to shifts in demand for blue jeans and the imposition of

39. Unilever, which owned 85 percent of UNIWAX, is a shareholder in both ICODI and COTIVO.

voluntary export restraints by importing countries, but the choice of product and the choice of technology can both be questioned. Denim is a product with high technical specifications. It permits only very limited tolerances in dyeing, streaking, and twisting. Although COTIVO's quality has improved, most denim firms operate with a 2−3 percent "second choice" whereas COTIVO's output still includes 15 percent or more "second choice." In addition to high quality-standards, denim production requires high volume and low cost to compete effectively with Asian producers who currently set world prices. COTIVO cannot meet these conditions.

COTIVO is also plauged by a number of inappropriate technological choices. The Saurer looms initially purchased by Schaeffer are not appropriate for heavy denim cloth and they have now been converted to the production of cotton graycloth for sale to ICODI and UNIWAX. But the use of expensive looms for such a simple product pushes the cost of graycloth well above that of imports and increases the price of printed cloth produced by these two firms.[40] UNIWAX, which has traditionally exported its "Indonesian 'Dutch' " style wax-prints to neighboring West African countries, has been particularly affected and has initiated talks with the government to import cheaper Asian graycloth rather than fulfill its commitment to use COTIVO's output.

COTIVO's denim spinners and other related equipment, moreover, are designed to produce enough input to weave 9 million yards of cloth, but COTIVO is only producing 2.3 million yards of cloth. Hence all spinners operate only two

40. Originally the Grand Ensemble in Gonfreville was intended to produce export-quality cloth and hence very costly Sulzer looms were chosen. The high costs of production and the protectionist tendencies of the EEC countries during the late 1970s made it difficult for Gonfreville to market its output in Europe. In 1979 these machines were converted to the production of polyester shirt fabric for the domestic market where tastes and incomes do not require production to such high technical specifications. As in COTIVO, the high costs of production are passed on to the consumer through the process of "price harmonization."

days per week and indigo baths similarly function at less than one-third capacity.[41] This further increases the cost of producing denim. As Blue Bell is having difficulty selling its output in Europe and has cut back production, further difficulties at COTIVO can be anticipated.

When pressures to reduce textile imports from the Third World intensified in the EEC during 1975 and 1976, it became politically expedient to place ceilings on ACP textile imports even though these were not the source of market disruption. In effect, the EEC was signaling its decision to abandon a strategy of African industrialization just as negotiations leading to Lomé II were getting underway. By 1978, as a result, a halt was called to planned second- and third-stage investments in Ivorian export-oriented textile ventures, and in line with World Bank and EC policies now favorable to an expansion of primary production in Africa, Ivorian energies and resources were redirected to increasing productivity in the export-oriented *agricultural* sector.

The Ivorian development strategy has not been without its costs. While Africa was most seriously affected in all the Third World by the crisis of inflation and recession in the advanced industrial countries, "[t]he picture is not uniformly bleak" according to the World Bank's controversial agenda for African development. "Of the 45 countries in the region, nine posted annual growth rates of over 2.5 percent per capita between 1960 and 1979." However, a quick look at table 5.6 shows that the Ivory Coast was not among them. The World Bank study continues: "the tragedy of this slow growth in the African setting is that incomes are so low and access to basic services so limited."[42] But this assumed correlation between low per capita income and limited access to basic services does not hold in the Ivorian case. On the

41. Underutilized capacity is quite typical in African industries for reasons having to do with the choice of product and the choice of technique discussed above. See also, Frances Stewart, *Technology and Underdevelopment* (London: Macmillan, 1977).

42. IBRD, *Accelerated Development in Sub-Saharan Africa: An Agenda for Action* (Washington, D.C.: IBRD, 1981), pp. 2, 3.

TABLE 5.6: Growth of Income and Access to Services in Selected African Countries

	Ivory Coast	Kenya	Nigeria	Cameroon	Tanzania
Population in millions (1979)	8.2	15.3	82.6	8.2	18.0
GNP/Capita (U.S. $, 1979)	1040	380	670	560	260
Growth of GNP/Capita: Avg. annual (1960–79)	2.4	2.7	3.7	2.5	2.3
Debt service as a % of exports					
1970	6.8	7.9	4.2	3.2	8.2
1979	15.2	7.5	1.5	9.5	7.4
Adult literacy % in 1976[a]	20	45	—	—	66
Life expectancy at birth in years (1979)	47	55	49	47	52
Percentage of population with safe water (1975)	19	17	—	26	39

SOURCE: Compiled from World Bank, *Accelerated Development in Sub-Saharan Africa: An Agenda for Action* (Washington, D.C.: IBRD, 1981), Statistical Annex, tables 1, 17, 37.

[a] Or a year within two years of this date.

contrary, per capita GNP in the Ivory Coast is second only to Gabon among sub-Saharan African countries. And yet, as the figures in table 5.6 reveal, its record in terms of access to services, measured by adult literacy, life expectancy, and access to safe water, places this rich country at or well below the average for the continent as a whole. The benefits of Ivorian growth have thus been concentrated among a relatively privileged few. It is this same segment of the Ivorian population which now stands to benefit from the shift back to export-oriented agricultural production and processing.

A RETURN TO PRIMARY PRODUCTION

As Lomé I reflected a concern with the changing global locus of manufacturing activities, Lomé II is primarily a response to the oil crisis of the mid-1970s and a growing concern in advanced industrial countries with a need to secure supplies of raw materials at reasonable prices.[43] To mitigate the ability of producer cartels to withhold supply and influence prices in other vital primary products, the advanced industrial countries have pursued several strategies. Prospecting to increase the number of suppliers and the amount of proven resources is one such strategy. Developing alternate systems to induce or maintain the flow of raw materials at a desirable level, and thus frustrate efforts at stockpiling as a price support technique, is yet another.

The EC pioneered in the latter approach with STABEX, and as nonferrous mineral exports from Africa fell by $2179.6 million current U.S. dollars f.o.b. from 1970–71 to 1973–76,[44] some efforts in this direction were made in the mineral sector through SYSMIN—the new minerals system created under Lomé II. Community financial guarantees covering investments in mining and energy, moreover, are intended to move beyond the maintenence of existing output and "to stimulate mining investment by firms from any Member State in any ACP state."[45] Data on the importance of mineral production in Africa for the EC are contained in table 5.7 which details the ACP share of non-EC imports of key commodities in 1978 and 1979.

Prospecting is also a feature of the new Lomé Convention, not only for minerals and petroleum but for food resources such as fish. With the adoption of a 200-mile economic zone, African coastal fishery resources are now being surveyed by the EC, and joint declarations on deep-sea fishing and shipping indicate an interest in developing fish exports to Europe.[46]

43. See, for example, *La Documentation Francaise, Huitième Plan: Options* (Paris: 1979); and Wolfgang Hager and Michael Noelke, *Community-Third World: The Challenge of Interdependence,* 2d ed. (Brussels: Commission of the European Communities, 1980).

44. UNIDO, "Recent Industrial Developments in Africa," p. 17.

45. Response to the written question No. 1147/80 by Mrs. Walz to the Commission of the European Communities, Brussels, November 7, 1980.

46. K. Focke, *From Lomé I towards Lomé II,* p. 33.

TABLE 5.7: EC: Extra-EC Imports of Commodities (Total value, % from Class 2, % from the ACP)

	1978	1979
Woods (logs)		
Value	774729	915262
% Cl. 2	61.3	62.1
% ACP	55.7	56.8
Plywood and similar		
Value	578522	714411
% Cl. 2	43.6	44.7
% ACP	3.2	3.4
Cotton		
Value	932357	914964
% Cl. 2	47.9	47.3
% ACP	16.0	18.9
Cotton woven fabrics		
Value	770343	996082
% Cl. 2	41.3	42.9
% ACP	3.5	3.3
Undergarments		
Value	547330	653694
% Cl. 2	41.6	43.2
% ACP	0.5	0.6
Outergarments		
Value	859370	1064368
% Cl. 2	55.7	52.1
% ACP	3.4	3.1
Manganese ores[c]		
Value	114165	147362
% Cl. 2	52.0	51.7
% ACP	31.8	36.1
(Gabon, Ghana, Zaire)		
Uranium, thorium ores		
Value	179100	174416
% Cl. 2	82.5	95.3
% ACP	82.5	95.3
(Niger, Gabon)		
Zinc ores		
Value	219817	298565
% Cl. 2	31.0	35.4
% ACP	.3	.2
(Congo)		
Copper ores[a]		
Value	144490	185179
% Cl. 2	80.8	72.4
% ACP	56.3	45.9
(Papua, N. Guinea)		

TABLE 5.7 (*continued*)

	1978	1979
Copper, unrefined, unwrought		
Value	422936	481655
% Cl. 2	54.8	59.4
% ACP	34.3	37.7
(Zaire, Zambia)		
Copper, refined, unwrought		
Value	1650075	2161887
% Cl. 2	53.3	61.3
% ACP	29.7	31.2
(Zambia, Zaire)		
Aluminium ores (bauxite)		
Value	188692	211617
% Cl. 2	61.6	56.9
% ACP	61.5	54.3
(Guinea, Sierra Leone, Ghana)		
Aluminium, unwrought, not alloy		
Value	461937	571208
% Cl. 2	56140	87467
% ACP	6.3	9.2
(Cameroon)		
Roasted iron pyrites		
Value	1781640	2130890
% Cl. 2	49.2	47.5
% ACP	17.5	16.9
(Liberia, Mauritania)		
Tin ores		
Value	127174	117573
% Cl. 2	82.9	84.6
% ACP	26.4	19.5
(Zaire, Rwanda)		
Chromium ores		
Value	59048	71396
% Cl. 2	28.4	15.3
% ACP	12.0	5.7
(Madagascar, Sudan)		
Petroleum, crude		
Value	40344912	48503088
% Cl. 2	94.0	93.5
% ACP	7.7	10.6
(Nigeria)		

SOURCE: *EUROSTAT* (1980).

NOTE: Total value = 1000 ECU; percentages are percent of value/extra EC.

[a] Manganese and copper ores in seabed manganese nodules along with nickel and cobalt.

A clause-by-clause analysis of the Lomé II Convention supports the argument that emphasis is now placed once again on developing Africa as a primary-producing hinterland for Europe. The preamble, for example, makes this shift evident in the two new paragraphs it contains. The first stresses agricultural production and the second the development of mineral resources.[47] Safeguard clauses which the ACP sought to have eliminated were not abolished and, in fact, were changed in such a way as to make them easier to apply. Thus, the implementation of safeguard clauses envisaged in Articles 10 and 11 of Lomé I were limited, temporary, and exceptional. Under Lomé II, safeguard clauses and "arrangements" [Article 13(2)] are the outcome of a process of negotiation and their scope and duration [Article 12(3) and Article 12(1)] are now open to continuous bargaining. Although Lomé II calls for prior consultation before the invocation of safeguard clauses [Article 13(1)], the need for such prior consultation is negated in a subsequent paragraph [Article 13(3)]. The EC thus has it both ways. It can negotiate "voluntary" limitations on exports, as the US has done numerous times with Japan and with Third World countries, and it can impose safeguard clauses unilaterally when market disturbances or financial difficulties warrant it. Continuous negotiation over "safeguard clauses and other arrangements," moreover, opens the possibility for the EEC to threaten closure of its market to future exports as a means of creating pressure on those who might be planning to invest in what the EEC views as competitive production. Indeed such threats lay at the heart of the hasty cancellation of planned textile investment in the Ivory Coast.

Other clauses give further evidence to the renewed emphasis in Lomé II on the development of African agricultural and mineral exports. STABEX has been broadened and SYSMIN created. As to Title V, which deals with industrial cooperation, scarcely a reference is made to secondary manufac-

47. The comparison is based on the following two documents: Commission of the European Communities, *The Convention of Lomé,* doc. no. 129/76/X/E (July 1976), and *Lomé II Dossier* reprinted from "The Courier," no. 58.

turing or to the capital goods sector, although agricultural and mineral processing are referred to specifically at several points in the Convention and again in this Title. Article 66(a), moreover, stresses that the promotion of industrial development should take place within the framework of a "dynamic complementarity" between the EEC and the ACP. For the EC, such dynamic complementarity clearly now lies in the area of mineral and agricultural processing.

CONCLUSION

In 1975 at Lima, Peru, the United Nations Industrial Development Oragnization (UNIDO) set as its goal the location of 25 percent of world manufacturing capacity in the Third World by the year 2,000. To appraise the realism of this target, the UNIDO secretariat developed an econometric model to test a number of possible industrialization scenarios. Their results, insofar as Africa is concerned, were most pessimistic. When historical trends are projected to the year 2000, the share of the advanced industrial countries in world manufacturing value added only falls from 91.5 percent to 86.1 percent, with all of the relocation going to Asia and Latin America. Africa just barely maintains its present .7 percent share (see table 5.7.) The UNIDO study concludes that:

Relative to other developing regions, the prognostication for Africa gives particular cause for concern. In 1975, *per capita* figures for GDP and manufacturing output in Africa were roughly comparable to those of South and East Asia. By 2000, *per capita* GDP would be considerably below that of South and East Asia, while the region's *per capita* manufacturing output would be less than one half that of the other regions.[48]

48. UNIDO, *World Industry Since 1960: Progress and Prospects* (New York: United Nations, 1979), pp. 57–58.

TABLE 5.8: Projections of Manufacturing Value Added Per Capita by the Year 2000

	1975	2000[a]	2000[b]
Developed Countries	861	2919	2392
Developing Countries			
Africa	24	51	96
South and East Asia	25	124	168
Latin America	164	548	944
West Asia	80	341	550

SOURCE: UNIDO, *World Industry Since 1960: Progress and Prospects,* (New York: United Nations, 1979), calculated from unnumbered tables on pp. 57 and 59.
[a] Based on the historical projection of trends from 1960 to 1975.
[b] Based on a high-growth scenario for the years 1975–2000.

If, instead of projecting historical trends, a high growth scenario is adopted, then the Third World share of manufactures would rise from its 1975 figure of 8.5 percent to 23.8 percent—quite close to the Lima target. But the African share of 1.5 percent still falls below the regional Lima target of 2 percent, and the manufacturing value added per capita in Africa as a percentage of the Third World average rises only slightly, 26 percent in 1975 to 31 percent in the year 2000. (see table 5.8)

Intermediate range projections by the World Bank are similarly pessimistic with respect to Africa's industrial growth and industrial export potential in the 1980s.[49] Indeed UNIDO, the World Bank and the IMF concur in projecting slow overall rates of growth and hence slow rates of growth in per capita incomes for most of sub-Saharan Africa.[50] The implication is then that African import-reproducing industrialization, designed as it has been by multinational corporations, will remain limited by the slow growth of domestic elite markets. And, as we have seen from the data presented above, export-oriented manufacturing, when or-

49. World Bank, *World Development Report, 1980* (Washington, D.C.: IBRD, August 1980), esp. ch. 2.
50. "IMF view of the African economy," Report of the IMF meeting in Libreville, Gabon in May 1981, *African Business* (July 1981), pp. 15–17.

ganized by foreign capital, does not appear to be a solution either.

Throughout Africa, within the context of a close relationship between the state and foreign capital, multinational corporations have managed the industrialization process, orienting product and process choices in such a way as to limit linkage and employment effects and reduce the efficiency of production. The resulting relatively high cost of African manufactures coupled with the imposition of quotas and "voluntary" export restraints by Africa's European customers, has frustrated exports and rendered even more fragile an already vulnerable industrial sector. Unlike their Asian competitors or Dutch, Austrian, and Swiss firms, African firms lack the technology, skilled labor force, and high productivity, as well as the communications, marketing, and transportation networks which permit rapid and flexible adjustment to trade barriers or consumer taste changes. Thus, the colonial legacy still weighs heavily upon Africa's industrial possibilities. Clearly Africans must devise a new development strategy, one in which primary emphasis is placed on using domestic factors of production to meet domestic needs. As the above analysis suggests, it is highly questionable whether a central role should again be accorded to foreign capital in the design and implementation of such a strategy.

PART II: THE SELF-RELIANCE PROBLEMATIC

6.

Selective Dissociation in the Technology Sector

HELGE HVEEM

IF THE CASE of South Korea, as analyzed by Haggard and Moon, shows that the location of developing countries in the international division of labor is by no means immutable, it also suggests several requisite conditions of a successful export-led development strategy, conditions that are not present in great abundance in the Third World. The character of domestic social and political structures in South Korea has been such as to expand the degree of flexibility in the external ties that link the country to the world economy, as well as to internalize some beneficial effects of growth.[1] The economic "miracle" in South Korea has not been achieved without social and political costs, however. And the current economic stagnation and political crisis in South Korea appear to be the product of the long-term accumulation of such costs. Hart's discussion of Venezuela indicates that even the substantial attenuation of external financial constraints is not by itself an adequate substitute

1. Stephan Haggard and Chung-in Moon, in this volume.

for the full range of requisite conditions.[2] Venezuela compares favorably to many developing countries in terms of economic performance and the progressive character of its political regime. Nevertheless, as Hart demonstrates, the pattern of domestic social coalitions and policy networks make it difficult for Venezuela, in the context of an associative development strategy, to deepen industrialization and follow through more fully on the state's commitment to meeting the basic needs of its people. Lastly, the case of the Ivory Coast, as described by Mytelka, suggests that where neither favorable external factors nor requisite domestic conditions are present, continued dependency and dislocation is likely to attend a close embrace of the world economy, and the welfare benefits of association are likely to be few and highly concentrated.[3]

That the prospects of success via close association are thus constrained and limited does not imply that a severance of all ties with the center economies is desirable for those countries which fall beyond the perimeters of successful association. A complete severance is likely to have deleterious consequences of its own, and even if it were thought to be desirable, it is difficult to see that it is feasible in today's world political economy. The present paper, therefore, explores the more complex middle ground of "selective dissociation" or greater "self-reliance." It does so in the context of a sector that is central to all development strategies, the sector of technology.[4] The centripetal forces are strong in this sector, as will be shown. But the potential

2. Jeffrey Hart, in this volume.
3. Lynn K. Mytelka, in this volume.
4. For the purposes of this paper, technology will be defined as the knowledge to control and exploit resources for the production of goods and services. Science in relation to technology is the generation of knowledge about the basic conditions permitting control and exploitation of resources, and about the effects of technology on nature and society. I stress, with Schumpeter, the process aspect and the innovative character of the science-technology relationship. Joseph Schumpeter, *Capitalism, Socialism, and Democracy,* 5th ed. (London: George, Allen & Unwin, 1976).

capacity of peripheral countries in the area of science and technology is frequently underestimated. Many people still believe that the periphery is a scientific and technological "desert," which will bloom and blossom only as a function of being properly and sufficiently watered by imports from the center. This view stems from several sources, of which the dualism thesis is the most pervasive. Its distinction between "modern" and "traditional" science and technology connotes a systematic bias against the latter. Often, there is simply a lack of information about or understanding of the existence of technical capabilities outside the so-called modern sector. In other cases, their existence may be deliberately ignored and even suppressed by those interests which dominate the modern sector, notably international capital and its local associates.

This tendency suggests that different types of technology enjoy the support of different kinds of "social carriers,"[5] so that choices concerning alternative technologies are not merely technical choices, but rather choices among contending ideologies and strategies of development. Four sets of conditions shape the character and consequences of such choices in the realm of center-periphery technology relations: (1) the goals of the seller, primarily center capital, and the form in which the seller puts technology into circulation; (2) the capacity and the will of the recipient to modify or control the form and content of the circulation process; (3) the international and domestic political-economic context within which circulation takes place; and (4) the character of the technology proper. These conditions may yield stresses and contradictions in any particular instance, as between the seller's profit aspirations and the recipient's development aspirations, for example. What I propose to look at in particular is whether there is room amidst such stresses and contradictions for periphery countries to adopt technol-

5. Charles Edquist and Olle Edquist, "Social Carriers of Technology," *Journal of Peace Research* (1979), vol. 16, no. 4.

ogy strategies that will enhance the prospects for more self-reliant development.

This chapter is organized as follows. In the first section, I review the centripetal forces in the international circulation of technology, relating chiefly to the transnationalization of production and the role of technology in transnationalized production networks. In the second section, I examine the experience of two developing countries, Algeria and India, in attempting to achieve "selective dissociation" in the technology sector, pointing out their degree of success as well as obstacles to success. In the third section, I combine the Algerian and Indian experiences with what is known about similar efforts elsewhere to suggest a more general strategy for dissociation in the technology sector. In the fourth section, I take up the issue of the welfare consequences of dissociation in this sector. The fifth section concludes my discussion.

TECHNOLOGY AND THE INTERNATIONAL DIVISION OF LABOR

There is a vast and growing literature on the role of technology in the international economy. Theories of direct private investments,[6] the international "product cycle,"[7] the "technology gap,"[8] industrial location,[9] and "technological dualism"[10] treat this role in a way relevant to the analysis of

6. Stephen Hymer, "The International Operations of National Firms: A Study of Direct Foreign Investment" (Ph.D. diss., Massachusetts Institute of Technology, 1960); and S. Hirsch, *Location of Industry and International Competitiveness* (Oxford: Clarendon Press, 1967).

7. Raymond Vernon, "International Investment and International Trade in the Product Cyle," *Quarterly Journal of Economics* (May 1966), vol. 80.

8. The OECD issued a series of studies on this topic in the early 1970s.

9. Robin Murray, "Underdevelopment, International Firms, and the International Division of Labour," in J. Tinbergen, ed., *Towards a New World Economy* (Rotterdam: Rotterdam University Press, 1972).

10. Hans W. Singer, ed., *The Sussex Manifesto — Science and Technology to Developing Countries During the Second Development Decade* (Sussex: Science Policy Research Unit, University of Sussex).

center-periphery relations. More recently, the thesis of a "new international division of labor"[11] has been empirically tested and further developed,[12] and its relationship to technology underlined.[13] According to these theories, in particular the last mentioned as well as the work by Hymer, the current reordering of the world economy is centrally coordinated and hierarchically executed and employs technology as its spearhead.

The View From the Center
The belief that center capital would never permit the periphery to industrialize clearly has turned out to be incorrect.[14] There are several reasons for this, the most important of which have to do with developments in the center itself.

In the 1960s the United States alone accounted for 70 percent of the capitalist world's R&D expenditures, Western Europe and Japan for 28 percent. In the mid-1970s, the percentages were estimated at 50 and 47, respectively.[15] Increasing intra-center competition, notably Japanese and West German corporations challenging U.S. corporations, and increasing R&D expenses due to huge investments in innovation, have necessitated growing economies of scale. Rapidly increasing labor costs also have pushed corporations to seek markets of cheap, skilled and semi-skilled labor. And mounting political opposition to direct investments or other forms of direct control over production has led center capital to look for other forms of relations with the periphery,

11. Jan Annerstedt and Rolf Gustavsson, *Towards a New International Division of Labour* (Roskilde, Denmark: Roskilde University Center, 1975).

12. Folker Fröbel, Jürgen Heinrichs, and Otto Kreye, *Neue Internationale Arbeitsteilung* (Hamburg: Rororo Aktuell, 1977).

13. Dieter Ernst, "International Transfer of Technology, Technological Dependence and Underdevelopment: Key Issues," in Dieter Ernst, ed., *The New International Division of Labour, Technology and Underdevelopment: Consequences for the Third World* (Frankfurt/Main: Campus, 1980).

14. See Paul A. Baran, *The Political Economy of Growth* (London: Monthly Review Press, 1957), for such a view.

15. Jan Annerstedt, "A Survey of the World Research and Development Efforts" (Roskilde, Denmark: Roskilde University Centre, 1979). Mimeo.

wherein technology is a key factor. As one industrialist has put it:

Markets closed to products are invariably open to technology. Even extremely closed markets will open to Western technology, provided the West gives them the credits to make the purchase! . . . as long as the United States is the predominant technological power in the world, closed product markets will always be open to American technology.[16]

These are some reasons why the international fractions of center capital have been favoring a reorganization of the international division of labor. As a result, there is no longer an opposition to industrialization efforts in the periphery, even efforts that take a "nationalist" line. This seems particularly true with large, resource-rich periphery countries (Brazil, Nigeria), though it is not always true with smaller "breakaway" socialist countries (Allende's Chile, Cuba) and resource-poor ones. The main emphasis in center headquarters is no longer on reserving production for the center, not even necessarily for facilities completely owned or controlled by the TNCs concerned. The emphasis is on controlling the most important (either the largest or the most profitable) market of the final product and the product line upstream through the manipulation of strategic advantages. Even for the majority of OPEC countries, investment capital has had to be imported after 1973. To the extent that it is, this constitutes a strategic advantage for center-based capital. Its major advantage, however, lies in the integration of technology, management, and global organization.

Effects on the Periphery
The new international division of labor does not involve simply a relocation of production from old to new sites. It entails in most cases a fundamental reordering of the pro-

16. Thomas A. Callaghan, Jr., "U.S.-European Economic Cooperation in Military and Civilian Technology," lecture at Georgetown University, September 1975.

duction process as a whole.[17] One of the main characteristics is its fragmentation, which makes it feasible to relocate the various component parts to new sites. Consequently, the machinery transferred and employed is designed for specific production tasks only. These tasks fit into a worldwide organization of production involving a number of sites in different locations. This pattern not only minimizes production costs, but also gives the TNC enormous leverage over the individuated production sites and allows it to control the accumulation process more effectively through, for example, the mechanism of transfer pricing.[18] Moreover, standards and specifications as to materials used, manufacturing design, handling, and transportation are laid down by the headquarters of the company. Therefore, the possibility for using local inputs, other than labor, is often limited. Logistical and similar reasons also favor centralization of activities.[19]

A growing share of production at periphery sites is located in "free zones." Goods are imported, processed to a further stage, and reexported. This kind of industrial production, which is largely separated from the rest of the economy, results in limited employment opportunities, and often leads to adverse consequences for social equality. As a rule, only some 5 to 15 percent of the labor force is touched by foreign technology and production,[20] and the income disparity between this sector and the rest of the labor force skews domestic income distribution.[21] At the same time, however, this kind of enclave production requires its own sophisticated infrastructure (transport, communication, and so on), which also is often separated from the rest

17. Fröbel et al., *Neue Internationale Arbeitsteilung.*
18. S. M. Robbins and R. B. Stobaugh, *Money in the Multinational Enterprise: A Study of Financial Policy* (New York: Basic Books, 1974).
19. Murray, "Underdevelopment."
20. ILO, *World Employment Programme Series,* various studies.
21. Frances Stewart, "Technological Dependence in the Third World," paper presented at OECD Seminar on Science, Technology and Development in a Changing World, Paris, 1975.

of the country save that it bears the costs. Scarce resources also have to be invested in systems to secure and protect the industrial enclaves (police, military) and to supply cheap but suitable labor (schools, vocational training).

On the side of the benefits for the host country, to the extent that production is oriented towards the domestic market, the periphery gets more standardized and thus cheaper mass-consumer-oriented goods as an extension of the international product cycle. However, the category of "mass" most probably covers only the middle class, the skilled working class and the better-off peasants, not the mass of the poor, un- or underemployed. If this is the case, the poor become marginalized not only as producers, but also as consumers.

Another positive effect is that an industrial infrastructure does get built up to some extent and necessary modernization is initiated. This has technological as well as social and political implications. Skilled labor and pioneering peasants, technicians and engineers, managers, and perhaps an "entrepreneurial bourgeoisie" in the Schumpeterian sense, emerge. Some of these groups are potential social carriers of technology. They also form the nuclei of social coalitions that may change society and lay the foundations for indigenously shaped development.

Finally, TNCs do contribute to the buildup of an S&T infrastructure in the periphery. While this observation will be strongly qualified below, it is true that U.S. TNCs, for example, spend about 1 percent of their total R&D expenditures in Third World countries. Foreign expenditure accounted for 8 percent of total R&D in LDCs in 1975. The Third World countries' share of TNCs' expenditure abroad was up from 3 percent in 1966 to 9 percent in 1975. These corporate R&D efforts are, however, extremely concentrated: Brazil and Mexico alone account for close to 2/3 of TNC-generated R&D in the periphery.[22] Although R&D relo-

22. The Conference Board, *Overseas Research and Development by United States Multinationals, 1966–1975* (New York: The Conference Board, 1976).

cation is on the increase, it lags far behind relocation of productive facilities.[23]

Implications for Development
Let me summarize the impact of these trends on development in periphery countries:

1. The science and technology gap between center and periphery continues to be dramatic. Periphery countries' share of capital goods production in the world was 3.2 percent in 1970, up from 2.9 percent in 1963. The share of the capitalist center was 61 percent and of socialist countries 36 percent in 1970.[24] Of all LDCs, only Argentina, Brazil, Mexico, and India had significant levels of capital-goods production and enjoyed a high degree of self-sufficiency with regard to engineering products.

In terms of the first stages of the scientific and technological process, R&D, the share contributed by the whole of the periphery to the capitalist world's R&D expenditures was 2 percent in 1963 and around 3 percent in 1973.[25] If socialist countries are included, the periphery's share drops to about 2 percent. The position of the periphery with regard to inventive and innovative capacity is, however, even worse than these figures indicate. Much of the actual R&D outlays of international capital and center governments are not included in the figures; military R&D is the best example. And some of the expenditure of the periphery countries is appropriated by international capital through subcontracting and other means.

Finally, about 85 percent of all patents granted and registered in periphery countries are owned by foreigners, most of them being owned by large corporations in the United

23. Sanjaya Lall, "Transnationals and the Third World: The R&D Factor," *Third World Quarterly* (July 1979), vol. 1.
24. Ernst, "International Transfer of Technology."
25. Annerstedt, *Survey of the World Research.*

States, West Germany, the United Kingdom, France, Japan, and Switzerland (see table 6.1). From 90 to 95 percent of these patents are not used in production in the periphery.[26] Similarly, 56 percent of all trademarks registered in periphery countries are controlled by foreigners.[27]

2. These facts reveal the dependence of the periphery on the capitalist center. (Transfers of technology from socialist countries play a significant role in but a few countries and seem to be decreasing.[28] This dependence relationship has a technical, structural, economic, as well as socio-political aspect. I take up the first two here, and the others as points three and four.

The *technical* aspect simply consists in the fact that technology circulating to the periphery in "embodied form" (machinery, turnkey factories, and various capital goods) is dependent on the center for its maintenance and reproduction. The *structural* aspect of dependence is illustrated in the "packaging" of technology, probably the dominant form of circulation internationally.

There are basically three types of technology circulation: "simple-direct" sales, "process-packaged" sales, and "project-packaged" sales.[29] The first covers supplier-to-buyer sales of capital goods, consultancy services, and so on, according to "ordinary" market behavior. The second normally provides part of a production line in such a way that the buyer is obliged to purchase the *whole* line. This form is particularly suited to suppliers who enjoy a monopoly po-

26. UNCTAD, *The Role of the Patent System in the Transfer of Technology to Developing Countries* (New York: United Nations, 1975).

27. Peter O'Brien, "The International Trademark System and the Developing Countires," *Idea* (1978), vol. 19, no. 2.

28. United States Congress, *Science, Technology, and American Diplomacy* (Washington, D.C.: USGPO, Subcommittee on International Security and Scientific Affairs, Committee on International Relations, House of Representatives, 1976).

29. Charles Cooper and Kurt Hoffmann, "Transactions in Technology and Implications for Developing Countries," University of Sussex, Science Policy Research Unit, 1978. Mimeo.

sition with regard to some element of the production process, and who link other elements in which no monopoly is enjoyed in order to increase sales and profits. Technology packages in this form of deal may range from the supply of subsystems for production lines (such as electronic equipment) to large turnkey projects. The third form, "project-packaged" deals, normally arises out of a concern on the side of suppliers to control the use of the technology. It may also be termed "vertical transfer." The supplier may take out a share in the production venture, perhaps even wholly own it through direct investment. Or he may exercise control over production through a management contract, sales contract, or by licensing technology supplied on specific conditions that control future use. Such conditions include restricting exports and specification of product requirements. This third type of deal seems to be the preferred one by international capital, among other reasons because it gives the best opportunity for practicing transfer pricing.[30]

These patterns of control of the circulation of technology to the periphery are a major factor in structuring center-periphery relations. Another is the dependence of the periphery on the innovative and reproductive capacity of center-based science and technology systems. As a rule, the periphery is at the receiving end of the last stage of a process, where each subsequent stage successively builds on

30. Several of these control mechanisms are at work in the Zambian government's agreements with the big mineral TNCs operating its copper industry. According to the agreements, the companies not only enjoy exclusive rights over technical and engineering services and over possible future R&D, they also exercise control through the organizational structure, staffing of leadership positions, management contracts, and through financial and entrepreneurial relations. Although the companies were minority shareholders after Zambia's nationalization in 1969, President Kaunda had this to say in 1973: "The effective control of the industry was vested firmly in the minority shareholders." In a similar agreement between the Sierra Leone government and the local subsidiary of the Roan Selection Trust, a clause was included which removed the sovereignty of the host government with respect to the operation of the technology. Raphie Kaplinsky, "Control and Transfer of Technology Agreements," *IDS Bulletin* (Sussex University: March 1975), vol. 6.

the prior stage. Put briefly and roughly, the science and technology chain is composed of invention, innovation, application, and final production. The chain is a sequence of steps from the initial one where an idea or a goal is born, to where it is finally converted into a process or a product. The great majority of periphery countries really does not take part in this chain, but receives the final product.

This observation may appear to contradict the fact, referred to above, that center capital does relocate R&D to the periphery. However, a closer look at the patterns of relocation shows that R&D transfer takes place mostly in low-technology sectors where monopolization is largely absent. In high-technology sectors, relocation even to other industrialized countries is negligible.[31] In other words, the division of labor in R&D is even more strict than that in production.

3. Scientific knowledge and technology are commodities with a price, at each stage of the S&T chain.[32] Outlays in the periphery countries on imports of technology have increased exponentially over the past two decades. Industrialization and "green revolution" programs, as well as the urge to modernize according to the standards set by the new international division of labor, have been the motor behind this trend. These factors, together with domestic pressure for rapid and visible growth, have resulted in what might be called "self-reliance substitution" in science and technology. Instead of channeling more resources into building up their own science and technology systems, periphery countries on the whole tend to devote more and more resources to finance imports. The ratio between resources invested in domestic S&T activities and those used

31. Lall, "Transnationals."

32. Constantine Vaitsos, "Estrageias Alternativas en la Comercializacion de la Technologia: El Punto de Vista de los Paises en vias de Desarrollo," JUNAC Doc. Jun/di 5 (October 20, 1970); Charles Cooper and F. Sercovich, *The Channels and Mechanisms for the Transfer of Technology from Developed to Developing Countries* (Geneva: UNCTAD, 1971); and Surendra Patel, "Le cout de la dependance technologique," *CERES, FAO Review of Development,* (March-April 1973), vol. 6.

on imports was 1:2.5 in 1968.[33] There is reason to believe that it is on the order of 1:4 today, and considerably more in OPEC countries, with vast currency surpluses, and in some of the highly externally oriented, "newly industrializing countries."

If imports were accompanied by active domestic adaptation and other efforts to integrate the imported knowledge into the development process, high import levels for some time might be a viable strategy. This was "the Japanese model,"[34] later copied, it seems, by Taiwan. They appear to be the exceptional cases, however, rather than the norm. In the absence of such integration, no real *transfer* of technology takes place. For it to occur, three conditions would have to be met. First, there would have to be an identifiable recipient in the periphery country with the capacity to make use of the technology according to self-defined goals. Second, all aspects of the technology concerned which are necessary for it to be put into stable productive use by this recipient would have to be transferred. Third, there would have to be a clear net gain for the recipient in the exchange process, so that the resources the recipient accumulates would have to be greater than the resources transmitted to the other side.

In actuality, if one adds to the direct financial outlays such second-order consequences of the existing pattern of technology transfer as the brain drain, one can begin to entertain the possibility of there being instances of a *reverse* transfer. For example, in the period from 1961 to 1972, three industrialized countries, the United States, Canada, and the United Kingdom, received skilled S&T personnel from peripheral countries that just about equaled in value the total flow of ODA from these same countries.[35]

33. Patel, *CERES*.

34. Kinhide Mushakoji, "La restructuration de la recherche et du dévélopment scientifique et technologies au service du Tiers Monds," *Revue Tiers Monde* (April-June 1979), vol. 20.

35. UNCTAD, "Technology: Development Aspects of the Reverse Transfer of Technology." Document Prepared for UNCTAD V, Manilla, TD/239, May 1979.

4. One major reason for this perversion of S&T efforts in the periphery is the lack of linkage between such efforts and local productive goals. As an example, local workshops and laboratories have developed and proven industrial technologies but have found it difficult to convince domestic manufacturing firms to take them up. Instead, these firms sign licensing agreements for corresponding technology with foreign suppliers. India is a case in point.[36] On the other hand, the Indian S&T system has been criticized for not linking up with efforts to develop agriculture and the countryside at the level of small peasants and poorer communities. Its work is directed toward the "modern" sector, to industry and high-productivity agriculture, while it is irrelevant to the needs of the masses.[37]

There are several possible explanations for this situation. Local capitalists prefer foreign technology because they believe a priori that it is better than the locally generated one. This is partly a result of the demonstration effect of the international division of labor, whereby those economies which "have made it" represent the model for those which have not. A second explanation is that periphery capitalism is tied to international capital and must buy its technology for reasons of ownership patterns and the like. Third, there is a class factor and the urge for social mobility, leading to what has been called an "internal brain drain."[38] R&D employees perceive career opportunities and other channels of personal mobility as being intimately linked to the foreign economic sector. This sector looks more rewarding socially, intellectually, as well as economically. Finally—and related to the first and third factors—is the process of "self-coloni-

36. Charles Cooper, "Policy Interventons for Technological Innovation in Less-Developed Countries" (Sussex: Sussex University, Science Policy Research Unit, April 1976), mimeo.; and V. A. Chitale, *Foreign Technology in India* (New Delhi: Economic and Scientific Research Council of India, 1973).

37. Amaluya Reddy, lecture at workshop on "Research Policy Programme," University of Lund, Sweden, May 31–June 2, 1977.

38. A. Cairncross and M. Puri, eds., *Employment, Income Distribution and Development Strategy: Essays in Honor of H. W. Singer* (London: Macmillan, 1976).

zation" or the acceptance of Western values and consumption patterns.[39]

The prestige, class character and the demonstration effect of modern Western technology are main elements in what I referred to as the political-cultural factor. It not only marginalizes large fractions of labor and the mass of consumers. It also excludes locally generated and available technology from systematic social use. In studies of Kenya and Indonesia, it has been shown that a wide range of technological knowledge as well as locally generated "embodied technology" were left out of the development plans of the state and the corporate-private sectors.[40] This knowledge is often noncommercial, or it is generated in an informal, intermediate sector, and thus is considered to be irrelevant to corporate interests. The state sector participates in the rejection and the marginalization of the village blacksmiths, carpenters, peasants, artisians, and other carriers of the locally generated technology. Even publicly owned workshops with a long tradition of maintenance, adaptation, and innovation are being marginalized.

Domestically generated technology is often referred to as "traditional." In such a reference lies a connotation of obsolescence and inferiority. Whether the "traditional" technology is, in fact, obsolete, or for what concrete purposes it may be so, is often not demonstrated. Indeed, we seem to know less about the obsolescence of "traditional" technology than we know about the irrelevance or inappropriateness of foreign imported technology.

In conclusion, while a full cost-benefit analysis of the circulation of technology between center and periphery at the global level is not possible at this stage, the major fac-

39. Karl P. Sauvant, "His Master's Voice," *CERES* (September-October 1976), vol. 9.

40. J. Moeliono and R. Dilts, "Count Them In," *Reports Magazine* (May 1979); Martin Bell, "The Exploitation of Indigenous Knowledge or the Indigenous Exploitation of Knowledge: Whose of What for What?" *IDS Bulletin* (Sussex University, January 1979), vol. 10; M. Godfrey and G. C. M. Mutiso, "Economics, Politics, and Education," *IDS Bulletin* (Sussex University, February 1975), vol. 6.

tors that would go into such an analysis may be summarized. Increased productivity, accumulation of productive
equipment and knowledge, some education and training of
some people, and limited inter-industrial linkages forward
and backward are among the potential *positive* effects.
Among the potential *negative* factors one may mention financial outlays—including the effect on balance of payments—brain drain, insufficient and/or inappropriate transfer, linking up national productive and intellectual potential
to foreign interests thus reproducing the "enclave economy," and the demolition of indigenous cultures through
the penetration of alien values. Thus, simple reliance on the
"technology transfer" brought about by the changing international division of labor is no solution to the development
problems facing most periphery countries.

SELECTIVE DISSOCIATION IN PRACTICE

If close reliance on the circulation of center technology
provides no universal cure, what options exist for pursuing
a greater degree of self-reliance? What are their prospects
for success? What are the obstacles impeding success? In
the present section, I examine the experience of two major
developing countries that have attempted to achieve greater
technological self-reliance by adopting a stance of selective
dissociation: Algeria and India. Both are, a priori, prime
candidates for success. Algeria combines resource richness
with a nationalist developmental ideology, and is attempting to exploit its resources in order to achieve long-term
self-reliance by state-managed relationships with center
capital. India has one of the largest S&T systems in the
global periphery (see table 6.1) and has deliberately resisted close association out of fear of its adverse consequences.

Algeria
The Algerian policy is an attempt to industrialize in the course of a few decades according to three strategic principles: (1) to link manufacturing and semi-manufacturing industry with the needs of agriculture; (2) to integrate the economy by developing inter-sectorial linkages (or what the Algerians call *noircissement de la matrice*) on the basis of certain "industrializing industries"[41] — or those capital and intermediate goods industries that are capable of generating the largest spread effects; and (3) to build up a national S&T capacity. The state assumes dominant nominal control over the economy; only some service sectors are still in private hands. The Algerian strategy, however, is highly dependent on imports of technology and management expertise and on exports to foreign markets.

Can "introversion" of growth effects be achieved by extrovert means? In other words, can short-run, state-managed reliance on the center lead to greater autonomy in the longer run? Probably in no other contemporary periphery country is the paradox of this strategy better revealed than in the case of Algeria. What follows is a brief description and analysis of the pattern and some hypotheses on possible future outcomes.[42]

The Import Syndrome. Algeria is rapidly building a modern productive base and trying to create a domestic

41. Gerard Destanne de Bernis, "Industries industrialisantes et contenu d'une politique d'intégation régionale," *Economie appliquée,* (1966), 3:3–4; (1968), 4:1.
42. I discuss the Algeria case at greater length in another paper: Hveem, "Technology and the Contradictions Between Internationalization of Capital and National Development: Some Notes on the Case of Algeria," in Dieter Ernst, *International Transfer.* Detailed accounts of the practices of technology imports since the 1960s may be found in Gerard Destanne de Bernis, "Les industries industrialisantes et les options algériennes," *Tiers monde,* (July-September 1971), no. 47; Pierre Judet, *Le processus d'industrialisation en Algerie* (Grenoble: IREP, June 1973); Dimitri Germidis, *Le Mahgreb, la France et l'enjeu technologique* (Paris: Editions Cujas, 1976); OECD, *Migrations et transfert de technologie: Etude de cas. Algerie, Maroc, Tunisie et France* (Paris: OECD Development Center, 1975); Abdelkrim Abib, *L'access à la technologie: le cas algerien* (Lausanne: Université de Lausanne, Ecole

market and national S&T capacities to match that base. Domestic investments in petroleum, raw material processing, and manufacturing industry grew rapidly from the late 1960s to mid- and late 1970s. The value of technology-import contracts with foreign suppliers almost trebled from 1970–72 to 1973–75 and has further increased, although less dramatically, since 1975. Petrodollars are literally oiling the economy.

Reliance on the center is thus clear. However, there are elements of selective dissociation in various measures adopted, such as attempts to establish new bargaining arrangements, demands for the fullest possible transfer of technology, centralized monitoring of technology imports, and diversification of suppliers. Bargaining with external suppliers and the acquisition of foreign technology is concentrated in the state sector. In principle, a mixture of centralization and decentralization is sought. Overall planning, decision making, and monitoring of imports are to be centrally performed. Negotiation of specific contracts, technology acquisitions, and applications are the responsibilities of the individual state companies in their respective sectors of activity. According to the model, the state, through the planning directorate and the principal ministries, either acts as a broker or imposes the general collective will whenever there are opposing claims or conflicts of interest among the conpanies.

Concerning attempts to strengthen the national bargaining position, a first observation is that negotiators, especially those of a weakly industrialized, peripheral economy such as Algeria, very often suffer from lack of information, especially information about information, when dealing with powerful technology sellers. The seller knows

des Hautes Etudes Commerciales, 1976); Carlos Anex, *The Transfer of Petroleum Technology to Algeria* (Sussex: Sussex University, Science Policy Research Unit, 1975); and Abdellatif Benachenhou, *Foreign Firms and the Transfer of Technology to the Algerian Economy* (Geneva: ILO, World Employment programme, 1976), mimeo.

what he is selling, but the buyer does not know precisely what he wants or can get. Bargaining on design, prices, and other contract specifications requires detailed knowledge on what to look for, what to ask for, what alternative choices exist to the offer made by the negotiating counterpart, and so on. The problem of getting access to the inner secrets of the technology circulated has been experienced in the case of training of management,[43] and more particularly in the case of the engineering department of SNS, the *Societe Nationale de Siderurgie*. In a project with the French firm Sofresid, for example, the SNS got basic instructions and was able to get calculations verified, but the French firm "was reluctant to reveal their methods of work."[44]

Second, it is questionable whether the principle of centralized monitoring really is applied as envisaged. If the individual state companies are not independent of the central organs of the state bureaucracy, at least they have considerable room for maneuver. The company does the real bargaining, possesses or commissions (when foreign consultants are required) the most detailed know-how and information, and normally takes care of all other aspects of the project concerned in addition to technology acquisition. Moreover, the position of the companies is enhanced by the fact that they are required to run their operations so as to generate a surplus of their own, thus they also deal competitively with other Algerian companies on prices and other terms of exchange.

Third, the relatively free hand which the state companies enjoy in the acquisition of technology, coupled with the efficiency demand to which they seem to be subject, leads to a degree of integration with the foreign technological milieu that is often greater than that of their integration with

43. Benachenhou, *Foreign Firms.*
44. Jacques Perrin and John Roberts, "Design Engineering and the Mastery of Knowledge for the Accumulation of Capital in Developing Countries," paper presented at the 23d Study Seminar, Institute for Development Studies, Sussex University, 1971.

other state companies in- or outside the sector concerned. Ever-growing increases in technology purchases from abroad is one indication of this.[45] Another is instances where locally available technological milieus, such as maintenance and repair shops, are virtually cut off from jobs because the state company concerned has chosen to let its foreign clients do the maintenance service.[46]

On the other hand, Algeria's role under Boumedienne as a leading spokesman for the Third World, as well as its position as a seller of quality crude petroleum and a potentially leading, future world supplier of natural gas, has helped its overall bargaining position vis-à-vis the center. For example, Sonatrach, the state oil and gas company, has been able to obtain concessionary technology transfers and market information from German firms.

A second element of selective dissociation is the diversification of foreign trade and assistance that Algeria has pursued ever since its independence, especially with respect to France. France's share of Algerian overall imports fell from 69 percent in 1966 to 27 percent in 1974 and its share of technology contracts from 60 percent 1962–66 to 33 percent in 1974 (in value terms). At the beginning of 1977, some seventy U.S. companies held contracts worth some 6 billion U.S. dollars, with several billion worth of more contracts in view.[47] A similar inroad into the former French *domene* has been made by West German companies.[48]

But does geographical diversification really matter? There are several reasons why it might not. First, the various fractions of center capital may coordinate their activities. In fact, they often do, through subcontracting, tacit market-sharing arrangements, and the like. The gas lique-

45. Abib, *L'access à la technologie*.
46. Abdellatif Benachenhou, "Économie Algerienne: Enjeux et realités," *Révolution Africaine* (December 1977), pp. 721–22.
47. *New York Times*, February 26, 1977.
48. U.S. Congress, *Science, Technology, and American Diplomacy*, and *Industries et Travaux d'Outre Mer*, February and November 1976.

faction plant in Skikda, the single largest industrial contract before 1971, illustrates the point. One French and one German engineering firm competed for the contract, based on two different processes of production. The French firm, *Technip*, won the contract valued at 900 million French francs at the time. Among the subcontractors chosen, counting only the most important ones, there were two French, one Swiss, and two West German firms; *Technip* was charged with paying and supervising the subcontractors. A noticeable trend away from contracts with Soviet and East European countries also may increase the prospects for such supplier coordination.

Geographical diversification internationally and sectorial diversification domestically have taken place in Algeria. However, there is a continued and sometimes deepened geographical concentration in certain sectors, such as in mechanical and electrical engineering (West German firms), liquefied gas (United States), and petroleum processing (France). Thus, a tendency to diversify overall international connections may be offset by a tendency to become dependent on *specific* fractions of center capital at the branch or sectoral levels. There is of course a logic to this pattern. To over-diversify suppliers within a single branch or plant may result in unacceptable efficiency losses. At the same time, however, sectoral concentration can also reach levels that may result in the reproduction of dependence, if only in different forms.

The "Introversion" Problem. Among Algeria's efforts to make the inputs of foreign technology a dynamic element in the domestic development process, three measures stand out as being particularly important: technical training of the labor force, and management in *produit en main,* or "plant in production," contracts; education and vocational training generally; and the building-up of an autonomous national science and technology system. As the three go very much together, I shall treat them jointly.

Algeria plans to master the research-and-development end of the S&T process by the year 2000. A timetable exists for achieving that goal in steps. Monitoring of imports already exists, as noted above. By the early 1980s, Algeria is supposed to master the assimilation of imported technology. By 1985 or so, according to plan, institutions will have been set up and properly staffed to cover the various aspects of engineering so that imported technology can be domestically reproduced.[49] With an increasing emphasis on basic research and R&D resources over time, it is believed that a relatively independent national S&T system will be established before the end of the century.

The policy pursued seems to be one of conscious effort to follow the plan, combined with a series of leaps into unknown territory with little certainty as to where the leaps will lead. The efforts to see to it that the reservoir and institutions of skill-formation keep pace with the buildup of the productive system are immense. Between 1974 and 1980, some 30 percent of overall public investments was directed toward research, training, and education. About 25 percent is spent on education alone, which means that the Algerian government is very conscious of the need to broaden the basis of knowledge in the society. The output of researchers, engineers, and trained personnel at different levels of skill is increasing rapidly.[50] Still, questions remain as to whether these efforts are enough to bridge the gap between the productive and the innovative systems. Indeed, after the big leap in productive investments from 1974 on, they may not even prevent a widening of the gap. The main problem may not be one of numbers; the level of qualification of the labor force and the capacity of scientific personnel must

49. Mohamed Benbouta, "Situation et rôle d'engineering dans l'integration du système industriel algérien" (Ph.D. diss. Université de Grenoble, UER Sciences Economiques, 1972).

50. Mohamed Benyahia, interview in *Impact* (Unesco) (May–September 1976), no. 26.

keep pace with, and be consciously linked to, the range and level of sophistication of the means of production.

Moreover, serious problems in the production system were unofficially reported during the late 1970s. Several factories produced at far below capacity-levels. Some would explain this as a temporary problem of infant industry. If so, although the economic costs are considerable, the burden can be carried by the petrodollar economy. But if the problem takes on a more lasting character, then both the causes and the remedies must be sought in other factors. It may be that this problem too reflects the fact that the level of skills is lagging behind the sophistication of the means of production.[51]

The *produit en main* contract is supposed to alleviate these problems. In many respects it is an interesting and important innovation in itself. The purpose is to train the labor force on-site and to get production going at desired levels and according to required quality specifications. The latter will sometimes take precedence over the former, because this type of arrangement calls for a part of the output to be bought or marketed by the foreign contractor. As a result, however, the Algerian company may consent to leave more of the operations of production in foreign hands for a longer period than it would otherwise have done.

The possibility that these tendencies may reproduce the export "enclave" has probably been underestimated by Algerian officials. Admittedly, there is bound to be a certain friction between the introversion and extroversion tendencies in the Algerian economy as in *any* economy which attempts to develop by making use of the international circulation of technology, finance, and products. And Algeria could not conceivably have done without taking advantage of her hydrocarbon resources through exports. The question is whether the Algerian industrialization strategy—with

51. Hveem, "Technology and the Contradictions."

its emphasis on international competitiveness and thus on meeting the standards of the industrialized countries' markets, economies of scale, maximum efficiency, and sophisticated technology—is not making long-term introversion through short-term extroversion a practical impossibility.

The "filling in of the matrix" is complicated not only for reasons of its own—because the planning and implementation of a very detailed system of interindustrial and intersectorial linkages is inherently difficult—it is also restricted because of the extrovert policy of seeking assistance in solving these problems. When a sector, or single industrial project, subjects itself to the norms, specifications, and the technical coefficients of the foreign supplier who has no a priori interest in the internal applications and linkages to other sectors, the coupling envisaged may turn out to be impossible. It may be doubly difficult then for the Algerian institutions to catch up with and adapt individuated production units if they, as seems to be the trend, are established primarily within or are related directly to external markets and companies.

Conclusion. Algeria stands at a critical juncture between extroversion, which is designed to build up an indigenous capacity but which has also produced an internally fragmented industrial structure, and "filling in of the matrix," which may become increasingly difficult unless introversion is soon effected. The international environment will affect the outcome by structuring the constraints and opportunities that Algeria faces. But the outcome will be determined much more directly by the evolution of political, social, and institutional factors in Algeria. And, whatever may hold elsewhere, in Algeria these domestic factors are not simply a mere reflection of international forces.

India

To a considerable extent, India has already created the industrial base that is characterized by the term "industrializing industries." India already possesses much of the scientific and technological capacity that Algeria plans to have by the end of the century. And it has accomplished this without extensive foreign penetration, deliberately guarding against it.

Indigenous Capacity. Indian capabilities include mastering both the intermediate stage of innovation, that is, product design and improving on design, as well as the advanced stages, that is, the setting up of complete production systems and designing new industrial processes. This capacity has been built up over a period of almost three decades.[52] The first concrete expression of the science and technology program was the Scientific Policy Resolution passed by the Indian Parliament in 1958, but the foundation for it in fact had been laid as early as 1938, in a plan drawn up by the Congress party under Nehru's leadership.[53]

Unlike Algeria, India did not have the possibility of rapid industrialization because she lacked the financial means to buy foreign technology in huge quantities over a short period. Moreover, India disposes of an important home market, an objective basis for introversion, and is thus much less dependent on exporting the final products of industrialization. And India's scientific and technological capacity reflects a knowledge base whose growth has kept pace with the evolution of its productive system.

India's capacity-building in science and technology has

52. For this discussion of the Indian experience, I draw on Ashok Parthasarathi, "India's Efforts to Build an Autonomous Capacity in Science and Technological Development," *Development Dialogue* (1979), no. 1; Ward Morehouse, "The Endless Quest: Science and Technology for Human Betterment in India," discussion paper no. 106, University of Lund, Research Policy Program, December 1976; Sanjaya Lall, "Developing Countries as Exporters of Technology: A Preliminary Analysis," Oxford University, Institute of Economics and Statistics, 1978, mimeo; K. K. Subrahmanian, *Import of Capital and Technology: A Study of Foreign Collaborations in Indian Industry* (New Delhi: People's Publishing House, 1972); Chitale, *Foreign Technology in India*; and V. N. Balasubramanyam, *International Transfer of Technology to India* (New York: Praeger, 1973).

53. Parthasarathi, "India's Efforts."

been under heavy state control and, perhaps an underestimated factor, under the effective leadership of the Prime Minister's office. The presence of strong political support probably is one of the decisive factors behind the relative success of India, differentiating it from the Algerian as well as other periphery countries.

India's substantial and growing capacity in these fields has even led to the penetration of foreign markets. India has outcompeted center countries for consultancy contracts in the Third World;[54] over the last few years consultancy services abroad have increased by 200 percent annually, and the exports of engineering goods grew by 30 percent.[55] This exceeds the capacity and performance of Argentina and other Latin American countries, whose advances in the engineering and capital goods sectors are also quite considerable, and it may soon represent a real breakthrough into international markets.[56] India is already becoming able to offer some comparable but cheaper technologies than West German or U.S. firms, possibly less packaged and potentially more appropriate to the needs of other periphery countries.

The Missing (Domestic) Link. The external brain drain from India has been considerable, as noted earlier. There has also been an internal brain drain, from the so-called traditional to the modern sector. As a result, the great bulk of the Indian S&T system is "not necessarily of immediate relevance to or used by the domestic productive sectors."[57] Thus, while India is capable of producing its own means of production, and has most of the capacity to achieve a per-

54. *Newsweek,* October 16, 1974.

55. Lall, "Developing Countries as Exporters."

56. Jorge Katz, lecture at the "Workshop on Technology," Science Policy Research Unit, Sussex University, July 1978; and Constantine Vaitsos, "The Role of Transnational Corporations in Latin American Integration Efforts," Report prepared for UNCTAD Secretariat, 1978. Mimeo.

57. UNCTAD, *Technology Planning in Developing Countries. A Preliminary View* (Geneva: UNCTAD, TD/B/C-6/29, May 25, 1978), p. 17.

manent innovation of it, the *objectives* in the pursuit of which the S&T system employs this degree of freedom at the national level is a "blurred xerox copy," as one critic has put it,[58] of the patterns and methods of Western industrial society. And while India exhibits a strong S&T export performance, it is not so much an alternative to as an indigenized conduit for center-based internationalization.

The reasons for this failure are in part politico-strategic, stemming from regional competition with China and Pakistan, as well as from a concern with the national prestige that the production of an atomic bomb, missiles, and conventional military hardware can procure in the international security system. In part it is class based, stemming from the fact that local capitalists have a vested interest in and the capacity to emulate the consumption patterns and lifestyles diffused through the capitalist division of labor. And in part it is cultural, reflecting the retarded process of decolonization in this realm.[59]

There is a long tradition in India favoring what has come to be known as "appropriate" technology, and it is reflected to some extent in national policy. Some 20 million people are employed in small-scale or village industries, with the state reserving certain branches of industry for them. Moreover, the introduction of the Swarash tractor has been a success.[60] And two government agencies have been established to support appropriate technologies, the Khadi and Village Industries Commission (DVIC) and the National Research Development Corporation (NRDC).

But these efforts are limited in their effects, for several reasons. First, the small-scale sector has not been provided with the kinds of incentives that would allow it to compete effectively with the large-scale industrial sector. And transnational corporations, large family businesses, and politi-

---

58. Reddy, lecture at University of Lund.

59. Jeffrey Harrod, "Transnational Power," *The Yearbook of World Affairs, 1976* (London: Stevens, 1976); see also David Laitin, in this volume.

60. Parthasarathi, "India's Efforts."

cally powerful traders control most of the inputs into the small-scale industry sector. As a result, locally generated technology has been outcompeted by Indian and indeed by foreign large-scale producers even in such industries as soap, cooking oil, eating utensils, low-cost building materials, and bullock-cart tires.[61] Second, state efforts to support appropriate technology have tended to marginalize it rather than to integrate it into the overall industrial configuration of the economy; some 80 percent of the processes developed by the NRDC and now in production has been in the small-scale sector.[62] Lastly, many of the so-called appropriate technologies developed for this sector turn out to be not appropriate at all. For example, a technique to isolate protein from ground nuts, developed by the Central Food Technological Institute in Mysore, promoted by the NRDC and commercialized under license by Tata, India's largest industrial house, produced a protein drink that was far too costly for the rural poor. And an electrically-powered *ghani,* a large mortar and pestle arrangement designed to extract oil from ground nuts, which was developed by KVIC, produced a system that provided fewer employment opportunities than a bullock *ghani,* was too costly for individual villagers, and provided insufficient returns on investment to be of interest to private capital. These are not isolated cases.[63] In sum, the prevailing picture at the national level is of an extrovert S&T system, an industrialization model that replicates the dominant production and consumption patterns of the center, and of a limited and marginalized sector within which alternative patterns are supported but, even these, often ineffectively so.

Local Technology Systems. Cooperative efforts employing local technologies are being undertaken in several parts of India, building on such precolonial experiences as, for example, communal water supply and irrigation projects

61. Joseph Hanlon, *New Scientist,* May 19, May 26, June 2, 1977.
62. *Invention Intelligence* (January-February 1977).
63. Hanlon, *New Scientist.*

in the Mysore area.[64] One such instance is the organization of peasant cooperatives to build *ghobar* gas plants, in the wake of some of the social effects of the "green revolution."[65] These plants were first developed and promoted by the KVIC in the 1950s, but had not been spread widely. More recently, the total count had reached some 40,000. They produce methane gas and manure from cattle dung mixed with water. The gas is used for heating and cooking, and in some cases even for small-scale power generation. The manure is used as a fertilizer. Studies from India, the United States and elsewhere show that this fertilizer is as effective as inorganic fertilizer for soil enhancement, water retaining capacity, and good aeration.[66] In addition, the process offers more job opportunities and uses local resources, whereas inorganic fertilizers are often imported. It is also more ecologically sound. In short, the *ghobar* gas plant seems to meet many of the criteria of an appropriate technology for the purposes of fertilizer production, and it also produces a source of energy as a by-product. Taking into consideration that some 50–60 percent of India's total energy consumption is non-commercial, mostly in the form of wood and cattle dung that is burned dry, greater use of the plant has a potentially vast positive effect on social as well as ecological aspects of development.[67]

However, given the existing income distribution, only 15 percent of the farmers can afford to invest in a family-sized plant.[68] Even the smallest plant requires the dung from

64. Per Olav Reinton, "Technology and Social Structure in Karnataka," *Third Report on the Karnataka Socio-Economic Development and Regional Plan Project* (June 1976).

65. Keith Griffin, *The Green Revolution: An Economic Analysis* (Geneva: United Nations Research Institute for Social Development, 1972); and F. Moore Lappé and J. Collins, *Food First* (New York: Ballantine Books, 1979).

66. Ananthakrishnan, "Techno-Economic Study of Biogas Plants," International Peace Research Institute, PRIO Publ. S02/77, 1976. Mimeo.

67. A. Makhijani, *Energy Policy for the Rural Third World* (London and Washington: International Institute for Environment and Development, 1976).

68. Ramesh Bhatia, "Economic Appraisal of Biogas Units in India: Framework for Social Benefit Cost Analysis," *Economic and Political Weekly* (August 1977), special number.

several cows. And private moneylenders are the only alternative for those who are not able to accumulate enough risk capital themselves. Further, the promotion of plants means that dung, which previously was free, now has a cash value. Landless villagers therefore can no longer pick it easily from the road. This in turn means that they get no fuel at all, since they cannot afford to buy biogas. These constraints and side effects mean that it is necessary to introduce national public regulation and incentives alongside local cooperative utilization of biogas and organic manure. But here the scheme has suffered from lack of central support, as well as from opposition by local, national and international interests that favor the use of inorganic fertilizer.

An example of more effective integration of the various levels of social organization, as well as of science and technology with mass needs, is the case of hand pumps used on wells in the Karnataka region that were appropriately modified by the ASTRA group at the Indian Institute of Technology. More than half the pumps, based on U.S. and British design, did not work. Using simple methods, ASTRA found out why and designed new equipment to repair the damage. ASTRA spent 2 percent as much on the problem as had three different international organizations and succeeded in solving it, while these organizations had not.[69] The new equipment is now adopted for all future hand-pump installations in the Karnataka region.

More broadly, to enhance their appreciation of the needs of their rural "clients," several academic-scientific institutions have begun to establish small extension units in rural villages. The idea is that these units will gradually be able to absorb the perspective and rationale of the farmers and the local entrepreneurs, so as better to focus their technical expertise on local problems. And a large part of the work is to be done by the local people themselves, not by R&D imported from the modern S&T sector.

69. Hanlon, *New Scientist*.

These cases constitute limited exceptions to the norm. But they demonstrate that the capacity to pursue alternative modes does exist in India today.

Conclusion. India has in many respects the most extensive, highly developed S&T capacity of any developing country. It has guarded against excessive dependence on external sources. It is capable of producing its own means of production, and in many sectors it does not need to import the inputs that go into producing its means of production. It has a vast potential for growth and development. Yet it suffers from a pervasive dualism, whereby its "modern" S&T system, and its attending incentive structures, as well as its production and consumption patterns, imitating those that prevail in the industrialized consumer societies, are divorced from the needs and the indigenous capacities of its own "traditional" sector.

TOWARD A STRATEGY FOR TECHNOLOGICAL SELF-RELIANCE

The "scientific and technological illusion," whereby individuals see technology "as a substitute for social and political choices,"[70] represents one of the greatest assets possessed by international capital wishing to penetrate the periphery. Because of this illusion, technology is perceived apart from its social carriers, and the belief gains hold that the means of development can be purchased—off foreign shelves. But all technology is linked to social carriers, and all social carriers have concrete interests. In the absence of compensatory measures, there is little doubt but that the interests of international capital will prevail. This is so not only because it possesses superior material capabilities, but

70. J. J. Salomon, *Science et politique* (Paris: Edition du Seuil, 1970), p. 110.

also because the technology illusion enhances those capabilities by undermining indigenous technological capacity. The socio-political and cultural context of technology, then, is decisive as to its impact. And it is on the ability to achieve appropriate linkages among these that successful development depends. In most cases, establishing such linkages will require measures of selective dissociation.

Domestic Linkages
S&T policies far too often have been implicitly based on a linear view of the innovation process, coupled in many instances with simple "trickle down" notions. In other words, the answer to *all* problems of innovation has been believed to lie in "the setting up of R&D institutions, usually with a token extension service to show that contact with industry is of concern. These approaches have usually failed."[71] There is often an absence of linkage in two respects: first, the "modern" productive sector is not linked to domestic mass needs, and second the S&T system is not linked to the domestic productive sector.

The problem in essence may be formulated in this way: in order for a social fabric to *develop*, the social system and the means of production ideally should evolve integrally. A developed society is one that is capable of producing and reproducing its own means of production. This does not mean that it imports no technology, but that it is capable of assimilating technology imports into well-articulated, intersectoral, and urban-rural linkages. The more a society resembles this state of affairs, the more it is able to benefit from an associative strategy without suffering its deleterious consequences. The less it does, the less is it able to avoid such effects without the buffering mechanism of selective dissociation.

71. Ivan Illich, "Alternative Technologies and the Three Dimensional Option," paper presented at the NGO Forum on Science and Technology for Development, Vienna, August 24, 1979. See also Laitin, in this volume.

Measures of selective dissociation fail to achieve their objective for a variety of specific reasons, many of which were encountered above. One general reason is that they are insufficiently responsive to the issue of linkages. This is true even of such relatively ambitious forms as "technology import substitution," which consists of replacing elements of packaged transfers with locally generated technology. But imports per se are not the problem. More often than not, the problem resides in the linkage between technology and demand, whether the technology is imported or not. All other things being equal, an imported technology responsive to indigenous demand is preferable to an indigenous technology responsive to foreign, but not to local demand.

Another general reason for the failure of selective dissociation measures is the time frame of decision making. Even governments whom no one can accuse of being knowing puppets or unwitting stooges for foreign capitalists are politically compelled to respond to domestic needs by purchasing a "quick fix" abroad rather than adapting or developing indigenous means. That the quick fix often fails to "deliver the goods" in the long run, by which time domestic means might have been in place at lesser expense and with more beneficial side effects, often is not a part of short-term calculations. The rationale is understandable at one level. Ultimately, though, it reflects a deep loss of confidence in one's own culture, raising the question of how far techno-economic dissociation can proceed without corresponding measures in the cultural realm.[72]

An "Ideal Typical" Model
If the various elements that seem to be related to success in achieving self-reliance in the technology sector are combined, and those apparently responsible for failure are eliminated, an idealized strategy results, the component parts of which I simply enumerate:

72. See the discussion by David Laitin in chapter 7.

1. A minimum size and endowment of national S&T systems is of course necessary, though it will vary considerably depending upon the levels and types of economic activities pursued. Table 6.1 indicates that few developing countries actually meet that minimum, even if it is set low and capacities are viewed optimistically. There is no question, therefore, that technology imports will continue. The issue is how it will be best accomplished.

2. Technology imports should take place through mechanisms that assure central monitoring and filtering in the first instance, and adaptation and assimilation subsequently. Experience seems to show that it is feasible to achieve monitoring immediately, filtering in the short run, adaptation and some assimilation in the medium run, and locally-based innovation as well as basic R&D in the long run.

3. Indigenous technology must receive a higher priority. Imports now consume the bulk of outlays. Instead, national S&T expenditures ought to reflect greater concern with: (a) improvements on existing production systems and local technologies; (b) systematic adaptation of new methods developed by others; and (c) funding R&D as a complement to (a) and (b). It follows that domestic S&T institutions and personnel need to be closely integrated into and made responsive to national-development objectives and needs.

4. Both imports and indigenous efforts must be embedded in an integrated development strategy. Agriculture must be linked with industry. And the so-called industrializing industries must be closely linked with one another. Moreover, the conventional wisdom concerning the necessary scale and capital intensity of these industries, including even cement production and hydroelectricity, must be questioned, as reduction has been achieved in many cases without loss of economic efficiency and considerable gains in levels of employment and ecological stability.[73] And

73. See footnote 42; and Hayrettin Erdemli, "La Minisiderurgie: Evolution des filières et quelques characteristiques" (Grenoble: IREP, 1979). Mimeo.

"appropriate technologies" should not be encapsulated within a marginal sector so labeled, but integrated into the mainstream of both agricultural and industrial production.

5. In the final analysis, achieving greater self-reliance will also depend on the redistribution of land, income, and social power. Where there is a highly unequal income distribution, and where those at the upper levels therefore are given privileged access to scarce resources, the products in demand and the technologies employed in their production are unlikely to satisfy the basic consumption and employment needs of the vast majority of the population. At the same time, however, it is inconceivable to change income distribution so drastically as to produce alternative technological configurations by means of changing effective demand alone. Thus, the entire sequence of component parts of a self-reliance strategy must be incorporated into a plan that deliberately links this strategy to the needs of the mass of low-income producers and consumers.

6. The lack of emphasis on international measures throughout this discussion has been deliberate. The evidence suggests that action at this level can only be supplementary to action at the national and local level. And it also suggests that international coordination of S&T policies by periphery countries should consist, first of all, of a *defense* against disadvantageous association, and second, of efforts to develop a system of exchange and support among these countries. By and large, the negotiations characterized as the North-South Dialogue do not embody this order of priority.

Just as there is no such thing as a typical developing country, so there is no single strategy that is equally applicable to all cases at all times. The features outlined here specify general criteria and orientations, not the detailed policies which perforce will depend on innumerable domestic and international factors attending any particular case.

TABLE 6.1: Some Indicators of Dependence, "Technological Autonomy," and Socioeconomic Development

	Total R&D Manpower, 1973 (in 1000s) (1)	General Expenditure on R&D, 1973 (US $ million) (2)	General Expenditure on R&D as % of GNP, 1973 (3)	Stock of Foreign Direct Investments, as % of GNP, 1973 (4)	% of Registered Patents Owned by Foreigners, 1971 (5)	% of Workforce Outside Agr., 1970 (6)	Infant Mortality Rates (deaths/ 1,000 live births). 1974 (7)
India	120,700[e,f]	276	0.4	2.2	83	31	134
Argentina	25,200	121	0.3	6.5	77	84	60
Indonesia	19,600[f]	47[f]	0.3	9.5	–	34	125
Brazil	16,200	313	0.4	9.4	78	54	82
South Korea	15,000	39	0.3	5.0	16	49	47
Cuba	13,200	51[b]	0.8	–	97	69	29
Vietnam*	12,000	20	0.3	2.8	–	24	200
Philippines	11,200	32	0.3	7.0	95	47	74
Egypt	10,700	76	0.8	–	98	46	98
Iran	9,900[d]	47[d]	0.2	3.5	93	54	139
Pakistan	8,800	15	0.2	6.3	93	41	124
Ghana	8,600[d]	20[c]	0.5	9.0	100	42	133
Sudan	8,200†	9	0.3	1.0	–	18	136
Thailand	7,800	39	0.4	4.9	–	20	78
Chile	6,500[b]	34[e]	0.5	11.6	95	76	71
Mexico	5,700[e]	108	0.2	5.9	–	55	61
Bangladesh	4,900	14[e,f]	0.2	–	–	14	132
Peru	4,200[f]	25[b]	0.4	15.0	–	55	110
Sri Lanka	3,600	4	0.1	–	91	55	45
Venezuela	3,500	67	0.4	20.4	87	74	50
Uruguay	3,000[c,d]	3[d]	0.1	2.8	65	85	45

Country						
Bolivia	3,000[b]	3[b]	0.3	7.0	83	44	108
Nigeria	2,800[b,c]	33[b]	0.2	15.3	–	38	162
Burma	2,200[f]	2	0.1	0.4	–	23	126
Iraq	1,900[e]	25[e]	0.2	1.5	93	53	99
Singapore	1,600[f]	2[f]	0.05	13.7	–	97	17
Jamaica	1,300	7	0.4	58.5	–	70	26
El Salvador	1,300[e]	4	0.3	7.5	91	44	58
Colombia	1,100[c]	13[c]	0.1	7.7	98	62	76
Tunisia	1,100[d]	6[d]	0.2	7.7	99	50	128
Zambia	1,000	9[d]	0.4	12.3	–	27	157
Panama	1,000[f]	3[e]	0.2	–	–	58	44
Senegal	900[d]	9[d]	0.9	–	–	20	159
Mongolia	800	3[b]	0.4	–	–	–	75
Ecuador	750	6	0.2	10.0	96	49	78
Guatemala	750[e]	5[e]	0.2	7.5	81	39	79
Morocco	650[b]	1[g]	0.02	5.0	93	43	149
Lebanon	550	8	0.2	3.1	81	80	59
Trinidad and Tobago	550[b]	3[b]	0.2	81.0	98	81	24
Ivory Coast	550[b]	5[b]	0.2	13.4	–	15	160
Kenya	550[f]	14[c]	0.6	10.0	99	18	115
Costa Rica	500[c]	1[c]	0.1	12.2	–	58	52
Honduras	500[c]	2[c]	0.2	22.2	91	23	115
Nicaragua	400[c]	1[c]	0.1	7.8	–	49	121
Central African Republic	400[f]	1[b]	0.3	14.4	–	9	163
Laos	350[b]	–	–	–	100	–	123
Cameroon	350[b,c]	6[b,c]	0.4	12.8	–	15	135
Algeria	350[d]	18[d]	0.2	3.7	99	39	126
Madagascar	300[b]	8[c]	0.9	–	100	11	–
Mauritania	300[f]	–	–	54.6	–	12	137

TABLE 6.1 (continued)

	Total R&D Manpower, 1973 (in 1000s) (1)	General Expenditure on R&D, 1973 (US $ million) (2)	General Expenditure on R&D as % of GNP, 1973 (3)	Stock of Foreign Direct Investments, as % of GNP, 1973 (4)	% of Registered Patents Owned by Foreigners, 1971 (5)	% of Workforce Outside Agr., 1970 (6)	Infant Mortality Rates (deaths/1,000 live births), 1974 (7)
Libya	300	48[g]	0.7	18.6	–	68	125
Togo	250[c]	4[c]	1.0	15.6	–	27	127
Chad	200[c]	1	0.3	5.3	100	10	160
Jordan	200	3	0.3	2.2	–	66	97
Paraguay	150[c]	1[c]	0.1	4.5	–	47	65
Papua New Guinea	150[c]	–	–	–	–	14	–
Upper Volta	100[a]	2[b]	0.4	5.6	–	13	180
Arab Republic of Yemen	100[e,f]	2[e,f]	0.2	–	–	21	152
Niger	100[e]	0.2[e]	0.04	6.9	–	7	175
Dominican Republic	30[d]	2[d]	0.1	13.5	94	39	98
Malawi	10[a]	2[c]	0.4	10.5	100	12	119
Somalia	–	4[g]	1.4	–	100	–	177
Syria	–	7[g]	0.2	0.9	96	49	93

SOURCES: Jan Annerstedt: A Survey of the World Research & Development Efforts (Roshilde, Denmark: University Center, Institute of Economics, July 1979), mimeo.; Ruth Leger Sivard: World Military and Social Expenditures (WMSE Publications, 1977); The World Bank: World Development Report, 1978 (Washington, D.C., August 1978); United Nations: 1976 Statistical Yearbook (New York, 1977); Industrial Property (Monthly Review of the World Intellectual Property Organization, December 1972), Annex, Chart 1a and Chart 1b.

* Where necessary, the data on South and North Vietnam have been combined.

† Probably overestimated according to Annerstedt, halved by author.

a 1967; b 1970; c 1971; d 1972; e 1974; f 1975; g 1976.

TABLE 6.2: Domestic Income Distribution in Selected "High S&T Capacity" LDCs (by highest and lowest quintiles' shares)

	1953		1963		1973	
	Low	High	Low	High	Low	High
Cuba	2.1	60.0	8.0	48.0	7.9	34.9
			(1960)			
Sri Lanka[a]	5.2	63.6	5.5	52.3	7.2	42.9
India			6.7	48.9		
			(1964 − 65)			
Brazil			3.5	54.3	2.7	66.0
					(1976)	
Venezuela					3.0	54.0
					(1970)	
South Korea					5.7	45.3
					(1976)	
Taiwan					8.7	39.2
					(1971)	

SOURCES: Alberts and Brundenius (1979); Gunatilleke (1978); The World Bank, *World Development Report, 1979*.

[a] Not a "high" S&T country; included for comparative purposes.

THE WELFARE IMPLICATIONS OF SELECTIVE DISSOCIATION

One of the great myths perpetrated by liberal economics is the "efficiency-equity" trade-off. The assumption here is that for a time, typically of unspecified duration, equity concerns must yield to efficiency concerns so that, in the long run, equity can be achieved. And for periphery countries, efficiency in turn is usually taken to imply close association with center capital. Having already argued that there is no necessary connection between association and efficiency, it is my final objective in this paper to demonstrate that dissociative strategies do as well as, and often better than, associative strategies in terms of human welfare as well.

The aggregate data reflect a great variety of situations in the global periphery concerning the relationship between S&T systems and the provision of human welfare. Table 6.1 presents seven indicators for about sixty countries. The countries included are simply those LDCs for which comparable data exist. The indicators represent national R&D capacity (manpower and public expenditures in R&D sector); the degree of foreign penetration of the economy and of the S&T system (stock of foreign direct investments as percentage of GNP, and percentage of patents registered in the country that are owned by foreigners); level of industrial development (percentage of work force outside the agricultural sector); and human needs satisfaction (infant mortality rate).

Table 6.1 makes clear that no overall pattern exists in the relationship between *any* attribute of S&T systems and the indicator of human welfare, except that *more* industrial development is roughly correlated with *lower* infant mortality rates. (Sri Lanka is an exception to the exception; more is said about it below.) To the extent that direct investments and patent ownership are valid measures of foreign penetration, cases such as Chile, Peru, Ghana, Indonesia, and Venezuela among the "high S&T capacity" countries are highly dependent on foreign S&T. But here we detect *no* systematic relationship, positive or negative, between external dependence and *either* the level of industrialization *or* infant mortality.

Table 6.2 takes a look at selected "high S&T capacity" LDCs from the point of view of domestic income distribution, another broad measure of human welfare. And it tells a similar story. Cuba rates very high, but so does Taiwan. Brazil exhibits high foreign penetration and rapid growth combined with great inequity, but Taiwan, as penetrated and as rapidly growing, shows that the link with inequity is not inevitable. South Korea combines high growth rates with a lower level of foreign penetration and has an internal income distribution that is more egalitarian than Venezuela or Brazil, but considerably less so than Cuba or Taiwan. India, with an exceedingly high S&T capacity by developing-country standards and a relatively low level of foreign penetration, does slightly better than the average among this group of countries in terms of income distribution (but fares worst in terms of infant mortality rates). Figures for income distribution in Algeria are not available; recent evidence shows that life expectancy, adult literacy, average index of food production, and daily caloric supply are all low by "middle-income country" standards, though on some health-related measures Algeria ranks higher than the average of this group.[74]

In sum, if there is a direct and simple relationship between S&T systems and the provision of human welfare, it is not apparent from these data. What is clear, however, is that dissociation does no worse (or better) in the aggregate in predicting human needs satisfaction than association. But to push on—if the close associators who also do well in welfare terms are examined, one finds a handful of newly industrializing countries: Taiwan, South Korea, Singapore, Hong Kong. These countries are hardly typical, even of the larger group of NICs let alone of periphery countries more generally. Singapore and Hong Kong are compact city-states, and Taiwan and South Korea are the "beneficiaries" of past colonial and occupation authorities that implanted a relatively more egalitarian social structure within them. Once such cases are filtered out, the relationship between welfare achievements and selective dissociation strategies become stronger.

Take the cases of Sri Lanka and Cuba. Sri Lanka, and Cuba even more so, have achieved relatively high levels of material needs satisfaction, even though both have relatively poor resource bases. Infant mortality rates are low and life expectancy is high. Illiteracy is virtually eradicated in Cuba, and down to about a fifth of the population in Sri

74. IBRD, *World Development Report, 1980* (Statistical Annex).

Lanka. Indeed, both countries have a sizable intelligentsia, even though Cuba lost some two-thirds of its professionals to emigration after the revolution, and Sri Lanka has suffered a consistent brain drain. Cuba ranks uniformly high on the provision of nutritional requirements, health services, and employment; Sri Lanka fares worse on all of these, though by developing-country standards it rates respectably on most (one major exception being access to safe drinking water). Income in the two countries is distributed about as equitably as anywhere.[75]

These similarities in accomplishment exist despite major institutional differences between the two countries. Sri Lanka has an important state sector, but is essentially a mixed economy. Cuba is pursuing a state socialist pattern, closer to the East European than the Algerian model. Cuba has an extensive S&T capacity, whereas Sri Lanka does not. Both countries are dependent on external economic relations, though of very different sorts. Sri Lanka imports some 40 percent of its food supply and has conducted almost one-half of its trade with other developing countries. More recently, however, Sri Lanka has established "export free zones" to attract foreign capital, in the hope of reducing growing unemployment,[76] which was in part produced by the green revolution,[77] and to ease foreign exchange strains, in part caused by food imports. Cuba's monocultural exports are destined almost exclusively for the Soviet Union and CMEA countries, from which Cuba also receives the bulk of its foreign aid—according to the CIA, some $8.2 billion between 1961 and 1976.[78] Sri Lanka under the previous government sought technology imports from the Soviet Union;[79] Cuba makes repeated overtures to capitalist coun-

75. *Ibid.*
76. Ann R. Mattis, "An Experience in a Need-Oriented Development," *Marga Quarterly Journal* (1978), vol. 5, no. 3.
77. Réné Dumont, *Paysanneries aux abois* (Paris: Edition du Seuil, 1972).
78. U.S. Central Intelligence Agency, *The Cuban Economy—A Statistical Review* (Washington, D.C.: CIA, December 1976).
79. A report from the Marga Institute has claimed these benefits from technology relations with the Soviet Union: "(a) a relatively free access to technology,

tries, which in turn see Cuba as a potentially important future market.[80]

Amidst these disparities lies the common element that both countries have achieved high levels of human needs satisfaction by deliberate internal social reorganization, the relatively decentralized pattern of social organization in Sri Lanka,[81] and political mobilization together with socio-economic redistribution in Cuba.[82] And this, in turn, has been coupled with forms of selective dissociation, radically different in substance and degree in the two countries, and brought on only in part by deliberate choice in Sri Lanka and entirely by external fiat in Cuba.

CONCLUSION

This paper casts doubt on both mainstream-liberal and stagnationist-dependency views on development. The relationship between national welfare and the international division of labor is not as simple as either would have it. At least in the realm of technology, which is absolutely central to any development strategy, close association with center capital does not provide the key to solving the development problems of vast numbers of periphery countries. At the

---

(b) the absence of restrictive conditions in regard to procurement of raw materials and marketing of products abroad, and (c) a genuine concern for creating the local technical capability to run the plant and for establishing research and development facilities at each plant to ensure the growth of technology." Marga Institute, "Transfer of Technology: The Sri Lanka Experience," and "Reverse Transfer of Technology from Sri Lanka: Problems and Policy Issues," *Marga Quarterly Journal* (1978), 5(2):13. On balance, however, while imports from the socialist countries may have had fewer negative side effects than imports from transnational corporations, they also yielded few positive effects.

80. *Cuba at a Turning Point: New Opportunities for Multinational Corporations* (Washington, D.C.: Business International Corporation, 1977).

81. Godfrey Gunnatilleke, "Participatory Development and Dependence: The Case of Sri Lanka," *Marga Quarterly Journal* (1978), vol. 3, no. 2.

82. Claes Croner, "Cuba: Labour Force Utilization and Mobilization, 1959–1979" (Stockholm: SAREC, 1979). Mimeo.

same time, complete dissociation is neither desirable nor feasible. Accordingly, this chapter has explored the more complex middle ground of selective dissociation. Some empirical cases were investigated, a more general strategy was outlined, and selective dissociation was shown to compare favorably to association in direct human welfare terms. The centripetal forces in the world political economy, especially in the technology sector, make selective dissociation a difficult strategy to follow. But, I have suggested that, ultimately, periphery countries exercise greater control over the obstacles to *this* strategy than they do over the alternatives.

7.

Linguistic Dissociation: A Strategy for Africa

DAVID D. LAITIN

WHILE FORMAL POLITICAL ties between the European metropoles and their former colonies in Africa have been nearly completely severed within the past generation, many aspects of the imperial relationship remain and even prosper. In this volume, the economic, military, and technological dimensions of these ties have been discussed. My concern here is with the more elusive but no less significant cultural ties. Of all the cultural ties that still bind Africa to Europe, it is the continued use of European languages as the official languages of African states that remains most significant. In this paper, I plan to explain the continued linguistic association between African states and their former metropoles and to show its consequences. I will also discuss certain trends which can best be described as emergent strategies

Extensive and helpful comments by Peter Cowhey, Henry Ehrmann, David Friedman, Peter Gourevitch, Ernst Haas, Jeffrey Hart, David Jordan, Gerd Junne, Mubanga Kashoki, Mary Katzenstein, Peter Katzenstein, John Ruggie, Richard Wood, and Crawford Young enriched this paper significantly. William O'Barr kindly invited me to deliver an earlier version of this paper to his colleagues at Duke University, and they helped me clarify my ideas.

of "linguistic dissociation." It is my contention that in the African case, despite perhaps insurmountable administrative problems, linguistic dissociation could yield benefits consistent with the hopes of those articulating the need for a more general dissociative strategy. Indigenous languages may be one of those latent resources available to new states in their quest for greater self-reliance.

LANGUAGE, NATIONALISM, AND THE STATE

Linguistic dissociation—the policy of decreasing the domains in which non-indigenous languages have official sanction—is often, at first blush, associated with anti-progressive nationalism. By progressive, I mean opening up opportunities for social mobility, political participation, and wealth among the less-advantaged segments of a country's population. Is not the promotion of indigenous languages playing into the hands of more-advantaged, traditional elites? To ascribe virtue to a state which legitimates itself by heralding its particularistic culture is to conjure up images of Hitler's National Socialism. Why should a paper in a volume concerned with equity and human welfare seek refuge in a traditional cultural institution?

What I wish to argue at the outset is that the promotion of national vernaculars is not in itself a progressive or anti-progressive policy. In different historical periods, and with support for development by different social groups, the promotion of national vernaculars has had a whole range of political implications. The social context in which language policy takes place is essential for an understanding of its social meaning. To emphasize this point, some historical perspective is clearly in order.

With the spread of the Roman empire, Latin became the language of political and ecclesiastical power throughout Europe. It was generally accepted that Latin was the language of the peoples within the imperial realm. But when Charlemagne authorized the development of a standardized pure Latin in the late eighth century, it became obvious that what had been perceived as impure dialects of Latin were in fact different languages. These vernaculars had low political status, and remained subservient to Latin until the Renaissance, when the Italian of Dante, the German of Luther's Bible, and the commitment to "le bon usage" in French by Racine signaled the challenge of national vernaculars to the supremacy of imperial Latin. Even though the vernaculars eventually became supreme throughout Europe, the historical and social context of their development must be examined carefully before the political meaning of their success can be ascribed. Here I will look briefly at the English and German cases.

In England, while Latin was the language of ecclesiastical and legal authority, French (after the Norman conquest) became the language of the ruling elites. It was not until the Francophobia of the Hundred Year's War that English began to gain status. In 1362 Parliament passed a statute suggesting that since the French language was "much unknown in this Realm," all argument in courts of law should be spoken in English and recorded in Latin.[1] It was in this same period that Wycliffe published an English Bible translated from Latin, directly challenging ecclesiastical hierarchy and intended for commoners. Meanwhile, the schools, which had relied on French, began employing English as the medium of instruction, and in the early fifteenth century, English grammer schools were founded. English was perceived by the aristocrats to be a vulgar island patois, to be sure; but indeed it was the language of the people.

These developments in the English language gave support to Henry VII's "new monarchy" (1485–1509). A strong English state was Henry's goal, and the centralization of administration his means. He was able to build legitimacy for

1. See G. M. Trevelyan, *History of England* (Garden City, N.Y.: Doubleday, 1926), 1:179–80, 308–11.

the monarchy (badly crippled by the War of the Roses) in part on a notion of the special worth of the English "yeoman." Through the acceptance of an indigenous culture as the basis for the English nation, and the forced spread of that culture through the realm (even among non-English-speaking minorities), Henry was laying the foundation for a nation-state. It took Henry VIII to destroy the power of Latin through his split with Rome and his authorization for the publication of the complete Bible in English in one volume.

The support of the English language, then, meant that the language of the people rather than the language of the Church or the aristocracy would become the language of the realm. The promotion of the English vernacular at the expense of French and Latin among the Tudors was (whatever their intentions) progressive. With the language of the people promoted as the language of the state, more people could understand and respond to public affairs. Once the state was defined by the cultural characteristics of the people, the groundwork was (inadvertently) laid for ideas of popular sovereignty.

In both England and France, the forces unleashed by the ideology of popular sovereignty were truly revolutionary. The national vernaculars had become tools of the middle classes to challenge the legitimacy of monarchy. After the Napoleanic wars, the great powers attemped to suppress this revolutionary nationalism, but the lid blew off in 1848 when again nationalism and popular sovereignty were equated. It is no wonder that among the German-speaking states, the aristocracy was deeply afraid of movements to forge a single *Staatsnation* (political nation) out of a common *Kulturnation* (cultural nation).

It took Bismarck to demonstrate to the Prussian Junkers the conservative potential of an ideology of nationalism. Bismarck attained through military conquest what the Holy Roman Empire and the German liberals both had been unable to achieve: political unity of the German nation. Bismarck recognized that the symbols of the German nation—

language and culture—could become tools of the Prussian aristocrats to legitimate his conquests. German and English aristocrats revered French. But unlike the English aristocracy, the Prussian Junkers identified with and held in high regard their national vernacular. Junkers were able to promote Hegelian idealism as a useful tool both to glorify the German nation and to legitimate conservative principles. If the expansion of the English language has been associated with opportunities for a liberal middle-class challenge to aristocratic rule, then the glorification of the German language has been associated with the reactionary hold over German society by the Prussian Junkers. The promotion of English as the language of the Tudor state and the use of the German language as a symbol to legitimate the political unity of the German *Kulturnation* had vastly different social meanings.

Yet another pattern emerged in the wake of World War I. This began the era of mass mobilization and the articulation of national demands by peoples who lived in states (Russia, Austria-Hungary, the Ottoman Empire) in which the monarchs had long been unable to create nations. While President Wilson of the United States espoused a doctrine of self-determination which was consistent with the English model of development, most of the debate concerning language and nationalism took place in socialist circles.

Many Eastern European Marxists, upholding an internationalist doctrine, could not easily accept the actual demands of their socialist allies in the imperial peripheries who wanted their own separate states. Rosa Luxemburg, for one, held to the logically consistent position that the national self-determination of subject peoples in the former Austro-Hungarian and Russian Empires had no place in socialist thought. In opposition to her, a group of Austrian Marxists, notably Otto Bauer and Karl Renner, attempted to demonstrate that it is possible and fruitful to conjoin a socialist program with a nationalist language policy. They believed that socialism dictated the equal opportunity of all subject peoples to fulfillment, and this required the recognition of national cultures.[2] Lenin, ever the pragmatist, saw the importance of supporting self-determination among the peoples who were not assimilated into the imperial state so that they would be able to be mobilized to stand up against their imperial rulers. But he saw no intrinsic merit to the idea of national solidarity of small states unified by a common language. The Soviet state has followed this line over the course of the century. It has promoted the languages and cultures of some of its national groups in order to gain support. On the other hand, it has divided other national groups through differentiating them by minor cultural differences. In either case, centralized economic and political control is exerted through the Russian language.[3] In both theory and practice within the socialist experience, the promotion of national vernaculars has had a variety of political meanings.

These European patterns developed still new meanings as Europe penetrated Africa. European languages evoked contrasting symbolic responses in the course of African nationalism. First, English and French were seen as the languages of lucrative foreign trade and subsequently imperial control. The colonial powers by the late nineteenth century had all but destroyed the authority of African states and stateless societies. Through colonial administration, new states were formed, and these were administered by means of the language of the colonial power. Within a short period,

2. Karl W. Deutsch's idea of assimilation builds on Bauer's insights, as Deutsch recognized the importance of the ability to communicate as a precondition for the success of participation. For Bauer, see *Die Nationalitätenfrage und die Sozialdemokratie* (1907); for Deutsch, see *Nationalism and Social Communication* (Cambridge: MIT Press, 1953). Interestingly, Jürgen Habermas uses the idea of "communicative competence" in a way similar to Deutsch's "assimilation." See Stephen K. White's discussion, "Reason and Authority in Habermas: A Critique of the Critics," in *American Political Science Review* (December 1980), vol. 74, no.4. An excellent discussion of the debate concerning nationalism and socialism among Russian jews is that of Jonathan Frankel, *Prophesy and Politics: Socialism, Nationalism, and the Russian Jews* (Cambridge: Cambridge University Press, 1981).

3. Richard Pipes, *The Formation of the Soviet Union: Communism and Nationalism 1917–1923* (Cambridge: Harvard University Press, 1957).

socially mobilized subjects sought political freedom through an ideology of nationalism. All people who resided within the colonially set boundaries, no matter what their previous identity, were defined by these nationalists as part of the new nation. Since these peoples were heterogenous linguistically in most cases, and because the colonial administrations were ill-equipped to process messages in local languages, the language of national self-determination was the very same as the language of colonial oppression.[4]

But that is not the only pattern in the complex relationship of Europe and Africa. To govern, the colonial states found it impossible to ignore the indigenous languages at the lower levels of administration. More important, though, is that many of the English and German missionaries were philosophic idealists and believed that the only true way to approach the "genius" of African peoples was through their own languages. One East African missionary, assuming that each state has its own "contribution . . . to the sum of human attainment," argued that the development of Swahili would provide the "medium of expression of the special genius of their race."[5] These idealists translated the Bible and other materials to make an important contribution to the development of African vernaculars. And so, one tool for radical opposition to European hegemony was fashioned by Hegelians. Some African socialist thinkers have therefore viewed European language competence as the tie that binds African "compradors" to international capitalism. Support of the vernaculars, these socialists contend, could weaken that bond.

That the European languages are associated with colo-

4. See Ali Mazrui, "The English Language and Political Consciousness in British Colonial Africa," *Journal of Modern African Studies* (1966), 4(3):303.

5. G. W. Broomfield, "The Development of the Swahili Language," *Africa* (1930), 3(4):516–22. For similar approaches, see P. W. Schmidt, S.V.D., "The Use of Vernacular in Education in Africa," *Africa* (1930), vol. 3, no. 2, and the anecdote in Gilbert Ansre, "Language Standardisation," in Thomas Sebeok, ed., *Current Trends in Linguistics*, vol. 7, *Linguistics in Sub-Saharan Africa* (The Hague: Mouton, 1971), p. 692.

nialism *and* with nationalism, and that the vernaculars are associated with missionary idealism *and* socialist internationalism, have led to complex patterns of language choice in contemporary Africa. Consider Leopold Senghor. As a socialist in the 1930s and an early intellectual proponent of the idea of negritude, Senghor romantically assumed—with Hegelian imagery—that European languages could never catch the African timbre nor capture the soul of Africa. But, as President of Senegal, in an attempt to unite his country and to court French aid, he marched to a different beat. Turning his Hegelian argument on its head, and adopting a position consistent with that of Rosa Luxemburg, he argued that the French language could only become truly universal when Africans help develop it to its fullest range. French would therefore remain the language of the Senegalese state, and Senegal would help the French language to become universal.[6]

Or consider this irony. Because of the Leninist line encouraging the development of national cultures in order to do battle with colonial and neocolonial authority in Africa, socialists have associated themselves with movements to promote African vernaculars. Socialist-inspired intercontinental congresses have often voted to propagate African languages, and UNESCO, in a typical statement, held that "we take it as axiomatic . . . that the best medium for teaching is the mother tongue of the pupil.[7] The development of the Wolof language became an important symbol in the socialist opposition to Senghor's role in Senegal,[8] and in Tanzania and Somalia, the two African countries in which African languages have full official status, language auton-

6. I. Markovitz, *Leopold Sedar Senghor and the Politics of Negritude* (New York: Atheneum, 1969), pp. 62–63.

7. See Pierre Alexandre, "Les Problèmes Linguistiques Africains Vus de Paris," in John Spencer, ed., *Language in Africa* (Cambridge: Cambridge University Press, 1963). The UNESCO quotation is from their *The Use of Vernacular Languages in Education,* Monographs on Fundamental Education, vol. 8 (Paris: 1953).

8. See issues of the newspaper *Kadu* — "speech" in Wolof — published by the Marxist branch of the National party.

omy and socialist ideology are conjoined. The viability of African languages has been an axiom of the political left.

Yet in South Africa—and here is the irony—the development of the African vernaculars is a tool of the "right." The political elite in South Africa is of Dutch descent, and their language, derived from Dutch, is called Afrikaans. In a clear policy to divide and rule, the Afrikaans-speaking elite has encouraged the development of the black African vernaculars. Although many of the African languages are similar (and could provide a basis for language unity), Afrikaner authorities have emphasized dialectic differences. For nearly all black Africans, Afrikaans represents the language of political reaction. Meanwhile English, the language of much of the business elite, represents to many black Africans the language of internationalism and possible freedom. As far back as 1939, the Head of the Department of Bantu Studies at the (moderately liberal) University of Witswatersrand noted that the Africans who saw English as the language of African unity "are suspicious [of] any desire by the education authorities to extend the use of the vernacular in schools for purposes of segregation and differentiation." In the 1976 riots in Soweto, it is no surprise that the issue which ignited the troubles involved the desire by the black African population to have English in their curriculum. Nor is it a surprise that on the eve of independence after more than sixty years of rule by South Africa, Namibians will expand English at the expense of Afrikaans and the indigenous languages. English is the language of international commerce; Afrikaans and the indigenous languages represent either repression or internal division.[9] The point: vernacular promotion is the

9. The quotation is from C. M. Doke, "European and Bantu Languages in South Africa," *Africa* (1939), 12(3):316. The issue of language choice in South Africa is fascinating, since Africaans development vis-à-vis the "imperialism" of English had its own separate battles. The whole issue deserves full political analysis. For historical background, see Pablo Eisenberg's essay on South Africa in Helen Kitchen, ed., *The Educated African* (New York: Praeger, 1962); Adriaan J. Barnouw, *Language and Race Problems in South Africa* (The Hague: Martinus Nijhoff, 1934); E. G. Malherbe, *The Bilingual School: A Study of Bilingualism in South Africa* (Lon-

policy of both the far Left and far Right in contemporary Africa.

A final irony. Tanzania, as has already been mentioned, has conjoined a socialist ideology with a commitment to expand the official use of the Swahili language. Research has demonstrated that because Swahili is a language widely known throughout Tanzania, in both urban and rural areas, yet is not associated with a dominant nationality within Tanzania, there has been a discernible egalitarian effect of Swahili development consistent with the socialist ideology.[10] Yet when looked upon from the village level, as J. O'Barr has, the egalitarian thrust of the policy becomes problematic. In a careful study of Pare District's Village Development Committees and Ward Development Commitees (where Swahili is best known to those who are most socially and geographically mobile), she found that the requirement of Swahili use for meetings consistently worked against the participation of the women and the less well-to-do.[11] The language policy which increases participation on the state level seems to work against that ideal when looked upon at the local level.

The development of national vernaculars has been associated with the liberal, the idealist, and the socialist traditions. It has been associated with the movement for the self-determination of African peoples and it has been asso-

---

don: Longmans, Green, 1946); and *Education in South Africa, 1923–1975* (Cape Town: Juta, 1977); and Marius F. Valkhoff, "Descriptive Bibliography of the Linguistics of Afrikaans: A Survey of Major Works and Authors," in Thomas Sebeok, *Current Trends*. The relationship of language policy to the Soweto uprising is discussed in the *New York Times* (June 20, July 7, and July 11, 1976). See also B. Hirson "Language in Control and Resistance in South Africa," *African Affairs* (April 1981), vol. 80, no. 319, and his *Year of Fire, Year of Ash, The Soweto Revolt: Roots of a Revolution?* (London: Zed, 1979). On Namibia, see M. Kashoki, "Achieving Nationhood Through Language: The Challenge of Namibia," UN Institute for Namibia (Lusaka) (May 1980).

10. See D. Laitin, "Language Choice and National Development: A Typology for Africa," *International Interactions* (1979), vol. 6, no. 3.

11. J. F. O'Barr, "Language and Politics in Tanzanian Governmental Institutions," in W. M. O'Barr and J. F. O'Barr, eds., *Language and Politics* (The Hague: Mouton, 1976), pp. 80–81.

ciated with the continued oppression of African peoples. It has been associated with policies to enhance local participation, yet it has often acted to restrict the possibility of participation by the poor. The point I wish to make here is that language policies alone do not signal progressivism or conservatism. In order to defend a policy of linguistic dissociation, for any African state, I must demonstrate that in this historical period, such a policy would be progressive. But before I can defend dissociation, the cogency of linguistic association must be made clear.

THE LOGIC OF LINGUISTIC ASSOCIATION

Despite the enthusiasm generated by such movements as negritude, which called for the promotion of African culture and languages, very few African states at the moment of independence became committed to the immediate return to the African vernaculars as languages of politics, administration, and education. Leopold Senghor's switch from nationalist politician supporting African culture to responsible leader supporting the language of the former metropole reflected a position typical of most of the new leaders in Africa concerning matters of language choice. Four basic reasons seem to explain why African leaders abandoned their earlier commitments to negritude and to cultural independence.

First, there was *inertia.* Innumerable problems faced the new leadership, and virtually no one was making demands for rapid linguistic dissociation. Governing coalitions had to be constructed, cabinets had to be chosen, the mechanics of imposed constitutions had to be understood. Furthermore, an endless series of demands by workers, students, and disaffected ethnic groups, usually disregarded by the waning colonial powers, had to be deflected. Finally, the overwhelming needs of economic development, health care, and primary education made the question of whether to sever ties of linguistic association seem an inappropriate one to ask. As one commentator on Zambia's linguistic history put it:

At independence Zambia was very heavily dependent on expatriate help in both its public and private sectors. In spite of an extremely rapid expansion of education and great strides in Zambianization, such dependence was still relatively heavy in 1970. Given Zambia's resources and the tasks that faced the new government, the continued use of English as the official language does not seem surprising, since many aspects of the life of the country had been conducted in English by the former government, and large numbers of Zambians had learned to communicate using the English language with varying degrees of efficiency.[12]

By this argument, linguistic dissociation is perhaps a second-generation movement in postcolonial states, as it was in Finland.[13]

Second, there is the need for *unity* in culturally heterogeneous states.[14] Throughout Africa the states which received their independence in this generation were not, with few exceptions, nations. What can become the language to express a new national culture other than the language of the former metropole? There is an egalitarian logic to this choice—all ethnic groups are more or less equally ill-equipped to speak it. No ethnic group has a "natural" advantage in getting those jobs associated with literacy in the official language of the state. Even though the language of the metropole was often spoken by not more than 10 per-

12. Sirarpi Ohannessian, "Historical Background," in Ohannessian and Mubanga Kashoki, *Language in Zambia* (London: International African Institute, 1978), p. 272.

13. See Keith Orton, "Dependency Avoidance: The Finnish Experience in Controlling Transnationals," paper delivered to the International Studies Association, West, Los Angeles, 1977.

14. Rupert Emerson, *From Empire to Nation* (Boston: Beacon, 1960), ch. 7.

cent of the population in the newly independent states,[15] and even though certain ethnic groups which had special relations with the colonial powers did have better access to its language, it came to be seen as the language of national unity.

Third, there is the need for *expertise.* Hordes of UN experts and aid officials, and agents of multinational corporations, none of whom could communicate in the African vernaculars, descended on the new states. English, French, and other European languages were seen as the keys to technical knowledge, to scholarly journals, to textbooks, and to links with the technologically advanced world. A resurgence of the vernaculars could only mean, it was argued, the inaccessibility of Western science to educated Africans.

This phenomenon was especially noticeable in the schools. As Fox and Abdulaziz have pointed out, in their private report to the Ford Foundation on its investment on a Survey of Language Use and Language Teaching in Eastern Africa, "English was the only language in which there were sequential, relatively up-to-date materials both for training teachers and teaching school children from upper primary on."[16] Or in the words of the "Report of the Kenya Education Commission of 1964," chaired by Professor S. H. Ominde:[17]

First the English medium makes possible a systematic development of language study and literacy which would be very difficult to achieve in the vernaculars. Secondly as a result of the systematic development possible in the English medium, quicker progress is possible in all subjects. Thirdly, the foundation laid in the

15. Pierre Alexandre, *Languages and Language in Black Africa,* F. A. Leavy, trans. (Evanston: Northwestern University Press, 1972), p. 81.

16. Mohamed H. Abdulaziz and Melvin J. Fox, "Evaluation Report on Survey of Language Use and Language Teaching of Eastern Africa" (September 1978), p. 12. I should like to thank Messrs. Fox and William Carmichael of the Ford Foundation for supplying me with a copy of this private report.

17. T. P. Gorman, "The Development of Language Policy in Kenya with Particular Reference to the Educational System," in W. H. Whiteley, ed., *Language in Kenya* (Nairobi: Oxford University Press, 1974), p. 441.

first three years is more scientifically conceived, and therefore provides a more solid basis for all subsequent studies, than was ever possible in the old vernacular teaching. . . . In short, we have no doubt about the advantages of English medium to the whole educational process.

Expertise, systematic learning, and science have all been associated with the language of the former metropole.

Each of these three reasons appears in the annual reports of the Ministries of Education in a variety of African states, but they are not, in themselves, compelling. Inertia should not stop the clear articulation of a future desire to break the ties of linguistic association. And the need for expertise should not rule out the strategies of the small European states which have made the dominant languages of technology available to students in their educational systems without abandoning their national languages. And finally, the argument concerning unity, while apparently valid, never made sense to me in light of my research on the Somali experience. Somalia, upon independence in 1960, was a linguistically homogeneous state. More than 95 percent of the population could understand the Somali language heard on the national radio. But due to the exigencies of Somali history, the new state had a diversity of languages of foreign contact. British control in the north, Italian colonialism in the south, and the Islamic influence throughout the country led to the emergence of (small) linguistic elites literate in English, Italian, and Arabic. Since a choice of any of these three foreign languages as the official language of state would bring differential advantage to different elites, the argument for unity would suggest that Somalia would make Somali its official language. But for the first twelve years of independence, English, Italian, and Arabic were the three official languages, with English beginning to predominate. Surely there was more to the choice of the European colonial languages as the official language of state in other newly independent African countries than a desire for unity.

Here one must assess the interests of the dominant ruling coalitions in the first generation of postcolonial leadership. Whether or not they form a "class" is irrelevant for
present purposes, but they correspond to those social leaders who have been called the "organizational bourgeoisie."[18] These are the higher civil servants, the managers of
transnational corporations, and the licensed distributors of
imported goods from the industrialized world. Most of them
derived their initial capital in jobs which required the ability
to write in a European language. In the civil service especially (still the most preferred route into the middle class in
most of Africa), literacy in a European language has been
the most important skill. The interest of the members of the
organizational bourgeoisie in protecting their capital investment in having learned a European language (a resource
that is easily transferred to the next generation) leads them
to stress the difficulties inherent in any strategy of linguistic
dissociation.[19] These are the very people who became the
political leaders of the new states, and their interests were
translated into political reality.

The linguistic interests of the ruling groups, supported
by arguments concerning national unity and technical access, and self-implemented through inertia, made the strategy of linguistic association in postcolonial Africa highly
probable.[20] But a similar confluence of interests and reason
support strategies of economic and technical association;
and as is shown elsewhere in this volume, these strategies

18. I. Markovitz, *Power and Class in Africa* (Englewood Cliffs, N.J.: Prentice-
Hall, 1977), ch. 6.

19. See Einar Haugen, *Language Conflict and Language Planning: The Case
of Modern Norwegian* (Cambridge: Harvard University Press, 1966); Antoine Meil-
let, *Les Langues dans L'Europe nouvelle* (Paris: 1928), and D. Cruise O'Brien, *Saints
and Politicians* (Cambridge: University Press, 1975), for discussions of bureaucratic interests, jobs, and language choice in Norway, Western Europe, and Senegal.

20. An excellent defense of the use of the language of the metropole in Nigeria (but applicable elsewhere) is Keith Allan, "Nation, Tribalism, and National
Language: Nigeria's Case," in *Cahiers D'Etudes Africaines* (Paris: Mouton, 1978),
18(3):71.

may not be best suited for a development program which fulfills the basic needs of the citizens of the new states. It is therefore important to reexamine old assumptions about linguistic association to see whether a case can be made for the fuller development of the African vernaculars.

THE PROMISE OF LINGUISTIC DISSOCIATION

The most common argument given in support of linguistic dissociation, among the five I shall raise here, has to do with the restoration of cultural autonomy and self-respect. Frantz Fanon was vehement in making the connection between use of the French language and the deep psychological problems of the colonized peoples vis-á-vis their masters.[21] A Haitian poet put it this way:

Sentez-vous cette souffrance
Et ce désespoir à nul autre égal
D'apprivoiser, avec les mots de France
Ce coeur qui m'est venu du Sénégal[22]

The former vice-president of Zambia expressed this same thought in 1969:

We should stop teaching children through English right from the start because it is the surest way of imparting inferiority complex in the children and the society. It is poisonous. It is the surest way of killing African personality and African culture. From my experience people defend what they have and not what they do not have. The African children will only defend the European culture because that is what they will be taught from the start to the finish.[23]

---

21. Fanon, *Black Skin, White Masks,* Charles Markmann, trans. (New York: Grove Press, 1967), pp. 17–18, 38. Fanon's work is a clear example of how idealist arguments in the European context can attempt to serve progressive social purposes in the colonial situation.

22. Quoted in Claude Wauthier, *The Literature and Thought of Modern Africa,* Shirley Kay, trans. (New York: Praeger, 1967), p. 31.

23. Simon Kapwepwe, quoted in Robert Serpell, "Developments Since 1971," in Ohannessian and Kashoki, *Language in Zambia,* p. 432.

And the President of Kenya concluded his first speech (which had been in English) to Parliament as President with these words (translated here from Swahili):

Mr. Speaker, I want to say a few words in Swahili because I personally think that the time is not far away when we will be able to speak Kiswahili, which is our own language, in this House. . . . Now that we have full independence we don't have to be slaves of foreign languages in our affairs, and consequently, brothers, I wanted to make this point, because everything has to begin somewhere. If I had left this House without uttering a word of Kiswahili, I would have felt somewhat humiliated.[24]

These sentiments are crucially important. To the extent that Africans must communicate with Africans in the language of their former colonial masters, the humiliations of colonialism may remain omnipresent, reinforcing those attitudes and actions which are inimical to the breaking of the bonds of dependence. To be sure, the European languages in Africa today are very much African languages, adopted and changed by the local population.[25] Nonetheless, whether there is a relationship between language use and psychological dependence is problematic and worthy of more systematic research.[26]

This first argument, despite the purposes of its proponents, is ultimately idealist and conservative. Language is seen as a cultural artifact, which, if rejected, would represent the very rejection of oneself. There is some truth to this, but that should not lead one to forget that language is as dynamic and changing as economic relations. Instead of viewing language as a treasure trove of a nation's past, why

24. Quoted and translated by T. Gorman, in "Language Policy in Kenya," paper presented at the 1970 meeting of the Language Association of Eastern Africa.

25. See the examples in Harold Reeves Collins, "The New English of the Onitsha Chapbooks," no. 1, Papers in International Studies, Africa Series (Athens, Ohio: Ohio University Center for International Studies, 1968).

26. See the pioneering work done by the Comité Linguistique Appliqués à Dakar, at the University of Dakar, Senegal; and A. Colot, "Notes sur L'Entrée A L'Ecole Dans L'Agglomération Dakaroise," *Psychopathologie Africaine* (Dakar: 1965), 1:1. See also, Mubanga Kashoki, "The African Language as a Tool of Development," OAU, Inter-African Bureau of Languages (October 1979).

not view language as a springboard for innovation and change? The second argument for linguistic dissociation views language as a potential source of cultural, economic, and technological innovation, and not as a source of psychological pride.

The basic insight behind this second argument — perhaps best called the argument of "linguistic relativity" — is that a study of language categories will demonstrate (to use Edward Sapir's formulation) "the tyrannical hold that linguistic form has upon our orientation in the world."[27] The thesis developed from this insight (now in the bolder formulation of Sapir's student, B. L. Whorf), "holds that all observers are not led by the same physical evidence to the same picture of the universe, unless their linguistic backgrounds are similar, or can in some way be calibrated" and "that users of markedly different grammars are pointed by their grammars toward different types of observation and different evaluations of externally similar acts of observation, and hence are not equivalent as observers, but must arrive at somewhat different views of the world."[28]

While the nineteenth century German and English idealists used an argument of this sort to explain the special role certain nations had in world history (some to rule; some to be ruled), surely there is a precedent for turning Hegelian arguments on their head. One can conceive of the contemporary world as one in which the problems of the peripheral countries in the international economy will get decreasing attention from the center. What is required from the periphery is vision, innovation. From where are the new ideas to come? Assume the plausibility of the linguistic relativity hypothesis. If speakers of different languages in some systematic manner perceive the same world from different perspectives, does it not follow that in a world of a multitude

27. Quoted in Dan I. Slobin, *Psycholinguistics* (Glenview, Ill.: Scott Foresman, 1971), p. 120.

28. Benjamin Lee Whorf, *Language, Thought and Reality*, John Carroll, ed. (Cambridge: MIT Press, 1956), pp. 214, 221.

of languages, there will be — as it were — a broader supply of innovation coming from the periphery?[29]

To what extent can one assume the plausibility of the linguistic relativity hypothesis? Scholars in socio- and psycholinguistics have all but abandoned Whorf's formulation. As John Carroll concludes from a (sympathetic) review of the literature, "the linguistic relativity hypothesis has thus far received very little convincing support. Our best guess at the present is that the effects of language structure will be found to be limited and localized."[30] In my own field research, however, in the Somali-speaking Northeastern Province in Kenya (in 1973), I attempted to reformulate the linguistic relativity hypothesis in order to see if language change in Africa carries with it changes in the way people think and act politically. The resultant data lend some support to the linguistic relativity hypothesis, and I shall summarize the findings here.

Bilingual (in Somali and English) secondary school students answered interview questions and participated in structured role-playing sessions in both languages. I had hypothesized — based on both linguistic and anthropological evidence — how and why approaches to certain kinds of problems would be different depending on which language the interview or role-playing session took place. Examination of the transcripts from these sessions demonstrated that a relationship existed between the language in use and the approach taken by the respondents to certain problems.[31]

29. The relationship between culture and scientific innovation is brilliantly and incomparably explored by J. Needham, *Science and Civilisation in China* (Cambridge: Cambridge University Press, 1954 ff.), 5 vols. See vol. 2, s. 13(b) for a skeptical view toward linguistic relativity. But the corpus suggests a cultural basis for scientific paths of discovery.

30. John Carroll, *Language and Thought* (Englewood Cliffs, N.J.: Prentice-Hall, 1964), p. 110. But see Alfred Bloom, "The Impact of Chinese Linguistic Structure on Cognitive Style," *Current Anthropology* (September 1979), 20(3):585 – 86.

31. David Laitin, *Politics, Language and Thought* (Chicago: University of Chicago Press, 1977). The thorny theoretical issues involved are treated in ch. 6; the even thornier empirical issues — concerning adequate controls, sample, etc. — are treated in ch. 7; the findings are reported in ch. 8.

The most telling difference between the two sets of answers concerned the concept of authority. In one role-playing situation, I structured a conflict between a "headmaster" (who wrote an exceedingly difficult final examination) and the "teacher" of that subject (who wanted to protest the difficulty of the examination). In the English dialogues, the Somali respondents tended to justify their stand by virtue of their *role*, i.e. who had the right set the questions. Again and again in the English dialogues, the respondents would make claims like this: "Since I am the English master, you leave the English to me. You are the headmaster of the school, but you are not supposed to interfere with my subjects." A typical response by the Headmaster was "in this school, I am the one who is supposed to know what is going on."[32]

Although there is nothing inherent in the Somali language which would prevent someone from making those claims, such claims were rarely made in the Somali dialogues, perhaps because Somali social structure had few formalized roles. Constructions making role claims (e.g., "I am the Headmaster.") in the Somali language seem odd. In fact, a few students who made a "role" claim in the Somali dialogues reverted to English to express their thoughts. In the Somali-language dialogues, authority was generally determined not by role, but by the substance of the issue. The teacher, the advocate of the easy test, would point out to the headmaster that "Progress is through understanding bit by bit," while the headmaster would point out that "the children will be accustomed to easy tests, and will not understand the hard one."[33]

These data (in which the differences were statistically significant) indicated that in the Somali-language dialogues, the "teachers" and the "headmasters" saw each other as equals, with equal claims to rightness on an educational issue. In the English dialogues, on the other hand, the

32. *Ibid.*, p. 198.
33. *Ibid.*, pp. 201–2.

teachers and headmasters saw each other as having certain rights and obligations which would have bearing on the educational claims being made. To an important degree, then, both the teachers and headmasters were seeing different people and making different claims depending on which language they were speaking.

Three other differences—based on data from a variety of questions—were also recorded in my study. In the Somali-language dialogues, political argument tended to take a more "diplomatic" style, while in the English-language dialogues, there was a more "confrontational" style. Also, the Somalis with whom I worked had ambivalent feelings about their own identities (Were they Kenyans or Somalis?), and tended to be more open to Kenyan self-conception when speaking in the English language. Finally, religious themes appeared apposite on a number of issues when the students were speaking in Somali; they were largely absent when speaking in English. In general, the concepts these students used, their approach to problems, their view of who they were, and their rights and obligations were different depending on the language in which they were asked to communicate.

The qualifications and limitations to these data are not relevant here.[34] At minimum, however, they should reopen the question of whether different languages do lead their speakers to different approaches to similar problems. To the extent to which the theory is valid, one might begin to see the Tower of Babel episode not necessarily as a curse, but perhaps a blessing to our world.

To be sure, imperialist powers throughout history have often been an important source of technological advance. One could hardly deny that the spread of the Arabic language throughout Africa and Asia in the period of Islamic florescence brought great advances in mathematics and

34. See the reviews by Carol Eastman in *American Anthropologist* (June 1979), vol. 81; and William O'Barr in *American Ethnologist* (November 1978), vol. 5, no. 4. Both emphasize the limits of my data.

philosophy. Nor can one deny that European colonialism and neocolonialism have led to the institutionalization of a vast corps of technical innovators in the Third World perfectly at home in French and English. Surely as well, American expansion after World War II has been a catalyst for technological advances by those people in Asia and Africa competent to read the English language. Any theory of linguistic relatively must accept this. But this does not deny that the development of technological breakthroughs might well be enhanced by multicultural (and multilingual) onslaughts.[35]

Let me push this argument a bit further. What has become accepted as "technological rationality" throughout the world encompasses a mixed bag of both highly efficient methods of production and a whole set of cultural forms which accompanied technical advance as it developed in England, France, the United States, and elsewhere in the West. The dominant mode of development theory has conflated the technical and cultural forms, and its proponents have argued that technological progress requires extensive "westernization." But in Japan, where linguistic barriers have been particularly high, there was an incentive to separate the "technical" from the "Western," making more probable the development of distinct organizations and market strategies, and with it the potential to break the hegemony of the economic order dominated by the advanced industrial states of the West. By this argument, while policies of linguistic association might induce "catch up," policies of linguistic dissociation might induce "challenge."

The third argument in favor of a linguistic dissociative strategy concerns the ability of a regime to create an *institutionalized audience* for its policy guidelines. Here I mean two interrelated things: whether supporters of the regime

---

35. Karl Mannheim, in *Ideology and Utopia* (New York: Harcourt Brace, 1936) pp. 98–108, identifies a cultural basis for utopian innovation. See also Marshall Hodgson, *The Venture of Islam* (Chicago: University of Chicago Press, 1974), 3:430–36, who sees in the dynamics of an active cultural tradition the source of multifarious innovations.

will properly understand the nuances of policy guidance coming from the center; and whether the people (nomads, peasants, workers) will accept and be motivated by the principles articulated by the regime. When any regime in the world's periphery attempts a selective dissociative strategy, its supporters must have a clear understanding of the tasks involved. And perhaps even more important, the productive classes must make changes in behavior which, from a short-term point of view, appear irrational. My contention here is that if linguistic dissociation were part of a general dissociative strategy, the tasks of guiding the regime's supporters and winning those people who must make personal sacrifices might well be easier.

For any policy of dissociation to succeed in Africa, it is quite clear that a regime must be able to modify its incentives to the productive sectors so that there is compliance with the spirit of its policies. When Dr. Nkrumah attempted to tax the cocoa farmers in Ghana in order to subsidize a policy of industrial development, he was too slow to respond to the fact that it became rational for Ghanaian cocoa farmers to smuggle their cocoa into the Ivory Coast (where a better price was available) or to abandon their cultivation of cocoa altogether in favor of subsistence crops. Behavior by peasants which is rational for them in the short run but harmful to their broader long-term interests is a well known phenomenon, and it was of course once argued that the abandonment of subsistence crops for cocoa in the first place was a perfect example.[36] My point here is simpler one: that for a regime to foster change in the direction that it wants, it must be attentive to the types of responses to its directives which tend to subvert its intentions. It must then be able to reformulate and transmit new directives which alter the incentive structure.

All this action and reaction by the regime and its cadres requires regular and precise communication—communica-

36. Karl Polanyi, *The Great Transformation* (Boston: Beacon, 1944).

tion which often must be transmitted through government radio. But European languages (especially English) are very hard to learn. With independence came the decreasing reliance on expatriate teachers and an expansion of educational opportunity in many new states. All this has led to the decline of the standardized international languages as efficient modes of communication. Thus the transmission of directives from higher to lower civil servants, if it hopes to alter behaviors in a nuanced way, must be through the medium of the indigenous language. Especially when a regime has radical socialist goals, what can be the purpose of criticism and self-criticism if the nuances of the dialectic are not appreciated by the cadres?[37] Although I have no empirical support for my proposition here, I think it impressive that any perusal of the speeches (all in European languages) on "authenticity" by President Mobutu Sese Seko of Zaire, or on "humanism" by President Kaunda of Zambia, or on the "Green Revolution" by President Shagari of Nigeria will show a level of generality and abstractness which can have no direct meaning to those who have an interest in implementing those lofty goals. While it is true that President Nyerere's policy of *ujamaa* villages (an indigenized version of collectivized agriculture) is hardly a ringing success, one can be impressed with the numerous adjustments in the implementation strategy over the years, especially inasmuch as the dialogue between the center and its functionaries has taken place in the Swahili language.[38]

The second component of institutionalized audience involves the transmission of the program to the people. To

37. My image of the problems of communications to the periphery for regimes implementing revolutionary programs is derived from Merle Fainsod, *Smolensk Under Soviet Rule* (New York: Vintage, 1963); William Hinton, *Fanshen* (New York: Monthly Review Press, 1966); and Kenneth Jowitt, "An Organizational Approach to the Study of Political Culture in Marxist Leninist Systems," *American Political Science Review* (September 1974), vol. 68, no. 3.

38. See Frances Hill, "Ujamaa: African Socialist Productionism in Tanzania," in H. Desfosses and J. Levesque, *Socialism in the Third World* (New York: Praeger, 1975).

elucidate this point, I must return to my Somali research.[39] In 1969 there was a military coup d'etat in Somalia, after which the new rulers adopted a socialist ideology. A year after its declaration of scientific socialism, the regime solved the major political problem holding back the writing of the Somali language, and declared that Somali would be written in a Latin-based script. In a matter of months, Somali became the language of politics, administration, and education throughout the republic. Problems and opportunities abounded, but what concerns me here was the necessity to translate the regime's statements on socialist ideology into the Somali language. The process of translation turned out to be a process of ideological debate which involved a broad segment of the Somali population. To be sure, a linguistic commission was appointed to make official translations, but it could not work in a vacuum. As soon as official translations were made, objections and demands for clarification came from a variety of sectors of Somali society.

The very word for socialism came under initial attack. The regime translated it as *hantiwadaag,* which means, literally, the sharing of wealth, with the word for wealth connotating wealth in livestock. Unlike *socialism,* which has no connotations whatsoever for a Somali nomad, *hantiwadaag* is a coinage with many denominations. To many nomads it meant that the regime was intent on confiscation of their livestock. The president of the country, Maxamad Siyaad Barre, had to go around the country explaining to the nomads that he had no intention of confiscating their livestock, and thereby setting limits to the program of hantiwadaag.

Similar problems emerged when the Russian-trained ideologues decided to make Somali socialism "scientific." First, *scientific* was translated as "sitting on knowledge" which would not do for the more activist socialists ("too

39. David Laitin, "The Somali Military Regime and Scientific Socialism," in T. Callaghy and C. Rosberg, *Socialism in Sub-Saharan Africa* (Berkeley: Institute of International Studies, 1979).

passive," they argued). So it was changed to *built on knowl-edge*. But then broad segments of the population wanted to know why it was not built on Islamic knowledge. President Siyaad had to tour the country refining his ideology to show the relationship of socialism and Islam.

The point that follows from this discussion is that the very process of exposition of goals in an indigenous language compels the regime to articulate and rearticulate its goals to a broader segment of the population than would be the case if the statements or ideological pronouncements were in a European language. In its clarifications, the regime will provide the opportunity for the constituents of social policy to engage in criticism of the programs. This criticism, while potentially destabilizing to any regime, is a necessary condition for the successful implementation of development-oriented social policy. Whether the audience is made up of cadres or citizens, linguistic dissociation provides opportunities for a regime to be "heard" in the periphery.

The fourth argument in favor of linguistic dissociation—and one that builds on the idea of institutionalized audience—is that such a policy will make a regime more attentive to the felt needs of the people in the periphery. To the extent that the language of politics, administration, and education is an indigenous one, basic literacy programs can more easily reach the people. Once nomads, farmers, workers, and shopkeepers are literate, they do not have to employ official letter writers or lawyers to petition government to redress grievances. They can (and will) do so directly. Heavier loads of communication to a political administration from the rural areas will compel it to become more attentive to those peoples' needs. To be sure, lowering the costs of communication from periphery to center cannot assure that rural people will be heard in the capital city. Nonetheless, communication in the language of the people will better enable frustrated citizens to petition higher civil servants in the ministries without having to rely on district officers who gain status by deflecting popular demands from their superiors. In an interview with a Somali official, I learned that the volume of petitions of the government from nomadic groups grew enormously in the wake of a general literacy drive after Somali became the official language of administration.

There is also some budget data to support the contention that not only will regimes in which an indigenous language is the official one be more attentive to grievances from rural areas, but they will be more generous to them in their capital allocations. In Somalia after the change in official language and in Tanzania (where Swahili quickly emerged as the official language of administration),[40] capital expenditures for projects to rural areas formed a larger part of the government development programs than in comparable states where English and French remained the principal language of administration.[41] In fact, in discussing the role of Swahili in Tanzania, M. H. Abdulaziz remarked, "Without the presence of this powerful medium the present egalitarian policies of socialism and self-reliance would have been difficult to implement in so short a time."[42] A basic "human needs" orientation toward development has been the general concern behind dissociative strategies generally. Here I am suggesting that linguistic dissociation will pressure regimes in Africa to be more attentive to the development needs of their citizens in the poorer rural areas. With a regime more attentive to the people, one might expect a populace more willing to take local initiatives to support regime programs.

A final argument which could be made for linguistic dissociation (although I have never seen it made) concerns

40. *Ibid.*, p. 182; David Laitin, "Language Choice and National Development," pp. 312–13.

41. It should be noted that Imperial Ethiopia was an exception here. The use of a single indigenous language in a linguistically heterogeneous state creates new inequalities. I shall be dealing with this problem in the next section.

42. "The Ecology of Tanzanian Language Policy," in E. Polomé and C. Hill, eds., *Language in Tanzania* (Oxford: University Press, 1980).

plugging the "brain drain"—a deep problem for many African states. Building on his inventive typology in *Exit, Voice and Loyalty*, Albert Hirschman has recently addressed the problem of the brain drain.[43] What were the incentives, he inquired, which brought exogenously educated personnel back to their own countries, in professional environments far less satisfying than where they had been educated? From his Latin American experience, Hirschman suggested that cultural "complexity"—those Byzantine procedures which must be learnt to get anything done in Latin America—might be viewed not as a blight on development, but as a resource for development. Latin American intellectuals are rather proud of their ability to understand the deeper meaning of social and political interactions—those nuances that gringos are most likely to miss. The understanding of the complexity and the enjoyment of participating in it is, Hirschman suggests, an incentive for intellectuals to resist "exit."

I am skeptical of this argument—however elegant and complex it is. As I chat with foreign-trained physicians in Nigeria, who tell stories of how they have to use culturally laden coaxing to order to get their nurses to pass them the proper piece of equipment, or to get them to participate in more than one operation in a morning, I cannot believe those interactions provide an incentive to remain in Nigeria. As I watch my professorial colleagues (I write this as a visiting faculty member of the University of Ife, Oyo State, Nigeria) spend a whole morning coaxing technicians to provide electricity for their lecture room that day (all in rich culturally significant imagery), I cannot believe that these encounters provide an incentive to resist teaching offers abroad.

Nevertheless, there is an application of the Hirschman argument which is less mysterious, and perhaps even valid. To the extent that education in African countries is provided primarily in the indigenous language, indigenously trained

43. Albert Hirschman, "Exit, Voice and the State," in *World Politics* (October 1978).

technicians will be less able to apply for and procure jobs abroad. The educational systems in many African countries are still based on the curricula and the economic structural needs of the former metropoles. Indigenously trained graduates, technically expert in a European language, are able to fit into advanced programs or job categories abroad with little adjustment. Surely this has advantages; but the costs should be made clear. When an African country is compelled to use its own texts—that is when it switches the medium of instruction—it begins to make its curriculum more relevant for the country's needs. As curriculum changes come in the wake of linguistic dissociation, the direct links between advanced degree and job category, which exist in Africa and Europe, will be weakened. Indigenously trained technicians under these conditions will be less able to "exit."

To be sure, highly trained technical personnel must have competence in at least one of the major world languages. The mobility of these people will never be constrained by indigenous language policies. But middle-level technicians do not need ready access to scientific journals, and their training can be competently provided through the indigenous language medium. Since these personnel would be geographically constrained, an indigenous language policy may bring a net benefit to the society.

In a major critique of neoclassical approaches to the problem of the brain drain, M. Godfrey has come to conclusions similar to mine. Analyses which focus on salary differentials, costs of transport, and the probability of getting employment, are, according to Godfrey, unable to predict migration patterns of professionals. Godfrey cites studies which show that professional affiliations and other institutional connections between countries are a necessary basis for large-scale migration. He therefore suggests training in Third World countries in which "nonnegotiable qualifications" are provided. This involves a policy of educational "disengagement," one component of which is to "use the national language as the medium of instruction in courses and textbooks." Godfrey points out that linguistic disengagement is in part responsible for Japanese technicians spurning higher salaries abroad.[44] Alternately, the massive spread of English in Israel has facilitated a middle-class exodus to the United States.[45]

Promotion of an indigenous language, although it does imprison many professionals in their own country, might provide at least one countervailing benefit. The few cases of promotion of the indigenous language I have seen in Africa (Somali in Somalia; Swahili in Tanzania; Yoruba in the southwestern states of Nigeria), have been associated with a cultural renaissance. Here I do not mean the re-creation of "native" dances or any treatment of culture as a museum piece, but rather the contemporary development of theatre, poetry, literature, and opera for local audiences. While I cannot believe African intellectuals enjoy going through Byzantine rituals to perform adequately their professional roles, I have seen these intellectuals delighted and excited by the development of indigenous language theatre and opera. To the extent that the indigenous cultures of Africa can avoid the stultification of being of archeological interest alone, contemporary intellectuals will derive deep pleasure in supporting the renaissance. This aspect of cultural complexity could provide an incentive to resist the appeal of professional advancement through emigration. Linguistic dissociation could then be one mechanism of plugging the brain drain.

A PROGRAM FOR LINGUISTIC DISSOCIATION

While the benefits of linguistic dissociation can be made to appear attractive, the implementation of this strategy is

44. Martin Godfrey, "The Outflow of Trained Personnel from Developing Countries 'Brain Drain': The Disengagement Alternative," UN, ECOSOC, E/CN.5/L.421, November 12, 1976.

45. Richard Wood suggested this example to me in his comments on an earlier draft.

fraught with difficulties — not dissimilar to problems of self-reliant strategies in other policy realms. In this section, I explore some trends and proposals in Africa in the direction of language dissociation.

It must be pointed out that although the pressures favoring linguistic association, as discussed in the second section of this paper, are very strong, it would be wrong to assume that linguistic association represents a stable policy outcome. The counterpressures for change are strong; if only because the social force of nationalist goals is often stronger than the force of technical goals. Trends in this direction are already discernible. Tanzania moved towards the official use of Swahili shortly after independence. In Somalia, after twelve years of independence, the three exogenous official languages were replaced by the indigenous Somali. In Uganda under Amin (who was raised in a combat unit and not a European university), Swahili gained stature. In Senegal, where the president was a gifted poet in the French language, some leftist groups used the promotion of the Wolof language as a symbol to discredit the Senghor regime in general. In Zaire, regional lingua francas such as Lingala, Swahili, and Tshiluba are gaining in stature. And in Zambia and Kenya, both countries where radical policies of employing English as the sole medium of instruction from Primary I were implemented in the 1960s, the Ministries of Education have retreated and now support more instruction through the media of indigenous languages.[46] From a variety of sources — military leaders who have less affect for the

46. Abdulaziz and Fox, "Evaluation Report," pp. 13 – 14, 88; and Ohannessian and Kashoki, *Language in Zambia*, p. 438. In Cameroon and Madagascar, there are already movements for the promotion of the indigenous languages. See Beban Sammy Chumbow, "Language and Language Policy in Cameroon," in Ndiva Kafele-kale, *An African Experiment in Nation Building: The Bilingual Cameroon Republic Since Reunification* (Boulder: Westview, 1980); and Denis Turcotte, "La planification linguistique à Madagascar: réaménager les rapports entre les langues française et malgache," in *International Journal of the Sociology of Language* (1981), vol. 32. The best available compendium of indigenous language experimentation in Africa is that of Mechthild Rey and Bernd Heine *Sprachpolitik in Afrika* (Köln: Institut fur Afrikanistik, 1982).

language of the metropole than their civilian predecessors, leftist intellectuals who seek ways to discredit the conservative trends among the first generation of nationalist leaders, educationists who are disillusioned with the slow progress of students who learn in a language foreign to them — pressures have been mounting for the increased status and use of African vernaculars.[47]

As should be apparent, the two countries which have made the most progress toward linguistic dissociation — Tanzania and Somalia — are both linguistically homogeneous states in the sense that a vast majority of the populations of these states is competent to speak the same indigenous language. (In another sense, to be sure, Tanzania is linguistically heterogeneous). For linguistically homogeneous states, the most difficult problem of dissociation — i.e., which indigenous language(s) should be official — does not arise.

Still, as I shall discuss in the section which follows, problems abound.[48] A linguistic commission must be appointed to standardize a single dialect and orthography. As the late W. H. Whiteley has pointed out, "Anyone who has worked on a local language committee knows how tenaciously people cling to unworkable, impracticable orthographies because they feel that somehow to tamper with the spelling is to tamper with the languages."[49] New words must be coined; and in coining new words the proper balance of indigenous root words as opposed to foreign words adjusted to the indigenous sound system must be worked out.

---

47. See the calls for an indigenous language policy in Onuigbo Gregory Nwoye, "Language Planning in Nigeria" (Ph.D. diss., Georgetown University, 1978), and in G. O. Onibonoje, Kole Omotoso, and O. A. Lawal, *The Indigenous for National Development* (Ibadan: Onibonoje Press, 1976). Regular appeals to the importance of indigenous language policies appear in the journal *Présence Africaine* (Paris). This genre of writing demonstrates the latent ideological power inherent in indigenous language political movements.

48. See Björn Jernudd and Joan Rubin, *Can Language Be Planned?* (Hawaii: University of Hawaii Press, 1971.)

49. Whiteley, *Language in Kenya*, p. 2.

Textbooks must be written. Civil servant examinations must be set and graded. Dictionaries and manuals for usage must be published. All this must be done in countries which do not have a large professional class of linguists, lexicographers, and grammarians. While I do not want to minimize the difficulties inherent in such a project, the Somali and Tanzanian experiences suggest that unlike economic dissociation, the seeds of linguistic dissociation can yield fruit within a few years.[50]

Among the linguistically heterogeneous states—the norm in Africa—the components of a linguistic dissociation strategy are more complex. Here I shall differentiate four trends which have some resonance in African language discussions.

Linguistic Empires

By far the most controversial language strategy for a linguistically heterogeneous state is the choice of the language of a dominant language group as the single official language of the state. While this strategy is hardly different from the policies of François Ier of France, the times are different today. In his Edict of Villers-Cotterêts (1539), he established Francien, the dialect of Île de France, as the only official language of the state. Latin, Norman, and Picard may well have had more prestige. Speakers of other dialects and languages could not understand Francien. But through this ruthless policy, a nation was forged from an empire. To ignore the claims of some minority language group in the sixteenth century was hardly a risky enterprise. Today, every "forgotten" minority has a "liberation front" and an easy call on international arms and media. The use of an imperial policy, creating a "nation" out of the forced assimilation into

50. See Hussein Adam, *The Revolutionary Development of the Somali Language,* UCLA Occasional Papers in African Studies (1979); and W. H. Whiteley, *Swahili: The Rise of a National Language* (London: Methuen, 1969) for the Somali and Swahili experiences.

the imperial culture of language minorities, may well be anachronistic.

Although in the twentieth century it would be extraordinary to replicate the success of François Ier, Haile Selassie made such an attempt in Ethiopia. In his 1955 Revised Constitution of Ethiopia, it is stated that "the official language of the Empire is Amharic."[51] And laws requiring all missionaries to evangelize and teach in Amharic, requiring all Ethiopians to display their name in Amharic letters, and requiring all schools to teach through the Amharic medium soon followed.[52] Although some other Ethiopian languages got limited official status, and although English became an important language for law and commerce, Amharic was the primary official language.

This strategy was implemented in a country of 25 million people, where only 7.8 million speak Amharic as a first language, and another 2.2 million are competent to speak it as a second language.[53] To a certain extent, this imperial policy bore fruit. The level of Amharic knowledge grew in the towns, in industrial establishments, and among school-leavers.[54] As the Ethiopian population became socially mobilized (a painfully slow process in that feudal empire), many non-Amhara groups began to adopt Amharic as the language of homelife—especially the Oromos, perhaps the largest nationality group in the Empire.

But the risks were great. First, Amharic speakers had easier access to government jobs and resources. In a survey of university freshman, 55.5 percent were Amharic mother tongue, while only 10.4 percent of the students were Oromo speakers. The Amhara and Oromo have approximately a third of the population each.[55] Worse, the former Italian colony of Eritrea, by 1962 annexed to Ethiopia, was

51. M. L. Bender et al., *Language in Ethiopia* (London: Oxford University Press, 1976), p. 188.

52. *Ibid.*, pp. 189–90.

53. *Ibid.*, pp. 15–16.

54. *Ibid.*, pp. 194, 212, 271.

55. *Ibid.*, ch. 16.

far more educationally advanced than other regions of the country. The Eritreans are predominantly Tigrinya speakers, and their access to jobs in an Amharicized civil service and intellectual life became severely threatened. There is little doubt that the regional separatist movements, which since the fall of Haile Selassie, have been rife among the Eritreans, the Somalis, and the Oromos, are in large part due to the imperial language policy of Haile Selassie. The present revolutionary Dergue has begun to backtrack on language policy to deflect the claims of the separatist movements and has begun to advocate the official use of ten Ethiopian languages as media of instruction.[56]

Imperial strategies have been considered in other African settings with similar resistance. In Nigeria, where about one-third of the population is competent in Hausa, and in which some 400 languages have been differentiated, a proposal was made in 1961 in the Nigerian House of Representatives that Hausa should become Nigeria's official language. Chief Anthony Enahoro, an Edo speaker from the Benin area led the (successful) opposition. He argued:

. . . as one who comes from a minority tribe, I deplore the continuing evidence in this country that people wish to impose their customs, their languages, and even their way of life upon the smaller tribes. . . . My people have a language, and that language was handed down through a thousand years of tradition and custom. When the Benin Empire exchanged ambassadors with Portugal, many of the new Nigerian languages of today did not exist.[57]

Leaving aside the dubious historical claims about the origins of other Nigerian languages, his sentiments reflect well the position of speakers of the "nonchosen" languages in an imperial language strategy.

Measured in centuries, then, imperial language policies may have merit. But in a reckoning of decades, social mo-

---

56. Abdulaziz and Fox, "Evaluation Report," pp. 17, 44.
57. Quoted in Allan, "Nation, Tribalism and National Language," p. 398.

bilization induced by the expansion of the state will outpace assimilation of minority groups into the imperial language and nationality. This is an equation, when nonassimilated groups are geographically distinct, likely to lead to separatist regional movements.[58] Without ruthless and visionary leadership, the short-term pressures against an imperial strategy will outweigh any long-term potential benefits for the creation of an indigenously based national culture.

Linguistic Confederations

Perhaps not France, but Switzerland, should be a model for African language strategy. The idea that each language group should have control over its own area, and its language become the official one is attractive. Despite attempts in the early independence years to create a linguistic empire, India is today working its way toward a linguistic confederation. The dynamics of Indian language policy—given India's multilingualism—have considerable resonance in Africa, and so its case deserves some scrutiny here.[59]

The Indian Constitution, although written in English, gave special place to the Hindi language. Hindi was scheduled to become the official language of the Indian state after a fifteen-year period—a time which would presumably enable Indians from non-Hindi speaking areas to learn the new official language. On the eve of the fifteen-year deadline—with very little preparation for its consequences—rioting throughout some of the non-Hindi areas and technical

58. This is part of the thrust of Deutsch's argument in *Nationalism and Social Communication.*

59. For an early appraisal of the Indian case, see Selig S. Harrison, *The Most Dangerous Decades: An Introduction to the Comparative Study of Language Policy in Multi-Lingual States* (New York: Columbia University, Language and Communication Research Center, 1957). This discussion will be based on the following sources: B. R. Nayar, *National Communication and Language Policy in India* (New York: Praeger, 1969); M. L. Apte, "Multilingualism in India and Its Socio-Political Implications: An Overview," in O'Barr and O'Barr, *Language and Politics;* and J. Das Gupta, "Practice and Theory of Language Planning: The Indian Policy Process," in *ibid.*

problems of implementation led the government to rescind the constitutional guideline and to continue using English as the language of the Indian bureaucracy and parliament.

Some observers have not given up hope. Nayar points out that should one focus one's attention away from the 1965 deadline, one would see that much has been done to promote Hindi as a national language. The author points out that, *inter alia,* "In 1962, a consolidated Glossary of Technical Terms (English-Hindi), running into 1,400 pages, representing work done over a decade, was published . . . [and that] the Ministry of Education is also carrying on the translation into Hindi of office manuals and forms. Some 1,400 manuals running into 74,000 pages and over 23,000 departmental forms are involved."[60]

Das Gupta agrees that there has been an impressive, even overwhelming, production of "Hindi words, books, dictionaries, encyclopaedias, lectures, and exhortations," but argues that "paradoxically, none of these impressive gains in Hindi production and development could be said to be directly related to the question of bringing Hindi closer to the unrivaled role of the official language of the Union." As evidence, he points to the fact that in Parliament, legislation is introduced in English, and that the main result of bilingual requirements for official acts is to "provide employment to a growing profession of translators." More important, he finds that in government publications, the bilingual publication norms have had virtually no impact "in the more technical fields of transaction involving contracts, licenses, and tenders. Where caution and precision are highly valued," the author concludes, "chances are rarely taken, and the logic of business presumably gains a premium on the progress of Hindi."[61]

If union language policy appears to be sinking in a bureaucratic quagmire, state language policy is on more solid

60. Nayar, pp. 127, 129.
61. Das Gupta, in O'Barr and O'Barr, *Language and Politics,* pp. 202, 204–5.

ground. Since the decision to develop states based on linguistic criteria, the states have accepted the dominant languages of their people as the official languages of state business. Less than a third of the twenty-eight states and union territories employ English as the official language of education and state business.[62] States have appointed special committees for language development, and the Union government, in its desire to placate the states in order to carry on its Hindi language policy, has heavily subsidized the states' efforts. The indirect effect of diffusing criticism for expenditure on Hindi language development by subsidizing state policies seems to be the planting of seeds for a multilingual confederation.[63]

There is some indication in Nigeria that a similar strategy is being pursued. Amid the civil war of 1967−70−in which the Igbo people attempted to secede from the Nigerian federation−the federal government decided that the three-region structure of the early independence years−in which there was a linguistic majority in each region along with a plethora of minorities−exacerbated interethnic tensions. A multistate Nigeria was envisaged, with language a key (but not sole) variable in the creation of new states. Today there are nineteen states. The existence of oil and the distribution of much of its revenues to the states has given the states considerable leeway in the development of their programs under the 1979 Constitution. Although English remains the dominant language of the federal government, the states are free to choose a state language.[64]

While it is still too early for most of the states to address the issue of state languages, there is some indication that in the southwest (Yoruba-speaking) states, that the indigenous language may be further developed. There are over eleven million Yoruba speakers in the Nigerian states

62. Apte, in *ibid.*, pp. 161–63.
63. Das Gupta, in *ibid.*, p. 208.
64. See C. M. B. Brann, "Some Linguistic Implications of the Constitution of the Federal Republic of Nigeria," *Africa* (Rome: March 1980), vol. 35, no. 1.

of Oyo, Ogun, Ondo, Kwara, Bendel, and Lagos (although the latter three have large non-Yoruba populations). Despite the Nigerian-wide language policy over the years, which designated English as the official language of civil service, higher education, and business, the Yoruba people have continued to press for growing official status for their language. In an exciting educational experiment conducted at the University of Ife, Yoruba-medium instruction was offered in an experimental school for the first six years of education. With careful controls, it was found that the students who learned all subjects through the Yoruba medium (and who learned English as only one subject, albeit an important one) performed better in all subjects, including English.[65] This experiment suggests that indigenous language development for use in most official domains does not need to hold students back from eventual acquisition of an internationally prominent language. Since the end of military rule in 1979, the legislature in Oyo State has successfully pressed for the acceptance of Yoruba as a language for official debate; and the governor has begun to give policy statements (and not just make ceremonial gestures) in Yoruba. Is it not possible to conceive of each state following this model— eventually to have the civil services and secondary schools to operate in the state languages—while the federal government and the universities operate in English?

Three problems can be predicted for such a model. First, it is a prescription (in Nigeria especially, but in other African

65. See Adebisi Afolayan, "The Six Year Primary Project in Nigeria," in Ayo Bamgbose, ed., *Mother Tongue Education: The West African Experience* (London: Hodder and Stroughton, 1976). The author notes that in the experimental group, the teacher best equipped to speak English became the English teacher. So the students there heard a good and consistent role model. This factor—and not the variable of whether it is pedagogically sounder to begin one's education in one's own language—may account for the findings. Nonetheless, the scarcity of good English speakers in African primary schools is a fact of life. Compare Afolayan's findings with those of Anders Andersson, "Multilingualism and Attitudes: An Explorative-Descriptive Study Among Secondary School Students in Ethiopia and Tanzania" (Ph.D. diss., University of Uppsala, 1967); and in Serpell, in Ohannessian and Kashoki, *Language in Zambia*, pp. 432–33.

states as well) for leap-frogging secessionist claims by small language groups. Nigeria went into independence with three regions, representing the dominant language groups of Yoruba, Hausa, and Igbo. Pressures by "minority" groups (including Chief Enahoro's Edos) increased that number to four, then twelve, now nineteen, and pressures exist in at least three states for still more separations. A confederationist language policy would create incentives for small ethnically distinct groups to claim mutual unintelligibility with neighboring language groups. With some scholars reckoning that there are over 400 languages in Nigeria, the logic of confederationism could lead to administrative decentralization ad absurdum.

Second, a confederationist policy tends to ignore the enormous geographical mobility of peoples throughout Africa. Numerous Igbos work in Nigeria's north; Hausas have large communities in the west; and minority groups have their communities throughout the republic. Can it be possible to provide for Hausa-language schools in Yoruba dominated states? What happens to minority children who learn through the foreign (to them) Yoruba medium for their early years, and then move to a different (but still foreign) part of the country? Nigeria has a patchwork of language groups, and the spacially static logic of confederationist policies may be inadequate to serve its linguistic needs.[66]

Third, a confederationist language policy can easily hide the real problem: what will be the language of the center? For Renner and Bauer, German would be the main language of the Austro-Hungarian state. For Lenin, whatever concessions were made to the nationalities, Russian would remain the language of power and mobility. In India, as the states develop their languages, English remains the language of the central state. In conditions of this type, the development of the national languages in the educational systems of the regions tends to be perceived as a mechanism to hold

66. See M. Kashoki on "language zoning," discussed in Serpell, in Ohannessian and Kashoki, *Language in Zambia*, p. 437.

the peoples from the peripheries away from the centers of power. (Indeed, this is how many Africans perceive the development of Bantu languages in South Africa). Educational curricula which teach primary school students in their indigenous tongues for the first few grades and then move "up" to the language of the center "teach" children that their language is not capable of transmitting higher levels of communication. Such a policy could work against the purposes of dissociation; or it could be used by a chauvinist center to restrict mobility opportunities in the name of dissociation.[67] The confederationist language strategy in India (and the potential for the same in Nigeria) has certain attractions as a model for Africa—it combines the technical and unity roles of the European language with the cultural and participatory rules of the indigenous languages. Yet the strategy has high costs. In the African context it can lead to leap-frogging demands for state creation. Also, it constrains the geographic mobility of families across state boundaries. Finally, it can work subtly to subvert the very values it wishes to promote.

Gradual promotion of an Indigenous Lingua Franca
In Kenya, unlike neighboring Tanzania, the Swahili-medium trade in the centuries before European colonization did not penetrate far beyond the coast. The spread of Swahili up-country in Kenya is far less impressive than in Tanzania, and this fact has had important consequences for Kenya's language policy. By 1967 the Kenyan government began to implement a series of policies which would essentially make most Kenyan schools at nearly all levels English-medium.

Meanwhile, however, other social forces were at play. The Kenyan African National Union, Kenya's sole political

67. See M. Kashoki, "The African Language as a Tool of Development," OAU, Inter-African Bureau of Languages (October 1979), p. 8. Kashoki is a supporter of indigenous language development. But he has a keen understanding of how, if badly done, the hidden curriculum would lead students to further belittle the possibilities of their mother tongues.

party, was active in promoting Swahili as a national language. The president, too, was supportive of Swahili, and he decreed in 1974 that Swahili become the language of Parliament. By 1978 the educational system began to turn away from sole reliance on the English-medium, and the 1978 National Committee on Educational Objectives and Policies proclaimed that at "Kiswahili is the national language for Kenya."[68] Also, the major ideological slogans, whether *Harambee* (literally, "let us pull together") under Kenyatta or *Nyayo* (literally "footsteps", as in following Kenyatta's, but more recently as in follow mine or else!) under President Moi, are self-consciously in Swahili, with deep resonance throughout many parts of the country.

Although estimates vary, it seems fair to say that about 50 percent of Kenyans speak Swahili well enough to use it in a variety of domains.[69] And, quite important, only about 10,000 are ethnically "Swahili". Swahili, then, has considerable spread, but is not associated with any one dominant nationality group.

The linguistic strategy in Kenya seems to be one of maintaining English as the language of power and privilege while paying lip service to the special role of Swahili. Yet an alternative conception would be to see in Kenya the gradualist promotion of an indigenous lingua franca. Even were this the intention of the regime, implementation would not be easy. Swahili in Kenya has long had a low social status,[70] and its social meaning—it is the language in which one orders one's servants—does not augur well for its progress. But this could gradually change. As Kenyan intellectuals and civil servants have continued to work and learn in English,

68. Quoted in Abdulaziz and Fox, "Evaluation Report," p. 14.

69. Whiteley, in *Language in Kenya,* estimates that 60 percent of the Bantu speakers (numbering about 7 million) and less than 10 percent of the non-Bantu speakers (numbering about 3.6 million) speak Swahili well enough to use it in a variety of situations. See pp. 59–60, 27.

70. *Ibid.,* pp. 4, 143. See also Carol M. M. Scotton, "Language in East Africa: Linguistic Patterns and Political Ideologies," in Joshua Fishman, *Advances in the Study of Societal Multilingualism* (The Hague: Mouton, 1978).

neighboring Tanzanian colleagues have been assiduously developing and modernizing the Swahili language. Over the years, as more and more students are required to learn Swahili to advance through the school system, and as more Kenyans become geographically mobile (and thereby forced to improve their Swahili), the 50 percent figure of competent Swahili speakers is likely to rise — to rise faster than any estimate for competent English speakers, where there is often a rapid loss of competence after a student leaves school.[71] In some future period (measured in decades), it is reasonable that the political climate could change and that Swahili could replace English as the official language of the Kenyan state.

How applicable this strategy is to other African states is questionable. In Uganda, the level of competent Swahili speakers is even lower than in Kenya. In Zaire, Lingala (the lingua franca of the armed forces, with considerable spread throughout that large country) is a candidate, but it hasn't the literature, the oral tradition, and the published grammars that Swahili has. The task of reducing it to a standard script for purposes of administering a large country would be enormous. Hausa has considerable spread in West Africa, but not in any one West African state. In Senegal, Wolof is not only the language of the dominant nationality group, but it is a spreading lingua franca as well. The gradual promotion of Wolof could put it as a candidate for a generally accepted official language within a generation. Or, more interestingly, the elevation by African states of English-affiliated creoles to official status would be consistent with the strategy of gradual promotion of an indigenous lingua franca. In Sierra Leone, for example, their Krio is as much an African language as is Swahili, but it has the same status as English had in England after the Norman invasion.

The examples are few, but the idea is attractive. It is in very few African countries that such a language could be

71. See Peter Ladefoged et al., *Language in Uganda* (Nairobi: Oxford University Press, 1971), p. 25.

found. But in those countries, a Machiavellian leader, sensitive to the realities of African language politics, might well begin to promote a relatively neutral language which has some geographical spread while still proclaiming the language of the former metropole as the language of state. He might well be planting the seeds of a linguistic revolution which he would not live to harvest.

Cultivated Multilingualism

Through this discussion of policy alternatives, linguistic heterogeneity has been assumed to be a "problem."[72] This assumption has recently been questioned by Zambian scholar and higher civil servant Mubanga Kashoki. In a series of recent papers, Kashoki has argued that in Zambia (and surely elsewhere in Africa) multilingualism is a fact of life. If ordinary citizens of different linguistic backgrounds can learn each other's language when necessary, why not build government policy on the strengths of its own citizenry?

Kashoki's studies have shown that in border areas, many Zambians speak between two and three languages, and if necessary, can learn more. The goal of language policy should not be toward the elimination of linguistic diversity, but rather "to harness and utilize it in Zambia to our best advantage."[73]

Unfortunately, Kashoki has not spelled out as yet exactly what this means in terms of what is to become the official language(s) of state. He talks vaguely about mutual respect, decentralized negotiation, and incentives for multilingual performance, but without concrete proposals for the (typically) complex Zambian situation. The Nigerians are now experimenting with ideas concerning multilingual compe-

---

72. Whiteley takes this common view in *Language in Kenya*, p. 4.

73. Kashoki's papers are summarized in Serpell in Ohannessian and Kashoki, *Language in Zambia*, p. 435. See also Kashoki, "Achieving Nationhood . . ." *Language in Zambia*, p. 8; and E. Palomé, "Tanzania: A Socio-Linguistic Perspective," in E. Polomé and C. P. Hill *Language in Tanzania*.

tence for students, considering a requirement that all Nigerian graduates learn at least one Nigerian language other than their own. Their policy of placing the university graduates who constitute the National Youth Service Corps in states different from their own would supplement this idea, if it were ever put into practice. Yet even here, one wonders how to avoid bureaucratic cacaphony unless a single language of wider communication were agreed upon.

In this context, the Austro-Hungarian experience is a useful one to consider. Amid the dissolution of the Empire, as was alluded to earlier in this paper, opponents of Rosa Luxemburg articulated a position in regard to the nationalities which attempted to conjoin support for national self-determination and socialism within the context of a heterogeneous and geographically mixed population. Karl Renner and Otto Bauer articulated a "principle of personality" which was explicitly opposed to the confederative "principle of territoriality." In Jászi's summary of Renner's position, it was held that "all members of each nation should be entitled to form local, intermediate, and central, national associations, so-called National Universities, endowed with a state-like jurisdiction in all matters pertaining to cultural life and educational system, disregarding the territorial divisions of the whole empire. . . . According to this program the joint state should be doubly organized; first, from a national standpoint; and second, from an administrative standpoint."[74] This position's brilliance lies in its cultivation of societal multilingualism without constraining individual geographic mobility. Unlike Kashoki's idea, however, Renner foresaw the societal dominance of a single language (i.e., German) and the continued centralization of finance.

That the Habsburg Monarchy did not survive meant that the Austrian Social Democrats had no chance to implement this program. But in Estonia in 1925, a law was passed permitting self-defined national groups to set up public cor-

74. O. Jászi, *The Dissolution of the Habsburg Monarchy* (Chicago: University of Chicago Press, 1929), p. 179, also p. 180, fn. 4.

porations, promulgate decrees, raise taxes, and supervise education. No territorial unit was needed.[75] Surely this is a precedent for Africa. A declaration that all civil servants to reach a certain grade level must become competent in two officially named indigenous languages (out of say, five) would not, it seems to me, be an excessive burden in the African context. All official documents would require extensive translation into five languages, and different schools would be required to offer a variety of languages as subjects along with one as the medium of instruction. Is this a bureaucratic load which no African government can afford? Perhaps. But perhaps also such a policy would create a language industry with vast employment prospects for people whose job it is to promote the development of African languages. This industry—serving the purposes of the state—would go a long way toward reviving—and not just preserving—African culture.

PROBLEMS IN IMPLEMENTATION

The future of languages in Africa over the next century will in most cases be in the hands of market forces rather than policy planners. One could predict, for example, that in some states, like the Ivory Coast, where French has penetrated widely with a good educational infrastructure, and where no indigenous language has wide currency, French could well become a true national language. In other cases, like Zaire, where a variety of regional languages are autonomously expanding in scope, one could predict the growth of these languages based on the economic and political fortunes of the regions in which they are based.

But because the issue of the official language of state remains on the political agenda, and because initial attempts at language change do not appear to be very expen-

75. See G. Von Rauch, *The Baltic States: Estonia, Latvia, Lithuania—Years of Independence 1917–1940* (Berkeley: University of California Press, 1974).

sive, African leaders will have an incentive to engage in language planning. One of the striking characteristics of language planning, however, as opposed to economic planning, family planning, or city planning, is that the level of success in terms of implementation appears to be extraordinarily different in different cases. While in retrospect one can explain why some programs failed in the implementation stage, one does not have a clear grasp of the technical, social, and economic conditions favorable for successful implementation. Why was the implementation of Hebrew as the official language of the Israeli state so easy to achieve, given that so few Israelis were capable of speaking it and that the language was technically ill-equipped to express the concepts of the twentieth century? Yet the implementation of a common Norwegian language for Norway led to nothing but internecine battles. In Tanzania, as we have seen, Swahili has found a fertile ground for development as a language which can handle the weight of the technocratic age. Yet in Uganda, since the language is seen as one for the "prostitutes," implementation of Swahili programs has met strong resistance. In Indonesia, a Malay dialect, the mother tongue of only a small minority of Indonesians, has made enormous progress as an official language, and this despite the fact that there is a large minority of Javanese who have loyalty to their own language. Yet in Malaysia, the heartland of the Malay language, the official Malay language is still, according to an expert, a decade or so behind Indonesia.[76]

76. On the Israeli case, see C. F. Gallagher, "Language Rationalization and Scientific Progress," in K. H. Silvert, *The Social Reality of Scientific Myth* (New York: American Universities Field Staff, 1969), p. 76. The Norwegian case is brilliantly analysed by E. Haugen, *Language Conflict and Language Planning: The Case of Modern Norwegian* (Cambridge: Harvard University Press, 1966). The quotation from Uganda is from Carol M. M. Scotton's excellent study, *Choosing a Lingua Franca in an African Capital* (Edmonton, Canada: Linguistic Research, 1972). On the Malay language, see S. T. Alisjahbana, "Language Policy, Language Engineering and literacy in Indonesia and Malaysia," in J. Fishman, ed., *Advances in Language Planning* (The Hague: Mouton, 1974). Professor Richard Wood has informed me that Malay has made enormous strides in Malaysia since Alisjahbana's article was published.

364   David D. Laitin

Technical issues are obviously not the crucial determining factor in whether language policy will be successfully implemented. Although it is hard to minimize the technical problems, that Malay development has been faster where there were fewer technical resources (that is, expertise in the language) and that the Swahili language has advanced at differential rates in different contexts suggest that the determining factor lies elsewhere. Summing up the results of a multidisciplinary study of language policy, W. M. O'Barr argued:

> We are led to the conclusion that the acquisition of a single language or the resolution of conflict between two or more languages will not automatically solve or eliminate the sorts of political difficulties which have been considered in this book. The real issues are political, not linguistic; their solutions must lie in the resolution of differentials in power relations.[77]

The question, however, is what the determining political variables are.

A first cut at this question might lead one to seek for the existence of a revolutionary situation. In revolutions, loyalties to language may become unhooked, as it were. Fishman demonstrates the problems with this hypothesis. Although he found revolutionary successes (orthographic reforms in the USSR; language reform in Turkey under Kemal) and nonrevolutionary failures (language reform in India and in Africa), he found as well an equal number of counterexamples. As for revolutionary failures, he cites the Soviet inability to "rationalize" Yiddish, and the Chinese Communist party's inability to address successfully the issue of the phoneticization of Han. Finally, for nonrevolutionary successes, he notes that "the initial orthographic distinctions between Serbian and Croatian or between Ruthenian (Ukranian) and Polish were decided upon by representatives of God and Caesar who sought to cultivate *ausbau*

---

77. O'Barr and O'Barr, *Language and Politics,* p. 19.

differences between speech communities that were "in danger" of religious, political, and linguistic unification."[78]

Four other variables, which I will briefly outline here, seem to be worth considering in assessing the likely success of a linguistic dissociation strategy. First, if the policy confronts the interests (or linguistic capital) of any socially mobilized region in the country, the pressures to subvert the policy will probably outweigh the pressures to support it. This is precisely what occurred in Madras and Andhra Pradesh in India when it looked as if Hindi might replace English as the language of bureaucratic mobility. Second, the policy must be advocated by a coalition of actors with sufficient resources to confront the organizational bourgeoisie. The interests of this group in retaining the preeminence of the European languages was discussed earlier.

Third, the language must be perceived by broad segments of the population to be worthy of learning and developing. In the cases of preliterate languages, as with the vernaculars in early modern Europe or most African languages today, there exist popular stereotypes which downgrade the language at the expense of the "world" languages. And so, there are now educated Ugandans calling the language they use most of the time a language for prostitutes, or educated Wolofs calling their mother tongue "barbaric".[79] These stereotypes inhibit the *necessary* popular acceptance of a dissociative language policy. I say *necessary* because in language policy, success is in large part determined by whether people actually converse in the promoted language. Much research effort has gone into understanding these stereotypes better, and this research can only be helpful to future language planners in Africa.[80]

78. J. Fishman, "The Uses of Sociolinguistics," in G. E. Perren and J. L. M. Trim, eds., *Applications of Linguistics* (Cambridge: Cambridge University Press, 1971).

79. See M. Calvet, "The Elaboration of Basic Wolof," in W. H. Whiteley, ed., *Language Use and Social Change* (London: Oxford University Press, 1971).

80. I am thinking in particular of the papers by D. J. Parkin in W. H. Whiteley, *Language in Kenya*, and J. Rhoades, *Linguistic Diversity and Language Belief in*

A final political variable focuses on those people B. Weinstein calls "language strategists."[81] In Norway, had there been a core of intellectuals and literati who had begun to write beautiful prose in the language of the planners, much of the opposition to its development might have evaporated. Instead, the literati held to the literary language of the past. But, the twelfth-century reduction-to-writing of *El Cid,* or the Lutherian translation of the Bible into German, or the Crowther translation of the Bible into the Oyo dialect of Yoruba, all had dramatic effects on the spectrum of possibilities available to the political authorities. A nationalist literary circle which has an interest in linguistic dissociation can do more for the development of African dissociative strategies than a score of linguistic commissions. That Ngugi, a prominent Kenya author who wrote in English, turned his talents to artistic creation in the Kikuyu language, resonates loudly throughout his country. The important role of these language strategists in the development of the idea of the nation deserves even more scrutiny. Any theory of the likely success of a linguistically dissociative strategy in Africa requires, then, an analysis of social, economic, and political variables. The limited point I wish to make here is that implementation successes in a dissociative language policy are not impossible in Africa, but that the precise social conditions favoring success are not known.

Kenya: The Special Position of Swahili (Syracuse, N.Y.: Maxwell School of Citizenship and Public Affairs, 1977). There is some interesting new evidence that the prestige of English in Tanzania is declining with the increased official use of Swahili. See C. P. Hill, "Some Developments in Language and Education in Tanzania Since 1969," in Polomé and Hill, *Language in Tanzania.* A promising approach toward understanding the conditions under which language planning might succeed is offered by Carol M. Eastman, "Language Planning, Identity Planning, and World View," *International Journal of the Sociology of Language* (1981), vol. 32.

81. See Brian Weinstein, "Language Strategists: Redefining Political Frontiers on the Basis of Language Choices," *World Politics* (April 1979), vol. 31, no. 3. Consistent with this line of argument is Paul Brass's idea of "symbolic congruence" in nation building. See his *Language, Religion and Politics in North India* (Cambridge: Cambridge University Press, 1974).

SUMMARY

While dissociative language strategies have no necessary connection with progressive social and economic policies, this paper has suggested that in late twentieth-century
Africa, linguistic dissociation has considerable merit. The
interdependence between the rich industrialized OECD states
and the less-industrialized states in Africa is clearly asymmetrical. These ties are rarely challenged, yet they work to
ossify the world division of labor. How is it possible to
weaken those ties without inducing capital flight and economic chaos? To a certain degree, unlike other forms of
dissociation, linguistic dissociation need not be perceived
as an immediate threat to international capital, and it could
be implemented without vast aid from advanced industrial
states.

It is to the challenge of how an African state can partially retreat from interdependence without paying exorbi-
tant costs that a linguistic dissociative strategy provides an
intriguing response. Indeed I recognize that even this partial answer has problems. The very elites who have an interest in the perpetuation of the colonial languages are those
who wield greatest political power in Africa. Furthermore,
the four alternative dissociative strategies suggested for linguistically heterogeneous states all have inadequacies. The
imperial strategy yields regional inequalities which might not
be overcome for generations; more important, it will yield
strong pressures for regional secession. The confederationist strategy assumes a geographically static population
which is hardly ever a reality in contemporary Africa. The
gradual promotion of an indigenous lingua franca, while an
attractive model, has few realistic applications in Africa. And
the cultivation of multilingualism, also attractive, has as yet
to be worked out in a concrete way for any particular state.

Nonetheless, despite the claims for efficiency and unity
that are made to support associative language policies for

Africa, there are a number of alternative considerations. I have presented arguments that linguistic dissociative strategies may: (a) help African peoples overcome the still delibitating psychological effects of colonialism; (b) be the source for technical and political innovation; (c) create an institutionalized audience for the successful promotion of progressive social policies; (d) bring greater regime attention to the development needs of the peripheral areas of their own societies; and (e) help policy planners to plug the brain drain. These potential benefits—even if they are limited and carry with them heavy burdens in developing old languages, translating vast numbers of books, laws, forms, and notices and coming to grips with the true linguistic diversity of Africa—make the continuing search for a viable linguistic dissociative strategy worthwhile.

8.

Security Strategies for Dissociation

BARRY BUZAN

THE PREVIOUS TWO chapters have articulated the desirability and examined the feasibility of selective dissociation for
certain groups of Third World countries as part of a strategy
of self-reliant development. They have shown to what extent, and how, indigenous economic and cultural capacities
may constitute a resource base to be exploited in the quest
for more independent and equitable development paths. The
present chapter deals with the realm of security relations. It
is unlikely that the types of dissociative measures discussed
by Hveem and those explored by Laitin would pose direct or
immediate security risks to the dissociating state. The assumption is made in this chapter that the state concerned
has opted for a broader and more thoroughgoing form of
dissociation than that discussed by Hveem and Laitin. Such
a decision could arise because a moderate posture of selective dissociation has proved difficult to maintain or because
it has, in the end, proved inadeqate to achieve the objectives expected of it. More general dissociation could also
come about as a result of an initial decision about devel-

opment strategy which required extensive delinking as part of a reorientation of the country's economy. In either case, the likelihood of security problems for the dissociating state would increase, and consequently security policy could become a critical element in the success or failure of dissociation in other sectors. Here I discuss the types of security problems that are likely to arise as a result of such dissociation, and I examine the costs and benefits of alternative security strategies that are available to dissociating states, paying particular attention to whether or not such security strategies themselves remain consistent with the self-reliance aims of overall dissociation.

A number of difficulties stand in the way of this analysis, not the least of which is a considerable vagueness about what is included in the meaning of dissociation. To restrict it to a rapid and complete break leading to autarky would be to create a caricature, but quite at what point a move toward greater independence qualifies as dissociation is not always clear. Indeed, in terms of the security problem created, what the dissociating actor is actually doing may be less important than how other actors perceive its intentions. In a different direction, there is a problem in distinguishing between dissociation aimed at greater self-reliance and dissociation aimed at reassociation with a different, probably rival, center power. As I shall show, what is an easy distinction in theory becomes much murkier in practice, especially when alternative associations involve very different structural patterns, as they do in relation to the United States and the Soviet Union. The case explored here is dissociation aimed at self-reliance, and the security analysis is oriented accordingly.

A further difficulty is that dissociation has a rather weak historical record. For this reason, an assessment of it based on the analysis of past cases alone would be too limited in scope and generalizability. Relatively clear cases of dissociation aimed at diminished dependence and increased self-reliance include the Chinese move away from the Soviet

Union in the late 1950s, the Hungarian and Czechoslova-
kian attempts to do likewise in 1956 and 1968, the Iranian
revolution of 1978, the developments in Chile under the Allende gavernment, in Nicaragua under the Sandinista regime, and, in a limited way, the long-term policies followed
by the governments in India and Tanzania. Dissociation
aimed primarily at switched association is illustrated by the
swings in allegiance of Somalia and Ethiopia in 1977. The
communist-led nationalist movements in Vietnam, Cambodia, and Laos might also be seen in this light, but the
earlier assumption that communism invariably implies
switched association is increasingly being undermined by
the spread of what might be called "national communism."
In this sense, Cuba, China, and Vietnam might all be seen
as genuinely mixed cases of self-reliance/reassociation. In
each case, the nationalist component was high, and alternative association seems to have resulted primarily from the
need to hold off strong counterpressures from the West. A
number of other cases must be considered borderline because of insufficient evidence; these include Iran (1953),
Guatamala (1954), the Dominican Republic (1965), Mozambique (1975), and Angola (1976). All of these experienced Western counterintervention, and in the first three
cases this extinguished the putative dissociation at an early
stage. Other cases of domestic political upheavals resulting
in perceptible weakening of associative links might be considered, including the ouster of monarchies in Egypt (1952),
Iraq (1958), and Libya (1969), but these are clearly at the
boundaries of dissociation.

The paucity of cases is easily explained. Dissociation is
only relevant to the postcolonial era, and until recently the
process of decolonization itself has occupied center stage
for most Third World countries. Dissatisfaction with the conditions of nominal independence, however, began to grow
almost as soon as the ink was dry on the formal transfers
of authority. In this sense, dissociation can be seen as the
successor to, or next stage of, decolonization. The demand

for it arises naturally as part of the evolution of Third World countries towards fuller independence.

At the same time, a number of particular conditions in the contemporary international system give more force to dissociation as an emerging trend. Foremost among these is the failure of existing economic models to meet the development aspirations of large segments of the Third World. Western models are increasingly seen as reinforcing, rather than ameliorating, both global and local inequalities, and consequently the erosion of confidence in capitalist modes of development has undermined some of the justifications for association. The Soviet Union has only made itself available as an alternative pole of association to a very limited extent, and its economic performance is not such as to kindle much enthusiasm as an alternative path to development. Under these conditions, dissociation and self-reliance become more attractive options despite the undertainties attached to them.

Moreover, a loosening of the global power structure provides Third World countries with somewhat more room for maneuver than they had previously. A number of factors stemming from the rediffusion of power in the system following the unnatural polarization caused by World War II are relevant to greater Third World independence. Military power, especially that effective in local conditions, has spread more widely in the system, partly as a result of arms trade activities, and partly as a result of political mobilization. Although military inequalities are still very great, the conditions no longer exist whereby advanced countries can easily occupy and hold extensive overseas territories. Add to this the assertion of global military reach by the Soviet Union as a counterbalance to the traditional Western dominance, and some measure of the increased room for maneuver in the system is revealed. The American failure in Vietnam symbolizes the potential of local military force supported by the Soviet Union against the full weight of Western intervention. Although the Vietnam case is obviously not grounds for writing off the significance of Western military intervention potential in the Third World, it does reveal the narrowing limits on what was once a virtually untrammeled Western capability to maintain association by the use of force. Military power is only part of the loosening in the system, and it is complemented by the growing experience of Third World countries as independent actors on the international stage. Whatever the inefficiencies that still attend many Third World actors, it cannot be denied that two decades or more of experience has greatly sharpened their skills as players. The creation of the Group of 77 and OPEC are the most outstanding examples of this, and can be seen as a natural development as the new states move away from the colonial orientation with which they started.

These trends in the international system suggest that the incidence of attempts to dissociate may increase in the future. However, they do not imply that such attempts will necessarily be any more successful in the future than in the past. Dissociation entails the substantial loosening or even breaking of certain patterns of center-periphery relations, and therefore poses threats to elements in both the center and the periphery. As a result, any government pursuing dissociative strategies is likely to encounter security threats from within and beyond its borders.

The first section of this paper examines the nature of the security problems generated by dissociation, emphasizing the linkages between external and domestic factors. The second section then explores four alternative security strategies that are available to dissociating states in the Third World, assessing their relative merits and demerits from the point of view of the self-reliance objectives assumed at the outset. The third section concludes with some observations about the prospects for successfully devising and implementing an appropriate security strategy for dissociation.

SECURITY PROBLEMS ARISING
FROM DISSOCIATION POLICIES

Third World countries as a group can be differentiated from more highly industrialized states along a number of lines relevant to security.[1] Although Third World states are an enormously diverse group, the following six factors give a useful guide to the most important ways in which their general security environment differs from that of the industrialized states. First, and with a few obvious exceptions, their resource base (in the broad sense of *resource*) is likely to be relatively small and narrow. This poses a hard set of constraints on security policy options. Second, many of them lack a modern military tradition associated with the state. Since the state itself is often a weak tradition, this makes them vulnerable to the temptation to copy military traditions developed and seen to be successful elsewhere. Third, there are very few stable security communities among Third World states, and active security problems with immediate neighbors are common. This problem is compounded by instability in the governing regimes of neighbors that can lead to rapid shifts in patterns of alignment and hostility. It contrasts with the security environment of many developed states which is relatively constant in its sources of threat and patterns of alignment. Fourth, domestic political instability is more widespread, resulting in a degree of civil role for the military much higher than is customary in Western states. Third World security perspectives are thus much more inward oriented, and problems of elite rivalry, insurgency and separatism have a relatively high security salience. Fifth, these countries are highly susceptible to intervention from larger powers. This is not unique to Third World countries,

1. The term *Third World* is used here to mean the countries in Asia, Africa, and Latin America, excluding China, Israel, and South Africa. Each of the latter three is in an important sense exceptional, and a more coherent group-meaning is obtained by making the term coterminous with the self-selected membership of the Group of 77.

but their domestic weakness makes them highly vulnerable to it. Sixth, they are generally dependent on foreign suppliers for advanced military equipment. This makes them vulnerable to manipulation by their suppliers, and it also makes them vulnerable to rapid, and relatively enormous, shifts in their local military balance through the sudden import by one state of even moderate amounts of modern equipment into a low arms environment. All of these factors combine to make the general security environment of Third World countries quite different from that largely assumed in the literature on East-West security. It is useful to retain some sense of the general instability and insecurity of the Third World environment when considering the more specific security problems arising from dissociation.

Dissociation, by its basic nature, is likely to generate threats to the government which pursues it. Assuming that the dissociating state (state D) was associated with a state or group of states at the center of the world political economy (state(s) C), then three types of threats to D's government can be anticipated:

1. Internal threats arising purely from domestic sources;
2. external threats of *direct* armed intervention from C (as in the American tradition of sending the Marines into Latin American countries); and
3. internal threats supported by *indirect* intervention from C (as in American action against the Allende government in Chile).

The nature and mix of these threats will vary greatly across cases. They may be of an explicitly military character, or they may occur on more subtle economic and political levels. Cases of a pure type will be rare, the norm being a complex mix of different types and levels of threat which changes over time (for example, the range of American threats to Cuba since 1960, stretching from economic sanction, through indirect armed invasion (Bay of Pigs), and threat of bombing and invasion (Cuban missile crisis), to various CIA attempts on the life of Castro). For this reason a general typology of cases is not feasible. A simple model (figure 8.1) is, however, a useful aid to discussion.

From this model it can be seen that at least two groups are likely to be severely disaffected by a policy of dissociation. One of these groups will comprise those interests in C who benefited from the associative links with D. If they perceive their interests as being very adversely affected by D's actions, then they can mount threats against D in two ways: either by mobilizing their own private resources in an indirect intervention; or by getting their government(s) to accept that their sectional interest is part of the national interest, thereby justifying the use of the instrumentalities of state(s) in either direct or indirect intervention against D. In pursuing these options, the interests in C might be able to strengthen their hand by gaining support from other interests in C whose welfare may not be linked directly to D. These might be persuaded that the precedent set by D constituted an important indirect threat to their associative links with states other than D. External threats from C to D will normally be directed against D's government, but can take the form either of specific action against the government, or of general action against state D which is designed to undermine the government's position. These distinctions will be explored in more detail below.

The second disaffected group likely to threaten D's government over dissociation policy comprises those interests in D that benefited from association with C. These may include any or all of economic, political, military, and cultural interests. Their links with C can range from virtually total dependence, as in the case of a well-rewarded neocolonial elite maintained by interests in C to provide optimum conditions for the exploitation of D, to interests with substantial domestic roots in D that benefit from, but are not dependent on, links with C. Displacing these interests from the seat of government is a necessary condition for dissociation

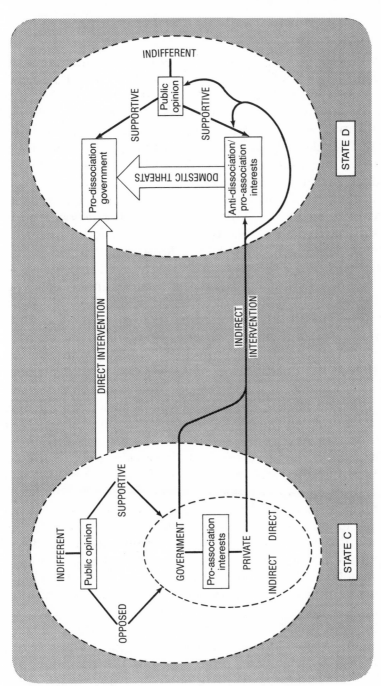

Figure 8.1. Source of Threat to a Dissociating Government

in that the policy requires control of the instrumentalities of the state. The transfer of power can, however, take many forms. If it involves extensive domestic conflict (civil war), as it did in China, then the power of the pro-association interests may well be largely broken in that process. If the transfer is relatively peaceful, as in Chile, then the anti-dissociation interests may retain their sectional positions with relatively small loss of power.

Except in the most extreme cases of prior civil conflict, however, it seems likely that substantial pro-association interests will remain in being after the transfer of power. If the association has existed for a long time, the network of interests tied to it will extend throughout the society of D. Such penetration cannot be eliminated either easily or quickly without causing extensive domestic disruption, and even if apparently eliminated may regenerate if opportunity offers. Any incoming government with plans for dissociation will be faced with this dilemma. If it tries to purge all opposition at the outset, it risks at least extensive dislocation and conflict, and at worst self-destructive chaos and external intervention. The rapid exodus or destruction of professional and skilled labor, as illustrated by the flights from Cuba, is only one of the more obvious hazards of this approach. If, on the other hand, it chooses to tolerate the opposition and attempts to achieve social transformation with a minimum of violence and upheaval, it runs the danger of either subtle or overt undermining of its policies from within. The existence of an extensive anti-dissociation interest within the country, most probably still in command of significant economic, political, social, and possibly military resources, is not only a domestic source of threat to the dissociating government, but also a possible channel for external intervention.

Internal threats can have two sources: elite opposition and mass opposition. The danger from the former is of a coup overthrowing the pro-dissociation leadership. The danger from the latter is of popular uprisings which either destroy the legitimacy of the pro-dissociation leadership, or else remove it from office by force. The frequent turnover of military leaders in Bolivia is an example of the former process, and the recent ouster of the Shah of Iran is an example of the latter, though in neither case was the issue opposition to dissociation. Where dissociation is the issue, it seems very unlikely that internal opposition would remain unsupported by external interests.

From the point of view of external interests, while the disposition to intervene is predictable from the general structure of relations between center and periphery, any particular intervention will be conditioned both as to probability and character by a large number of specific factors that are themselves complex, interactive and unstable.[2] Among the situational determinants are geopolitical and geostrategic factors, how substantial and important to C the associative links are, how much of an affront the dissociative break poses to C, and a variety of domestic factors in both C and D.[3] In general, indirect intervention in the form of assistance to pro-association groups within D is by far the best option for external interests. It enables them to pursue their objectives at relatively low cost and risk to themselves, and with a maximum cloaking of local legitimacy for the outcome. Quite small amounts of money, arms, advice, and equipment, when combined with promises of future support, might well be enough to tip the domestic balance against the pro-dissociation government, as happened in Chile. This is especially so if the military establish-

2. John L. S. Girling, *America and the Third World: Revolution and Intervention* (London: Routledge and Kegan Paul, 1980).

3. See the discussion in Girling, *America and the Third World*, R. Jackson, "The Great Powers and the Indian Subcontinent," *International Affairs* (1973); 49(1):35–50; C. Legum, "The Soviet Union, China, and the West in Southern Africa," *Foreign Affairs* (1976), 54(4):745–62; M. D. Wolpin, "Egalitarian Reformism in the Third World versus the Military: A Profile of Failure," *Journal of Peace Research* (1978), 15(2):89–108; R. B. Stauffer, "The Political Economy of a Coup," *Journal of Peace Research* (1974), 11(3):161–77; and Ian Lustick, "Stability in Deeply Divided Societies: Consociationalism versus Control," *World Politics* (April 1979), 31(3):325–44.

ment from association days is still largely intact. Such establishments are often heavily penetrated by center states as part of past association policy, and if they remain intact, they are ideally placed to intervene against a pro-dissociation government. Penetration is achieved not only through arms and equipment supply by C, but by extensive military training programs in C for foreigners. The United States, for example, trained some 483,000 foreign military personnel from 70 countries, mostly at institutions in the US, between 1951 and 1977. An explicit part of this training was to "promote a pro-U.S. orientation," including the teaching of English, as a way of cultivating future allies.[4] In 1977 the U.S. International Military Education and Training Program covered 5,012 students from fifty countries, of which 4,421 were from forty-four Third World countries. More than half of these were from Latin America, and most of the training was in the context of regular courses and institutions serving the American armed forces.[5] Obviously, if the self-interest and the cultural orientation of the military can be tied to maintenance of associative links, then the military establishment will be a major domestic impediment to policies of dissociation.

Indirect intervention can take many forms, and can have many sources, but it is usually aimed at either or both of two objectives:

1. to strengthen domestic groups that are opposing the pro-dissociation government; and/or
2. to manipulate external conditions so as to generate such an excessive burden of problems for the government that it will be unable to operate effectively.

4. Hearings before the Subcommittee on International Security and Scientific Affairs of the Committee on International Relations of the House of Representatives, 95th Congress, 1st Session, "Policies on Arms Transfers and Military Assistance Programs," March—April 1977, p. 34. See also Miles D. Wolpin, *Military Aid and Counter-Revolution in the Third World* (Lexington, Mass.: Heath, 1972), pp. 143—54; and G. J. Pauker et al., *In Search of Self-Reliance: U.S. Security Assistance to the Third World* (Rand-1092-ARPA, June 1973), p. 64.

5. *Congressional Presentation, Security Assistance Program* (FY 1979), pp. 12—15.

Separately or together, these tactics can make life extremely difficult for a pro-dissociation government. An increase in the intensity of domestic opposition forces it to devote more material and mental resources to ensuring both civil order and its own survival. Normally, this would have direct adverse effects on its ability to pursue the complex business of transforming the domestic structure away from the patterns of association.

Similarly, a *sudden* worsening of external conditions, such as credit squeezes, trade restrictions, restrictions on aid and investment, industrial closures, and threats of direct intervention, can create severe and immediate domestic problems of the kind experienced by Cuba. Coping with these again takes the government away from its desired course, and may well force it into relatively extreme and unpopular policies. In effect, pressure of this sort pushes the government into *complete* dissociation at a very rapid rate and can create transition problems of such magnitude as to discredit the policy overall.

Combined pressure along these lines might well overwhelm a government whose limited human and material resources are insufficient to cope with the range and intensity of problems raised. At the same time as the pro-dissociation government is being "destabilized," indirect intervention can be applied to building up pro-association elements as an alternative government. At its most blatant, this might involve arms supply, military training, and the finance, advice, and equipment necessary to overthrow the government by force. In its more subtle forms it may simply be the mobilization or encouragement of pro-association elements by promises of terms of association which appear advantageous either for the country as a whole or for the particular group concerned.

The threat of indirect intervention against D can come from a variety of sources. Many types of indirect intervention, short of major military and economic moves which require state resources, can be undertaken by nongovernmental actors, such as large corporations in C. These could apply a variety of economic sanctions against D, with particularities depending on the nature of D's economy and the structure of associative links. They could also, to a limited extent, provide aid relevant to the use of force. Transnational intervention can be either supplemented or replaced by state action from C. In this case a much wider variety, and a much higher level, of resources becomes available for indirect intervention. State C may act alone, or it may seek assistance from other states or interests adversely affected by D's policy. The possibilities here are legion. C may be able to keep a low profile itself by directing more extreme forms of intervention through other states—perhaps neighbors of D. Indeed, D's neighbors may intervene independently if their ruling interests see developments in D as a threat to their own legitimacy. The South African interventions into Angola, which started in 1975, illustrate both of these options to some extent. The situation becomes even more complex if competitive interventions develop. Different outside interests may support different factions opposed to dissociation, or competition may develop between outside interests opposing dissociation and other outside interests which support it. In this latter case, D risks the danger of becoming a battleground for interests and issues much larger than itself, and thus of finding its own interests submerged. In such a case, the objectives of dissociation may be almost as much threatened by allies as by enemies, inasmuch as the dependencies arising from receipt of assistance clash with the aims of dissociation. The situation in Iran after the fall of the Shah illustrates some of these possibilities, as does the experience of Cuba.

External threats of direct intervention—that is to say, the use of external military forces against D—constitutes the last resort of the anti-dissociation interests outside D. Compared with indirect methods, invasion is a clumsy, costly, and risky option. Possibilities for disguise are very limited, as illustrated by the Bay of Pigs episode, and the overt use of force makes explicit patterns of control that work better when they are subtle. The need for blatant use of external forces bespeaks failure of policy, and does not, in the long run, escape the need to put together a viable pro-association government in D. Many conditions affect the propensity to intervene directly, but it seems reasonable to surmise that, as a rule, outside states will prefer indirect to direct forms of intervention. One exception to this might be the case where C desires to make an example of D, and therefore prefers the visible exercise of its own strength. Other than this, however, direct intervention can only be justified by urgent threats to important interests, and by the absence of alternative, reliable courses of action.

A number of conclusions can be drawn from this brief overview of security problems arising from dissociation policies. First, dissociation is a posture that is likely to generate security problems. Natural opposition groups exist both inside and outside the state, and these are likely to take the policy shift seriously enough to justify hostile actions against the government. Second, the security problems arising from dissociation policies are likely to be extremely complicated and highly politicized because of the existence of both internal and external sources of threat, and the potential for links between them. Under these circumstances, security questions become inextricably tangled with domestic politics, and foreign relations assume disproportionate domestic importance. The normal security orientation of threats to the state or to the nation ceases to be the central issue, and the much more highly political issue of threats to the *government* becomes dominant. If the security of the government is what is at stake, then economic and political factors, as well as military ones, become relevant to security in a way that would not happen if security threats remained state oriented. The security of the government can be threatened in nonmilitary, as well as military, ways, and thus security perspectives will tend to invade the government's thinking in all policy areas. As a rule, governments will be much more vulnerable targets than states.

A third conclusion is that a sound security policy is a necessary condition for any success with dissociation. Unless security problems are anticipated and met successfully, the chances for successful dissociation are small. Appropriate responses will, of course, vary according to the particularities of specific cases. Nevertheless, it seems reasonable to posit as a general rule that a high level of effective domestic consensus in support of, or at least not opposed to, the government is a necessary condition for successful dissociation policies. Domestic dissent creates ideal conditions for external intervention, and a government fighting on two fronts is likely to be short-lived. If it does survive, it will have little time or energy to devote to a major policy shift like dissociation. Quite how such internal harmony is to be achieved in the face of a naturally divisive policy like dissociation is a question largely outside the scope of this paper, but it seems unlikely to be done easily or painlessly.

SECURITY STRATEGIES FOR DISSOCIATING STATES

There are examples of successful external intervention against governments pursuing dissociation measures: Czechoslovakia, Chile, Guatemala, Iran (1953), and so forth. There are also examples of states that have succeeded in implementing dissociation measures against varying degrees of external opposition: China, Cuba, and possibly Angola and Mozambique, though in these latter two cases, dissociation is entangled in a delayed process of decolonization. Countries like Tanzania, India, and Libya have achieved moderate levels of dissociation without suffering really serious intervention pressures. Defense strategies in these states are only one of a number of factors that might explain success or failure in each case, and it is not my intention here to argue that there are any foolproof means of guaranteeing security. These cases are useful as indicators of the range of defense options available, and of the advantages and disadavantages of different options, rather than as precise guides to future action. The intention in this section is to explore four alternative security strategies in this light: appeasement, alternative security association, conventional self-reliance, and unconventional self-reliance. These strategies, and the arguments in favor of and against them, might be applied generally to the security problems of Third World countris. As presented here, however, the discussion is particularly oriented towards the problems of dissociating states. Given that security problems are likely to be of high priority among the issues facing dissociating states, the objective in this section is to discern which policies are most likely to meet the kind of threats faced by dissociating states *without* at the same time imposing costs, risks, or conditions likely to cripple the posture and objectives of dissociation itself.

It is perhaps worth stating here the author's view that there are no compelling grounds, either moral or intellectual, for the automatic posing of armament and development as mutually exclusive objectives.[6] The perspective informing what follows is more in line with Gavin Kennedy's observations, that "Nobody has yet devised a substitute for armed forces," and "[the] monopoly of violence is an inescapable part of the burden of government."[7]

Appeasement
Appeasement is a political approach to security. It involves the use of political action to remove or reduce threats, rather than the deployment of military strength, whether your own

6. This is done in, for example, *North-South; A Programme for Survival,* Report of the Brandt Commission (London: Pan Books, 1980), p. 117; Alva Myrdal et al., "Disarmament and Development," *Development Dialogue* (1977), no. 1, pp. 3–33; and SIPRI, "Disarmament and Development," *Yearbook of World Armament and Disarmament 1978* (Stockholm: Almqvist and Wiksell, 1979), ch. 10.

7. Gavin Kennedy, *The Military in the Third World* (London: Duckworth, 1974), pp. 1 and 245.

or somebody else's, to deter threats or to turn aside hostile actions. Specifically, it would require in the context of this discussion that D take positive action to remove or to reduce whatever it was doing that was causing serious offense to C.

The potential appeal of appeasement is that it is inexpensive and does not require the diversion of scarce resources into some form of military establishment. The avoidance of military instruments may have a moral as well as an economic appeal, though this is less likely in a society undergoing a divisive social transformation. As Robin Luckham argues, "the fact that military force settles things in the last resort is critical, particularly in societies in permanent crisis, where the last resort is always close to hand."[8] Avoidance of military options may also be argued on practical grounds. It may be argued that even with a maximum willingness to divert resources to military ends, a small, poor, developing country will still be unable to mount a military capability that would make any difference against the forces of an intervening center state. In such a case the resources would be better used in domestic development projects than wasted in a heroic but fruitless gesture.[9] In addition, it may be the case that military forces tend to incite more hostility than they deter, but this is not susceptible to general proof and will depend on the values of the leaders concerned.

Whatever the appeal of a nonmilitary security policy, it seems unlikely that it can be the basis of a viable security policy for D. The basic reason is that the very essence of

8. Robin Luckham, "Militarism: Force, Class and International Conflict," *IDS Bulletin* (July 1977), 9(1):27.

9. A number of countries have exceedingly minimal armed forces, sometimes indistinguishable from police, coast guard, and other civil bodies. *The Military Balance 1979—80* (London: IISS, 1980) gives no listing for Iceland, Bhutan, Trinidad and Tobago, Swaziland, and Lesotho. Costa Rica and Panama have no formally constituted armed forces, but have paramilitary bodies containing several thousand men. Fiji, Luxembourg, Malta, and Botswana all have armed forces containing 1,000 men or fewer.

dissociation is inimical to C. Assuming that C is both structurally and ideologically oriented towards association, then D's actions will necessarily cause C direct economic loss, ideological affront, and the humiliation of seeing the pro-association group in D displaced at best and persecuted at worst. If D is to retain dissociation as a central objective of its policy, then its room for political manoeuvre vis-à-vis C will be very limited. Appeasement of C would mean, in effect, abandonment of dissociation.

Assuming that D's commitment to dissociation is given precedence, then the only appeasement option open to D is to make the process of dissociation as moderate and as polite as possible in relation to C. This could be done by such actions as: avoiding extreme ideological postures known to be offensive to C; avoiding the characterization of C as an enemy; avoiding the mistreatment of C's nationals; proceeding moderately in the nationalization of C's property in D; avoiding open incitement of other states to follow D's example; and suchlike. This may serve to appease C, but it is not without costs and risks to D. A moderate line may well involve substantive policy sacrifices for D in terms of reducing the range, and slowing the implementation of, preferred policies. More seriously, a moderate line will require that D's leadership forego the use of many dramatic actions and images that might be valuable tools in the process of social mobilization. Possession of a unifying negative may even be an essential tool for the leadership in the turbulent transition implied by dissociation. If this is the case, then D's leadership may welcome a certain amount of hostility from C, and may need to cultivate that hostility as part of the process of establishing its own legitimacy. However, a problem with this tactic is that events in D may move beyond the control of the government. Mass action against the symbols and interests of C may take on a life of its own, as it did in Iran after the fall of the Shah. Policy towards C may also be a sensitive issue within the ruling group of D, and splits between radicals and moderates may mean that D does not command unconstrained rational choices with regard to its policy towards C.

Even if D's leadership were prepared and able to make the sacrifices necessary to pursue a moderate line toward C, there would still be no guarantee of stemming intervention. In part, this reflects the classic critique of appeasement—that it is more likely to be seen as expressing weakness on the part of the appeaser than as expressing a genuine and reasoned concession. As such, it might backfire for D either by stimulating C to increase its demands, or by tempting C to intervene on the assumption of low resistance. This last possibility is especially dangerous for D because the policy of appeasement would probably have meant relatively moderate treatment of pro-association interests in D, that would thus still be in a position to facilitate effective indirect intervention by C. The case of Chile is instructive in this regard.

On this basis, it must be concluded that appeasement by itself is probably an inappropriate security policy for dissociating states.

Alternative Security Association
Alternative security association involves D finding a third state to act as its protector against C. This can take a variety of forms ranging from a treaty of alliance, through less-formal guarantee arrangements, to the covert supply of military aid. Links might be established directly with another major power, as in the case of Cuba and the Soviet Union, or indirectly as in the case of Angola, Cuba, and the Soviet Union, where Cuba seems to act partly as a proxy for the Soviet Union, and partly as a supporter in its own right. Alternative security associations might be set up with either a center power rival, R, of C's, or else with a sympathetic local power if one is available. Large and relatively independent

regional powers like China, India, and Brazil might fill this role. Normal commercial arms trade deals would not necessarily indicate a security association. The idea of association implies measures of guarantee extended to D, and/or the supply of arms and military assistance on political rather than on purely economic grounds. While commercial arms supply might be associated with political links, as in the case of the United States and Saudi Arabia, there is no necessary inference of a tie. France, for example, sells its arms on a fairly opportunistic basis, and a number of arms importers like Libya and Nigeria try to diversify sources of supply and keep them on a commercial basis in order to avoid entanglement.

The attractions of alternative security association are fairly obvious. Acquisition of a patron may offset both immediate and longer-term threats of direct intervention from C. In the heat of a dissociation crisis between D and C, where D has high fears of direct intervention, a security association may appear to be the *only* means of preventing a looming disaster. That must have been the view from Cuba around the time of the Bay of Pigs intervention. Castro seemed to face imminent attack from the United States. Given the paucity of Cuba's military resources, he had only three basic alternatives:

1. appeasement, and the abandonment of his political objectives;
2. continued lone defiance, and the high likelihood of his revolution being crushed by American intervention; or
3. finding outside support against the United States that could be obtained at a cost to domestic policy objectives lower than that likely under appeasement.

Castro's position at this time is a good test case to indicate the circumstances in which alternative security association may have very strong appeal to dissociating states. In this case, the initiative for association seems to have come much more from Cuba than from the Soviet Union.[10]

In addition to its appeal as an emergency measure, alternative association offers not only longer-term diminution of D's security problems through the availability of an ally, but also the prospect of a quick and easy upgrading of D's own military strength. While its ally provides deterrence against intervention, D's own armed forces can be strengthened and modernized by inputs of technology and training. The presence of the ally minimizes the chances of direct intervention, and the supply of arms not only makes direct intervention more problematical for C in the longer run, but also might offset external support for armed opposition within D. It is possible also that an alternative security association might have political uses for D's leadership. It might serve as an additional goad to C, especially if the ally is R, which could enhance a "unity of negatives" campaign within D aimed at C. It might also enhance the legitimacy of D's leadership by giving it some international recognition and perhaps also some ideological support, although this would depend very much on the particular circumstances of the case.

These considerable pragmatic attractions of alternative security association are, however, offset by some very substantial drawbacks. The first, and most obvious, of these can again be illustrated from the Cuban case: a commitment to a protector implies another form of dependency. At its most extreme, the danger here is that one form of association (that with C) will simply be replaced by another (for example with R), with dissociation getting lost in the process. An alternative association might undermine not only the ends of dissociation, by, for example, creating new dependencies between D and R, but also the means, possi-

10. Robin Blackburn, "Cuba and the Superpowers," in E. de Kadt, ed., *Patterns of Foreign Influence in the Caribbean* (Oxford: Oxford University Press, 1972), p. 132; and Hugh Thomas, *Cuba* (London: Eyre and Spottiswoode, 1971), pp. 1278, 1281–82, 1389.

bly, by the creation of military or economic structures in D modeled on those of R. Cuba received very substantial military aid from the Soviet Union during the early 1960s[11] and has continued to receive substantial economic aid for the last two decades. The former was necessary to meet the threat of American direct intervention, whether by U.S. forces or by U.S.-aided Cuban exiles. The latter has been necessary to keep Castro and the image of his revolution afloat in the face of a stringent American boycott of Cuba. Cuba is an extreme case, both because of its physical proximity to the United States, and because of the depth of the association ties that linked the two countries together before the revolution. The American economic action *inflicted* nearly total dissociation on Cuba at a stroke, in the hope that the withdrawal symptoms would undermine Castro's government. Without massive Soviet assistance to Cuba, the American strategy might well have worked.

Although Soviet support was necessary to preserve Castro's government, Cuba looks more and more like a case of switched association than like a case of dissociation for self-reliance. Soviet support has allowed the Cubans to achieve many of their basic human needs objectives, if not to progress much beyond. There has been, however, a steady increase in Soviet influence over Cuban economic structures, practices, and planning, particularly during the 1970s. The Soviets allowed Castro considerable leeway in both domestic and foreign policy in the early years, but increasing debt, and the failure of many idealistic Cuban projects, brought Cuba more and more into line with the Soviet Union from the late 1960s onward. Cuba's joining of COMECON in 1972 was perhaps a milestone in this process. The sustained American blockade produced a self-fulfilling prophecy by forcing Cuba to depend so heavily on the Soviet Union.[12]

11. See SIPRI, *The Arms Trade with the Third World* (Stockholm: Almqvist and Wiksell, 1971), pp. 189, 869–70; and SIPRI, *The Arms Trade Registers* (Stockholm: Almqvist and Wiksell, 1975), pp. 95–96.

12. On Soviet economic and political influence in Cuba, see Andres Suarez, "Soviet Influence on the Internal Politics of Cuba," in A.Z. Rubinstein, ed., *Soviet*

Alternative security association thus tends to work against the values and structures of self-reliance that are an integral part of dissociation. This is especially the case when the security threat to the *government* takes economic as well as military forms, and so requires a broad commitment to association with the supporting ally. Such reassociation may be the only alternative for states wishing to break loose from highly sensitive associations. The case for so doing would depend on the differences in effect of association with different types of states.

It is clear at least from the Cuban experience that association with the Soviet Union is quite different in its effects from association with the United States, and that, therefore, a real choice exists. Nevertheless, other hazards arise from alternative association which would make its avoidance the preferred option wherever a choice exists.

The second drawback of alternative association is the severe danger it raises of politicizing dissociation in terms of the Cold War or the balance of power. So far we have largely been assuming that dissociation was generated by processes within D, and that C's propensity to intervene stemmed from its reaction to D's policy. R has been brought into the picture as the third actor in a sequence of events beginning in D. While this model may be appropriate to a hypothetical first case, once the precedent of alternative association has been established, dissociation will cease to be

---

and Chinese Influence in the Third World (New York: Praeger, 1975), ch. 8; Thomas, *Cuba,* pp. 1252, 1265–66, 1292, 1450; Blackburn, "Cuba and the Superpowers," pp. 134–47; W. R. Duncan, "Cuba," in H. E. David and L. C. Wilson et al., *Latin American Foreign Policies* (Baltimore: Johns Hopkins University Press, 1975), pp. 155, 163–74; Fidel Castro (excerpts from speeches), in Stephen Clissold, ed., *Soviet Relations with Latin America 1918–68: A Documentary Survey* (Oxford: Oxford University Press, 1970); and G. F. Treverton, "Cuba After Angola," *The World Today* (January 1977) pp. 19–24. For a sympathetic, but insightful, account of the domestic problems in Cuba caused by rapid forced dissociation, see L. Huberman and P. M. Sweezy, *Cuba, Anatomy of a Revolution* (New York: Monthly Review Press, 1960); and *Socialism in Cuba* (New York: Monthly Review Press, 1969). On this topic, see also A. P. Schreiber, "U.S. Economic Measures Against Cuba and the Dominican Republic," *World Politics* (1973), 25(3):387–405.

seen as a matter between C and D, and will increasingly be interpreted in the light of competition between C and R. Neither dissociation nor the domestic interests of subsequent D's will remain at the center of the stage once D gets absorbed into the framework of great power rivalry. The tendency will be for C to view any signs of dissociation as the work of R, and perhaps for R to justify this by encouraging pro-dissociation groups as a means of promoting its own interests against C. Rivalry in this form would be characterized by extensive indirect intervention by both C and R in the domestic politics of prospective D's. Domestic politics within these countries would tend to become excessively polarized, and local issues would get submerged or distorted by the larger issues between the great powers.

From this perspective, alternative association is a diminishing asset as a security policy for would-be dissociating states. While it may serve the interests of some early D's, it can do so only by increasing the difficulties of those that follow. Given the enormous disparity in resources and capabilities between C and R on the one hand, and prospective D's on the other, it is frequently possible for the larger states to intervene in the politics of the smaller ones at a relatively low cost to themselves. Although it may be difficult for them to control local politics to such an extent as to determine major policy direction, it will be much easier to exercise the negative control of preventing policy from going along wholly adverse lines. Competitive intervention will tend to paralyze domestic politics in D by creating an irreconcilable polarization supported by external resources. It must be remembered that in the absence of mass mobilization, C or R can easily put more resources into the politics of D than can be mobilized by domestic political interest within D itself. Cases like Angola, Afghanistan, and El Salvador, all during the late 1970s and early 1980s, illustrate the dangers to Third World states of becoming the objects of competitive interventions.

It is clear that in the contemporary international system, dissociation has already become politicized in terms of the competition between the United States and the Soviet Union. As Yergin observes, since the onset of cold war mentality in the United States, in situation assessment "the global antagonism was always given priority over the nature of the local conflict and the appeal of nationalism."[13] In other words, the tendency for the superpowers to react to local movements and initiatives in developing countries *as if they were primarily due to the machinations of rival superpowers* is already deeply rooted in the international system. If this is the case, it might be argued that alternative association is the *only* means of breaking an associative link, and therefore must be accepted despite its hazards and drawbacks for the D concerned, and despite its adverse effects on subsequent attempts. This is an appealing, if rather drastic, conclusion, and can only be evaluated in the light of other alternative security strategies.

A third difficulty with alternative association is that it may magnify, as well as ameliorate, security threats to D. As we have seen, part of the price D pays for security support from R is that it gets identified with R in the eyes of C. Thus while D benefits to the extent that the threat to it from C is offset by R, it may suffer to the extent that it acquires new threats as a result of its association with R—i.e., part of the threat previously directed towards R by C is now transferred to D. A striking example of this is provided by the Cuba missile crisis. Although the Soviet reasoning behind the decision to emplace strategic nuclear weapons in Cuba is not known, it is clear that for a few weeks Cuba was faced with a threat much greater than anything arising from Castro's disputes with the United States. Clear prospects for a major American military attack against Cuba were related almost entirely to issues between the United States and the Soviet Union, and only marginally to American concerns about Castro. Continued rumblings in the United States about So-

13. Daniel Yergin, *Shattered Peace* (Boston: Houghton Mifflin, 1978), p. 406.

viet troops and naval facilities in Cuba provide an ongoing extension of this example.

This problem can arise in many forms. R may take advantage of D to make military deployments (bases, observation stations, stationing of forces) relevant mostly to its own strategic concerns. In this case, these forces will reasonably attract the attention of R's rivals, leaving D as a potential area of "collateral damage." Even if R's deployments in D are, in its eyes, wholly intended to assist in the defense of D, they may still be treated by R's rivals as forward deployments, thus again raising threats to D. The more D becomes involved in the rivalry between C and R, the more it will either tend to be pushed into dependence on R or have to devote its own scarce resources to defense. Both of these developments run against the needs of dissociation.

A variant of this problem is an increase in local and regional security threats to D arising from its association with R. D's neighbors may respond in alarmed fashion to an inflow of modern arms from R into D. They may fear the regime in D and see its arms more as a threat against them than as part of D's defense against C. They may also fear R and see D as a base, or as a proxy, for the spread of R's influence in their region. Local arms races and rivalries may thus add to D's burdens as a result of its association with R. The reaction of other Latin American states to Castro's Cuba, the arms race in the Gulf area during the 1970s, and the rivalry between India and Pakistan in the context of their competing external links, illustrate the disruptive local effects which external security associations can have on local relations.

A fourth possible problem with alternative association is one raised by Girling in relation to association.[14] This is the tendency for security links between a major and a minor power to result in increasingly repressive domestic policies in the latter. The argument is that since the major power's

14. Girling, *America and the Third World,* pp. 147–51, 192–94.

interest in the minor is primarily in relation to its security rivalry with other major powers, its concern over the minor power will be more in terms of the minor power's loyalty and stability than in terms of the particularities of its domestic politics. Consequently, the major power will tend to drift into encouragement of repressive measures against any domestic discontent arising either from the association or from wholly internal causes. This tendency would be exacerbated if the major power's rivals meddled, or were thought to be meddling, in the minor power's domestic politics, and the general result would be a militarization of the minor power along lines largely determined by the interests and disputes of others. Girling makes this argument in the context of Third World countries associated with the United States. However, there seems no reason that the logic should not apply to a considerable extent to alternative associations, as the heavy supply of modern arms which is a feature of Soviet cultivation of Third World countries would indicate.[15]

The drift of this discussion increasingly has shifted away from the issue of dissociation for self-reliance, and toward alternative association as a strategy in its own right. As pointed out above, there is considerable room for ambiguity on the boundary between these two strategies. For our purposes, however, it seems clear that alternative association is a distinct strategy in its own right, and that pursuit of it to any great depth would raise incompatibilities with a broader self-reliance approach to development. It may be possible under some conditions to combine a limited alternative association in the security sector with a broader policy of dissociation, but as the arguments above indicate, this would run considerable risks inasmuch as the alternative association may create new pressures for its own intensifi-

15. On the character of the Soviet Union as an arms supplier, see Hearings, Before the Subcommittee, "Policies on Arms Transfers," pp. 23– 24; and Raymond Hutchings, "Soviet Arms Exports to the Third World: A Pattern and Its Implications," *The World Today* (October 1978), pp. 378– 85.

cation. The case of Cuba is instructive as to the *process* by which alternative association tends to deepen, although the distinctive features of the case deny it any status as a model for what is likely to happen under different circumstances.

Conventional Military Self-Reliance

Conventional self-reliance as used here refers to the whole range of policies aimed at producing a national defense modeled on that of advanced industrial countries. High technology weaponry and a standing professional military establishment are the main features of this approach. Nuclear weapons and their delivery systems are an optional feature. The notion of self-reliance means that the desired capability must be obtained in such a way as to leave the government relatively unconstrained in its maintenance of, control over, and use of the armed forces. The preferred way of achieving self-reliance is by developing appropriate construction, maintenance, and training facilities within the country, thus assuring government control. A measure of self-reliance can also be gained by careful control of imports, but wherever imports are necessary, there is always a risk that the supplier will attempt to exert leverage. The classical models for this strategy are Japan and Russia/the Soviet Union, both of which achieved independent, great-power, military status in the twentieth century after having been weak, backward, and dependent in the nineteenth.

Since I am dealing here with Third World countries (as possible candidates for dissociation), it is necessary to raise the question of feasibility before the pros and cons of this approach are examined. Can such countries achieve conventional self-reliance even if they want to?

For reasons that are largely self-evident, domestic production of sophisticated weapons is an exceedingly tall order for developing countries. Indeed, in the short and medium term it would appear to be virtually impossible. Although many Third World countries are in the business of arms production, their activities are on a small scale compared with the production of developed states, and are very largely concentrated in the simpler, low-technology end of the market. It is not uncommon to find Third World production of such items as infantry weapons, light artillery, light aircraft, trucks and armored cars, light naval vessels, and so forth;[16] and some countries, such as Brazil, India, and China, have made a small impact as exporters.[17] Only a few Third World countries have actually tried to become independent producers of a broad range of modern weapons, and their example is instructive. They are Iran, China, and India, all countries either very large or very wealthy by Third World standards.

Iran under the Shah was embarked on a very ambitious program of imports which was designed to result eventually in an independent production capacity.[18] Since the revolution in Iran has ended this program, little can be said about its utility except that the enormous amount of capital required would exclude it as an option for most Third World countries.

India has had independent arms production as an objective almost since independence. Initially under the stimulus of Nehru's nonalignment policy, and later pushed by India's rivalries with China and Pakistan, India has developed a broadly based and moderately sophisticated arms industry. Small arms, artillery, light naval vessels, military vehicles, light aircraft, and some electronic components are all produced independently. High-technology weapons are

16. For details, see SIPRI, *The Arms Trade with the Third World*, ch. 22.

17. SIPRI, *The Arms Trade Registers.*

18. See Shahram Chubin, "Implications of the Military Build-Up in Non-Industrial States: The Case of Iran," Institute for Political and Economic Studies, Teheran (May 1976); *U.S. Military Sales to Iran*, Staff Report to the Sub-committee on Foreign Assistance, Senate Committee on Foreign Relations, 94th Congress, 2d Session, July 1976, USGOP; S. Chubin, "Iran's Security in the 1980s," paper presented to the ISA Annual Meeting, St. Louis, Missouri, March 1977; and L. Martin, "The Future Strategic Role of Iran," in H. Amirsadeghi and R. W. Ferrier, eds., *Twentieth-Century Iran* (London: Heinemann, 1977), ch. 8.

purchased from abroad, but almost always with arrangements leading to licensed production in India. On this basis, deals have been made with Britain, France, Czechoslovakia, and the Soviet Union to produce tanks, armored vehicles, frigates, surface-to-surface and air-to-air missiles, helicopters, transport aircraft, and a variety of jet fighters. India's experience with licensed production does, however, illustrate the limits of this approach. Although the Indian content in production sometimes reaches over 50 percent, as in the case of the "Gnat" jet fighter, basic dependence on the foreign supplier remains, and opportunities for complete transfer of technology are rare. At worst, the Indian role is restricted to assembly of foreign components, with little actual transfer of design and construction knowledge. Cost savings over direct import are minimal because of the need to import many specialized components, and the necessity to duplicate production and assembly facilities. Improvements in independence are marginal because continued production depends on foreign supplies, and licensers have proved very reluctant to release the level of information necessary to enable a full production takeover by India.[19] Indian attempts to circumvent this barrier by undertaking independent design and development of jet aircraft failed because of inability to master indigenous production of jet engines.[20] Given the large size, and relatively advanced industrial and technological capacity of the Indian

19. Although the general argument against increased independence holds, it is possible that licensed production may give a measure of freedom from the threat of embargoes. Components, spare parts, and ammunition are much-less-sensitive export items than complete weapons systems, and may well escape or leak through an embargo by the supplier, especially if the embargo were being pursued without enthusiasm by the government for reasons of public face. Local production of spares and ammunition may also be sufficiently independent to mitigate the immediate impact of an embargo.

20. On the struggles of the Indian armaments industry, see Emile Benoit, *Defence and Economic Growth in Developing Countries* (Lexington, Mass.: Lexington Books, 1973), ch. 4; SIPRI, *Arms Trade Registers*, pp. 33–37; SIPRI, *The Arms Trade with the Third World*, pp. 472–86, 737–58, 781–82; and Raju G. C. Thomas, *The Defence of India* (Delhi: Macmillan, 1978).

economy as compared with other Third World countries, the Indian example does not augur well for any others considering independent arms production. Entrance into the club of advanced weapons producers requires a level of capital expenditure on plant and research and development combined with a level of industrial capacity which are beyond the reach of developing countries for the foreseeable future.

Less is known about the Chinese case, but such evidence as there is points in the same direction. After the break with the Soviet Union in 1960, China was able, after a lag of some years, to get some of the arms industry left behind by the Soviets into operation. The "gift" of this industry was already an advance on the position of most Third World countries, and even so it was not without great effort that the Chinese were able to produce limited quantities of obsolete Soviet models. While the production of MIG 19s and F-9s is a major achievement in its own right, there seems little point to it when such weapons are two or three generations behind those of China's enemies and, therefore, can offer them no meaningful opposition. The lesson here seems to be that although large developing countries might be able to produce modern weapons independently, they could do so only at a high cost (in terms of scarce capital) and would end up with a product vastly inferior to those on sale from advanced industrial countries. Recent Chinese shopping in European markets for jet engines and aviation electronics would seem to confirm the Indian experience.[21]

The conclusion from this discussion seems to be that independent arms production is not a viable security policy for dissociating states. For many states, the limits of capital, technical skill, and industrial capacity would rule it out

21. On Chinese defense production and the problems of the break with the Soviet Union, see John Gittings, *Survey of the Sino-Soviet Dispute* (London: Oxford University Press, 1968); H. Gelber, *Nuclear Weapons and the Chinese Policy* (London: IISS, Adelphi Paper 99); R. L. Garthoff, ed., *Sino-Soviet Military Relations 1945–66* (New York: Praeger, 1966); and S. Jammes, "China's Defence Burden," *Survival* (1976), vol. 18, no. 1.

immediately. Even for larger and wealthier states it seems unattainable except in the very long term, and so the question of security policies for the short and medium term would still be left open. If achievable, it would have the merit of avoiding the risks and dangers of both appeasement and alternative association, but the high costs, the dangers of falling into new dependencies, and the uncertainty of outcome greatly detract from its initial appeal. In addition, the opportunity cost to social and economic development of a large diversion of resources into military research, development, and production would need to be considered.[22]

22. On the record of domestic defense production in Third World countries, see SIPRI, *The Arms Trade with the Third World*, ch. 22. On the problems involved, particularly concerning research and development, see U. Albrecht, P. Lock, and H. Wulf, "Arms Production and Technological Dependence," in Peter Lock and Herbert Wulf, *Register of Arms Production in Developing Countries* (Hamburg: Study Group on Armaments and Underdevelopment, March 1977), pp. vi–xxxvi; SIPRI, *Yearbook of World Armament and Disarmament 1978* (Stockholm: Almqvist and Wiksell), p. 313; U. Albrecht, D. Ernst, P. Lock, and H. Wulf, "Militarism, Arms Transfers and Arms Production in Peripheral Countries," *Journal of Peace Research* (1975), 12(3):199–200; and Peter Lock and Herbert Wulf, "The Economic Consequences of the Transfer of Military-Oriented Technology," in Mary Kaldor and A. Eide, eds., *The World Military Order* (London: Macmillan, 1979), ch. 8. For a more enthusiastic view of arms production in Third World countries see Kennedy, *The Military in the Third World*, chs. 15 and 16. For an updated listing of arms production capabilities in Third World countries, see *The Military Balance* (London: IISS, annually). Precise figures on military research and development are hard to obtain, but those available indicate clearly the scope of the problem confronting any Third World country desiring to enter into the major league of weapons producers. J. V. Granger, *Technology and International Relations* (San Francisco: Freeman, 1979), pp. 17–36, estimates that in 1976 in the United States, both government and industry spent some 36 billion dollars on R & D—about 2.2 percent of GNP—of which around 70 percent related to military projects. Just over half of government funded R & D was for defense. SIPRI, *Yearbook of World Armaments and Disarmament 1976*, pp. 125–31, estimates that some 12 billion dollars of the American Defense Department's budget for 1976 was earmarked for R & D. By contrast, India, one of the biggest and most ambitious arms producers in the Third World, manages to devote only .3 percent of its GNP to R & D, and only about 2 percent of its defense budget goes to R & D as compared with around 10 percent in the major Western arms-producing countries. See Thomas, *The Defence of India*, pp. 111–112; and SIPRI, *Arms Trade with the Third World*, pp. 384, 757. The implication of these figures is that countries like India have no hope of narrowing the gap, let alone catching up with the central arms producers. So long as disproportions of this order remain, and the disparity in available resources

Nuclear weapons fall to some extent outside this argument and so demand separate consideration. Because of their status as superweapons, it takes very few of them to make a large impact on security considerations. Even a moderately credible threat that such weapons are available, as in the case of Israel, can have a substantial impact on the behavior of friends and enemies. Given the spread of capabilities associated with civil nuclear reactors, an increasing number of Third World countries may be able to contemplate building small numbers of crude fission weapons at a relatively moderate cost. Such an option might have particular appeal where the threat of direct intervention is seen to be high, and where options for conventional military resistance to such a threat are restricted by the factors outlined above. Various practical problems attend this option—how to obtain a credible delivery system, how to avoid the dangers of local and regional nuclear proliferation, how to avoid stimulating a preemptive attack like that of Israel on Iraqi nclear facilities in June 1981, and suchlike—but it would nonetheless be foolish to ignore the appeal of this approach to defense. The imperatives underlying the nuclear programs of China, Pakistan, Israel, Iraq, South Africa, and India are not unique to those countries.

The alternative path to conventional self-reliance is not by indigenous manufacture of modern weapons, but by importing such weapons from other producers. Given the international record to date, this option would appear to apply only to conventional, and not to nuclear weapons. Given the desire for modern weapons, several advantages accrue to Third World countries from taking the purchase option.

---

makes it hard to see any other likely future, the pace of military innovation at the center will outpace any conceivable effort in the periphery. For a somewhat dated, but still very useful, attempt to produce comparative statistics on R & D, see SIPRI, *Resources Devoted to Military Research and Development* (Stockholm: Almqvist and Wiksell, 1972). This study underlines the enormousness of the gap between a handful of leading military R & D states and the rest. The pattern of concentration revealed is significantly greater than that associated with levels of defense expenditure.

Imported weapons will be, for the most part, of tested quality, and their delivery will be fairly reliable. They will be much better than anything home produced, and may well be cheaper. They will also be available much more quickly than home-produced alternatives.

The obvious disadvantage of importing weapons is the danger of dependency on, or identification with, the supplier. It is not difficult for an exporter-importer relationship to take on the form of an alternative association, as illustrated by the case of India and the Soviet Union.[23] Trends in the arms market have, however, reduced this risk by increasing the number of sellers and the level of competition among them. The overtly political norms of arms transfers which reflected Anglo-American domination of the arms trade in the 1940s and 1950s, have been increasingly, though by no means totally replaced, by commercial considerations. First the Soviets and later the French and Chinese entered the arms supply market and broke the Anglo-American monopoly. Although the Soviet Union, the United States, and China still attach considerable political weight to arms transfers, France and Britain have adopted more purely economic approaches. Many types of modern weapons can also be obtained from smaller producers like West Germany, Sweden, Switzerland, Israel, Italy, Belgium, Austria, and Canada. Thus, arms are accessible economically and also from a politically diverse array of sources. This competition among suppliers creates something of a buyer's market, and thus provides purchasers with the opportunity to manage their affairs in such a way as to minimize the effects of dependence on foreign arms supplies. Libya, Nigeria, and Tanzania are all examples of states that

23. By continuously offering arms to India at extremely concessional rates since the early 1960s, the Soviets have managed to draw India away from nonalignment and into the beginnings of security association. The 1971 treaty between the two marked the end of Indian neutralism, and with the recently concluded 1.6 billion dollar deal for tanks, missiles, and electronics (*Weekly Guardian*, June 8, 1980), the Soviets have moved into a dominant position as the main licenser for the core elements of Indian military production.

have achieved a measure of self-reliance by choice and diversity of arms suppliers.[24]

It is possible also that political suppliers might view self-reliance in some purchasers as an asset, and therefore be disposed to facilitate self-reliance—by—import strategies. There were some signs of this line of thinking in discussions in the United States concerning the Nixon doctrine of 1969.[25]

Within limits, then, conventional self-reliance by the import of modern weapons may be a feasible strategy. Achievement of the same objective by indigenous manufacture seems much less likely, and anyway could not meet short- and medium-term needs. Given that this strategy is to some extent feasible, is it *desirable* as a security policy for dissociating states? The arguments in favor have been made in the discussion above. There are at least four interlinked arguments against, and on balance they seem to carry more weight.

The first criticism of conventional self-reliance is that it results in a military force that is at best inappropriate and at worst ineffective in relation to the needs of dissociating state. Armed forces modeled on those of the advanced industrial states will be organized around sophisticated heavy weapons like supersonic aircraft, tanks, and frigates, and will reflect tactics and strategies evolved in the weapons' country of origin. Arrayed against a direct intervention from C, such forces will be ineffective because of the inferior

24. SIPRI, *Arms Trade Registers,* pp. 68–69, 81–83, 87–88; SIPRI, *The Arms Trade with the Third World,* pp. 587–90, 634–38, 852–53; SIPRI, *Yearbook, 1976,* pp. 137–38, 160–61, 168, 226, 229, 232–33. Recent French maneuverings in relation to aircraft sales to India illustrate some of the difficulties of managing self-reliance by purchase. The French have attempted to pressure India into buying the Mirage F2000 advanced strike aircraft by threatening to sell the plane to Pakistan should India refuse it. *The Times,* July 20, 1980.

25. Pauker, et al., *In Search.* Girling, *America and the Third World,* pp. 147–51, 191–94, argues against the utility of this development for Third World countries.

quantity, quality, training, and logistical support.[26] Against domestic opposition or insurgency, such weapons will be largely ineffective because of a lack of appropriate targets. They might well be effective against interventions by the forces of neighboring states, and their merits in this capacity would need to be assessed on a cost-efficiency basis against the alternative proposed in the next section. As Kemp argues, high-technology forces are extremely expensive in comparison with more labor-intensive configurations: as a rough example, a package of 200 airborne troops plus 20 helicopters will cost as much to acquire and maintain as a package of 6,000 ground troops with 350 light trucks.[27] Given the scarcity of skilled labor and sophisticated maintenance facilities in developing countries, the opportunity costs may well be higher than the strict economic costs. There is always a danger that sophisticated weapons will be-

26. This point is illustrated by the recent war between Britain and Argentina over the Falkland Islands. Even where the Third World country concerned was a relatively powerful one, and the center state a decidedly second-rank power, the Third World country was not well served by its conventional self-reliance forces. They proved adequate to get it into trouble, but seriously deficient when facing numerically inferior British forces operating on a very long supply line and inadequately provided with air cover. Although the military assessments are not yet fully in at the time of writing, some points are clear. The Argentine navy was useful only when unopposed. The threat from British submarines was sufficient to keep the Argentine navy out of the fighting. The Argentine army, though apparently quite well equipped and supplied, and with considerable advantages in terms of numbers and defensive positions, was beaten with apparent ease by a better-trained British force. Only the Argentine air force performed well, and then at a very serious cost in pilots and aircraft. The war suggests that precision-guided munitions (PGM) like Exocet might make a big difference to the effectiveness of Third World armed forces, but such a conclusion cannot be sustained as a simple assertion. Countermeasures exist against PGM, as the Israelis have demonstrated in Lebanon. In addition, it seems that the center states that control the sale of advanced PGM do try to ensure that the countermeasures remaining under their control are adequate to deal with the use of their weapons by others against themselves. The war also demonstrated some of the problems of supply which states dependent on imports face during a military crisis.

27. Geoffrey Kemp, *Classification of Weapons Systems and Force Designs in LDC Environments* (Cambridge: MIT, Arms Control Project, January 1970), pp. 29–31, 46–47.

come useless because of insufficient maintenance and un-skilled handling. In other words, forces configured along these lines will strain the capacity of a Third World country without meeting any of its more crucial security needs.

The second criticism is closely related to the first—that the forces resulting from conventional self-reliance policies are likely to precipitate wasteful, security-reducing, local and regional arms races. Precisely because they are usable against D's neighbors, the import of such weapons will stimulate the neighbors to take similar action. Where the forces concerned are small, and where the level of forces can be changed rapidly by imports, the idea of a stable balance is very tenuous indeed.[28] Arms racing under these conditions cannot be compared to races between arms produc-ing countries where force levels are high, and the rate of change relatively slow. Because of this, the import of ad-vanced weapons runs a substantial risk or precipitating un-wanted and debilitating arms races, and of inflaming local disputes that otherwise might lie dormant because of the inability of either side to pursue them. It need hardly be added that an inflamation of local tensions provides fertile ground for indirect intervention and the involvement of the great powers, a development unlikely to be welcomed by a dissociating state.

The third criticism is based on the opportunity costs of this style of defense for other aspects of development. There are two lines to this argument. The first is that the cost of this approach is very high. Not only are the weapons them-selves expensive, but so are their maintenance, resupply, and support services.[29] The impact of these costs is magni-

28. *Ibid.*, pp. 26–27, 190–91; and J. L. Weaver, "Arms Transfers to Latin America: A Note on the Contagion Effect," *Journal of Peace Research* (1974), 11(3):213–14.

29. *Defence and Foreign Affairs Digest* (March 1979), p. 26, lists the price of a Chieftain Tank at over 400,000 dollars, a Leopard I Tank at 1,000,000 dollars, and an M198 towed 155mm Howitzer at 263,000 dollars. *The Military Balance 1979–80*, p. 106, lists an American sale of F-15 fighters to Japan at 18 million dollars per aircraft. Once acquired, sophisticated weapons are subject to signifi-

fied in developing countries where the kind of resources consumed by these systems are more scarce and more expensive than they would be in developed states. In addition, the adoption of a policy based on modern technology implies a commitment to keep up with new developments. If this is not done, the systems acquired will become obsolete fairly quickly, and thus make nonsense of the rationale for acquiring them in the first place. In other words, states opting for this type of defense policy tie themselves to the pace of weapons development at the center, particularly if local arms competitions develop as discussed above. The policy thus implies a *continuous* heavy commitment to military expenditure, and not just a one-off purchase. This is true whether the policy is based on imports or on domestic manufacture. If imports are used, then new and more expensive models must be purchased periodically to keep up the standard of modernity. If domestic manufacture is used, then very large amounts must be devoted to military research and development in order to keep up with the pace of evolution at the center.[30] A priori reasoning would suggest that

cant attrition rates even with normal peacetime use. Amelia C. Leiss, Geoffrey Kemp, et al., *Arms Transfers to Less Developed Countries* Cambridge: MIT Arms Control Project, Center for International Studies, MIT, C/70-1 (February 1970), lists annual attrition rates of 10 percent for combat and trainer aircraft and helicopters, 7.5 percent for other aircraft and 5 percent for other military systems. Lock and Wulf in Kaldor and Eide, *World Military Order,* p. 214, note that the running costs of an A-7D aircraft over a fifteen-year life add up to about one-third more than the total acquisition cost. SIPRI, *The Arms Trade with the Third World,* app. 4, gives some idea of the skilled manpower requirements for maintaining sophisticated weapons systems: 100 tanks require 150 mechanics, one destroyer requires 45,000 man hours of skilled personnel for annual maintenance purpose, and an average jet fighter requires 30 man hours of maintenance for each hour of flight. The skilled labor required for these tasks is at a premium in most Third World countries, and without appropriate maintenance, sophisticated weapons systems quite quickly become inoperable.

30. On the problem of keeping up with developments in center arms technology, see Report of the Secretary General to the UNGA, "Economic and Social Consequences of the Armament Race," UN Document A/32/88, August 12, 1977; Ulrich Albrecht, "The Costs of Armamentism," *Journal of Peace Research* (1973), 10(3):274–78; Robin Luckham, "Militarism: Arms and the Internationalisation of Capital," *IDS Bulletin* (March 1977), 8(3):39; Albrecht, Lock, and Wulf, "Arms Pro-

high capital outlay on defense in capital-short economies should have adverse effects on other aspects of development. The empirical literature, however, is ambiguous, suggesting that defense spending is not adversely correlated with growth, but saying little about its effect on other aspects of development.[31] More research would be needed to substantiate the weight of this line of criticism.

The second line of the opportunity costs critique is also based on an a priori argument which needs to be empirically tested. The argument is made by Luckham that the high cost of arms imports, presumably including imports associated with domestic production attempts, virtually forces the country concerned to participate in the center economy in order to generate the foreign exchange to pay for them.[32] This would have implications for the entire economic structure of D that would run directly against the structures necessary for dissociation. At a minimum, the maintenance of modern armed forces would require the adoption of export-oriented economic structures. At a maximum, it would require subsidies from center states (e.g., if declining terms of trade, rising defense needs, or suchlike made D unable to maintain its armed forces on its own account), that would create a relationship of close association. Inasmuch as the economics of dissociation imply a restructuring of production to satisfy domestic welfare demands, this argument has force against a defense policy of conventional self-reliance.

The fourth and final criticism concerns the creation of a military establishment incompatible with the social structures necessary for dissociation. As suggested in the first

duction," p. xviii; Lock and Wulf, *ibid.*, ch. 8; and Lock and Wulf, *Register of Arms Production in Developing Countries.*

31. See, for example, D. Dabelko and J. M. McCormick, "Opportunity Costs of Defence: Some Cross-National Evidence," *Journal of Peace Research* (1977), vol. 14, no. 2; Luckham, *ibid.*, p. 44; Emile Benoit, *Defence and Economic Growth;* Gavin Kennedy, *The Military in the Third World,* ch. 10; and Gavin Kennedy, *The Economics of Defence* (London: Faber and Faber, 1975), ch. 8.

32. Luckham, "Militarism: Arms," pp. 46–47; and "Militarism: Force," pp. 25–26. See also Albrecht et al., in *JPR,* p. 196.

critique, modern arms tend to bring with them not only an elitist view of the role and social position of the military, but also the whole baggage of social values associated with the society from which the arms come. Modern weapons necessitate training programs run by, and often in, the supplier country, and these are an effective means, intentional or not, for the political socialization of military elites in ways incompatible with dissociation.[33] This links up with the third critique inasmuch as the military sees the maintenance of modern equipment as a necessary condition for its own institutional well being. If this is the case, then the military would become a vested interest in favor of domestic economic structures and foreign alignments which would enable the supply of modern weapons to be maintained. These views would conflict with the imperatives of a dissociation policy.

A further problem here is the emergence of the military as a powerful force in domestic politics. As one Latin American observer put it: "What we are doing is building up armies which weigh nothing in the international scale, but which are Juggernauts for the internal life of each country. Each country is being occupied by its own army."[34] The major resource allocation to the military required by conventional self-reliance almost inevitably means that the military grows into a leading political actor, whether directly by forceful intervention into the political sphere, or indirectly as an institutional influence on government. If the arguments about military attitudes made directly above hold true, then a substantial role in politics for *this type of military establishment* would be disastrous for dissociation. Although military governments in general do not appear to differ much from civilian ones in the range of effectiveness of their performance,[35] a government already committed to

33. See fn. 4, plus Kemp, *Classification of Weapons Systems*, p. 24.
34. Eduardo Santos, quoted in Edwin Lieuwen, *Arms and Politics in Latin America* (New York: Praeger, 1961), pp. 236–38.
35. On the performance of military governments see, among others, Luckham, "Militarism: Force," pp. 20–22; R. D. McKinley and A. S. Cohen, "A Compar-

dissociation would have no desire to create the risk of a political rival with alternative ideas.

Unconventional Military Self-Reliance

Unconventional self-reliance as used here refers to the range of possible defense policies based on maximizing use of indigenous resources in circumstances where those resources are insufficient to pursue conventional self-reliance. Reliance on external inputs is not excluded entirely, but a heavy emphasis on self-sufficiency means that it is kept to a minimum. Defense strengths are sought in areas where the country has, or can develop without undue strain, plentiful resources. Defense policies requiring scarce resources or major distortions in development are avoided. For developing countries, such a policy normally implies avoidance of advanced weapons, and may also mean elimination or minimization of separate, professional, Western-model armed forces. The kinds of indigenous strengths on which unconventional self-reliance can be based include:

1. mass mobilization to bring a large section of the population under arms;
2. intensive organization to enable the efficient use of large numbers dispersed over the country;

---

ative Analysis of the Political and Economic Performance of Military and Civil Regimes," *Comparative Politics* (October 1975), vol. 8, no. 1; and R. W. Jackson, "Politicians in Uniform: Military Governments and Social Change in the Third World," *American Political Science Review* (1976), 70(4):1078–97. See also S. C. Sarkesian, "A Political Perspective on Military Power in Developing Areas," in Sheldon W. Simon, ed., *The Military and Security in the Third World: Domestic and International Impacts* (Boulder: West View Press, 1978), ch. 1. Sarkesian argues that his survey of the literature suggests that: "distinctions between civilian and military regimes are not supported by empirical evidence. Moreover, there is also some basis to argue that military regimes do not substantially differ in their overall impact on social and economic change from civilian regimes" (p. 10). He argues further that the notion of civil versus military regimes is a false dichotomy—that most LDCs are ruled by civil-military elite coalitions with varying mixes of strength between the two groups (p. 3).

3. cultivation of nationalism or ideology to create a highly motivated mass force;
4. maximum use of knowledge of terrain and local conditions;
5. use of simple infantry equipment which can be locally maintained and resupplied.

The typical instrument of unconventional self-reliance is the militia, based on some minimum of universal military training, organized on a local basis, and with some system for rapid access to light arms. This may or may not be complemented by more professional, elite bodies to perform specialized functions like training, or to perform highly skilled tasks such as those associated with naval and air forces. The typical task of these forces is local policing and defense, combined with the general objective of making the country difficult to occupy. Their logic is based on Mao Tse-tung's principles of the people's war, in which local forces are mobilized against a better equipped invader. The idea is not to defeat the occupier in a direct battle, which would pit your weakness against the occupier's strength, but to make the occupation too expensive and too difficult to sustain over the long run, which pits your strength against the occupier's weakness. In the last resort this constitutes a defense policy, but the principal objective of its preorganization would be to deter would-be invaders.[36]

Although it is not without difficulties, some of them serious, this type of security strategy has a lot to recommend it to dissociating states. On military grounds, it can be argued that unconventional self-reliance will serve the secu-

36. On the theory of the people's war, see Lin Piao, *Long Live the Victory of the People's War* (Peking: Foreign Languages Press, 1965). On the idea of Territorial Defense, see Adam Roberts, *Nations in Arms* (London: Chatto and Windus, 1976). Roberts' discussion is mostly with reference to Western states but many of the ideas are relevant to Third World countries, even though application strategies would need to be reconsidered. For arguments against the efficacy of people's war, see Chalmers Johnson, *Autopsy on People's War* (Berkeley: University of California Press, 1973), especially pp. 43–47.

rity needs of dissociating states as well as or better than alternative policies. On political and economic grounds, it can be argued that it fulfills security objectives at a lower cost and risk to the policy of dissociation than alternative policies.

To look first at the arguments about military utility, it is clear that unconventional self-reliance is by no means foolproof. Although it does offer both deterrence and defense potential against direct intervention, and probably compares favorably in cost-effectiveness terms with conventional self-reliance in this regard, it would seem to offer less certainty than alternative association. As a strategy it is vulnerable to swift, short-term, military intervention, and if called into action as a defense mechanism, there is a high probability of extensive collateral damage to the country (scorched-earth-style defense). There is also some danger attached to the spreading of weapons through the population. Should the unity of support for the government begin to decay, an armed population would be ripe ground for civil war.

In addition to its general deterrence and defense potential, unconventional self-reliance has the following military utilities to recommend it. It offers a relatively low threat to neighboring countries and is therefore not likely *in its own right* to stimulate either local arms races or preemptive attacks (though it will not attenuate any political hostilities generated by dissociation). It will be relatively effective against domestic opposition in that the forces are of appropriate type (manpower based) and well distributed throughout the territory on the basis of local organization and basing. On technical grounds, it can be argued that the simpler weapons implied by unconventional self-reliance will optimize cost-efficiency for military utility in societies not yet fully permeated by the norms and skills of industrialization.[37]

37. Kemp, *Classification of Weapons Systems,* argues this point with a wealth of technical detail, especially pp. 29–32, 46–47, 96–99, 143–46, 196. Pauker et al., *In Search of Self-Reliance,* pp. 2–11, comes to similar conclusions.

Armed forces equipped at a level appropriate to the technical skills of the country will be more effective, more reliable, and more sustainable than those which are equipped at an over-sophisticated level. It might also be argued that the sustainable self-sufficiency implied by unconventional self-reliance provides the best basis for limiting unwanted side effects of either arms imports, major domestic arms production projects, or alternative association strategies as discussed above. If conditions appear to necessitate D either purchasing some sophisticated weapons (such as anti-tank or anti-aircraft missiles) or accepting protection guarantees from R or others, a baseline of unconventional self-reliance will ensure that it does not become overly dependent and therefore vulnerable to pressure. If D is unable to manufacture even light infantry weapons for its own needs, it can obtain these by import at much lower risk of dependency than would be the case for more sophisticated weapons. There are far more manufacturers of small arms than of jet aircraft and tanks, and the highly competitive market, including an active secondhand sector, would serve to shield the importer from leverage attempts on the part of exporters. It is also worth noting that under contemporary historical conditions, the mode of warfare (guerrilla tactics and territorial defense) implied by unconventional self-reliance enjoys high credibility as a military policy. Its effective use in independence campaigns in Mozambique, Zimbabwe, and Angola, its association with the Vietnam War, and its successful use in the Chinese and Cuban revolutions have established a reputation which by itself is a major asset as a deterrence factor.

In terms of political complementarity, it can be argued not only that unconventional self-reliance does not contradict the basic imperatives of dissociation, as the alternative strategies do, but also that in several respects it can enhance them. The low capital costs and self-sufficiency aspects of unconventional self-reliance, for example, avoid many of the economic and structural problems associated with conventional self-reliance. Necessity for reliance on foreign resources is minimized, and where unavoidable can be bargained for from a position of some independence. In domestic terms, the transfer of substantial military power to the masses either avoids, or at least counterbalances, the problems of intervention associated with conventional elitist military establishments in Third World countries.

On the more positive side, defense by unconventional self-reliance and development by dissociation would appear to be complementary in several respects additional to the ways in which defense normally complements government. If, as some authors argue,[38] the purging or dismantling of the existing military establishment is a necessary part of the dissociation revolution, the mass-based militia forces supporting the government are a useful, perhaps necessary, part of that transition process. The necessity for a fundamental restructuring of the existing armed forces is one of the critical points in the security of dissociation because the attempt may itself precipitate domestic action against the government. Militia forces may thus start out as part of the domestic revolutionary process, and later develop into an alternative form of defense establishment. The costs and risks of this transformation process are one of the major hazards of dissociation and must be weighed carefully in the balance when the merits of the policy as a whole are considered.

The armed forces can also be used as a major instrument of political socialization in line with the vanguard approach taken in the People's Republic of China. The relatively uncontroversial obligation of military service can be used to process large sections of the population through a training program designed to impart attitudes, ideologies, and skills considered useful for development. The armed forces thus become a model for and a leading edge of the social revolution, a process which can be expanded, as in

38. Wolpin, "Egalitarian Reformism," pp. 98–100.

Cuba, by means of semimilitary organizations for those out-side the militia structure.[39] In this way, the armed forces un-der unconventional self-reliance can become an important part of the machinery for restructuring society, though it needs to be stressed again that there is nothing guaranteed about this process.

On a more mundane level, the armed forces can be used to mobilize mass labor for occasional projects (harvesting, civil engineering projects) and to provide useful dual ser-vices (transportation, road and airport maintenance, air traffic control).[40]

For all these reasons, unconventional self-reliance ap-pears to be much the most appropriate security strategy for dissociating states in the Third World. Whether by itself or in combination with limited aspects of other approaches, it offers a cost-effective means of acquiring security without involving the contradictions to dissociation implicit in the alternatives.

THE PROSPECTS FOR SUCCESS

Given the nature of dissociation as a policy, there seems little doubt that it is highly likely to generate security prob-lems. Many of its basic features invite forceful opposition on several levels, most obviously in its need for a rupture in existing patterns of external relations, and the need for a transformation in domestic social structures and relations. Both the propensity of dissociation to stimulate opposition, and its vulnerability to forces unleashed by its own imple-mentation, are illustrated by the cases of Cuba and Chile.

39. See W. R. Duncan, "Development Roles of the Military in Cuba," in Simon, *The Military and Security in the Third World*, ch. 4.
40. For some useful thoughts on the economics and possibilities of military-civil cooperation/integration, see David K. Whynes, *The Economics of Third World Military Expenditure* (London: Macmillan 1979), esp. chs. 6 and 7.

In both instances, the basic American response was to force a moderate dissociation into a much more extreme mold, in the expectation that the internal pressures resulting in the target state would be sufficient to both discredit the policy of dissociation and undermine the government supporting it. This intrinsic vulnerability of dissociation is enhanced by the competitive intervention of the superpowers, which is an institutionalized feature of the present international system. Inasmuch as the larger powers tend to treat the Third World as an arena for their own status and security rivalries, independent self-reliance movements in Third World countries are faced with severe additional problems in establishing their own legitimacy. There will be a strong tendency for such movements to be treated by the major powers largely, if not wholly, as if they were simply extensions of major power rivalries. The more this is so, the more there is a tendency on the part of the major powers to make it a self-fulfilling prophecy by intensifying their interventions along promotional and preventive lines. Given the resource disparity between the major powers and the rest, it is not hard to imagine conditions in which a genuinely independent, local, self-reliance movement would be impossible due to the pressures created by an already existing level of foreign meddling.

If dissociation for self-reliance is to be a credible or even a possible policy under these conditions, the governments undertaking it must establish the legitimacy, stability, and above all the independence of their local base at an early stage. Failure to do so enhances the already ominous risk of becoming absorbed into the larger game of great power politics. For all these reasons, security policy is likely to be a key element in the success or failure of dissociation. Not only must a security strategy for dissociation be able to cope with the internal and external threats which the policy raises, but also it must avoid interacting with the security concerns of greater powers in such a way as to generate additional threats. This is a tall order. In many cases it may be impossible. As the discussion above indicates, there are no trouble-free options even in the refined world of ideal-type models. All of them contain major difficulties which may of themselves be sufficient to wreck the policy they are intended to support.

This paper can have no firm conclusions since the nature of its argument is inherently exploratory. Its objective has been to examine the character of a particular security problem and to outline possible solutions to it, commenting on advantages and disadvantages along the way. This has been done in the preceding sections and requires no further elaboration here. There are, however, three general observations arising from the argument which are worth separating out here by way of final comment.

The first is that dissociation is not likely to succeed unless pursued by a strong-willed and explicitly dissociation-oriented leadership. Both the policy itself, and the security needs arising from it, seem likely to intensify the volatile conditions within which government has to be attempted in most of the Third World. Vague objectives, dithering implementation, or uncertainty of leadership seem likely to succumb quickly to the numerous and powerful cross-pressures leading down the variety of paths to dependence of some sort. In this regard, the vulnerability of moderate dissociation to the counterstrategy of forced, rapid, and extreme dissociation/ejection, as in the Cuban and Chilean cases mentioned above, would seem to argue in favor of more extreme dissociation as the basic policy for periphery actors in the first place. This raises questions beyond the scope of the present discussion, but would constitute a central issue for any political movement considering dissociation as part of its program.

The second observation is that domestic unity is likely to be a factor of crucial importance in any dissociation attempt. Excessive disunity has two adverse consequences for dissociation. First, it enormously compounds the security problem, both by creating a domestic "second front" and by opening the country to indirect intervention. The liability entailed by this needs no elaboration. Second, it severely constrains, and perhaps even makes impossible, the use of an unconventional self-reliance strategy. Since this strategy is the one that appears to be best suited to the general needs of dissociation, its exclusion not only denies a useful measure of support for the policy, but also entails the additional burdens associated with an alternative strategy. While a relatively high degree of domestic unity is an easy enough criterion to specify in the abstract, it may well be impossible to meet in the real world. The inherently divisive nature of dissociation has been a central theme in this paper, and there seems no escaping the conclusion that here there is a core contradiction of dissociation policy. Add to this the preexisting divisions within most Third World countries, and the measure of the problem becomes apparent.

This contradiction points in the direction of the argument that creation of domestic consensus by a process of revolutionary civil war may be a necessary condition for successful dissociation. In such cases, the process of revolution and the process of dissociation would become almost indistinguishable, and the failure of either would mean the failure of both. There is no guarantee of success in this combined course of action, and the hazards of civil war, and of outside intervention which it entails, provide the prime reason for trying to find more moderate approaches. The case of Cambodia during the 1970s illustrates most of the adverse possibilities.

The argument for a revolutionary approach to dissociation ties in neatly to the point made about the case for more extreme dissociation policies in relation to the first observation above. It also, however, raises a whole host of questions about the compatibility of human welfare assumptions (underlying this paper) with an implementation strategy that requires a major, probably very bloody, political upheaval. The arguments on this matter again are beyond the scope of the present discussion, but would need to be considered very carefully by anyone making a case for dissociation on basic human-needs grounds. The mass mobilization and socialization potential of revolutionary situations may have much to offer in terms of the self-sustaining, nation-building transformation which is the object of dissociation. Against this, however, would have to be set the considerable risks and losses inherent in a large-scale resort to violence. It is vital that this question not be evaded, as it often is by those who cease to think once they have criticized existing military arrangements and practices.

The third and final observation is that the neat categories and strict lines of argument presented above will probably never, in practice, fit accurately into the analysis of any particular case. Each case of dissociation will be pushed and constrained by a complex mix of factors unique to itself, and although there may be broadly similar features in some cases, there will almost certainly never be a universal formula for either analysis or policy prescription. Despite the academic arguments in favor of the radical and relatively thorough dissociation made above, most cases in the real world are likely to be partial, sectoral, incremental, and messy. Limitations of leadership, constraints of political and economic situation, domestic inertia, foreign pressure, quagmires of factional dispute and compromise, and the temptations of reformist approaches, will all tend to sidetrack any thoroughgoing drive toward radical dissociation. Within these constraints, a certain measure of evolutionary dissociation may be possible. This may have some useful potential in relation to human welfare objectives, and if it doesn't, it may still pave the way for conditions in which more effective dissociation might be possible.

From this perspective, elements of the four strategy models presented here may be more combinable than they appear to be when considered in the abstract. International politics is full of events that, at the time of their occurrence, seemed bizarre or unlikely in the light of the events and attitudes preceding them. Landmarks like the Triple Entente of 1907, the Nazi-Soviet Pact, the Chinese alliance with Pakistan, the Soviet emplacement of missiles in Cuba, and the defeat of the United States in Vietnam, should teach, if nothing else, that more things are possible than would appear to be the case from a priori reasoning. For particular governments in particular circumstances, it may be feasible to combine elements of the four strategies in such a way as to gain limited advantages in several directions while minimizing the risks of whatever side effects are deemed least desirable. Military self-reliance for Third World countries might also be considered a useful objective in its own right, aside from its connection here with the broader objectives of dissociation. If that is the case, then consideration might be given to the potential for particular countries to devise mixed strategies that are aimed at a degree of self-reliance appropriate to their circumstances. For example, a basic national/local militia might be supplemented by small specialized forces with specific tasks in air defense and coastal patrol. These forces could be supplied to some extent by national small-arms industries, with limited imports of advanced technology defensive weapons purchased on the open market. Elements of appeasement might be pursued for tension-reduction purposes, and limited guarantees from larger powers might be sought in relation to specific threats. Regional cooperation schemes with neighboring states might also be pursued, both for economies of scale (e.g., arms production, coastal zone surveillance) and in an attempt to build local security communities. What is achievable and what is desirable in this regard will vary from case to case, and indeed within cases as circumstances change. What is important is that options for greater self-reliance *do* exist. They should not be lost by default, either because of failure to explore alternatives to prevailing military arrangements, or because of a utopian disinclination to consider armaments and military forces as anything other than part of the problem.

PART III: SYSTEMIC CONSTRAINTS AND OPPORTUNITIES

9.

Political Structure and Change in the International Economic Order: The North – South Dimension

JOHN GERARD RUGGIE

THE PRECEDING CHAPTERS in this volume have focused on the national structures and strategies vis-à-vis the international economy by means of which a variety of countries have sought to achieve significant and sustainable welfare gains. We opted for a comparative rather than a global approach largely to balance the recent bias in the political economy literature, which has come to stress the determin-

I acknowledge with appreciation the material support provided by the Institute of War and Peace Studies at Columbia University, the research assistance of Jay Speakman, and the comments of Jock Finlayson, Jeff Frieden, Ernst Haas, Robert Keohane, and Mark Zacher.

ing role of international factors. We concluded that international factors constitute constraining and disposing forces, to be sure. But the ability to compensate for the one while exploiting the other is not itself simply a reflection of systemic determinants, as our case studies have shown. In this final chapter, however, we turn back to the international realm, in the attempt to discern the evolving patterns of systemic constraints and opportunities that await currently emerging and future industrializers.

Accordingly, my focus is the international economic order. This term is meant to comprise international economic regimes, on the one hand, and the international division of labor, on the other. Both depict institutional features of international economic relations. Broadly speaking, international economic regimes are governing arrangements, constructed by states, to coordinate their expectations and organize aspects of their behavior in such economic issue areas as monetary and trade relations. And the international division of labor refers to the configuration of productive capacity in the world economy, together with the patterns and terms of transaction flows among its constituent units. The relationship between the two, as the balance between authority and market domestically, is not fixed permanently but varies over time.

Protagonists in the so-called North—South Dialogue have tended to polarize around one or the other component part of the international economic order as embodying the key to enhancing the welfare of developing countries. The Group of 77, through its proposal for a New International Economic Order, has sought to restructure international economic regimes on the basis of redistributive principles. From their vantage point, changes in the international division of labor may alter the forms but not the fact of dependency. On the other side, those adhering to liberal economic principles stress the progressive contribution to national economic change that inheres in the international division of labor, which can be captured by instituting outward-oriented development strategies. From this vantage point, international regime change of the sort proposed by the developing countries is both politically unrealistic and economically inefficient.

My purpose here is to discern how much elasticity there is in *either* international economic regimes *or* the international division of labor to accommodate the welfare demands of developing countries. This purpose involves me in two tasks. The first is to *describe* the recent evolution of international economic regimes and the international division of labor, with an eye toward any patterns of change that materially affect the developing countries. The second task is to *explain* such patterns of change that I uncover. To anticipate the gist of my argument: I find that neither international economic regimes nor the international division of labor is as elastic as the respective protagonists assume. At the same time, neither is quite as rigid as its detractors maintain. And in both cases, the range of possibilities is circumscribed by the deeper political structure that gives shape to the international economic order.

The paper is divided into three parts: first, I take up the issue of international economic regimes and regime change; second, I examine recent trends in the international division of labor; and third, I conclude with a brief depiction of the relationship between political structure and the international economic order, from which I infer future prospects for developing countries.

INTERNATIONAL ECONOMIC REGIMES

No representative of the developing countries claims that negotiations on the New International Economic Order have been a success. A recent report by the United Nations Director General for Development and International Economic Cooperation offers this assessment:

International economic co-operation since the sixth special session [of the UN General Assembly, held in 1974] has largely failed to overcome the world economic crisis and to move towards putting in place a viable economic program of international development. In particular, progress towards achieving the objectives of the new international order has been limited. Advances have been registered in several areas, but in some crucial fields, including money and finance, protection of the purchasing power of exports of developing countries and access to markets, the process of change is at an early stage. Most developing countries continue to be at a fundamental disadvantage in the principal markets in which they are either suppliers (commodities, manufactures and labour) or customers (finance and technology). Participation by the developing countries in the management of the international economic system remains inadequate.[1]

And yet, despite this record, and despite the inability of participants after three years of preliminary talks on the so-called global round of negotiations to agree to its terms of reference, representatives of the developing countries persist in their expectation that fundamental change in the world economy can be accomplished through negotiations that would create new international economic regimes in areas where none now exist (commodities, transnational corporations, transfer of technology), and restructure existing regimes (as in monetary and trade relations) to reflect their particular needs. They have gained support from Northern social democrats, who maintain that a more equitable set of international economic relations would also be a more efficient one, in that the redistribution of wealth to the developing countries would, for example, trigger non-inflationary recovery in the world economy as a whole.[2]

1. Report of the Director General for Development and International Economic Cooperation, *Towards the New International Economic Order* (New York: United Nations, 1982), pp. 4 – 5; cf. Note by the Secretary General, "Reports of Organs and Organizations of the United Nations System on Progress Made Towards the Establishment of the New International Economic Order and Obstacles that Impede Its Success," UN Document A/S-11/6, July 25, 1980.

2. See, for example, the Report of Brandt Commission, *North-South: A Programme for Survival* (London: Pan Books, 1980).

The major industrialized countries have responded to demands for international economic regimes in new domains largely in a damage-limitation mode: drawing out negotiations as long as possible, making sure that their final instruments do the least possible harm to the ongoing conduct of private international economic transactions, and introducing their own concerns where and when possible. As for the second objective, the existing international regimes for money and trade were constructed by the capitalist countries to regulate critical aspects of their own behavior, and they directly affect their own collective welfare. Accordingly, one would expect this domain to be even more inhospitable to Third World demands for fundamental change. And it has been on such questions as internationally created reserves, the link between reserve creation and development assistance, and majoritarian control over the International Monetary Fund (IMF) and the World Bank. But there have also been some changes, as in the increased quantity and flexibility of IMF assistance, and in the granting of tariff preferences to developing countries. None of these changes fully reflects the substance of Third World demands, but, at the same time, they indicate that *some* change is possible even in the core regimes.

In sum, the continued commitment by the developing countries to the collective strategy of international regime change, together with the fact that the very core regimes have not been entirely immune to change, occasion the first set of analytical questions I hope to answer in this paper: what is the degree of elasticity in international economic regimes to accommodate the welfare demands of developing countries, and what explains it? I proceed by analyzing in some detail the evolution of the monetary and trade regimes, which, because of their centrality in the international economic order, serve as critical test cases, and then drawing on this experience to fashion a more general response to the questions I have posed. But first a definitional prolegomenon.

A more or less precise—and what is perhaps most important, a shared—definition of international regimes now exists in the literature: regimes are "sets of implicit or explicit principles, norms, rules, and decision-making procedures around which actors' expectations converge in a given area of international relations. Principles are beliefs of fact, causation, and rectitude. Norms are standards of behavior defined in terms of rights and obligations. Rules are specific prescriptions or proscriptions for action. Decision-making procedures are prevailing practices for making and implementing collective choice."[3] These distinctions are important, if we are to keep track of what has and has not changed. Changes in principles and norms—in what I will call the normative structure of regimes—amount to a change *of* regimes. Changes in rules and procedures—in what I will call the instrumentalities of regimes—amount to a change *within* regimes. Since the challenge of the Third World is to the very principles of the monetary and trade regime, this will be my point of departure.

Governing Principles

In the earliest days of their respective ruminations about postwar international economic arrangements, both Harry Dexter White and John Maynard Keynes had concerned themselves with the problem of international investment.[4] One of the mechanisms of systemic equilibration that had broken down during the interwar years was the timely provision of sufficient sums of investment capital. Great Britain

3. Stephen D. Krasner, "Structural Causes and Regime Consequences: Regimes as Intervening Variables," *International Organization* (Spring 1982), 36:186; Krasner's paper is the introduction to a special issue of *IO* on the topic of international regimes.

4. Richard N. Gardner, *Sterling-Dollar Diplomacy in Current Perspective* (New York: Columbia University Press, 1980); Armand van Dormael, *Bretton Woods: Birth of a Monetary System* (London: Macmillan, 1978); and Sir Roy Harrod, "Problems Perceived in the International Financial System," in A. L. K. Acheson et al., eds., *Bretton Woods Revisited* (Toronto: University of Toronto Press, 1972).

had supplied them before World War I; after that war, the United States, having the capability to do so, instead behaved erratically, and succeeded in becoming an unbalanced creditor country.[5] Neither White nor Keynes thought that private sources of investment funds could do the job alone. Accordingly, they both turned to intergovernmental schemes. White's first draft plan for an "Inter-Allied Bank" was even more ambitious than the corresponding design he produced for an "Inter-Allied Stabilization Fund." The Bank would have a capital stock of $10 billion, the Fund's resources being set at $5 billion. The Bank would have the short-term purpose of aiding postwar reconstruction, relief, and recovery. But, for the longer term,

It was designed also to eliminate worldwide fluctuations of a financial origin and reduce the likelihood, intensity, and duration of worldwide depressions; to stabilize the prices of essential raw materials; and more generally to raise the productivity and living standards of its members. It was specifically empowered to buy and sell gold and securities of participating governments, to discount and rediscount bills and acceptances, to issue notes, and to make long-term loans at very low rates of interest.[6]

Keynes' proposal was more tentative, since for him much would hinge on the fate of his "Clearing Union," a vastly more substantial version of a stabilization fund based on liberal overdraft provisions. Keynes had first addressed the problem of international investment in the series of prescriptive commentaries that he published on the occasion of the World Economic Conference in 1933, recommending concerted efforts by national authorities to provide sufficient levels of investment capital via loans.[7] He returned to this theme and carried his recommendation a step further when, in draft plans for the Clearing Union, he made reference to

5. Charles P. Kindleberger, *The World in Depression, 1929–1939* (Berkeley: University of California Press, 1973).

6. Gardner, p. 75. The very first draft of this plan is undated, but apparently was produced in late 1941 or early 1942.

7. J. M. Keynes, *The Means to Prosperity*, as cited by Harrod.

a separate "International Development Board." This was an institutional analogue of White's Inter-Allied Bank, though presumably it would have done more coordinating of national investment plans and less international lending.[8]

The point to note about these schemes is their underlying vision: apart from dealing with immediate reconstruction needs, both sought to internationalize a measure of public authority so as to facilitate the counter-cyclical management of the international economy as a whole. As implied by the term Keynes chose to describe the institution he proposed, the result would have been a regime with the *development* of *the world economy* as its mission—much the sort of thing the Brandt Commission would propose again forty years later. Neither the United Kingdom nor the United States were interested in so constraining their national discretion or the future of their national capital markets. And the International Bank for Reconstruction and Development (World Bank) that ultimately emerged from the Anglo-American negotiations of course was barely a pale shadow of White's first draft plan.

Development in a different sense than that denoted by Keynes' Development Board become an issue of contention during the negotiations on postwar monetary and trade arrangements. Here, the developing countries urged that specific references to the objective of *their* development be included in the instruments being negotiated. In the event, such references were systematically excluded from the Final Acts.

For example, in the monetary negotiations, the working draft of Article I (ii) of the International Monetary Fund, delineating the Fund's second of six purposes, read as follows: "To facilitate the expansion and balanced growth of international trade and to contribute in this way to the maintenance of a high level of employment and real income, which

---

8. I say "presumably" because the terms of reference of this Board were never clearly stipulated.

must be a primary objective of economic policy."[9] The Indian delegation contended that the concepts of high levels of employment and real income had little meaning in countries like India, and urged that the draft article be amended so as also to reflect the special conditions and needs of developing countries. This was resisted by the United States and the United Kingdom, on the grounds that it would confuse the functions of the Fund with those of the Bank. Debate continued until the very end of the Bretton Woods conference; in the final compromise, helped along by Australia, "promotion" was added before "maintenance" of employment and income, and "the development of the productive resources of all members" inserted as a third presumed by-product of the facilitation of the expansion of international trade.[10]

On the trade side, during the negotiations on the Charter of the International Trade Organization (ITO), Britain succeeded in having the pursuit of full employment raised to an international obligation of governments, and to gain exceptions to nondiscrimination and the nonuse of quantitative restrictions on imports for a variety of specified purposes. At the Geneva and Havana sessions of these negotiations, the developing countries sought similarly to have their economic development raised to the level of one of the primary objectives of the ITO, and to gain specified exemptions so as to safeguard national economic development plans. "The United States and Britain joined forces in opposing these exceptions."[11] While many of the former

9. This debate is discussed in detail in Joseph Gold, " '. . . To Contribute Thereby to . . . Development . . .': Aspects of the Relations of the International Monetary Fund with its Developing Members," *Columbia Journal of Transnational Law* (Fall 1971), vol. 10.

10. The final version of Article I (ii) thus reads: "To facilitate the expansion and balanced growth of international trade, and to contribute thereby to the promotion and maintenance of high levels of employment and real income and to the development of the productive resources of all members as primary objectives of economic policy."

11. Gardner, p. 365.

provisions found their way into the General Agreement on Tariffs and Trade (GATT) after the defeat of the ITO Charter, none of the latter did. Nor, of course, did the GATT encompass several areas of commercial policy included in the ITO Charter which were of particular importance to developing countries, above all international commodity agreements.

Thus, we can readily see the effects of *state power* in the negotiations on the postwar economic regimes. But—if toward neither the development of the international economy as a whole, nor the development of what were then called economically backward or underdeveloped countries—toward what *collective purpose* or "actors' expectations" was state power deployed? The answer lies in a particular configuration of forces that had emerged in the international political economy by the end of World War II. This configuration was the product of two transformations, one in interstate power and the other in domestic authority. The first was reflected in the ascendancy of the United States, which assured that liberalization would be part of any postwar institutional reconstruction.[12] The second was reflected in the shift that had occurred in all of the advanced capitalist countries, in the mediating role of the state between market and society, whereby the state had come to assume far greater responsibilities for securing high levels of domestic income and employment. This transformation assured that domestic stabilization would be part of any postwar institutional reconstruction.[13] The conjunction of these two principles defined the fundamental parameters— the collective purpose—of the postwar economic regimes.

12. This was particularly important on the trade side of the negotiations, where liberalization would have been unlikely without extensive U.S. prodding. It was less important on the monetary side, where broad consensus existed on the general features of a desirable postwar arrangement.

13. The shift in domestic authority occurred unequally among the major capitalist countries, and remained most ambivalent in the United States. This difference complicated negotiations on postwar arrangements, as well as their subsequent evolution, but did not fundamentally alter the fact that stabilization would be one of their two integral components.

Under the classical gold standard, levels of domestic prices and economic activity were strongly conditioned if not directly determined by the balance of payments. The adjustment process ultimately was geared toward securing external stability, that is, the gold parity of one's currency, an objective that was widely adhered to in the last third of the nineteenth century. The interwar period had established the primacy of domestic economic and social objectives over external financial discipline, but by the 1930s the international economic order lay in ruins. The task of postwar institutional reconstruction was to maneuver between these two extremes, and to resolve the dilemma between internal and external stability by striking a compromise between the two rather than by sacrificing one to the other. An institutional formula was devised that I have elsewhere termed the compromise of embedded liberalism: "unlike the economic nationalism of the thirties, it would be multilateral in character; unlike the liberalism of the gold standard and free trade, its multilateralism would be predicated upon domestic interventionism."[14] Under this compromise formula, the postwar regimes for money and trade would be designed to provide, at one and the same time, vehicles for liberalization as well as means for stabilization. And they would be designed to stabilize, at one and the same time, the *domestic consequences* of *external developments* that impinged on the pursuit by governments of their new economic and social objectives, as well as the *external consequences* of

14. Ruggie, "International Regimes, Transactions, and Change: Embedded Liberalism in the Postwar Economic Order," *International Organization* (Spring 1982), 36:393; the following paragraph paraphrases pp. 393–97 of that paper. The concept is adapted from Karl Polanyi, who distinguished two polar types of economic orders: *embedded*—wherein economic relations are systematically constrained by and made to serve broader social relationships and ends, like redistributive exchange for the sake of social integration and harmony; and *disembedded*—wherein economic relations are taken to be autonomous and responsive only to their own endogenous laws of motion. Laissez-faire liberalism falls toward the latter end of the continuum; the notion of embedded liberalism is designed to denote a modification in the direction of the other polar type. Polanyi, *The Great Transformation* (Boston: Beacon Press, 1944), ch. 4.

the *domestic measures* that governments undertook in the pursuit of these objectives.

This formula was reflected in the terms of reference of the IMF and the GATT. Briefly, the IMF provided for free and stable exchanges, on the one hand, and, on the other, a "double screen" to cushion the domestic economy against balance of payments constraints. The double screen in turn consisted of short-term assistance, made available "conditionally" by the IMF,[15] to finance payments deficits on current account, and so as to correct "fundamantal disequilibria," the ability to change exchange rates with Fund concurrence. If the exchange rate change was less than ten percent, the Fund could not object, nor could it oppose *any* exchange rate change on the grounds that the domestic social or political policies of the country requesting the change had led to the disequilibrium that made it necessary. As for the GATT, it made obligatory the most-favored nation rule and prohibited quantitative restrictions on imports. But it allowed a blanket exception for all existing preferential arrangements and quantitative restrictions were deemed suitable measures for safeguarding the balance of payments — explicitly including payments difficulties that resulted from domestic full employment policies. The substantial reduction of tariffs was also called for but not made obligatory, and it was coupled with several escape mechanisms that would make it possible under specified circumstances to protect domestic producers or to avoid altogether obligations assumed under the GATT. Multilateral surveillance of

15. References to IMF conditionality in the form it subsequently took are nowhere to be found in the Articles of Agreement. Countries were required to make "representations," but there was no clear indication what, if anything, the Fund could do if it disapproved of such representations. At the insistence of the United States, the Executive Directors adopted an "interpretation" of the Articles in 1947, to the effect that the Fund could "challenge" or "postpone or reject the request, or accept it *subject to conditions.*" The relevant documents are excerpted in J. Keith Horsefield, *The IMF, 1945–1965,* vol. 3 (Washington, D.C.: International Monetary Fund, 1969); the citation is from p. 227, emphasis added.

most escape mechanisms was also provided for, as were procedures for the settlement of trade-related disputes.

What specific arrangements were made, then, for the developing countries in the initial postwar scheme of things? Once the World Bank discovered that it had little if any role to play in European reconstruction, it turned to become an agency for concessional project lending exclusively to developing countries.[16] The United Nations instituted what it called an Expanded Program of Technical Assistance in 1949, and in 1957, after much resistance by the industrialized countries, created a modest and voluntary Special Fund for the purpose of stimulating capital investment in developing countries. (Eventually, these two bodies were merged to form the United Nations Development Program.) From these beginnings in the limited provision of international technical and financial aid for specific projects in developing countries, a "quasi-regime" for international development assistance gradually came into being. It included a generalized commitment to increase the aggregate volume and the concessional component of resource flows to developing countries, to share the burden of these flows equitably among donor countries, and to ensure that the terms of assistance not give a competitive advantage to any of the donor countries.[17] Andrew Shonfield dates the advent of this quasi-regime to coincide with the creation of the Organization for Economic Co-operation and Development (OECD) and its Development Assistance Committee in 1961 — which also marked the first year of the First United Nations Decade

16. The early evolution of the Bank is traced by Raymond F. Mikesell, "The Emergence of the World Bank as a Development Institution," in Acheson, et al., *Bretton Woods Revisited*. Mikesell points out that the Bank got off to a slow start; by 1950, it had authorized only $350 million in loans to developing countries, and disbursed but $100 million.

17. I use the term "quasi-regime" for three reasons (1) it was fully understood by the donor countries that certain norms, particularly those concerning the quantity of aid (0.7% GNP for ODA, for example), represented aspirations rather than commitments; (2) the various component parts of the would-be regime were al-

for Development. However, even at this late date, Shonfield
maintains,

That nations should seek to establish international rules and conventions about it [development assistance] was an unfamiliar idea.
The colonial empires were still in the last stages of being dismantled, and the natural answer seemed to be to leave it to each of
the Western nations concerned to take the lead in looking after its
colonies or ex-colonies. It was the United States which insisted
that the issue was a serious international problem. Its practical
aim was to induce other nations, particularly those without colonial ties and traditions, like Germany, to share with the Americans
the burden of providing aid for development.[18]

In sum, the interstate ascendancy of the United States,
coupled with the prevailing form of state/society relations
that emerged in the advanced capitalist world from the Great
Depression, produced a mutually conditioning relationship
between international liberalization and domestic stabilization as the governing principles of the postwar monetary
and trade regimes. The norms of uniformity and reciprocity
defined the fundamental standards of behavior in the two
regimes. Development of the international economy as a
whole remained collectively unregulated. And development
assistance to the developing countries became the subject
of a quasi-regime, the informing logic of which initially derived from potential inter-capitalist competition and the desire for burden-sharing as much as it did from a positive
commitment to the goal of development.

Regime Performance
Until the concept of a New International Economic Order
came to constitute the agenda for the North—South Dia-

---

most completely unrelated; and (3) the compliance mechanisms were few and weak
(e.g., the prisoner's dilemma situation with regard to avoiding competitive terms
of aid was partially attenuated by OECD collective review processes).

18. Shonfield, "Introduction: Past Trends and New Factors," in Shonfield, ed.,
International Economic Relations of the Western World (London: Oxford University
Press, for the Royal Institute of International Affairs, 1976), 2:10.

logue, the major efforts by developing countries to change the institutional arrangements of the monetary and trade regimes were devoted to appending "developmental" components to them. That is to say, they sought to take care of their own particularistic needs *within* the two regimes. This began to change in the trade field with the creation of the United Nations Conference on Trade and Development (UNCTAD), and with the advent of the NIEO the objectives of developing countries came to encompass nothing short of recasting the very normative structure of the two regimes. This is to be accomplished by redefining their governing principles, so that the liberalization-stabilization nexus would yield to redistributive concerns, and by operrationalizing the principle of redistribution as norms of positive discrimination in favor of developing countries, to replace the norms of uniformity and reciprocity. My intent below is to discern and assess the patterns and determinants of change in the two regimes toward accommodating the developing countries.

To assess patterns of regime change, it is necessary first to establish a baseline in the actual performance of the regimes in question. For obvious reasons, no comprehensive examination of the monetary and trade regimes can be attempted here. Nor, however, is one necessary for present purposes. Both of these regimes allocate tangible resources that are easily measured and summarized, and the distribution of which yields indicators that speak to the specific issues at hand.

1. IMF Drawings. One set of convenient indicators is the drawings made available by the IMF. As noted above, they are one of the "stabilization" components of the postwar monetary regime, designed for short-term balance of payments assistance (historically for one year, though back-to-back arrangements were evolved) to cushion the domestic economy from temporary imbalances in its external accounts. I therefore begin my brief baseline sketch with an

overview of IMF drawings by several groups of countries between 1947 and 1981.[19] These years can be divided into
three analytically district periods: reconstruction (1947–60),
growth (1961–73), and adjustment (1974–81). Table 9.1
presents various summary measures.

As is well known, the IMF got off to a slow start as a
lending institution. Countries benefiting from Marshall Plan
aid were prohibited from drawing on the resources of the
Fund, and in those early years the Fund made it extremely
difficult for developing countries to qualify for assistance.
As a result, new drawings dropped to zero in 1950, and did
not exceed 1947 levels again until 1956.[20] For the period as
a whole, the total drawings disbursed by the IMF were not
quite $3.7 billion, a very modest sum.[21] The pattern of
drawings indicates few surprises. The United States of course
required no assistance at this time. The industrialized "primary exporters" also emerged from the war with relatively
strong economies, and drew very little. The small European
industrialized states drew a proportion of Fund resources
that was roughly commensurate with their quota. The major
beneficiary was the group of "other" major industrialized
countries, which utilized by far the largest proportion of Fund
resources. However, as a ratio of quotas (and, even more
so, of their share of world trade), the non-oil developing
countries drew more heavily.

During the second period, a time of rapid growth in the

19. Two criteria determined the categorization of groups. First it had to reflect distinct attributes of countries in terms of foreign trade and, presumably,
therefore, in terms of their respective needs for payments financing. Second, I
wanted as much as possible to have the categories reflect similar distinctions used
elsewhere in this book. No major anomalies resulted from applying these two different criteria; Denmark, which by the first criterion might have been placed in the
industrialized "primary exporters" category, remains in Katzenstein's group of "small
European industrialized" countries.

20. Fred L. Block, *The Origins of International Economic Disorder* (Berkeley:
University of California Press, 1977), ch. 5; and Susan Strange, *International Monetary Relations,* vol. 2 of Shonfield, ed., ch. 4.

21. For example, even in nominal terms, the amount was less than the $3.75
billion stabilization loan from the United States to Great Britain in 1945.

TABLE 9.1: Drawings from International Monetary Fund, 1947–1981 (All Facilities)

	1947–60				1961–73				1974–81			
	% Total Quotas (1960)	% Total Drawings	$\frac{D}{Q}$ (%)[a]	$\frac{\%D}{\%Q}$[b]	% Total Quotas (1973)	% Total Drawings	$\frac{D}{Q}$ (%)	$\frac{\%D}{\%Q}$	% Total Quotas (1981)	% Total Drawings	$\frac{D}{Q}$ (%)	$\frac{\%D}{\%Q}$
United States	28.0	—	—	—	23.0	16.3	53.0	.71	20.8	6.4	18.0	.31
Other major industrial[c]	29.1	44.2	37.9	1.52	27.7	44.7	120.3	1.61	24.5	21.9	52.5	.89
Small European industrial[d]	8.2	7.6	23.3	.93	8.4	1.5	13.3	.18	8.0	.7	5.3	.09
Industrial "primary exporters"[e]	7.8	3.2	10.2	.41	8.5	6.4	56.4	.75	7.6	4.9	37.8	.64
Non-European NICs[f]	not applicable[h]				5.1	1.8	26.7	.35	4.4	5.9	127.7	1.34
Other non-oil LDCs[g]	20.3	33.8	44.1	1.67	17.3	22.3	96.4	1.29	19.5	43.4	130.7	2.22

SOURCE: International Monetary Fund, *International Financial Statistics, 1947–81.*

NOTE: Drawings are cumulative drawings during each period, from all available facilities. Quotas are as of the last year of each period. As a result, ratios involving the two have no precise meaning in absolute terms, but do indicate general orders of magnitude and permit valid intergroup comparisons to be made.

[a] Cumulative drawings during the period, divided by end-of-period quotas, multiplied by 100.

[b] Column 2 divided by column 1. This is a measure of "relative use," which averages to 1.0 for all members.

[c] France, Germany, Italy, Japan, United Kingdom.

[d] Austria, Belgium, Denmark, Finland, Netherlands, Norway, Sweden.

[e] Australia, Canada, Finland, New Zealand, South Africa. This is a group of industrialized countries for which agriculture constitutes a relatively high proportion of GDP and the export of primary products a relatively high proportion of total exports.

[f] The OECD currently categorizes as non-European NICs Brazil, Mexico, Hong Kong, South Korea, Singapore, and Taiwan; all but Hong Kong, which is not an IMF member, are included here.

[g] Non-oil developing countries are defined as non-OPEC LDCs (Mexico is included among the non-European NICs); the category therefore does not include some net exporters of oil, though all of them are capital deficient.

[h] Since the term NICs was not applicable before the 1960s, this row has been merged with "other non-oil LDCs." In any case, only Brazil and Mexico from among the future NICS made drawings, and Brazil accounted for over 80/ of their combined total.

world economy, the Fund disbursed almost $22 billion. Two new low-conditionality facilities were established within the IMF during this period to benefit primarily the developing countries. In 1963, a Compensatory Financing Facility was established to help finance payments deficits due to short-falls in export earnings from primary products over which the exporting country had no control. And a Buffer Stock Facility was added in 1969, to be used under certain circumstances to help finance national contributions to existing multilateral buffer stocks. Access to the former was so restrictive that it was little used until the 1970s, when it was made more flexible; and the eligibility rules of the latter were such that total drawings during its entire first decade barely exceeded SDR 100 million. The most striking feature in the distribution of drawings in the second period is its utter dominance by the industrialized countries. Of all industrialized groups, only the small European states decreased their proportionate claims on Fund resources, and the decrease was substantial.[22] The United States, which had been financing its growing payments deficits unilaterally by virtue of being the reserve currency country, drew on the Fund. The share drawn by the industrialized "primary exporters" doubled. And the "other" major industrialized countries, due largely to successive sterling crises, exceeded every group on every measure.[23] The newly industrializing countries

22. This is consistent with Katzenstein's hypothesis in chapter 2, above, concerning the greater reliance by these countries on internal adjustment mechanisms.

23. For the purposes of lending to the largest industrialized countries, and particularly out of fear of the possible consequences of a simultaneous run on sterling and the dollar, the General Arrangement to Borrow was instituted in 1962. By means of this arrangement, the so-called Group of 10 industrialized country members of the IMF plus Switzerland, agreed among themselves to supplement allocations of resources to themselves. The Fund formally initiates the process and administers the drawing in accordance with its standard procedures, but serious negotiations on the lending package are confined within the group. It should be noted that Fund borrowing from its member countries and Switzerland for the purpose of relending has since become common; in 1981, a higher proportion of Fund commitments involved borrowed resources than ordinary resources (*IMF Survey*, August 30, 1982, p. 269). The GAB is distinct, however, in formally cir-

emerged as a distinct subset of developing countries during this period; their use of Fund resources was relatively slight. The share of other non-oil developing countries, of whom there were far more than in the first period, was considerably less in relative terms than it had been in the first period.

The period of turbulence and adjustment since 1974 exhibits a sharp reversal from previous patterns. The Fund disbursed more than $35 billion. And it established several new facilities: a low-conditionality Oil Facility (1974—75), from which the industrialized countries drew some 60 percent of the total available, and the high-conditionality Extended Facility (1974) and Supplementary Financing Facility (1977), aimed primarily at developing countries. The relative share of total drawings accounted for by the non-oil developing countries, including the NICs,[24] more than doubled during this period. The relative shares of all groups of industrialized countries declined with small European states virtually disappearing from the scene. These overall patterns, however, mask the suddenness of shifts within the period. Between 1974—78, drawings by all industrialized and all developing countries were roughly even. Indeed, in 1977 and again in 1978, the developing countries actually repaid the Fund more for previous drawings than they took out in new drawings. Then came 1979. From 1979 to 1981, the industrialized countries made no drawings at all; they had come to rely exclusively on private capital markets for their payments financing.[25] Drawings by the developing countries doubled from 1979 to 1980, and then rose by another 50 percent from 1980 to 1981. New commitments ap-

cumscribing eligible recipients and in limiting the decision-making power of the IMF Executive Directors as a whole essentially to ratifying an arrangement reached by one of its subgroups. (At the time of writing, there are reports of negotiations to transform the GAB into an emergency fund with no a priori access restrictions.)

24. As a group, the NICs drew relatively little; over half of their combined total is accounted for by South Korea alone.

25. For a general discussion of this trend, see Benjamin J. Cohen, "Balance-of-Payments Financing: Evolution of a Regime," *International Organization* (Spring 1982), vol. 36.

proved by the IMF during 1981 totaled SDR 15.2 billion, all to developing countries.[26] This total included a drawing by India in the amount of SDR 5 billion, the largest drawing in IMF history and equivalent to 291 percent of India's quota, made for the purpose *not* of traditional short-term balance of payments assistance, but to facilitate "structural adjustment . . . with a view to achieving balance of payments viability in the medium term."[27]

In sum, the patterns of IMF drawings over the course of the past thirty-five years do indicate some degree of change affecting the developing countries. The questions of how much change there has been in this direction, what has determined it, and what are its limits, are taken up after a corresponding overview of the postwar trade regime.

2. Trade Liberalization, Preferences, and Escape Mechanisms. On the trade side, several convenient indicators exist that can be appropriately utilized for our purposes. One of these is simply the effect of trade liberalization over time on the distribution of world trade. A major purpose of the GATT has been to reduce tariff barriers to trade. And, as a result of seven rounds of multilateral negotiations since 1947, industrial tariffs have been virtually eliminated as trade barriers. Though it is not possible to establish a direct cause/effect relationship, it is the case that world trade during these same years has grown at historically unprecedented rates, both in absolute terms and proportionately to world production.[28] Despite these trends, however, the share

26. *IMF Survey,* January 25, 1982, table, p. 28.
27. *IMF Survey,* November 23, 1981, p. 365.
28. For example, from 1963 to 1973, world exports of all products rose at an average annual rate of six percent, of manufactures by eleven percent; world production of all products during that decade rose at a corresponding rate of three percent, and of manufactures by seven percent. During 1973–80, the rate of increase of both exports and production was smaller, but, except for 1975 (and again in 1981), trade continued to putpace production. "World Interdependence: Trade," *OECD Observer* (January 1982), no. 114, p. 6, and *IMF Survey,* August 16, 1982, p. 241. The problem of relating liberalization directly to gains in trade

of world exports accounted for by developing countries decreased steadily from 1950, when it stood at just under one-third, until 1973, when it stood at less than one-fifth. The non-oil developing countries accounted for roughly one-fourth of world exports in 1950, one-tenth in 1973. Overall shares of developing countries have since risen, led by the oil-exporting countries, and followed by a modest increase for the newly industrializing countries. The relative share of all other developing countries continues to decline.[29]

Ironically, while the only claim that can be made about the impact of the trade regime on trade expansion "is that since World War II it has provided a favourable environment for the expansion of trade, within which all factors tending towards this expansion have been given a pretty free rein,"[30] the character of the trade regime *can* be related more directly to the declining share of the developing countries. The overwhelming proportion of the expansion in world trade from the 1950s into the 1970s resulted from simultaneous increases in exports and imports within the same industrial sectors, that is, from intra-sectoral or intra-industry specialization.[31] Thus, the division of labor reflected in international trade flows increasingly was based on "individual firms narrowing their product range," not individual countries dif-

---

volume is one of multiple collinearity: too many factors were pushing in the same direction; see Gerard Curzon and Victoria Curzon, "The Management of Trade Relations in the GATT," in Shonfield, ed., *International Economic Relations,* vol. 1. A review of econometric studies going back to 1959 suggests that the direct effects of specific tariff reductions in fact have been modest: Mordechai Kreinin and Lawrence Officer, "Tariff Reductions Under the Tokyo Round," *Weltwirtschaftliches Archiv* (1979), no. 115.

29. UNCTAD, *Trade and Development Report, 1981* (New York: United Nations, 1981), table A.4, p. 116. The effects of the Tokyo Round are not expected to alter this trend: Peter J. Ginman, Thomas A. Pugel, and Ingo Walter, "Tokyo Round Tariff Concessions and Exports from Developing Countries," *Trade and Development* (August 1980), vol. 2.

30. Curzon and Curzon, p. 143.

31. For a good discussion of intra-industry trade in the context of developments in the trade regime, see Charles Lipson, "The Transformation of Trade: The Sources and Effects of Regime Change," *International Organization* (Spring 1982), vol. 36.

ferentiating their export structures.[32] This division of labor until recently bypassed the developing countries, except in their derivative capacities as suppliers of raw material inputs and as marginal export markets. And it is a division of labor that has been strongly shaped by the successive rounds of GATT tariff reductions, which "very much favor intra-industry over interindustry specialization."[33] A variety of economic explanations have been advanced to account for this departure from the classical case for free trade,[34] but on reflection it may be seen as a direct and even necessary consequence of the governing principles of the postwar trade regime. For governments pursuing stabilization along with liberalization, it was quite safe to liberalize this kind of trade. As a recent GATT study has found, in relative terms domestic adjustment costs have been "surprisingly" low.[35] Moreover, intra-sectoral specialization poses none of the political vulnerabilities to states that inter-sectoral specialization poses. And all the while it offers gains from trade. In contrast, the GATT has made little progress in liberalizing agricultural trade. And where international trade *is* based on a more classical notion of comparative advantage, as with the newly industrializing countries exploiting the advantage of low labor costs, quantitative restrictions on exports ("voluntary export restraints") and imports ("orderly marketing arrangements") abound.

The GATT has initiated no major changes to reverse the declining share of developing country exports. In 1957, it adopted a new text for Article XVIII of the General Agree-

32. Richard Blackhurst, Nicolas Marian and Jan Tumlir, "Trade Liberalization, Protectionism, and Interdependence," *GATT Studies in International Trade* (November 1977), no. 5, p. 11.

33. Gary C. Hufbauer and John C. Chilas, "Specialization by Industrial Countries: Extent and Consequences," in Herbert Giersch, ed., *The International Division of Labour* (Tübingen: J.C.B. Mohr, 1974), p. 6. This and related sources are cited by Lipson.

34. For an early but still pertinent discussion, see Richard N. Cooper, *The Economics of Interdependence* (1968; New York: Columbia University Press, 1980).

35. Blackhurst et al., p. 11.

ment, which made it easier for developing countries with development-related payments difficulties to invoke this escape provision. And in 1964, coincident with the convening of the first UNCTAD, the GATT added a new chapter to the General Agreement concerning "Trade and Development." This chapter released members from the obligation of reciprocity in trade negotiations with developing countries without requiring anybody to undertake preferential action, and it established a Trade and Development Committee to scrutinize trade restrictions affecting the exports of developing countries without mandating it to seek their reduction.[36] UNCTAD, on the other hand, at its very first session in 1964, initiated a set of proposals for generalized, nondiscriminatory, and nonreciprocal tariff preferences in favor of all developing countries. The Generalized System of Preferences (GSP), it was hoped, would stimulate industrialization in developing countries through increased exports to the industrialized countries.[37] In 1971, the GATT agreed to waive the provisions of Article I of the General Agreement, initially for a ten-year period, to permit this departure from the most-favored-nation norm. (The Tokyo Round of trade negotiations instituted a permanent enabling clause to this effect.) During the course of the GSP negotiations, the concept of all developing countries benefiting equally under a common system was replaced by individual national and regional schemes, within which the separate preference-granting parties would differentiate among beneficiaries and products. The last of the major schemes, that of the United States, was implemented in 1976.

Table 9.2 gives some indication of the effective coverage of the U.S. GSP, which differs in detail but not signifi-

36. For a recent overview of the relationship between international trade organizations and the developing countries, see Jock A. Finlayson and Mark W. Zacher, "International Trade Institutions and the North/South Dialogue," *International Journal* (Autumn 1981), vol. 36.

37. Branislav Gosovic, *UNCTAD: Conflict and Compromise* (Leiden: A. W. Sijthoff, 1972), ch. 3.

TABLE 9.2: United States Imports from GSP Beneficiaries, 1979

| | (US $ Million) | | | | Percentage Shares | | |
	Total (1)	MFN Dutiable (2)	Covered by GSP (3)	Actual Preferential Imports (4)	(4)/(1)	(4)/(2)	(4)/(3)
All Beneficiaries	94531.7	38163.8	11725.2	6280.0	6.6	16.5	53.6
Major suppliers[a]	24597.6	16630.0	9581.8	4955.1	20.1	35.8	51.7
Least developed[b]	812.6	215.1	118.1	43.5	5.4	20.2	36.8

SOURCE: UNCTAD, Trade and Development Board, Special Committee on Preferences, "Generalized System of Preferences: Replies Received from Preference-Giving Countries: United States of America," UNCTAD Document TD/B/C.5/PREF/8 (February 20, 1981), Annex, table 1.

[a] Includes Argentina, Brazil, Chile, Dominican Republic, Hong Kong, South Korea, Mexico, Philippines, Singapore, Taiwan.

[b] Includes some twenty-four of the poorest developing countries.

cantly in order of magnitude from the other two major schemes, those of the EEC and of Japan (together, the three account for roughly 90 percent of all preferential imports by OECD countries). The GSP, of course, grants preferential treatment only to dutiable imports from beneficiary countries; as table 9.2 shows, these imports represent less than half of all imports from these countries, since raw materials and nonagricultural primary products, the major exports of many of them, by and large enter duty free to begin with. The table shows furthermore that only a fraction of dutiable imports are eligible for GSP treatment. So-called *ab initio* exclusions are based on a variety of criteria, including product type, country of origin, quotas, ceiling limitations, and safeguards to protect industry in the importing country. Lastly, the table shows that not all covered products actually obtain preferential status, since they may be subject to further exclusions based on, for example, how competitive a particular beneficiary is becoming with respect to a particular product.[38] The table also differentiates between the more

38. A good review of the various exclusion criteria and their effect may be found in UNCTAD, Trade and Development Board, Special Committee on Prefer-

industrialized and the least-developed of the developing
countries, indicating that the former not only do better in
relative terms, but account for nearly 80 percent of all preferential imports into the United States; the five newly industrializing countries listed in table 9.1 plus Hong Kong in turn
account for fully 90 percent of all preferential imports from
the "major supplier" category. The question that the table
cannot answer is the extent to which the GSP has expanded
developing country exports as opposed to having diverted
them from one set of sectors to another. Specific findings
vary widely, depending on the assumptions and methods of
analysis used. The general consensus appears to be that
the GSP has expanded developing country exports compared to what they would be in its absence, but only modestly so.[39]

A third set of trade-related indicators is the use of GATT
escape mechanisms. A number of these, it will be recalled,
reflect the stabilization side of the embedded liberalism
compromise, conditioning, and in turn being conditioned
by, the counterpart principle of liberalization. These mechanisms give countries in difficulty the opportunity to control
the extent of short-term adjustment and the pace of long-
term adjustment necessitated by economic fluctuations and
changes in international specialization. And they give the
international trading community the opportunity to monitor
their use and to insist that certain standards of behavior be
adhered to. Table 9.3 summarizes patterns of invocation of

ences, "Differential Treatment in the Context of the Generalized System of Preferences," UNCTAD Document TD/B/C.5/74, February 23, 1981.

39. Cf., Tracy Murray, "Evaluation of the Trade Benefits Under the United States
Scheme of Generalized Preferences," issued as UNCTAD, Trade and Development
Board, Special Committee on Preferences, "Review of the Operation and Effects of
the Generalized System of Preferences, Including the Effects on the Least Developed Among the Developing Countries, Landlocked and Island Developing Countries," UNCTAD Document TD/B/C.5/66, February 20, 1980; Ginman et al., "Tokyo
Round Tariff Concessions"; and Gerald K. Helleiner, "The New Industrial Protectionism and the Developing Countries," Trade and Development (Spring 1979),
vol. 1.

TABLE 9.3: Invocation of Major GATT Escape Clauses, 1947–81

	1947–60 (n=213)					1961–73 (n=217)					1974–81 (n=150)				
	Balance of Payments[a]	Domestic Injury[b]	General Waiver[c]	% Total	% Total / % World Trade	Balance of Payments	Domestic Injury	General Waiver	% Total	% Total / % World Trade	Balance of Payments	Domestic Injury	General Waiver	% Total	% Total / % World Trade
United States[d]	—	12	1	6.1	.44	1	4	2	3.2	.26	—	9	—	6.0	.52
Other major industrial	29	1	1	14.6	.51	7	5	—	5.5	.17	2	—	—	1.3	.04
Small European industrial	25	1	1	12.7	.99	4	3	—	3.2	.22	—	1	—	.7	.05
Industrial "primary exporters"	42	5	4	23.9	2.7	34	22	—	25.8	3.3	4	30	—	22.7	3.6
Non-European NICs						9	—	—	4.6	1.0	12	—	1	8.7	1.5
Other non-oil LDCs	55	—	5	28.2	1.7	46	1	13	27.6	3.7	50	—	3	35.3	4.4

SOURCES: For escape clauses: Contracting Parties to the General Agreement on Tariffs and Trade, *Basic Instruments and Documents*, vol. 1–4 and Supplements 1–28, 1952–1981; *idem*, *GATT Activities, 1959–81*, 1960–82; GATT, "Modalities of Application of Article XIX," GATT Document L/4679, July 5, 1978; Indexes to GATT Documents, INF Series, 1955–81.

For trade statistics: IMF, *International Financial Statistics*, Yearbook, 1982; United Nations, *Monthly Bulletin of Statistics*, August 1982; The Economist Intelligence Unit, *Quarterly Economic Review of Taiwan*, Annual Supplement, 1982.

NOTE: Coverage includes entire universe of cases, save for purely technical uses of the General Waiver provision (e.g., Canadian delay in full implementation of Kennedy Round concessions due to dissolution of Parliament), and its use by industrialized countries to permit preferential treatment of specific imports from individual developing countries. Repeated waivers for the same exemption are not counted separately. Except where indicated otherwise, the figures reflect the actual number of cases.

[a] Articles XII and XVIII, the former being the standard balance of payments safeguards clause, the latter specifically tailored for the developing countries.

[b] Article XIX, permitting emergency action to protect domestic producers threatened with injury from import competition due to past tariff concessions. The emergency action cannot exceed the magnitude of the injury which is due to past concessions.

[c] Article XXV, granted by 2/3 vote of the contracting parties.

[d] Country groupings are defined as in table 9.1.

three such mechanisms, for various groups of countries, from 1947 to 1981. The entire era is again divided into the periods of reconstruction, growth, and adjustment.

During the period of reconstruction, the non-oil developing countries availed themselves most often of these GATT escape mechanisms, usually on balance of payments grounds. The industrialized "primary exporters" were close behind in the frequency of invocation, but as a proportion of world trade they were much more frequent users. The United States claimed domestic injury on twelve occasions, five of which involved Japan.[40] Balance of payments problems are reflected in the figures for both "major" and small European states; their use of GATT escape mechanisms no doubt would have been higher had they not also maintained exchange controls until 1958.

During the period of rapid growth, from 1961 to 73, the industrialized "primary exporters" increased both their absolute and proportionate use of the three escape mechanisms, domestic injury being an increasingly important cause. The non-oil developing countries also increased the frequency of their invocation of these mechanisms, but there were many more such countries in this period than there had been in the previous. There is little difference in the uniformly low rate of the United States and the other two groups of industrialized countries. But only for the small European states does this fully reflect the actual situation. In the case of the United States, and even more so the major European states, toward the end of this period governments increasingly went "straight to the heart of the problem by negotiating a minimum price agreement, or a 'voluntary' export restraint arrangement with the presumably reluctant exporter who has previously been 'softened' with threats of emergency action under GATT."[41] Japan was the first country to be targeted by these initiatives, and tex-

40. It should be kept in mind that until 1960 or thereabouts, the United States absorbed much of the adjustment cost of Japan's entry into the GATT in 1955.

41. Curzon and Curzon, "Management of Trade Relations," p. 225.

tiles the first sector. By the end of the period, a growing number of "new entrants," from Eastern Europe and the non-European NICs, faced similar quantitative restraints on the unimpeded flow of their exports into developed country markets. And the sectors included a wide array of labor-intensive, wage-sensitive, and standardized manufactures and basic industries.

A similar pattern has continued throughout the third period. The industrialized "primary exporters" and the non-oil developing countries still make frequent use of the formal GATT escape mechanisms. The major European states and to a lesser extent the United States press for safeguarding devices outside the GATT with greater frequency.[42] And the small European states manage to get by without either. Brazil and South Korea account evenly for the entire non-European NICs total.

This table suggests the following conclusion. Since the late 1960s, the use of GATT escape mechanisms has been concentrated among those countries that lack either the external negotiating power of the major industrialized states or the capacity for internal adjustment of the small European states. Whether or not their invocation of these mechanisms is economically wise, presumably the same deficiency would make it difficult for these countries to

42. While such agreements may not be sanctioned by the GATT, it does not follow that they necessarily violate the governing principles of the postwar trade regime. In point of fact, they may be the quintessential expression of these principles, particularly in times of rapid change. The boundary between embedded liberalism and "illiberal protectionism" is not a precise one, as others have pointed out (see Lipson, "Transformation of Trade," p. 425), but keep in mind that most such agreements have allowed for a continued increase in imports. Private agreements between the respective industries in importing and exporting countries are more pernicious because they violate the norm of transparency; in some bilateral trade relations they seem to have proliferated even more rapidly than intergovernmental agreements. Their effect has been noted in British imports from Japan, and Japanese imports from developing countries, by Thomas R. Graham, "Revolution in Trade Politics," *Foreign Policy* (Fall 1979), no. 36, p. 60. The more frequent recourse to Article XIX ("domestic injury" in table 9.3) by the United States may simply indicate that U.S. firms are legally constrained from striking such deals.

safeguard domestic economic activities were the mechanisms not to exist. Thus, this feature of the GATT provides some degree of international compensation for domestic economic and institutional weakness, though neither its existence nor its operation has anything to do with instituting redistributive concerns.

In sum, the relative distribution of benefits under the trade regime has not shifted over time in the direction of the developing countries, though it exhibits a partial response in the form of the GSP.

Regime Change

The first and most obvious generalization suggested by these cases is that the mechanisms of the monetary and trade regimes examined above have operated largely for the direct benefit of the industrialized countries.[43] The industrialized countries as a whole have benefited from liberalization, and different groups among them have been the major beneficiaries of the different stabilization mechanisms. With the exceptions of the post-1979 period in the monetary regime, and the GSP in the trade regime, there have been no significant departures from this baseline in favor of the developing countries. Therefore, our analysis of regimes changes that accommodate the developing countries, a task to which I now turn, can commence by exploring further these instances of change. For reasons that will become clear momentarily, I will discuss first the case of the GSP; then the increase in the volume of IMF lending to developing countries; and lastly changes in the conditionality provisions of IMF assistance to developing countries. I conclude with an analytical summary on the conditions under which the monetary and trade regimes have accommodated what kinds of Third World demands.

43. This generalization is not meant to exclude the possibility that the developing countries may be *absolutely* better off as a result of indirect benefits derived from these regimes than they would be in their absence.

1. The GSP. In theory, the GSP represented a violation of the norm of non-discrimination, thus requiring a GATT waiver to bring it into existence. "That decision constituted a landmark in trade relations between developed and developing countries, because for the first time the developed countries had agreed to grant tariff concessions exclusively to developing countries without seeking reciprocity from them."[44] Moreover, the GSP implies a shift in the governing principles of the trade regime, to accommodate redistributive concerns. In practice, however, the departure is not nearly so far reaching. Briefly, how did the GSP come about, and what does it signify?

The United States was vehemently opposed in 1964 to the UNCTAD-initiated scheme, and would have remained so had it not been for two interrelated factors. First, individual European countries had maintained selected trade preferences as a remnant of colonial ties with certain developing countries. The EEC was contemplating extending such preferences to the Mediterranean region in an arrangement that would involve reverse preferences for the EEC. Latin American countries, who would be excluded from this arrangement, as a result sought compensation for potential export losses to European markets by obtaining preferences from the United States. The United States came to perceive the GSP as a means to counter both.[45] United States support for the GSP was announced in 1967, though it took another nine years for its scheme to be implemented.

The design of the GSP that was ultimately instituted by the industrialized countries made it clear that the major purpose of the arrangement was to avoid discriminatory trade diversion among themselves, *not* to strive for trade creation between themselves and developing countries. Most

44. UNCTAD, "Differential Treatment in the Content of the Generalized System of Preferences," p. 2.

45. The change in the U.S. position is traced effectively by Ronald J. Meltzner, "The Politics of Policy Reversal," *International Organization* (Autumn 1976), vol. 30.

agricultural products are excluded from the GSP, and the exclusion provisions affecting the products that are included were determined by the desire for equal burden-sharing among the importing countries. Once it became clear that the GSP was not likely to disrupt the pattern of world trade flows, some of these restrictions were relaxed.[46] But in the final analysis, the GSP is a diminishing asset, as individual beneficiaries become internationally competitive in specific products and thereby "graduate" to lesser and lesser preference margins, and because multilateral tariff reductions have eroded all margins of preferences and eliminated some altogether.[47]

Thus, the GSP does not represent any fundamental shift in the governing principles of the trade regime to reflect redistributive concerns, but an extension of existing principles to regulate a potentially destabilizing phenomenon. Moreover, while the GSP technically violates the regime norm of nondiscrimination, it is a temporary violation involving a relatively small proportion of world trade, and one necessitated by the desire to maintain nondiscrimination as a standard of behavior among the industrialized countries themselves.

2. Increased IMF Lending to LDCs

The sheer magnitude of recent IMF drawings by and new commitments to developing countries represents a striking departure from past patterns of IMF lending. What is more, the change was accomplished by the effective erosion of one of the rules of the monetary regime, that access to balance of payments assistance from the Fund be strictly determined by the size of a country's quota. This rule has been

46. UNCTAD, "Differential Treatment in the Context of the Generalized System of Preferences, p. 3; United Nations, *Operation and Effects of the Generalized System of Preferences* (New York: United Nations, UNCTAD Document TD/B/C.5/71, 1980), ch. 1.

47. *Ibid.*, ch. 4.

stretched to the point where it is now possible for all countries to draw up to 450 percent of their quota over a three-year period, and for some developing countries to go as high as 600 percent.[48] How did this change come about, and what does it signify?

To answer these questions, we have to look back to the mid-1970s. Between 1974 and 1978, the cumulative balance of payments deficits of all non-oil developing countries was $182.3 billion; net drawings from the IMF by developing countries during the same period came to but SDR 5.3 billion.[49] What little the developing countries did draw from the Fund they obtained largely from the low conditionality Oil Facility and Compensatory Financing Facility, so that there was minimal conditional lending to developing countries during this time. Developing countries had long chafed under the conditionality provisions of the IMF. And in view of the low level of resources the Fund had available relative to the massive payments imbalances of the mid-1970s, the developing countries avoided using the high conditionality credit tranches if they could.[50] The Fund subsequently came to see its own "recycling-oriented approach" via the Oil and Compensatory Financing Facilities to have been in error, because it delayed the necessity to make domestic adjustments to the new international energy terms of trade. But it also realized that it would need a "critical mass" of re-

48. The difference is accounted for by the fact that the 450 percent figure does not include drawings under the Compensatory Financing Facility and the Buffer Stock facility, which traditionally have been regarded as LDC facilities. Note, however, that South Africa in the autumn of 1982 made the largest single drawing ever under the low-conditionality Compensatory Financing Facility arrangement. *New York Times*, October 15, 1982.

49. Balance of payments figures calculated from *IMF Survey*, September 21, 1981, table, p. 287; net drawings calculated from *IMF Survey*, January 25, 1982, table, p. 28.

50. That this avoidance of the Fund was a deliberate choice by some developing countries, in part irrespective of the availability of alternative sources of payments financing, is documented in Sidney Dell and Roger Lawrence, *The Balance of Payments Adjustment Process in Developing Countries* (New York: Pergamon Press, 1980), ch. 1 and 2.

sources in order "to entice member countries to agree on meaningful and realistic programs. . . ,"[51] that is, to accept the Fund's conditionality provisions. According to the IMF, the second oil shock, of 1979—80, provided the catalyst for change. By 1980, the scale of assistance the Fund could make available had been increased substantially, thanks to a 50 percent quota increase and the new "enlarged access" guidelines allowing countries to draw higher multiples of their quotas. And these resources were made available on the basis of strict conditionality, as indicated by the fact that the number of upper credit tranche arrangements in effect by 1981 was four times the annual average between 1974 and 1978.[52]

Though the IMF makes no explicit reference to it in official accounts of these developments, a second catalyst clearly has also been at work. One reason some developing countries managed to avoid high conditionality borrowing from the Fund in the mid-1970s was their greater access to private international capital markets. Indeed, throughout this same period, the external debt of developing countries has soared: according to World Bank figures, their medium- and long-term debt increased from $117 billion in 1973 to $426 billion in 1980;[53] an unofficial source put their long-term debt alone at $524 billion by the end of 1981;[54] a third source has estimated their debt to private banks to have been roughly $280 billion as of early 1981.[55] By 1980, the

51. "A Conversation with Mr. de Larosière" (Managing Director of the IMF), *Finance & Development* (June 1982), 19:5.

52. In 1981—82, some three-fourths of new commitments by the Fund involved high conditionality, whereas in the mid-1970s two-thirds of the resources provided by the Fund were extended on a low conditionality basis. "Fund Can Play an Important Role in Providing Conditional Finance to Support Economic Adjustments." Statement by J. de Larosière, Managing Director of the IMF, to the annual meeting of the Board of Governors of the Fund, September 29, 1981, as reprinted in *IMF Survey*, October 12, 1981.

53. IBRD, *World Debt Tables* (EC-167/81, December 1981), p. xv, table 1.

54. "A Nightmare of Debt: A Survey of International Banking," special supplement to *The Economist*, March 20, 1982, p. 99.

55. These are figures reported by the Bank for International Settlements, as

standard profiles of past debt problem cases came to describe an ever-larger number of developing countries,[56] and
the exposure of some private banks was such that the stability of the international financial system became and remains an issue of serious concern to the industrialized
member states of the IMF.[57] Though the payments deficits
of the non-oil developing countries have begun to decline
again, after reaching a record $99 billion in 1981, an addi-
tional IMF quota increase to take effect in 1983 has been
negotiated. Several major industrialized countries favored a
doubling or more. The United States initially favored only a
modest quota increase, together with the creation of a new
"borrowing arrangement which would provide additional resources to the IMF in the event a potential disintegration
might occur that would threaten the international monetary
system."[58] Under this new arrangement, the industrialized
and capital surplus developing countries would make the
additional resources available to the IMF in case of such
need, and the IMF in turn would lend them out on condi-

cited in IBRD, *Private Bank Lending to Developing Countries,* World Bank Staff
Working Paper, no. 482 (August 1981), p. 3, table 2.

56. An IMF staff report has analyzed twelve countries that required debt renegotiation between 1972–79, examining a number of standard debt-related and
more general macroeconomic indicators; IMF, *External Indebtedness of Developing Countries* (Occasional Paper No. 3, May 1981). A look through the *World Debt
Tables* reveals, for example, that the *average* debt service/exports ratio of *all* non-
oil developing countries now is roughly what used to be thought of as dangerously
high for any individual country. And, in point of fact, twenty-five countries were in
payments arrears on their external debt in 1981, compared to three in 1974, and
there were more debt reschedulings in 1981 than in any previous year. IMF, *External Indebtedness,* and *The Economist,* March 20, 1982.

57. "Governors' Statements Express Strong Support for Expanded Assistance
by Fund Members," Summaries of statements made at annual meeting of Board
of Governors of the Fund in September 1982, *IMF Survey,* October 4, 1982. The
$80 billion Mexican external debt in particular was very much on their minds, as
reported in *The Economist,* September 11, 1982, pp. 61–62.

58. Transcript of an exclusive interview with Beryl W. Sprinkel, Under Secretary of the Treasury for Monetary Affairs, conducted by Frederic Eckhard, editor
and publisher of *The Interdependent,* October 19, 1982; I am grateful to Mr. Eckhard for sharing this transcript with me prior to publication of the interview in his
newspaper.

tions at least as strict as those now prevailing in the upper credit transches. In the end, a 47.5 percent quota increase *and* a new emergency facility were agreed to.

What, then, do we make of these changes? The value of Fund quotas relative to total national reserves has declined steadily since 1966, so that inadequate Fund resources alone explains little.[59] Apparently, this factor had to interact with more proximate catalysts before producing change. There were two such catalysts. One was that those developing countries which could do so avoided using the regular credit facilities of the Fund at the very moment of the greatest turmoil in the postwar international economy. This was institutionally disconcerting to the Fund. And it denied the monetary regime access to the only part of the adjustment mechanism over which it had exercised any direct control.[60] The second catalyst was provided by the growing threat the external debt of certain developing countries posed to the international financial system. The 1980 changes were initiated primarily by the first set of concerns, together with a generalized apprehensiveness about the latter. Negotiations on the 1983 quota increases and the new borrowing facility proposed by the United States explicitly reflected the concern with international financial stability.[61]

In sum, the post-1979 pattern of IMF lending exhibits a partial rule change in the monetary regime in favor of de-

59. In fact, the decline has barely leveled off: "Payments Needs of Members Have Outpaced the Growth of the Fund's Usable Resources," *IMF Survey,* July 5, 1982; on the ratio of quotas to reserves since 1948, see chart, p. 199.

60. That is to say, no multilateral influence has been exercised over the policies of surplus countries, or of deficit countries that have had means other than Fund drawings to finance their deficits. The developing countries, therefore, have borne the brunt of multilateral adjustment policies under the Bretton Woods regime.

61. The interview with Under Secretary Sprinkel, cited above, suggests that the American administration's initial position at least in part was inspired by the so-called moral hazard problem, whereby the provision of adequate and easily accessible insurance may increase risk by reducing prudence. For a general discussion, see Kenneth J. Arrow, *Essays in the Theory of Risk-Bearing* (New York: Elsevier, 1974).

veloping countries, in that "enlarged access" goes some way toward severing the link between quotas and access to Fund resources. But, as we have seen, this is a rule change that remains well within the normative structure of the regime. It may be that a more fundamental departure is occurring in the role of the IMF itself. Reluctantly but ineluctably, it is coming to play a part in a broader effort to provide lender of last resort facilities for the international financial system. This effort includes industrialized country governments, the IMF in conjunction with private banks, and the Bank for International Settlements in conjunction with central banks. Such an institutional innovation of course would affect developing countries, but only by regulating their behavior as borrowers more closely than was possible in the past.

3. *Changes in IMF Conditionality.* Another departure from past patterns of IMF drawings was signaled by the "extended arrangement" entered into with India in 1981. India can draw up to SDR 5 billion over a three-year period and take up to ten years to repay, thus making this the largest and longest drawing in IMF history. The request from India was triggered not by an immediate crisis in its balance of payments, but by "the gloomy outlook for medium-term external payments." And it was granted not to finance a temporary deficit, but to enable India to undertake the "early adoption of adjustment measures, with a view toward structural change" in its economy. Moreover, the investment program that India proposes to undertake as part of these adjustment measures "envisages a continued key role for the public sector," with 53 percent of total gross investment being earmarked for it. The macroeconomic emphasis is on expanding the supply potential of the economy, with demand management being assigned the complementary task of mobilizing greater domestic resources for this purpose. The objective of rapidly expanding exports and liberalizing the import regime is coupled with promoting efficient import substitution. And no currency depreciation is called

for.[62] Each of these provisions stands in stark and pointed contrast to traditional "IMF orthodoxy." How did these changes come about, and what do they signify?

The factors that explain the Fund's reassessment of conditionality provisions include those that account for the expansion of lending to developing countries.[63] But they go well beyond them, into the realm of economic theory and ideology. Jürgen Habermas has defined legitimacy as "a political order's worthiness to be recognized," where recognition implies the willing acknowledgment of authority.[64] So defined, the legitimacy of the Fund has long been questioned by representatives of developing countries as well as by sympathetic Northern observers.[65] To these critics, the irreducible essence of the problem is that the Fund was born with an "original sin":

The Fund's financial mechanisms were designed to cope with a typical problem of industrialized economies: to provide short-term breathing space to enable countries to work their way out of payments deficits. . . . A deficit in the balance of payments of an industrialized country normally implies the existence of stocks of unsold goods and services, or of idle production capacities. An occasional deficit is considered a simple "maladjustment". . . . The IMF could extend credit to such a country in the legitimate expectation that deflation would make its exports more competitive and the above-mentioned stocks or idle capacities would enable the economy to respond almost immediately. . . . Deficits in Third World countries, on the contrary, are of a structural character. Hence the inanity of persisting with treatment for "malad-

62. Abstracted from In-Su Kim, "India's Program Seeks Higher Rate of Growth, Improved Payments Position, Lower Inflation," *IMF Survey*, November 23, 1981, pp. 374—77. I have deliberately emphasized what I perceive to be discontinuities from past practice.

63. They are so treated in Manuel Guitian, *Fund Conditionality: Evolution of Principles and Practices* (IMF Pamphlet no. 38, 1982).

64. Jürgen Habermas, *Communication and the Evolution of Society* (Boston: Beacon Press, 1979), p. 178.

65. *See* Cheryl Payer, *The Debt Trap: The International Monetary Fund and the Third World* (New York: Monthly Review Press, 1974).

justment". . . . To try to "correct" the development deficit is to halt the development effort itself.[66]

The norm of "uniformity" institutionalized in the Fund's past program parallels what Albert Hirschman has called the "monoeconomics claim" held by mainstream economists, admitting only quantitative but not qualitative differences between economies at different levels of development.[67] Under this norm, acceptance of the notion that there exists any "structural" or "development deficit," and that the balance of payments problem of developing countries therefore required a fundamentally different approach, was out of the question. However, neoclassical trade theorists have come to work with and accept the validity of asymmetrical models of Northern and Southern economies.[68] And a quasi-official account of recent changes in Fund conditionality states that "central to these modifications was the premise that the prevailing payments imbalances were *structural* and unlikely to be transitory."[69] Has the Fund abandoned uniformity and thus gained absolution from its "original sin"? Only in part.

During the mid-1970s, the Fund staff was finding that, by its own criteria, the success rate of its conditionality provisions had dropped precipitously. One published study reviewed the experience of twenty-one conditional drawings made by developing countries between 1973 and 1975. It concluded that only about a third could be deemed to have

66. Ismail-Sabri Abdalla, "The Inadequacy and Loss of Legitimacy of the International Monetary Fund," *Development Dialogue* (1980:2), pp. 38–40. Abdalla, a former professor of economics and Minister of Planning in Egypt, is chairman of the Third World Forum.

67. Albert O. Hirschman, *Essays in Trespassing: Economics to Politics and Beyond* (New York: Cambridge University Press, 1981), ch. 1; on the norm of uniformity in the Fund, see Joseph Gold, "Uniformity as a Legal Principle of the International Monetary Fund," *Law & Policy in International Business* (Summer 1975), vol. 7.

68. An analytical overview of this evolution may be found in Ronald Findlay, "Growth and Development in Trade Models," in P. B. Kenen and R. W. Jones, eds., *Handbook of International Economics* (Amsterdam: North-Holland, forthcoming).

69. *IMF Survey*, March 8, 1982, p. 70, emphasis added.

been successful, and they were qualified successes. On balance of payments targets, for instance, fourteen of the twenty-one countries did as well as or better than expected. But of these fourteen, eleven did *not* put into effect "adequate domestic policies." And three countries that *did* put "adequate" policies into place *failed* to achieve their balance of payments targets.[70] The failure of its programs, together with the relatively minor role in the international adjustment process to which the Fund had been relegated at this time indicated that not simply its worthiness to developing countries but its worth to the international monetary system as a whole was at issue. The Fund faced a serious legitimation problem, in that its official doctrine and the outcomes its programs produced were increasingly disjoined. The new conditionality provisions, in part modifying the doctrine, were its result.

However, three qualifying factors circumscribe the scope of the subsequent change. First, not all new drawings by developing countries will be of the "extended arrangement" type, so that the Fund has by no means accepted the argument that payments deficits of developing countries are inherently "structural" in character.[71] Second, the "structural imbalances" to which the Fund refers are not those envisaged by its Third World critics, but the "brutal" deterioration in developing countries' terms of trade brought about by the second oil shock, the global recession, and high interest rates prevailing in international capital markets.[72] There

70. T. M. Reichman, "The Fund's Conditional Assistance and Problems of Adjustment, 1973– 75," *Finance & Development* (December 1978), vol. 15; the one-third success rate compares to a 76 percent rate, for seventy-nine programs, between 1963 and 1972, as calculated by the same author; Thomas Reichman and Richard Stillson, "How Successful are Programs Supported by Stand-By Arrangements?" *Finance & Development* (March 1977), vol. 74.

71. To date, the Indian extended arrangement stands out as the exception in size of drawing, though not in duration; as of the end of 1981, other three-year arrangements had been made with Yugoslavia (SDR 1.66 billion), Romania (SDR 1.1 billion), and Zaire (SDR 912 million). *IMF Survey,* January 25, 1982, p. 28.

72. Speech by Jacques de Larosière, Managing Director of the Fund, *IMF Survey,* October 12, 1981, p. 313; see also the Interim Committee Communiqué, issued after the 1981 annual meeting of Board of Governors, *ibid.,* p. 302.

is more involved in this distinction than salvaging a theoretical/ideological point. Acceptance of the notion of "development deficits" would imply a more-or-less permanent state affairs, with the new lending policy remaining in effect so long as there are developing country economies exhibiting fundamental qualitative differences from the industrialized economies. The structural imbalances invoked by the IMF are expected to be a more temporary sort, so that the new conditionality provisions conceivably could be revoked more readily as the economic climate changes. Third, the increased quantity of resources and the extended arrangements now made available by the Fund have been accompanied by a much more rigorous application of performance criteria, with new commitments that become "inoperative" because countries are unable to meet specified targets rising more rapidly than the number of instances of expanded and extended assistance.[73]

In sum, though it remains highly constrained and contingent, the extended arrangement program of the Fund, granting medium-term assistance to facilitate structural adjustment in developing country economies, comes closest to reflecting a basic norm change in favor of the developing countries.

An Analytical Reprise
Each of these three instances of change reveals a different mechanism of change. In the case of the GSP, the benefits gained by the developing countries and the temporary and partial norm change effected in the trade regime were by-

73. For example, for the first six months of 1982, canceled arrangements *exceeded* by SDR 1.1 billion new commitments made by the Fund. And at the end of fiscal 1981–82, undrawn balances from outstanding commitments totaled 68 *percent* of those commitments; this figure in part reflects the fact that drawings are phased over the life of an arrangement, but also that a great many arrangements became inoperative because countries were unable to meet performance criteria. *IMF Survey,* July 19, 1982, p. 215 and August 30, 1982, p. 269, respectively.

products of the desire by the industrialized countries to minimize the competitive advantages and equalize the burden-sharing of particularistic trade ties with developing countries. The initiative by UNCTAD sought to generalize past preferences that were selective and entailed reverse obligations, and to gain them on the basis of nonreciprocity. It succeeded only in part, and only because the United States came to see the scheme as contributing to its own material interests and to its defense of a more central regime norm. Thus, the potential for rivalry and competition among the industrialized countries comprises one mechanism of change that developing countries, in exceptional circumstances and to a limited degree, are able to exploit. However, the impetus for change remains with the regime-making states.

In the case of increased IMF assistance to developing countries and the erosion of the regime rule that access to Fund assistance be determined strictly on the basis of national quota, the developing countries played a somewhat more active role in producing change. The inability of the Fund to exercise "corrective" influence over the policies of developing countries without substantially increasing its allocation of resources to them, together with the growing threat posed by developing countries to international financial stability, provided them with a source of negative power—that is, the power to create systemic disturbances. This capacity has served as a second mechanism of change for the developing countries, with potentially more far-reaching effects than the first, though their opportunities to utilize it are limited by the relatively small number of points at which either monetary or trade relations are susceptible to disturbances emanating from the developing countries.

The legitimation problem faced by the Fund reveals the workings of a third mechanism of change, which potentially affects the very normative structure of the monetary regime in a manner long advocated by the developing countries. The developing countries may be said to have initiated the process that ultimately led to the adoption by the Fund of the program of medium-term, structural adjustment assistance, through their long-standing rejection of the norm of uniformity and their insistence that the balance of payments problems of industrialized and developing countries are fundamentally dissimilar. However, the loss of legitimacy by the Fund and the subsequent reformulation of its program also required that its worth to the monetary regime as a whole be questioned on terms that the regime-making states themselves regarded as being legitimate. Hence, though this change approximates the kind of change hoped for by adovcates of the NIEO, the number of occasions on which such a conjunction of forces can be expected to occur is not likely to be large.

No claim can be made that these mechanisms exhaust the full range of possibilities. But they do serve to illustrate the range of possibilities, which in turn suggests two partially contrary conclusions. On the one hand, international regimes are not nearly as elastic as proponents of the regime-change strategy appear to assume. There is no sign that the liberalization-stabilization nexus of principles has yielded in any instance to redistributive concerns, either in response to warnings of the perils that lie ahead, or to the prospects of mutual gains that could be reaped. Instead, what we see is that the existing set of principles govern the adaptive redeployment of regime rules and, in a more limited fashion, regime norms so as to accommodate new situations.

On the other hand, international regimes are not quite as rigid as critics of the regime-change strategy imply. Each of the cases examined here has materially enhanced the level of regime resources allocated to the developing countries. This suggests that redistributive *consequences* to some extent can be achieved without redistributive *principles* being instituted as a motivational force. Moreover, the cases show, perhaps paradoxically, that while the core regimes in general may be particularly inhospitable to Third World demands for fundamental change, precisely because these regimes do matter to the regime-making states, their adaptive redeployment is a prize not entirely beyond the reach of the developing countries.[74]

THE INTERNATIONAL DIVISION OF LABOR

It is now a widely accepted proposition that the world economy, in addition to facing its worst conjunctural crisis since the Great Depression, is undergoing profound structural shifts. And these structural shifts, some would argue, are offering new and perhaps historically unique opportunities to those developing countries that are prepared to take advantage of them. Here is how the World Bank has put it:

In a certain sense, the 1970s may be remembered for giving new shape to the world economy. This is not the product of the search through negotiation for greater equality of economic opportunity among nations which the developing countries have pursued; little progress has been made along that route. Rather, what has evolved is a different pattern of economic power, with new centers of production, finance and trade, and new forms of interdependence.[75]

74. Although I have not analyzed it here, I would contend that the same set of generalizations holds for the evolution of the quasi-regime of development assistance as well. Its multilateral component, especially that part of it represented by the World Bank, has been expanded, but the ODA results are mixed, with some of the smaller donors approximating the agreed targets but the major donors falling far short. For an analysis of the changing patterns of the World Bank lending which complements my discussion of the monetary and trade regimes, see Robert L. Ayres, "Breaking the Bank," *Foreign Policy* (Summer 1981), no. 43; Ayres argues that "the underlying political rationale behind the Bank's poverty focus is the pursuit of political stability through what might be called defensive modernization" (p. 111).

75. IBRD, *World Development Report, 1981* (Washington, IBRD, 1981), p. 7. The Bank does not assume that success is automatic for all comers: "the 1980s will determine whether the opportunities can outweigh the difficulties, even for the poorest countries."

My purpose here is to sketch a brief overview of these new patterns, so as to provide some basis for informed speculation about how fundamentally they are likely to alter the matrix of constraints and opportunities the developing countries face in the international division of labor. Since the documentation of these new patterns perforce remains fragmentary and often impressionistic, we shall have to settle for indicative "stylized facts" that address the issue at hand.

Trends in World Industrial Production

The notion of "post-industrial society" has embraced a great many attributes since Daniel Bell first introduced it nearly twenty-five years ago, [76] some expressing insight, others folly. It is enjoying a resurgence because, leaving aside questions of intellectual history, recent trends in world industrial production do reflect several of the specifically economic dimensions of change that Bell had in mind. The final report of an OECD project known as "Interfutures" documents these dimensions of change. [77] The role of manufacturing industry in national production and employment in the advanced capitalist societies is shown to be on the decline. A new generation of industries, especially those organized around the so-called electronics complex of automation, data processing, and telecommunications, is emerging as central future growth poles. And the very concept of industrial activity is becoming increasingly blurred at the frontier, because of the close links there between industry and scien-

---

76. Bell traces the roots of the concept in his book, *The Coming of Post-Industrial Society* (New York: Basic Books, 1973), ch. 1. The five dimensions of post-industrial society, as he saw them in 1973, were a change from a goods-producing to a service economy; the preeminence of professional and technical classes; the centrality of theoretical knowledge as a source of innovation and policy formulation; the deliberate social control of technology; and the greater use of what he called "intellectual technology" or technology-based management systems (*ibid.*, p. 14).

77. OECD, *Facing the Future* (Paris: OECD, 1979).

TABLE 9.4: Regional Distribution of Industrial Value Added (%)

	1970	2000	Assumed Growth Rate 1970–2000
OECD	68.5	50.5	3.4
Third World			
(including China)	11.3	26.3	7.2
Eastern Europe/USSR	19.3	23.2	5.6

SOURCE: Adapted from OECD, *Facing the Future* (Paris: OECD, 1979), table 49, p. 331, Scenario B2.

NOTE: Moderate growth rate scenario.

tific research on the one hand, and between industry and many service activities on the other.

This transformation of industrial structures involves not only the advanced capitalist economies, but also Southern Europe, to some extent Eastern Europe, and parts of the Third World as well. Table 9.4 summarizes OECD projections of the regional distribution of industrial value added by the year 2000. The OECD scenario is somewhat more optimistic about the prospective share accounted for by the developing countries than corresponding projections by UN-IDO, whose political constituency is the Third World.[78] But both foresee a demonstrable "southward" shift. However, this shift is expected to remain concentrated among a relatively small number of newly industrializing countries, primarily in East Asia and Latin America. And it is likely to bypass altogether large parts of South Asia and much of sub-Saharan Africa.[79] At the same time, within the areas that are affected by this shift, the current newly industrializing countries have already gone beyond competing solely on the basis of low wages and labor-intensive products, such as tex-

78. Mytelka cites the relevant UNIDO figures in chapter 5 of the present volume (table 5.8 and text, p. 269). The discrepancy in starting bases (a higher 1970 Third World share in my table 9.4 than the 1975 share reported by UNIDO) is due to my having included China in the Third World category; UNIDO treats China as a category apart. The differences in the shares projected for the year 2000 are also due to somewhat different growth assumptions.

79. OECD, *Facing the Future,* part 5, ch. 2.

tiles, apparel, and footwear, to produce consumer durables, including automobiles and electronic products, as well as capital goods, such as steel and some basic petrochemical products.[80] And there is evidence to suggest that other developing country suppliers are making marginal gains in commodity groups in which the shares of the first tier of newly industrializing countries are leveling off.[81]

Trends in World Production Processes
This shift in industrial deployment has coincided with a transformation in the global organization of production processes. At the heart of this transformation are changes in the magnitude, character, and role of direct foreign investment. I first summarize some overall quantitative trends.[82] Since the mid-1970s, the extraordinary rate of growth in direct foreign investment that had prevailed from about 1960 on has moderated considerably, though it has remained more buoyant than domestic investment and GNP growth rates in the advanced capitalist countries, and it has kept pace with world trade. Moreover, there is a somewhat greater balance among countries now than there was before. The share of outward flow accounted for by the United States in the period 1974–79 was approximately 30 percent, or half of what it had been in the 1960s, whereas its share of inward flows, insignificant earlier, now is nearly one third of net international direct investment flows. The share of inward flows accounted for by developing countries has also increased, thus reversing a postwar trend that had held up to 1974, though two thirds of these flows are captured by only thirteen countries, and direct investment flows to developing countries in the 1970s were substantially outdis-

80. *Ibid.*
81. "OECD and the NICs: Current Trade Patterns," *OECD Observer* (November 1981), no. 113.
82. This summary is based on OECD, *International Investment and Multinational Enterprises: Recent International Direct Investment Trends* (Paris: OECD, 1981).

tanced by private bank lending. In addition, Third World countries today are more likely to be the "home" countries of multinational corporations than they were in the 1960s,[83] though the most important newcomers by far are Germany and Japan, and six OECD countries continue to account for more than 80 percent of the total stock of direct foreign investment. Lastly, there have been significant sectoral shifts. Mining has declined in importance everywhere. The service sector has increased in importance everywhere. And the share of total direct foreign investment accounted for by manufacturing in the OECD area is declining, while the share of world total accounted for by manufacturing in the developing countries is increasing.[84]

Even more indicative of the transformation of global production processes are two recent institutional changes exhibited by direct foreign investment. Neither was specifically designed with the developing countries in mind, but both are becoming more prominent in the North—South context. The first is an increasing fragmentation of the productive process, making it possible to transfer specific parts of it to new locations and thereby to exploit the relative advantages of different production sites worldwide. This innovation has its origins in a reorientation of multinational corporations in the 1960s:

During the early postwar period business investment abroad was predominantly designed to serve the local market and replace imports. There was comparatively little attempt to establish an inter-

83. According to a report published in the Harvard Business Review, as cited in the *New York Times,* the number of LDC-based MNCs on *Fortune* magazine's "Largest Overseas 500" list more than doubled to 34 between 1974 and 1979; of the top eighteen, those with 1977 sales of approximately $1 billion or more, ten were exclusively in petroleum; one in petroleum, electronics, and appliances; two in copper; one in textiles; one in industrial equipment, electronics, and textiles; one in steel; one in shipbuilding; and one in motor vehicles. Clyde H. Farnsworth, "Third World Companies Achieving Global Reach," *New York Times International Economic Survey,* February 3, 1980, p. 20.

84. Not every country in each group reflects the aggregate trends; for a fuller treatment, consult OECD, *International Investment* (1981).

dependent and integrated production operation abroad, and so trade between the affiliates of any given company was limited. But from about the mid-1960s onwards these companies increasingly turned toward exports and developed an integrated strategy for worldwide production and sales.[85]

First employed in the automobile and electronics industries, the incidence of segmented production networks has since become more common: "large multinational firms with production units in different countries producing semi-products to be further processed by the same company or group in another location in the framework of regional or worldwide networks of integrated production units, rendered possible by modern information processing and transmission systems."[86] A closely related tendency is toward a greater concentration of production capacity at each stage of the production process, thereby making possible the fuller exploitation of economies of scale offered by increasingly integrated world markets, so that local production units truly become "world market factories."[87]

The second fundamental institutional change is the evolution of new forms of international investment, in which the investor does not hold controlling interest in terms of equity participation.[88] Instead, investment may take the form of joint ventures, turnkey operations, international subcontracting, licensing agreements, or management contracts.

85. Andrew Shonfield, "International Economic Relations: The Western System in the 1960s and 1970s," *The Washington Papers* (Beverly Hills and London: Sage Publications, 1976), 4:72.

86. OECD, *International Investment* (1981), p. 3.

87. This term is used by Folker Fröbel et al., *The New International Division of Labour* (New York: Cambridge University Press, 1980), which contains the most detailed case studies yet available of the phenomenon. The general tendency is also described in OECD, *Facing the Future,* part 5, ch. 2.

88. The following discussion draws heavily upon Charles Oman, "Changing International Investment Strategies: The 'New Forms' of Investment in Developing Countries—A State-of-the-Art," OECD, Development Centre, Foreign Investment and International Banking Research Programme, CD/R(80)1314—Working Document No. 7, a summary of which is published as "New North-South Investment Strategies," *OECD Observer* (September 1981), no. 112.

These arrangements may be said to constitute investments rather than sales because the investor provides capital in *some* form, though not necessarily in the form of financial flows, and returns on this capital at least in part derive from the value created during the life of the arrangement. The new investment forms reflect the increased shares of outward flows accounted for by European and Japanese firms, who have long displayed a greater willingness to depart from the U.S. norm of establishing foreign subsidiaries; as well as factors in host countries, such as the East European's insistence on joint ventures or turnkey operations, and greater pressure in developing countries for participation in or control over direct foreign investment in their territories. No quantitative estimates are available of the overall magnitude of these new forms of international investment, but it is known that they have grown substantially since 1973, both in absolute terms and relative to traditional forms. Accordingly, the fact that international financial flows now exceed direct foreign investment flows to developing countries does not necessarily mean that the latter have therefore become less important.[89] These new forms of investment represent an unbundling of the traditional investment package that facilitates an optimization of functions for the international firm, a new role for the financial sector, and greater involvement in ownership and operation by host countries and local entrepreneurs.

89. *Cf.*, Jeff Frieden, "Third World Indebted Industrialization: International Finance and State Capitalism in Mexico, Brazil, Algeria, and South Korea," *International Organization* (Summer 1981), vol. 35. There is no question but that bank lending increasingly outpaced direct investment flows to developing countries during the 1970s. However, and leaving aside the fact that recent levels of bank lending have proven to be unsustainable, a simple comparison of the two sets of figures tells only part of the story. This is so because direct foreign investment statistics understate the flow of nonequity capital from international firms, and they exclude altogether direct investment financed by reinvested earnings, which have become the single most important source of asset acquisition abroad by international firms. Moreover, international firms themselves have increasingly turned to borrowing as a source of their foreign asset acquisition. OECD, *International Investment* (1981), pp. 28–29.

Thus a new division of responsibilities may be emerging among the three actors in which the *firms* will tend to concentrate more on provision of technology, some aspects of management, and control over access to international markets, as their major activities. The *banks,* on the other hand, will increasingly control the financial aspects of the international investment process, and the *host country* will retain ownership over the investment operation and be responsible for those managerial tasks (industrial relations is one) which they are best equipped to handle.[90]

In some cases, international firms may lose effective control as a result of this "new division of responsibilities." But in other cases, the reverse may be true. The risk of nationalization is reduced, the mechanisms of control that are embedded within worldwide production and distribution networks remain unaffected and, because they are less obtrusive and are operated in conjunction with the state or local entrepreneurs, the new forms of investment may be able to penetrate sectors of the host-country economy that were beyond the reach of traditional direct foreign investment.[91]

Trends in World Trade
The 1970s have also witnessed substantial shifts in patterns of world trade. Many of these can be attributed to the role of the OPEC countries as a source of imports to, and the destination of exports from, all other groups of countries. But beyond these effects of new international energy terms of trade, recent world trade patterns reflect as well the changes in world industrial structures and in the global organization of production processes which were described above.

    In terms of overall geographical distribution, the major impact of these changes has been on the growing share of world trade in manufactures accounted for by the newly in-

90. OECD, "New North-South Investment Strategies," p. 15.
91. Oman explores these and related possibilities with a good deal of sensitivity and sophistication.

TABLE 9.5: Total OECD Imports of Manufactures from NICs (%)

	1963	1973	1977	1979
OECD NICs[a]	0.8	1.6	1.8	2.1
East Asian NICs[b]	1.2	3.8	4.8	5.3
Brazil and Mexico	0.3	0.9	1.0	1.1
Total NICs[c]	2.6	6.8	8.1	8.9

SOURCES: For 1963: OECD, *The Impact of the Newly Industrializing Countries on Production and Trade in Manufactures* (Paris: OECD, 1979), table 4, p. 23. Other years: "OECD and the NICs: The Current Trade Pattern," *OECD Observer* (November 1981), no. 113, p. 13.
[a] Greece, Portugal, and Spain.
[b] Hong Kong, South Korea, Singapore, Taiwan.
[c] Includes all of the above plus Yugoslavia.

dustrializing countries. Table 9.5 summarizes OECD-NICs trade in this sector since 1963. If Greece, Portugal, Spain, and Yugoslavia are included among the newly industrializing countries, their total share of OECD imports of manufactured goods now is more than 9 percent, compared to less than 3 percent in 1963. The rate of increase has been most rapid for the four East Asian NICS, which now account for nearly 60 percent of OECD imports of manufactures from all newly industrializing countries. The non-European NICs have also made impressive inroads into OPEC markets, and have made moderate gains in the manufactured imports of the non-oil developing countries. At the same time, however, it should be noted that more than 85 percent of manufactured imports of the OECD countries still come from among themselves. Every OECD country except the United States and Canada has a surplus in its trade balance with the NICs, thanks largely to exports of investment goods, and the overall surplus has been increasing.[92] Moreover, only twenty-two developing countries earn one-fifth or more of their export earnings from manufactures. And nearly half of all developing countries earn less than 5 percent of their

92. "OECD and the NICs"; "World Interdependence: Trade," *OECD Observer* (January 1982), no. 114.

export earnings in this manner.[93] Lastly, to put recent changes into their broadest context, the share of total world exports accounted for in 1980 by all non-oil developing countries, including the NICs, was still *less than half* their share in 1950.[94]

The growth in industrial output and trade among the industrialized countries during the 1960s and 1970s was marked, as we have seen, by intra-industry specialization, whereby an expansion of trade often involved simultaneous increases in exports and imports within the same industrial sector. There are some indications that this pattern of specialization may be extended to the newly industrializing countries in the 1980s and beyond.[95] Recent sectoral diversification in exports by the NICs lends some support to this notion. For example, the share of NICs imports into the OECD accounted for by the products with which they first penetrated OECD markets, such as textiles and "miscellaneous manufactures," has declined markedly in recent years, while the relative importance of the two product groups in which their share of OECD imports in 1977 was highest (clothing and leather, footwear and travel goods) has either stabilized or declined slightly. "In contrast, substantial increases were registered [between 1977 and 1979] in practically all product groups where NICs were fairly small suppliers in 1977."[96]

Finally, the recent changes in global industrial structures and production processes are also reflected in the

93. Kathryn Morton and Peter Tulloch, *Trade and Developing Countries* (New York: Wiley, 1977), pp. 155–58.

94. UNCTAD, *Trade and Development Report, 1981*.

95. OECD, *Facing the Future*, part 5, ch. 2.

96. "OECD and the NICs," p. 12. The earlier OECD survey of trade with the NICs, referenced in table 9.5, found that the NICs tended to concentrate on very specific products within sectors (for example, their 12 percent share of "electrical machinery" imports into the OECD in 1977 masked the difference between a 30 percent share for "electronic components and radio receivers" and a 1 percent share for "medical and radiological apparatus"). Their pattern of specialization therefore remains both for weaker internally and more vulnerable externally than that of the OECD countries.

growing importance of intra-firm trade. Here, the data are extremely sketchy, and it is not universally agreed even what range of phenomena ought to be included in them. What little systematic data there is, is most complete for the United States. The United Nations has estimated that imports into the United States by U.S.-based multinationals from their *majority-owned foreign affiliates* was roughly one third of total U.S. imports in the mid-1970s.[97] Gerald Helleiner has found that if the less restrictive category of *related-party* imports is employed, the figure was nearly one half of total U.S. imports for all sectors in 1977, and over one half for manufactures.[98] There is every reason to believe, therefore, that if the new forms of direct foreign investment, discussed above, were to be included, what we might call *corporate-administered trade* accounts for perhaps as much as 60 percent of all U.S. imports, particularly in the manufacturing sector.[99] Fragmentary data for other countries and for world totals, even when the centrally planned economies are excluded, suggest similar general tendencies.[100]

As for the geographical distribution of this type of trade, to date its relative importance is clearly greater for intra-OECD trade than for North — South trade. However, since, in

97. United Nations, *Transnational Corporations in World Development: A Re-Examination* (New York: United Nations Sales No. 78.II.A.5, 1978), p. 220, table III-16.

98. Gerald K. Helleiner, *Intra-Firm Trade and the Developing Countries* (London: Macmillan, 1981), table 2.2, p. 28. Related-party trade is defined as trade among parties where one holds 5 percent or more of voting equity in the other.

99. This is a guess-estimate based on the growing use of nonequity forms of investment, as discussed above, and on the rapid expansion of manufactured imports from developing to industrialized countries under so-called off-shore assembly provisions (OAP). Under the latter, the industrialized countries export components, which are assembled in the developing countries, with the end-product then being exported back to the industrialized countries. No customs duty is charged on the reimported components. Between 1966 and 1972, OAP manufactured imports into the United States from developing countries grew at 60 percent per annum, compared to the corresponding growth rate for non-OAP imports of 12 percent per annum. OECD, *International Investment*, p. 31. This kind of trade of course is tied in some fashion, generally by subcontracting.

100. U.N., *Transnational Corporations*, pp. 41–45.

the case of the United States at any rate, there appears to exist a positive correlation between the level of manufacture of imports on the one hand, and related-party trade on the other, it is reasonable to expect that further industrialization in the Third World will also increase its share of related-party trade.[101] Some sectoral trade figures, as well as the rapid rate of growth in manufactured imports from developing countries under "offshore assembly provisions," seem to bear out this expectation.[102]

Helleiner concludes that "it is unfortunately not yet possible—because there are not yet enough observations—to establish rigorously whether intra-firm trade behaves significantly differently from arms-length (market) trade."[103] Speculation has focused on the "corporate internalization" of economic mechanisms and functions that arms-length market transactions performed in the past, which some believe to result in worldwide "zones of administered economic systems within which the notion of market has little if any meaning."[104]

101. Helleiner, *Intra-Firm Trade*. Elsewhere, Helleiner points out that while the manufactured exports of developing countries at present are less subject to being "managed" by private firms via related-party transactions, compared to intra-OECD trade in manufactures, they are more likely to be subject to intergovernmental management via such devices as orderly marketing arrangements. Indeed, Helleiner's sectoral figures suggest an inverse relation between the two types of "managerial efforts," as he calls them. Gerald K. Helleiner, "The New Industrial Protectionism and the Developing Countries," *Trade and Development* (Spring 1979), vol. 1.

102. For example, three fourths of U.S. imports of "electrical machinery, apparatus, and appliances" from developing countries in 1977 was conducted by related parties, chemical fertilizers were equally high, and several other sectors of industrial products fell into the forty to sixty percent range. Helleiner, *Intra-Firm Trade*, table 23. For OAP imports, see fn. 97.

103. Gerald K. Helleiner and Real Lavergne, "Intra-Firm Trade and Industrial Exports to the United States," *Oxford Bulletin of Economics and Statistics* (1979), vol. 41, no. 4.

104. Constantine V. Vaitsos, "The Visible Hand in World Production and Trade: Corporate Integration," paper presented to the Conference on Integration and Unequal Development: The Case of Western Europe, Institute of Development Studies, Sussex University, May 1979, p. 11.

A New International Division of Labor?

In sum, the structural shifts affecting the world economy today involve changes in patterns of international specialization, together with the global integration and rationalization of networks of production and exchange. These changes in the real economy in turn are paralleled and reinforced by corresponding changes in the world financial system.[105] The question of concern to us here is how extensively and profoundly these changes alter the matrix of constraints and opportunities faced by developing countries.

There are two prevailing interpretations, both of which stress the natural unfolding of intrinsic laws of capitalist development. The first interpretation is reflected in the statement by the World Bank which I cited at the outset of this section, and it expresses the position of neoclassical economics more generally. From this vantage point, these changes are concrete manifestations of the inherently progressive character of the international division of labor, responding to the laws of comparative advantage and yielding gains from trade. Moreover, they are viewed as signaling a new era in North—South relations, as successive tiers of developing countries now have the opportunity to upgrade their niches in the international division of labor. Lastly, the institutional transformations in production and trade that have

105. Good overviews of the evolution of the Euromarkets may be found in M. S. Mendelsohn, *Money on the Move* (New York: McGraw Hill, 1980), and Eugene Versluysen, *The Political Economy of International Finance* (New York: St. Martin's Press, 1981). Jeff Frieden has made the interesting observation that the worldwide interpenetration of financial markets to some extent reinforces global shifts in comparative advantage, on the assumption that finance capital will seek out ascending and avoid declining industries. "It seems clear that the increased importance of finance has . . . quickened the pace and deepened the impact of the structural transformation of the U.S. economy and, given the international commitments of U.S. finance, has tied this structural transformation very tightly into trends in the world economy." Frieden, "International Finance and the U.S. Economy," paper presented at the annual meeting of the International Political Science Association, Rio de Janeiro, August 9—14, 1982, esp. pp. 19—23, at 23. However, the relationship between productivity, profitability, and lending decisions by banks are too indeterminate for any direct correspondence between sectoral shifts and credit allocation to hold.

coincided with the sectoral shifts are thought to be beneficial, more effectively transferring technology to Southern
producers and in turn securing access for them to Northern
markets.

The second interpretation is inspired by neo-Marxist
economic theory and the dependency perspective. Not surprisingly, it offers the mirror image of the first. From this
vantage point, the recent changes in the international division of labor reflect the laws of "valorization and accumulation" of capital on a world scale.[106] Until recently, "the reproduction of capital on a world scale merely generated the
'classical' international division of labor: a few industrial
countries producing capital-goods and consumer goods on
one hand, confronting the vast majority of underdeveloped
countries which were integrated into the world economy as
producers of raw materials."[107] Under this arrangement,
capital was able to "valorize" itself in the developing countries only in the primary sector. By the 1960s, however, capital had produced the conditions which now permit a much
more effective and complete global accumulation process:
"the chief of these conditions are the existence of a worldwide industrial reserve army, the possibility of far-reaching
subdivision of the production process into fragments, and
an efficient transport and communications technology."[108]
Once these conditions were in place, the "traditional bisec-
tion" of the world economy was undermined and made to
yield to "the new international division of labour."[109] Forms
of exploitation and dependency have been altered as a result, but the phenomena themselves if anything have been
strengthened.[110] Those variants of this perspective which

106. Fröbel et al., *The New International Division of Labour*. The term "valorization" comes from the German *Verwertung*, used by Marx; in everyday language
it translates roughly as "realization of value."
    107. *Ibid.*, p. 44.
    108. *Ibid.*
    109. *Ibid.*, p. 45.
    110. It is not completely clear, though, who benefits from these relations,
since in the scheme developed by Fröbel et al., the periphery loses via exploitation

draw on the work of Stephen Hymer foresee intra-corporate hierarchies being reproduced as the dominant patterns of economic and social stratification within the world system as a whole.[111]

Both interpretations highlight important dynamic aspects of recent structural shifts in the world economy. But both exaggerate the determining role of the international division of labor by magnifying out of proportion those aspects of these changes that reflect their own a priori views. The neoclassical perspective stresses the sectoral shifts. These have been important for individual developing countries. However, when viewed in a global context, they remain relatively modest, shallow, and highly concentrated. Moreover, while there have been some spillover effects from the upgrading of exports by the first tier of newly industrializing countries for subsequent tiers of developing countries, the OECD itself has described these as "marginal."[112] In point of fact, one reason the first tier of NICs shifted out of certain sectors and other developing country suppliers have had difficulty simply stepping into the niche vacated thereby is precisely because trade barriers have been erected in the industrialized countries so as to slow the pace and limit the extent that the laws of comparative advantage are allowed to operate. This fact suggests two further sets of constraints. The first is the so-called fallacy of composition, which I addressed in the Introduction to this volume: for future industrializers to follow the route taken by the first tier of NICs, the absorptive capacity of world markets would have to increase by an order of magnitude the realization of which is difficult to foresee. Second, even the sustainability by the first tier of their own past trajectory depends critically

---

but the core also loses via the export of jobs to the periphery. Where the abstract "capital" that gains is located remains unspecified.

111. Stephen Hymer, "The Multinational Corporation and the Law of Uneven Development," in Jagdish Bhagwati, ed., *Economics and World Order* (New York: Macmillan, 1972).

112. "OECD and the NICs."

on what the OECD euphemistically calls "positive adjustment policies" in the industrialized countries. That is to say, it would require state intervention there so as to give greater play to the laws of comparative advantage in allocating economic resources.[113] In no small measure, positive adjustment policies would entail governments in the industrialized countries going well beyond the compromise of embedded liberalism in two directions: first, to "disembed" liberalization from the sociopolitical constraints that have guided it throughout the postwar era; and second, to redirect the economic activities of affected individuals, regions, and sectors more actively and extensively than the major capitalist states have been willing to do in the past.[114] It is not surprising that some developing countries, in a striking reversal of their previous ideological posture, have recently sought to raise "a system of trade based on a dynamic pattern of comparative advantage" to the level of "a fundamental objective of the international community."[115] However, as the first part of this chapter has demonstrated, the embedded liberalism compromise, at least as it is reflected in the evolution of the monetary and trade regimes, remains relatively robust and has held up under increasingly unfavorable international economic circumstances.

113. "Positive Adjustment Policies (PAPs)," *OECD Observer* (July 1979), no. 99. The economic rationale for these policies is argued by Stephen Marris, Economic Advisor to the OECD Secretary General, on the grounds that "we can improve our living standards by trading capital-intensive for labor intensive products." Consumers in the OECD countries "are able to buy the same quantity of goods as before while employing fewer people. And the people thus freed can be employed producing something else which is more capital-intensive and where labour is more productive." Marris, "The Case of the Newly Industrializing Countries (NICs)," *OECD Observer* (January 1979), no. 96, p. 10, and "OECD Trade with the Newly Industrializing Countries (NICs)," *OECD Observer* (July 1979), no. 99, p. 30.

114. That is, it would require that the major capitalist countries adopt policies similar to those of the small European states, as described by Katzenstein in chapter 2, above. For a listing of recommended policies, see "Positive Adjustment Policies."

115. *Report of the Preparatory Committee for the New International Development Strategy* (New York: United Nations), p. 176.

If the neoclassical perspective exaggerates the sectoral shifts, the neo-Marxist view distorts the scope, effects, and determinism of the institutional changes in production and trade. First of all, the picture of the newly industrializing countries supplying masses of cheap labor, in free production zones, under subcontracting arrangements with foreign capitalists, importing industrial inputs and converting them into standardized products for export, in a manner that neither requires nor teaches skills and yields few if any other economic or social benefits, is a caricature of their actual experience. Moreover, it exaggerates the developing country share in intra-firm trade and the share of intra-firm trade in developing country exports. It ignores altogether the opportunities in developing countries created by the new institutional arrangements for indigenous entrepreneurs, the state, and the process of local capital accumulation. Lastly, the sudden intellectual conversion that this interpretation requires is somewhat disconcerting: neo-Marxists have been insisting all along that it is an iron law of capital for developing countries to be cast in the role of a primary-producing hinterland;[116] now this iron law turns out to have been a mere inconvenience not a necessity of capital, waiting only for the appropriate technological breakthrough in production processes in order to be transcended by the *real* iron law, which had simply lurked behind the scenes for the duration. The notion that many of the institutional changes in production and trade reflect changing balances of economic power among the OECD countries, and between investors and host countries, is discounted.[117]

In sum, I conclude my assessment of the elasticity of the international division of labor to accommodate the wel-

116. For a classic statement of *that* law, see Paul A. Baran, *The Political Economy of Growth* (New York: Monthly Review Press, 1957).

117. The outlines of an approach that combines a focus on accumulation with greater sensitivity to domestic and international political factors may be found in James A. Caporaso, "Industrialization in the Periphery: The Evolving Global Division of Labor," *International Studies Quarterly* (September 1981), vol. 25.

fare demands of developing countries on much the same note as my assessment of international regimes. It is not nearly as elastic as its advocates assume, but not quite as rigid as its detractors insist. And its degree of elasticity, as in the case of regimes, depends ultimately on the political structure that shapes both component parts of the international economic order.

POLITICAL STRUCTURE

Domestic and international society differ fundamentally in the extent to which distributive justice and the laws of economic specialization can take hold. The difference is structural. In domestic society, patterns of economic opportunity and outcomes can be altered by the desirability of the greater social good, as defined and enforced by central agencies. And economic units can feel free to go about trading cloth for wine because any vulnerabilities that result from their mutual differentiation can be regulated by central agencies. Due to its political structure, domestic society can achieve what Durkheim called "organic solidarity."[118] Legitimate authority is not centralized in international society. No one by virtue of authority is entitled to command; no one in turn is obliged to obey. International society, therefore, remains a self-help system, limited to expressions of

118. Emile Durkheim, *The Division of Labor in Society,* translated by George Simpson (New York: Free Press, 1964). The distinction is between organic solidarity, linking highly differentiated units in a complex society, and mechanical solidarity, linking like units in a segmental society—that is, units that are alike in the tasks they pursue, though not necessarily in their ability to perform them. Organic solidarity represents a quantitatively greater extent and qualitatively higher form of interdependence. This distinction was first applied to the comparison of domestic and international society by Kenneth N. Waltz, *Theory of International Politics* (Reading, Mass.: Addison-Wesley, 1979). A more elaborate theoretical exploration of this model of international society may be found in my paper, "Continuity and Transformation in the World Polity: Toward a Neorealist Synthesis," *World Politics* (January 1983), vol. 35, which is a review article of Waltz's book.

"mechanical solidarity." As a result, what is desirable and acceptable in domestic society remains problematical in international society. And, due to the political structure of international society, its institutional orders closely reflect prevailing configurations in the relations of force. The international economic order is no exception to this rule.

The international economic order at any moment reflects three configurative attributes of the relations of force. The first is the degree of concentration or diffusion of economic capabilities among the major powers. Through the projection of *state power*, this determines whether a single international economic order prevails, or whether several such orders coexist. The second is the degree of congruence in the ends and means of state intervention in the economies of the major powers. Through the projection of *social power*, this determines the collective purpose that is instituted in the international economic order. The third is the degree of adherence by the major powers to a body of economic theory on the basis of which to formulate and legitimate economic policy. Through the projection of *epistemic power*, this determines how collective purposes are operationalized and the apparent limits of the possible circumscribed. A situation in which the three are in equilibrium may be termed a hegemony, in the Gramscian sense of the word.[119]

The *pax Americana* of the post World War II era comprised such a hegemony. U.S. economic and military predominance forged an invisible empire, which, while it never achieved the status of a singularity in the world economy, nonetheless completely overwhelmed its rival in scope and economic strength. Moreover, a sufficient degree of congruence existed in prevailing state-society relations among the major economic powers for the embedded liberalism compromise to define the social objectives in pursuit of which

119. For a useful introduction to Gramsci's concept, see Joseph Femia, "Hegemony and Consciousness in the Thought of Antonio Gramsci," *Political Studies* (1975), vol. 23, no. 1.

state power was deployed in the international economic order. It was reflected in the liberalization-stabilization nexus of governing principles of the regimes for money and trade, and in the sociopolitical constraints that shaped the evolution of the international division of labor by, to cite but one example, providing incentives for intra-industry specialization. Lastly, Keynesian demand management came to provide the scientific basis on which to operationalize the prevailing collective social objectives into specific policies, while at the same time serving as a mode of legitimation that allowed predominantly capitalist societies under the pressure of universal political participation to respond to distributional challenges without fundamentally altering the domestic social relations of production.

This hegemony has eroded. But the international economic order that was its expression has not collapsed, notwithstanding premature announcements of its demise. The balance of economic power among the major industrialized countries has shifted. As a result, the transnational economic order that was initially generated by U.S. predominance is becoming a more truly multinational one, within which economic processes are organized in an evermore complex fashion, and within which rivalry and competition among the major powers will continue to be an engine of change. But the constitutive basis of this order has not altered fundamentally, in part because the major beneficiaries of the relative decline of U.S. economic power, Western Europe and Japan, thus far continue to share with the United States a commitment to the maintenance of a single, integrated, capitalist world economy. At the level of collective social purpose there has been little fundamental discontinuity, which means that the governing principles of the monetary and trade regimes remain largely in place, even though the United States has abandoned its earlier role as the guarantor of both regimes.[120] The current conjunctural

120. I am referring to the decision taken by the United States in 1971 to abandon the gold-convertibility of the dollar, and the less discrete but no less

crisis in the world economy has tempted governments in several of the major industrialized countries to depart radically from the prevailing balance of state-society relations, toward both the left and right. To date, however, it seems that the class structure of these societies, together with the pressures of international competition on their domestic economic policies, have served to restrain these would-be departures and to keep policies more or less within the framework of the embedded liberalism compromise. Third and finally, the efficacy of Keynsian demand management in all probability has been permanently undermined. But even this development is muted in its impact by virtue of the legitimation role that Keynesianism played, for which any alternative would have to provide a substitute. Fred Hirsch has put this well:

Keynes's opponents, from the beginning, have seen his system as an engine of inflation, above all because of its manipulability. The charge can now be seen to be basically correct, and yet misplaced, reflecting a blinkered vision. . . . Both Keynesianism and inflation can be seen as defensive responses by capitalist societies challenged by the new political and economic imperatives of a democratic age. If these defences are now losing force, the underlying stresses will become more exposed. . . . But that the convulsion of both systems has been held back for so long is a reminder of the fecundity of their defence mechanisms and their capacity for mutation.[121]

In conclusion, then, what does all of this signify for the developing countries? I simply enumerate four major implications.

---

visible reluctance to accept a disproportionate share of the costs of trade liberalization. The latter is demonstrated by Stephen D. Krasner, "The Tokyo Round: Particularistic Interests and Prospects for Stability in the Global Trading System," *International Studies Quarterly* (December 1979), vol. 23.

121. Fred Hirsch, "The Ideological Underlay of Inflation," in Fred Hirsch and John H. Goldthorpe, eds., *The Political Economy of Inflation* (Cambridge, Mass.: Harvard University Press, 1978), pp. 283–84; see Goldthorpe's contribution in the same book, entitled "The Current Inflation: A Sociological Account." I have benefited from both papers in my discussion of the dual nature of Keynesianism.

First of all, in any self-help system, effective demand is the chief allocative mechanism. Not cries of anguish, not a sense of peril and doom, and not the promise of mutual gains *alone* can alter patterns of outcomes. Each "may lead to a clear definition of ends that must be achieved. Their achievement is not thereby made possible. . . . Necessities do not create possibilities."[122] The possibility of effective action depends on the ability to project effective demand. Where and when effective demand has been projected by the developing countries, as we have seen, the international economic order does exhibit a degree of elasticity to accommodate it. But at best the international economic order, whether via international regimes or via the international division of labor, provides a facilitative framework for change, which must rest, in the final analysis, on self-help measures.

The niche in the international division of labor that the newly industrializing countries have come to occupy reflects a permanent transformation. These countries are unlikely to be able to sustain their own past rates of increase in exports to the industrialized countries, but most now exhibit sufficient internal economic strength, diversity of external ties, and potential for systemic disturbance that their place in the "semi-periphery" seems secure.

The same is not true of the next tier of would-be newly industrializing countries. They are unlikely to benefit from the same degree of access to OECD markets as the first tier, whose "take-off" coincided with a booming world economy. If, therefore, the countries in the next tier adopt export-led strategies, the capital surplus oil exporters and the NICs will have to absorb an increasing share of those exports. Whether such a redirection of trade flows is characterized as resulting from regional growth poles, sub-imperialism, or collective self-reliance is merely a matter of rhetorical preference; the facts, as indicated by econometric studies

122. Waltz, p. 109.

of the recent past, suggest only limited growth to date of trade in this direction.[123]

Last, and least, we come to the poorest of the developing countries. The United Nations includes thirty-one countries in the category of least developed, having an average per capita income of $183 per year.[124] Any beneficial effects of the sorts of changes and tendencies discussed in this chapter are likely to bypass them altogether. Indeed, attempts through multilateral assistance agencies and other means to incorporate them into the international division of labor may do more harm than good for the foreseeable future. This is so because, if the European historical evidence is any guide to their future, market relations will undermine and erode self-provisioning and communal support arrangements long before their promised benefits begin to materialize.[125] Thus, if the advocates of unorthodox, basic-needs oriented, self-reliant development strategies have any province, this surely is it.

123. For a recent survey of patterns of LDC trade flows from 1963 to 1977, see Oli Havrylyshyn and Martin Wolf, "Promoting Trade Among Developing Countries: An Assessment," *Finance & Development* (March 1982), vol. 19.

124. Some of the other characteristics of these countries include a population growth rate that averages 2.7 percent annually; infant mortality rates of 142 per 1,000 live births, compared to 94 per 1,000 in all developing countries and 30 in the industrialized countries; life expectancy of 45 years; two of every three children malnourished; literacy rates of roughly 25 percent of the male population; and access to safe water limited to one third of the population. United Nations, "UN Conference on the Least Developed Countries," DPI/DESI NOTE/585, August 17, 1981.

125. Some of the relevant statistics are cited the second section of the Introduction to this volume. The most compelling "soft" account of this experience remains that by Polanyi, in *The Great Transformation,* chs. 6–10. Cheryl Payer presents persuasive illustrative materials that this outcome has been produced by the World Bank's lending program to small farmers in developing countries, though I remain unconvinced by her general argument that the Bank's underlying purpose is the deliberate appropriation of land to serve the markets of the core countries. Payer, "The World Bank and the Small Farmer," *Journal of Peace Research* (1979), vol. 16, no. 4.

Name Index

Subject Index

Adams, John Quincy, 58, 78

Africa: European languages, 322-25, 327-33, 338; export performance (1970–1976), 254-55; from import reproduction to export-led manufacturing, 240-46; industrialization, 240, 251-53, 255; linguistic dissociation, 317-68; manufacturing, projection of, 268-69; mineral exports, 265-66; primary production, return to, 263-68; trade and investment relations with Europe, 247-255

Afrikaans, 325

Agency for International Development, 153

Agrarian reform, *see* Land reform

Agriculture: United States (1776–1815), 53, 60; Venezuela, 200-2, 219-20

Algeria, 34-35, 195; education and vocational training, 294-95; human welfare, 313; selective dissociation in technology, 288-96, 309

American System, 75

Amharic language, 350

Andean Pact, 230-31

Anglo–French wars, 52-56

Angola, 371; dissociation with external opposition, 384; security association with USSR and Cuba, 388; South African intervention, 382; unconventional military self-reliance, 413

Appeasement, as political approach to security, 385-88, 420

Appropriate technology, India, 299-301, 307

Argentina: exports, 245; Falklands/Malvinas, 405n; import substitution, 135; labor, 145; technology, 308

Arms trade, 389, 399, 402-4, 406-8, 413; India, 399

ASEAN, *see* Association of Southeast Asian Nations

Asia: manufacturing, projections of, 269; newly industrializing countries, 27, 132-36; *see also* specific countries

Association, strategy of, 16, 18-20, 274; alternative security association, 388-97; dangers, 88; economic, political, and social costs, 44; and human welfare, 313; landed elites, benefits to, 88; small European states, post-World War II, 25-27; South Korea, 185-87; United States (1776–1860), 23-24, 43-90; Venezuela, 191-238

Association of Southeast Asian Nations (ASEAN), 170, 172

Austria: corporatism, 118-19, 125; dependency, 91; domestic compensation, 102, 114; export of services, 100; Social Democratic regime, slow

strikes, 108

Dependency, 14-15, 23, 140, 155-56; Africa, 240-41, 249; attenuation of external constraints, 196; market diversification and, 166; small European states, 91-93, 95-96, 98-99, 101, 115-17, 121-23, 127-28; social-structure distortions, 187; South Korea, 140, 156, 166; technology, 282; United States (1830s), 65; Venezuela, 193-96, 236-38

Developing countries (Third World): compared with European states, 129; debt (mid-1970s–1981), 455; dissociation, 12-13; exports, 443-45, 473-74; foreign investments, 468; GATT escape clauses, invocations of, 448-50; Generalized System of Preferences, 446-47; gross national product, 4; IMF drawings, 438-42, 453-58, 463; IMF negotiations, 430-31; industrial value added projections, 467; international division of labor, 477; international economic order, effect of changes on, 485-87; international regimes of money and trade, effect on, 8; International Trade Organization negotiations, 431; least developed countries, 487; manufacturing, projections of, 269; neo-Marxist theory, 481; New International Economic Order, 11; objectives of, in monetary and trade arrangements, 437; outward-oriented strategies, 9-11, 16; postwar monetary and trade arrangements, 430-31, 435-36; security environment, 374-75; self-reliance, 12-13; see also Newly industrializing countries

Dissociation, strategy of, 12, 16-17, 20, 34, 37, 370; appeasement as political approach to security, 385-88; conditions favoring, 372; consequences, 37; conventional military self-reliance, 397-410; domestic unity, importance of, 417-18; external threats and intervention, 375-76, 379-83; intellectual roots of, 14-15; inter-nal dissent and threats, 375-76, 378-79, 383-84; linguistic, 36-37, 317-68; as long-term option, 86; as next stage of decolonization, 371-72; revolutionary approach to, 418-19; security strategies for, 38, 369-420; self-reliance/reassociation cases, 371; strong leadership, necessity of, 417; unconventional military self-reliance, 410-15; United States, 90, (to 1815), 24, 59, 75-76, 83, 86, 89, (1815–Civil War), 77-79, 85; vulnerability of dissociating countries, 415-16; see also Selective dissociation; Self-reliance

Division of labor, international, see International division of labor

Domestic compensation, small European states, 94-95, 102-3, 106-14, 127-28

Domestic markets: small European states, 95

Dominican Republic, 310, 371

EC, see European Communities

Economic Commission for Latin America (ECLA), 14, 183

Economic openness: small European states, 95-101, 115-17, 121-23, 125; and public economy, 126; and unionism, 123

Economic specialization, 156; intrasectoral, 444; small European states, 95, 97-99, 101; trends in, 474

Economies of scale, small European states, 95, 101

ECSC, see European Coal and Steel Community

Ecuador, 309

Edo language, 351

Education: Algeria, 294; in indigenous languages, 344-45, 347-48, 355, 357

Efficiency-equity trade-off, 311

Egypt, 308

Electronics industries, 466

El Salvador, 309

Embargo, U.S., 48, 56-60, 75-76, 83

Embedded liberalism compromise, 433,

NICs (*Continued*)
  drawings, 439-41; industrial value added projections, 467; market diversification, 139; South—South ties, 171-72; trade, 444, 447, 473-74; trade barriers, 479; and trade regime, 138, 160-65
Nicaragua, 371; technology, 309
NICs, *see* Newly industrializing countries
NIEO, *see* New International Economic Order
Niger, 310
Nigeria, 249, 251, 263, 344; arms imports, 389, 403; language, 346, 351, 354-57, 360-61; technology, 309
Nonimportation Act, U.S. (1806), 56
Nonintercourse Act, U.S. (1809), 58-59, 76
North—South negotiations, 10-11, 18, 22-23, 425-26
Norway: collective bargaining, 114; corporatism, 117, 125; dependence, 91; domestic compensation, 102; export of services, 100; language, 363, 366; public economy, 110-11; economic specialization, 97; strikes, 108
Nuclear weapons programs, 402

Organization for Economic Co-operation and Development (OECD), 435; imports from newly industrializing countries, 473-74
Oromo language, 350
Outward-oriented development strategies, 9-11, 16, 23; newly industrializing countries, 27; political infrastructure, 19; possible consequences, 19-20; state intervention and direction of, 18-20; theoretical basis, 14; *see also* Export-led development strategies

Pakistan, 395; technology, 308
Panama, 309
Papua New Guinea, 310
Paraguay, 310
Park Chung-hee, 142-45, 150, 153-54, 158-59, 172-73, 175, 178-80, 188

Patents, ownership of, 281-82; foreign-owned, 308-10
People's war, Mao Tse-tung's principles of, 411
Peru, 308
Petroleum, Venezuela, 199-200, 202-5, 207, 225, 229-30, 237
Philippines, 308
Plantation economy, U.S., 24, 47, 67
Positive adjustment policies, 480
Post-industrial society, 466
Prebisch, Raul, 14
Primary-export substitution, 136
Production processes: fragmentation of, 469-70; trends in, 468-72
Protectionism, 105; and GATT, 434; newly industrializing countries, 136; South Korea, 163; United States (pre-Civil War), 68-69, 75, 77-79
Public economy: economic openness and, 126; small European states, 109-14; Venezuela, 206

Quasi-War (U.S.—France), 54

Randolph, John, 58, 78
Reassociation, 370-71
Research and development: Algeria, 294; expenditures, 277, 280-81, 308-10; India, manpower, 308-10; transfer, 284
Resource nationalism, 158
Revolutionary processes: and dissociation, 418-19; and language, 364
Rhee, Syngman, 142-43, 146
Ricardo, David, 6-7, 14
Rothschild, House of, 66

Saudi Arabia, 195, 389; and South Korea, 168, 172
Science and technology gap, 281
Security strategies, 38, 369-420; alternative security association, 388-97; appeasement, 385-88; conventional military self-reliance, 397-410; prospects for success, 415-20; unconventional military self-reliance, 410-15
Selective dissociation, 17, 34; Algeria, 288-96; and human welfare, 311-15;

THE POLITICAL ECONOMY
OF INTERNATIONAL CHANGE
JOHN GERARD RUGGIE, GENERAL EDITOR